AFRICAN ETHNOGRAPHIC STUDIES
OF THE 20TH CENTURY

Volume 28

THE WEB OF KINSHIP AMONG
THE TALLENSI

THE WEB OF KINSHIP AMONG THE TALLENSI

The Second Part of an Analysis of the Social Structure of a Trans-Volta Tribe

MEYER FORTES

LONDON AND NEW YORK

First published in 1949 by Oxford University Press for the International African Institute.

This edition first published in 2018
by Routledge
2 Park Square, Milton Park, Abingdon, Oxon OX14 4RN

and by Routledge
711 Third Avenue, New York, NY 10017

Routledge is an imprint of the Taylor & Francis Group, an informa business

© 1949 International African Institute

All rights reserved. No part of this book may be reprinted or reproduced or utilised in any form or by any electronic, mechanical, or other means, now known or hereafter invented, including photocopying and recording, or in any information storage or retrieval system, without permission in writing from the publishers.

Trademark notice: Product or corporate names may be trademarks or registered trademarks, and are used only for identification and explanation without intent to infringe.

British Library Cataloguing in Publication Data
A catalogue record for this book is available from the British Library

ISBN: 978-0-8153-8713-8 (Set)
ISBN: 978-0-429-48813-9 (Set) (ebk)
ISBN: 978-1-138-59198-1 (Volume 28) (hbk)
ISBN: 978-0-429-49020-0 (Volume 28) (ebk)

Publisher's Note
The publisher has gone to great lengths to ensure the quality of this reprint but points out that some imperfections in the original copies may be apparent.

Disclaimer
The publisher has made every effort to trace copyright holders and would welcome correspondence from those they have been unable to trace.

THE
WEB OF KINSHIP
AMONG THE
TALLENSI

*The Second Part of an
Analysis of the Social Structure
of a Trans-Volta Tribe*

by

MEYER FORTES

READER IN SOCIAL ANTHROPOLOGY IN THE
UNIVERSITY OF OXFORD

Published for the
INTERNATIONAL AFRICAN INSTITUTE
by the OXFORD UNIVERSITY PRESS
LONDON NEW YORK TORONTO

Oxford University Press, Amen House, London E.C.4
GLASGOW NEW YORK TORONTO MELBOURNE WELLINGTON
BOMBAY CALCUTTA MADRAS KARACHI
CAPE TOWN IBADAN NAIROBI ACCRA SINGAPORE

First published 1949
Second impression 1957

PRINTED IN GREAT BRITAIN

TO MY WIFE
AND FELLOW-WORKER
SONIA L. FORTES

FOREWORD

THIS book concludes the investigation of Tale social structure begun in *The Dynamics of Clanship among the Tallensi*, 1945. It carries the analysis into the domain of family life and the social ties that grow directly out of marriage and parenthood. This is the domain of kinship, in the current usage of social anthropology.

No subject in the whole range of anthropological studies has been so voluminously investigated and debated as kinship. It is no exaggeration to say that every anthropologist of repute has, at some time or another, written about kinship. Nor has this interest been confined to anthropologists. The marriage customs of primitive peoples, their modes of domestic organization, their rules of inheritance and descent, the laws, morals, and religious beliefs associated with family life among them, have furnished material for scholars of many kinds. It is nearly a hundred years since Bachofen's reconstruction of primordial mother-right and McLennan's theory of exogamy and endogamy upset long-standing beliefs about the nature of the human family. It is exactly a century since Lewis Morgan, who may justly be regarded as the father of the scientific study of kinship in primitive society, first wrote about the Iroquois clan. Since then psychologists and philosophers, sociologists, jurists, historians, and others have drawn constantly on the mounting quantity of data concerning primitive kinship to support their theories or confute their opponents.

Fortunately for the anthropologist who ventures to write about kinship, the vast mass of literature on the subject contains only a small amount of generalization that has stood the test of modern field research. But this alone would not excuse the omission of reference to the work of other students of the subject in a book on kinship. The chief reason why I have, in this book, referred only to those authorities whose writings have direct bearing on my material is because the general problems of kinship lie outside the scope of a descriptive monograph.

At the same time the truism that facts only acquire meaning for science in the light of an adequate theory is specially relevant to the study of kinship. 'No systematic thought has made progress apart from some adequately general working hypothesis, adapted to its special topic', says Whitehead.[1] Kinship studies, right up to

[1] Whitehead, A. N., *Adventures of Ideas*, p. 286.

the present time, have suffered from working hypotheses not adapted to the topic. I was fortunate in that both my chief teachers on this subject, the late Professor Bronislaw Malinowski and Professor A. R. Radcliffe-Brown, approached it with working hypotheses founded on the realities of field observation. Their theories have the merit of being adapted to the methods of observation available to the anthropologist in the field and to the kind of data within his reach. They can be tested in the field, as is most cogently shown in Raymond Firth's book *We, the Tikopia* (1937), which appeared while I was among the Tallensi. I found this book a mine of ideas and a most valuable stimulus to observation.

I have not, however, attempted to give a comprehensive account of family life and kinship among the Tallensi in this book. I am concerned only with kinship in relation to the social structure—that is, in my view, with the fundamental principles of Tale kinship relations as they enter into the organization of collective life. In a society as homogeneous as that of the Tallensi the common denominators of thought, feeling, and action stand out very clearly and the principles governing social behaviour are not so difficult to discern as might be supposed.

It is of interest to add that I was able to pay a very short visit to the Tallensi in 1945, after this book was finished. I found that as far as their social structure was concerned there had been no appreciable change since my wife and I first went to Taleland in 1934. But there are many signs that they are on the threshold of a period of rapid change. The war has opened up wider horizons to many of the young men who saw active service. Native Administration has developed greatly; schools are being established; missionaries have started work inside Taleland. The social structure I have described may well undergo many modifications in the next few years, though I do not believe it will alter much in fundamentals for decades.

M. F.

CONTENTS

FOREWORD vii

LIST OF PLATES xiii

CHAPTER I. INTRODUCTORY 1
    The Large-scale Framework of Tale Society . . . 1
    The Maximal Lineage and Clanship Ties . . . 4
    The Internal Constitution of the Maximal Lineage . . 6

CHAPTER II. KINSHIP AND THE LINEAGE SYSTEM . 12
    The Connexion between Kinship and the Lineage System . . 12
    Cognatic and Agnatic Kinship 13
    The Generic Concept of Kinship 16
    Two Classes of Kinship Relations 18
    The Native Theory of Conception 19
    The Significance of Paternity and Patriliny . . . 21
    The Ritual Coefficient of Patriliny 28
    The Significance of Maternal Parentage and the Uterine Line . 30
    Uterine Kinship and the Notion of Witchcraft . . 32
    Uterine Kinship and the Notion of *Tyuk* . . . 35
    Uterine Kinship as a Personal Bond 37
    The Dispersion of Uterine Kin 40

CHAPTER III. THE HOMESTEAD AND THE JOINT FAMILY 44
    Homestead and Family—a Single Social Entity . . 44
    The Ideas and Values embodied in the Homestead . . 45
    The Architecture of the Homestead in Relation to the Structure
        of the Domestic Family 47
    The Developmental Cycle of the Joint Family . . 63

CHAPTER IV. HUSBAND AND WIFE IN THE STRUCTURE
    OF THE FAMILY 78
    The General and the Particular in the Pattern of Domestic
        Relations 78
    The Significance of Marriage 81
    The Stability of Marriage 84
    The Wife's Ties with her Paternal Family and Lineage . 87
    The Opposition between the Kinship Ties and the Marital Ties
        of Spouses, and its Resolution 90
    The Relationships of a Wife with her Relatives-in-law . 93
    The Relationship of Husband and Wife . . . 97
    The Sexual Relationship in Marriage 100
    The Economic and Property Relations of Spouses . . 101

CONTENTS

The Husband's Authority over his Wife	104
The Sexual Relationship as the Corner-stone of Marriage	106
The Sexual Rights of the Husband and the Corporate Interests of his Clan	109
The Husband's Relationship with his Affines	118
Sex in the Relationship of Affines	123
The Adjustment of Co-wives to one another	126

CHAPTER V. PARENTS AND CHILDREN IN THE FRAMEWORK OF THE LINEAGE 135
Some General Principles recapitulated . . . 135
The Importance of 'Rearing' 136
Rights and Duties of Parents 137
Classificatory Parents and Own Parents . . . 140
The Significance of 'Having no Father alive' . . . 147
Change of Status Due to Death of 'Father' shown in Property Relations 156
Parallel Significance of 'Not having a Mother alive' . . 160

CHAPTER VI. THE MORAL BASIS OF THE RELATIONSHIP OF PARENT AND CHILD 162
The Fundamental Axiom of Parenthood . . . 162
The Tribulations of Parenthood 162
The Parent–Child Bond as an Absolute Bond . . . 169
Filial Piety 171

CHAPTER VII. THE GENETIC DEVELOPMENT OF PARENT–CHILD RELATIONSHIPS . . . 187
Babyhood 187
Childhood 190
Parents and Children in Everyday Intercourse . . . 196
Adolescence and the Principle of Reciprocity . . . 198
From Adolescence to Adulthood 203
The Duty of supporting the Parents in Old Age . . 216
A Methodological Point 220

CHAPTER VIII. TENSIONS IN THE PARENT–CHILD RELATIONSHIP 222
Rivalry between Parents and Children 222
The Native Theory of the Tension between the Generations . 226
The Discrimination between Oldest Children and Youngest Children 230
The Ancestors as Parent Images 234

CHAPTER IX. GRANDPARENTS AND GRANDCHILDREN . 236

CONTENTS

CHAPTER X. SIBLINGS IN THE SOCIAL STRUCTURE . 241
   The Concept of *mabiirət* 241
   The Equivalence of Siblings 242
   Factors modifying the Sibling Bond 243
   The Solidarity of *soog* Siblings 244
   Solidarity and Equality among *sunzɔ* Siblings . . 256
   The Social Equivalence of Siblings reconsidered . . 269

CHAPTER XI. THE WEB OF EXTRA-CLAN KINSHIP . 281
   Some General Points restated 281
   Kinship Terms 284
   The Socio-spatial Aspect of Extra-clan Kinship . . 286
   Kinship Amity 293
   The Classificatory Extension of Extra-clan Kinship . 295
   The Nuclear Relationship of Mother's Brother and Sister's Son 299
   The Place of Gifts in the Relations of *Ahəb* and *Ahəŋ* . 305
   The Status of an *Ahəŋ* as a Foster-child in his *Ahəb*'s Family . 313
   The *Ahəŋ* as Intermediary 317
   The Ritual Relations of Matrilateral and Sororal Kin . 321
   The Father's Sister 332

CHAPTER XII. THE FUNCTIONS OF KINSHIP . . 337

INDEX 349

LIST OF PLATES

1. The relationship of mother and child   *facing page* 32
2. *a.* The domestic family is the matrix of kinship . . 33
   b. A domestic sacrifice 33
3. *a.* Interior of a woman's *Dug* 48
   b. The homestead of a maximal lineage head, the Gbizug Tɛndaana 48
4. *a.* The central granary in the homestead of an elder . . 49
   b. In the *Dɛndɔŋo* of the senior woman of the family . . 49
5. *a.* A senior wife (*pɔyakpeem*) in her *dɛndɔŋo* sorting newly harvested millet 112
   b. Homeward bound from a visit to her father's house . 112
6. *a.* Kinship *versus* affinal relationships . . . 113
   b. A husband goes to inform his parents-in-law of the birth of his wife's first child 113
7. *a.* A senior wife takes care of her junior co-wives' infants . 128
   b. A pair of devoted co-wives 128
8. *a.* A domestic sacrifice of fowls, guinea-fowls, and beer . 129
   b. Ɔmara and his four youngest daughters . . . 129
9. *a.* The tribulations of motherhood 192
   b. The husband's mother and a co-wife of the new mother give her new-born baby its daily bath 192
10. *a.* Kinship patterns are not specific in public etiquette or domestic intercourse 193
    b. A father eating with his youngest son while his oldest son lounges beside them 193
11. *a.* The first-born son of a Namoo is ritually 'shown' his father's granary 208
    b. The youngest son and the youngest daughter of a dead woman wear the *dooluŋ* during the concluding rites of their mother's funeral 208
12. *a.* A grandfather with his son's children . . . 209
    b. The effective minimal lineage 209
13. *a.* Children of a single domestic family . . . 272
    b. Four generations 272
14. *a.* Siblings by the same parents have breakfast together . 273
    b. Successive (*nyeer*) *soog* brothers 273

LIST OF PLATES

15. *a.* Classificatory sisters' sons (*ahəs*) 288
    b. A group of 'siblings' of the same inner lineage dividing a lizard which they have killed 288
16. *a.* The members of a segment of a maximal lineage gather at the homestead of the head of the segment to sacrifice to their immediate founding ancestor 289
    b. Matrilateral kin come to set up a new shrine . . 289

CHAPTER I

INTRODUCTORY

The Large-scale Framework of Tale Society

THE central subject of the first part of this analysis of Tale social structure was the lineage system.[1] Our attention was fixed on the permanent large-scale framework of the society in relation to which individuals behave primarily as members of corporate groups. We observed that according to native belief and usage this framework has maintained its form from time immemorial and must continue to do so as long as their social system lasts. Our data left little doubt that in fact the macroscopic social structure of the Tallensi has been highly stable in form for at least five generations and probably for many more. We found evidence, however, that a continuous process of adjustment in the grading of structural relations between the component units of the total social structure underlies its stable form. These adaptations take place in response to economic, structural, and religious stresses. Though they do not alter the established forms of corporate grouping by means of which Tale collective life is organized, they do affect the social relations of persons as individuals and as members of corporate groups. Nor can there be any doubt that they are inherent in the social structure; whatever sets them in motion at any given time or in any given sector of the society, they are made possible by the dynamic factors inherent in the constitution of the stable large-scale units of social organization. We saw that units of Tale social organization can only be defined by reference to the way in which they emerge in corporate action in relation to other like units, and not by mechanical criteria.

For convenience of orientation I shall here sum up the principal results of our previous study. The Tallensi[2] are typical of the great congeries of Mole-Dagbane-speaking peoples that occupy the basin of the Volta rivers in the French Ivory Coast and the Northern Territories of the Gold Coast.[3] In race, speech, culture, social organization, and economy they constitute a completely homogeneous community of sedentary farmers. But there is no 'tribal unity' among the Tallensi in the ordinarily accepted sense of this phrase. They have no fixed territorial boundaries, nor are they precisely marked off from neighbouring 'tribes' by cultural or linguistic usages. They have no political unity in the sense of being uniformly and exclusively subject to a single, centralized tribal government (other than that imposed by the British

---

[1] *The Dynamics of Clanship among the Tallensi*, hereafter referred to as *Dynamics of Clanship*.

[2] Population (1931), approx. 35,000; density, approx. 170 per square mile.

[3] See *Dynamics of Clanship*, ch. i.

Colonial Government),[1] and no judicial or administrative machinery such as goes with a centralized form of government.[2]

The 'tribal unity' of the Tallensi is, in general terms, the unity of a distinct socio-geographical region forming a segment of a greater region of similar cultural type, economic organization, and social structure. This region can be demarcated only by dynamic criteria. The Tallensi have more in common among themselves, both in sentiment and in nuances of cultural usage, and closer social and politico-ritual bonds *inter se*, than the component segments of Tale society have with other like units outside what we have called Taleland. This characteristic of Tale society has a special relevance for the investigation we are undertaking in this book. For, like the network of clanship ties and the bonds of common custom and of politico-ritual association analysed in our first book, the web of kinship spreads far beyond the social frontiers of the Tallensi. This is one of the ways in which the field of inter-personal relations is congruent with the structure of relations between corporate groups among the Tallensi.

The principle of segmentary differentiation and the associated principle of dynamic coherence operate in every department of Tale social organization. We described in our previous work how the Tallensi are internally divided by a major cleavage into two clusters of clans, the Namoo clans on the one hand, and the Talis[3] clans and their congeners on the other. These two groups are distinguished by differences in their myths of origin, their totemic and quasi-totemic usages and beliefs, the politico-ritual privileges and duties connected with the Earth cult and the ancestor cult, and to some extent by their local distribution. The clans belonging to each group are more closely interlinked by clanship and politico-ritual ties than any one of them is linked to clans of the other group. But very close bonds of local contiguity, and of politico-ritual interdependence and co-operation in assuring the maintenance of the common interests of the society—peace and

---

[1] Since 1937, under the new system of local government introduced by the Administration, the Tallensi have a centralized Native Authority built up on federal principles and closely related to indigenous forms of political institutions. I am speaking, however, of the period prior to 1937. Moreover, the new political constitution has not yet been wholly integrated with the indigenous system of politico-ritual relations.

[2] This is further discussed in *African Political Systems*, ed. by M. Fortes and E. E. Evans-Pritchard, Introduction and pp. 239 ff.

[3] As explained in *Dynamics of Clanship* I use the following terminology for the sake of clarity: *Tallensi* (sing. *Talǝŋ*) means all the inhabitants of *Taleland*; *Tale* is the adjective derived from Tallensi and is used to refer to things common to all Tallensi. *Talis* (sing. *Talis*) is used both as a substantive and as an adjective to refer to the 'real' Tallensi, as the natives call them, who live on and around the Tong Hills. They are usually contrasted with *Namoos* (sing. and adj. *Namoo*) who are also Tallensi but a different section of the population. This nomenclature is artificial, though derived from native speech forms.

the rule of custom, fertility of soil and of man, health and prosperity—unite the two groups. In particular, inter-personal ties of kinship and of affinity link the members of the two groups of clans to one another, so that practically every Namoo has kinsmen among the Talis and vice versa.

These two groups of clans, we learnt, never combined for defence against or attack on neighbouring 'tribes'. Indeed, they were the traditional enemies of one another, and war sometimes broke out between Namoos and Talis in the Tongo area. But these wars were short and sharp. They were acute forms of internal dissension rather than wars as we understand the term, and they immediately set on foot actions to restore the *status quo ante*. Thus they served to emphasize the inescapable interdependence of the two groups.

The unity and moral solidarity of all the Tallensi emerge most conspicuously during the annual cycle of the Great Festivals. At these times the divergent interests that normally dominate the corporate actions of clans or groups of clans are set aside in obedience to ritual sanctions. A series of rites and ceremonies requiring the co-operation of both major groups of clans takes place, in which the greatest common interests and values of the whole society are dramatized and affirmed. The solidarity of the widest political community to which every Taləŋ belongs thus becomes temporarily supreme, and no intestine dissensions at other times can destroy it.

The Great Festivals bring out two points of special importance. They show, firstly, that the widest unified political community in which Tallensi participate is not a fixed group but a functional synthesis based on a dynamic social equilibrium. This equilibrium is maintained by the balancing against one another of like corporate units; by the play of the counterpoised ties and cleavages of clanship, kinship, and ritual allegiance; and through the agency of complementary politico-ritual-institutions. And secondly, they show that the whole system hinges on the complementary roles of two types of politico-ritual functionaries, chiefs (*na'ab*, pl. *nadɛm*) and Custodians of the Earth (*tɛndaana*, pl. *tɛndaanam*). The office of chiefship (*na'am*) is considered to be characteristic of the Namoos, the tɛndaana-ship of the Talis and their congeners, but neither office is the exclusive prerogative of either group. The picture is further complicated by the existence of other politico-ritual offices, in particular among the Talis, connected with their cult of the External *Bɔyar*. The complementary functions of chiefship and tɛndaana-ship are rooted directly in the social structure, but are also validated by myths of origin and backed by the most powerful religious sanctions of the ancestor cult and of the cult of the Earth. The Namoos are believed to be the descendants of immigrant Mamprusi who fled from Mampurugu many generations ago. Hence they claim remote kinship with the ruling aristocracy of Mampurugu. Their chiefship is derived from that of the Paramount Chief of the Mamprusi, and this is the ultimate sanction of its politico-ritual status in Tale society. The Talis and other clans that have the tendaana-ship claim to be the aboriginal inhabitants of the country, and the ritual sanctions of their office are derived from the Earth cult.

The Maximal Lineage and Clanship Ties

All politico-ritual offices are vested in particular maximal lineages or clans. These are the basic units of Tale social organization that emerge in corporate activities. They are defined primarily by the canon of agnatic descent. A maximal lineage is the most extensive group of people of both sexes all of whom are related to one another by common patrilineal descent traced from one known (or accepted) founding ancestor through known agnatic antecedents. The exact agnatic relationship of every member of a maximal lineage to every other member is, in theory, known or can be ascertained by genealogical reckoning. All the agnatic descendants of the founding ancestor, both male and female, belong to the maximal lineage. But in practice the male members are supreme in the conduct of lineage affairs and the *de facto* corporate unit is the group of male members. This is due in part to the fact that women members are bound to marry out of the lineage, by the rule of lineage exogamy. As marriage is patrilocal, a woman is usually separated from her male lineage-kinsfolk, and cannot easily take part in regular lineage counsels. What is more important, her children do not belong to her patrilineal lineage and they do not therefore contribute to its physical and social perpetuation. This is one manifestation of the dominance of males and the male line in jural and ritual institutions which, as we shall see in the following pages, is the principal factor governing the inter-personal as well as the corporate relations of individuals.

The maximal lineage is the basis of the Tale clan. A clan (or sub-clan, in a few instances) is a localized unit consisting of a defined segment of a maximal lineage, or a whole maximal lineage; or of two or more linked maximal lineages, augmented, frequently, by one or more accessory lineages incorporated into the clan by a fiction of kinship through a woman of the authentic male line. The commonest type is the composite clan, consisting of two or more linked maximal lineages of independent patrilineal descent whose association is accounted for by a myth of remote kinship or of age-old local solidarity. Every maximal lineage is exogamous, and with very few exceptions this rule applies also to the associations of maximal lineages we have called clans. Apart from local unity and putative genealogical linkage, clans are internally unified by common ritual cults connected with the worship of the ancestors and the earth.

An important corollary to the rule of exogamy in the maximal lineage and clan is the right of a man to inherit the widow of any male member of his lineage or clan, other than those whom he describes as his 'fathers' or 'sons'.

Every Tale clan is anchored to a particular locality from which it takes its name. In the central area of Taleland, around the Tong Hills, the present clan settlements appear to date back not less than eight to ten generations. But they have not been and are not territorially static. There are no strict territorial boundaries between adjacent settlements. The homesteads of a settlement merge with those of the adjacent settlements, and the boundaries between them are definable only in social terms, as a function of their ecological and politico-ritual relations at a given time. In the same way every segment of a clan—that is, each of its component maximal lineages—is anchored to a local subdivision of the clan settlement, though many of its members may be dispersed elsewhere.

A striking feature of Tale social organization is the system of inter-clan linkages which constitutes one of the principal forces of cohesion in the society. The genealogically and socially autonomous maximal lineage or clan is not a closed group. The component maximal lineages that form the segments of adjacent clans have ties of clanship identical with those that unite them to one another within their respective clans. Thus if two adjacent clans have segments A, B, C, and D, E, F, G, respectively, then A (but not B or C) may have clanship ties with D (but not with E, F, or G); B may have clanship ties only with E, and C with F. Each of these maximal lineages also has clanship ties with segments of other neighbouring clans. Thus each component maximal lineage of a clan has a field of clanship that includes the other segments of the clan as well as segments of other clans. This results in a network of interlocking clanship ties that embraces all the separate clans of Taleland. All the Talis clans and the main block of Namoo clans are interlocked in this way in two clusters which are in turn similarly connected at certain points. Moreover, this system of linkages ties the Tale aggregate on to adjacent clans of other neighbouring 'tribes'. Thus we observe that at this level of social structure—the skeletal level, so to speak—as in its territorial and cultural relationship to neighbouring 'tribes', Tale society is a segment of a greater society. The network of inter-clan linkages is one of the principal factors by which the socio-geographic region we have called Taleland is differentiated as a distinct segment of this greater society.

It is also one of the main factors of social equilibrium in Tale society. Dissension between neighbouring clans is kept in check by the mediation of maximal lineages linked by identical ties to both; and warfare is inhibited from disrupting the entire social order by the intervention of social and ritual obligations arising *inter alia* out of the fact that enemies are related directly or indirectly by clanship ties. It is this, in part, that gives Tale wars the complexion of acute family quarrels.

A maximal lineage is not only an organic genealogical unit, it is also *ipso facto* an organic ritual unit. The focus of its genealogical differentiation from and relative autonomy in relation to other like units, as well as of its corporate solidarity and its continuity in time, is the cult of its founding ancestor. The material symbol of this is the shrine (*bɔɣar*) of that ancestor, custody of which is vested in the head (i.e. the most senior male) of the lineage. Among the Talis each segment of a composite clan has its lineage *bɔɣar*, distinguishing it from the other segments of the clan. But, in addition, groups of maximal lineages belonging, severally, to *different* clans, and not necessarily united *inter se* by ties of clanship, collaborate in the cult of their collective ancestors. The collective ancestors are believed to dwell in a *bɔɣar* known as an External *Bɔɣar*. An External *Bɔɣar* is usually a sacred grove, or a shallow cave in the hill-side, where the community meets for the ritual of the cult. The most important rites of the cult occur during the Harvest Festival, when thanksgiving sacrifices are offered and young men of the group are initiated into its mysteries by special ceremonies.

Clanship ties, as we have mentioned, constitute the principal factor of social integration among all the Tallensi. Among the Talis the cult of the External *Bɔɣar* is another important factor of cohesion and equilibrium. It unites segments of different clans in the worship of the ancestors, and is common to the majority of Talis clans. It represents a system of social bonds that cut across and counterpoise those of clanship. But this system is itself counterpoised, on the plane of religious values, by the organization of the Earth cult. Groups of maximal lineages belonging severally to *different* clans, which are not associated in the cult of the External *Bɔɣar*, collaborate in the rites of the Earth cult. Each such group has its special Earth shrines, generally in the form of sacred groves (*tɔŋgban*). Thus each maximal lineage of a composite clan among the Talis has one field of corporate social relations in terms of clanship ties, a different field of corporate social relations in terms of the External *Bɔɣar* cult, and yet a third field of corporate social relations in terms of the Earth cult. The system as a whole forms a remarkable structure of mutually balancing fields of social and politico-ritual relations integrated into a complex unity. Sectional loyalties in one direction or on one level are counterpoised by similar loyalties in another direction or at another level. And the system as a whole stands under the governance of the supreme sanctions of Tale social life, the ancestor cult and the Earth cult. To crown it all, moreover, there is the ritually sanctioned and regulated polar opposition of Talis and Namoos focused in the relationship of the chiefship and the tɛndaana-ship.

The Internal Constitution of the Maximal Lineage

In this scheme of clanship ties and politico-ritual relationships the maximal lineage emerges as a corporate unit irrespective of its internal constitution. The main characteristics of the latter can now be briefly summarized.

A *maximal lineage* is divided into a number of segments all of the same form as the whole lineage but of regularly diminishing order of segmentation. Each segment is identified by reference to its founding ancestor. He marks the point on the genealogical tree of the whole maximal lineage at which that segment's line of descent connects with the other lines of descent sprung from the founding ancestor of the maximal lineage. Thus every maximal lineage is divisible, in the first instance, into two or more Major Segments. This is the highest order of segmentation. Each Major Segment embraces (or is believed to embrace) all the agnatic descendants of one of the sons of the founder of the maximal lineage. At the next level each Major Segment is itself divisible into Major Segments, each embracing the agnatic descendants of one putative son of a son of the founding ancestor of the maximal lineage; and this formula holds at every generation level of the maximal lineage structure (see Fig. 1). The lowest order of segmentation, at the opposite end of the lineage scale to that represented by the maximal lineage, is that of the *minimal lineage* or *minimal segment*, which we define as the group comprising only the children of one man. This is the narrowest agnatic group to which a person can belong.

It is clear from the above that every person belongs to a hierarchy of lineage segments lying between the minimal and the maximal limits of his maximal lineage. Different orders of segmentation become relevant for his conduct in different degrees and in accordance with variations in the social situation. As a farmer, for instance, his productive activities are mainly determined by his membership of his minimal lineage. If he wishes to marry, membership of his maximal lineage is one of the factors limiting his choice of a bride; but the completion of the jural formalities is governed by his membership of a segment of intermediate order. At the same time a very important aspect of the lineage organization is the fact that even when only a segment of a lineage emerges in any corporate activity its status and functions are influenced by the total lineage field including, at the limit, the field of clanship. A lineage segment emerges in action only as a relatively autonomous unit. Its activity is regulated by its relationship to other like segments of the lineage and to the whole. Conversely, a lineage or lineage segment always functions as a combination of segments, not as a collection of individuals of common descent. Every lineage or lineage segment, in fact, represents a dynamic equilibrium of mutually balancing segments.

To the contemporary observer a maximal lineage is fixed in form and dimensions, and all its segments except the minimal segments are fixed in relation to one another. Only the complete extinction of a segment can alter the balance. But the degree of relative autonomy which the segments

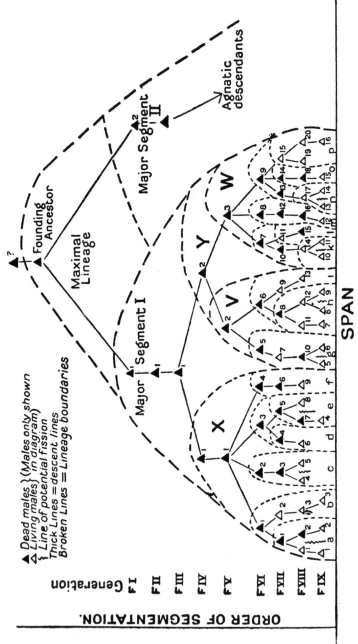

Fig. 1. (Reproduced from *Dynamics of Clanship*, p. 34.)

INTRODUCTORY

of a particular order have in ritual, jural, and economic affairs gradually alters with each generation. Thus, while their father is alive, two or more brothers have no jural or ritual or economic autonomy, either severally or as a group. The minimal segment of which they are the nucleus is submerged in the more inclusive lineage segment of which their father is the head. If their grandfather is still alive they and their father come under his jurisdiction and have no autonomy as a lineage segment independently of the segment of higher order of which the grandfather is the head. Thus the *effective minimal lineage*, as we have labelled it in order to simplify our analysis (that is, the narrowest lineage segment which is recognized in corporate activities), is not the same as the morphological minimal lineage. It may include two or three generations of agnates.[1] But the group that constitutes an effective minimal lineage in one generation may, in the next generation, split into two or more effective minimal segments.

In the same way, to simplify our exposition, we have distinguished three other grades of segmentation in the maximal lineage,[2] the *nuclear* lineage or segment, the *inner* lineage or segment, and the *medial* lineage or segment. These grades of segmentation vary in dimensions from one maximal lineage to another and from one generation to the next in the same maximal lineage. They cannot be precisely defined by morphological criteria, for they are distinguishable only in functional terms, by the incidence of jural, ritual, and economic rights, duties, and privileges.

The effective minimal lineage is marked by the fact that it commonly forms the basis of a domestic family which usually constitutes a single unit of food production and consumption.

The nuclear lineage generally forms the basis of what we shall later designate the expanded family. Its male members have a common interest in, and joint rights of inheritance to particular patrimonial farm-lands; and the head of the lineage bears the formal jural responsibility for any of the members in such matters as the payment of bride-price. The founding ancestors of such a lineage may be placed from four to six generations back, reckoning from contemporary minimal lineages. A nuclear lineage may include two or more effective minimal lineages.

The inner lineage, which may include two or more nuclear lineages, may, but does not necessarily, have a common interest in patrimonial land. Like the nuclear lineage, it is not the basis of a unit of production or consumption. Its characteristic feature is that it is the widest lineage within which generation differences are socially recognized. From this it follows that incest with a woman member of the same inner lineage is strongly reprobated and sexual intercourse with the wife of any other

[1] Very rarely four generations; never, to my knowledge, more.
[2] Cf. *Dynamics of Clanship*, ch. xii.

member of the lineage is regarded as a grave sin. The head of the inner lineage still bears jural and ritual responsibility for all junior members of the lineage but to a lesser extent than the head of the nuclear lineage. The founding ancestor of an inner lineage may be placed five to seven generations back.

A medial lineage includes two or more inner lineages. It may be a major segment of a maximal lineage or a major segment of a major segment. Its founding ancestor may be placed from six to eight or nine generations back. Its segments do not, as a rule, have a common interest in patrimonial land. The seduction of a co-member's wife is not invariably considered to be a sin. If it is a lineage of wide span, embracing several sub-segments, and the parties are distant agnates, this might be treated simply as a jural offence.

Generation differences are usually no longer recognized for jural purposes at this range of patrilineal connexion, and the lineage head has no jural responsibility for or ritual obligations on behalf of individual members who are not of his nuclear or, at most, inner lineage. A significant index of the medial lineage is that it marks the limits within which a man is prohibited from marrying a patrilineal kinswoman of his mother. He cannot, as a rule, marry a woman of his mother's maximal lineage who belongs to her medial lineage; he is almost always allowed to marry one who falls outside this range of agnatic kinship with his mother.

It must be emphasized that these distinctions are not made by the natives. The lineage units thus identified are often fairly clearly defined in practice in certain maximal lineages at a given time. But what holds for one maximal lineage does not hold for another of the same clan or for the same maximal lineage at another time. And borderline cases are common, so that a lineage which functions as an inner lineage in one situation may be treated as a medial lineage in another. These distinctions are based on the gradation of rights and duties observed in Tale jural and ritual relations in which lineage segments emerge as corporate units. Hence in considering the incidence of jural or ritual rights and duties, or in determining the scope of kinship sentiments, we cannot always lay down exact limits within which they apply, in accordance with this set of labels. In function as in form the different grades of lineage segments tend to merge into one another; and distinctions that hold at one period will not do so a generation later. As a lineage ramifies, the relative autonomy of its component segments tends to increase in proportion; so that a segment that functioned as a nuclear lineage at one time may, twenty or thirty years later, exhibit all the characteristics of an inner lineage, in corporate activities.

Finally, it should be noted that the Tallensi have no term for the lineage. A lineage of any order is designated the 'house' (*yir*) or the children (*biis*) of the founding ancestor, as in most West African societies which utilize the lineage principle in social organization. In contexts where the emphasis is on the lineage considered as a segment of a more inclusive lineage, it is commonly described as a 'room' (*dug*) of the more inclusive 'house' (*yir*). But when Tallensi speak of a *dug* without further specification they generally mean a segment of the order of an inner or medial lineage.

As this nomenclature shows, the internal constitution of the lineage is modelled on that of the polygynous joint family. The standard pattern is that the segments of a lineage trace their descent from the sons by different wives of their common founding ancestor. We shall consider this subject more fully in this book. In consequence, co-ordinate segments of a lineage are referred to as 'brother' (*sunzɔ*) lineages, and their reciprocal rights and obligations, as well as the conventional patterns of sentiments holding between them, are modelled on the mutual relations of brothers.

At the end of our previous book we pointed out that our study of the structure of corporate groups and their interrelations in Tale society covered only one aspect of the total social structure. We spoke of the first part of this study as an analysis of the warp of the social fabric. Our task now is to examine what might be called the woof of the social fabric. Our starting-point, this time, is not the organized corporate group or the framework of continuity and stability in the social structure, but the individual. Our main interest will be in the standard forms and processes of person-to-person relationships and their connexion with the large-scale framework of the society. Our subject, in other words, is Tale kinship in the narrow sense, viewed in relation to the lineage system.

CHAPTER·II
KINSHIP AND THE LINEAGE SYSTEM
The Connexion between Kinship and the Lineage System

THE method of analysis we have followed in this study has required, for purposes of description, the isolation of the lineage system from the domestic organization of the Tallensi. In the actual life of the natives, however, these two planes of social structure do not emerge in isolation from each other. Like blood and tissue in the animal organism, they constitute interpenetrating media of Tale social life. Membership of a family and membership of a lineage are equally and often concurrently decisive for the conduct of the individual and for the course of his life. Yet the analytical separation of these two planes of social structure is not entirely artificial. It corresponds to the fact that the interests and ends (primarily political, jural, and ritual) subserved by the lineage system differ significantly from those (primarily economic and reproductive) subserved by the family system, both in their bearing on individual conduct and in the values attached to them by the society.

The lineage system is the structural basis of Tale political, jural, and ritual institutions, whereas the domestic organization is the structural basis of person-to-person relations in the sphere of kinship in the narrow sense. One of our main tasks in the present investigation will be to observe how these two categories of interests and ends, and the institutions and practices in which they emerge, are co-ordinated and integrated. For the individual's rights and duties, sentiments and values, manners and moral conduct, his thinking, feeling, and acting, in the context of lineage relationships, on the one hand, and in the context of family relationships on the other, are organically integrated, as are lineage and family in the social structure. This appears most clearly, we shall see, from the way in which segmentation in the domestic family parallels segmentation in the lineage, the two processes being not only simultaneous in time but complementary in function. Fission in the lineage[1] follows the pattern of cellular segmentation in the joint family; and fission in the joint family, as we shall see, follows the lines of cleavage in the effective minimal lineage. The local and the functional groupings of families are regulated by the agnatic distance of the family heads from one another. In the study of Tale kinship usages and values we are confronted, at every step, by the interaction of domestic organization and lineage structure.

The Tallensi apply the concepts of kinship to describe and define domestic relations and the person-to-person ties that are derived from them. They use the same concepts in dealing with lineage relations. In

[1] Cf. *Dynamics of Clanship*, ch. iii.

the social structure as a whole kinship is the fundamental binding element. It furnishes the primary axioms of all categories of interpersonal and inter-group relations.

From the standpoint of the individual, all the norms and conditions that govern his social behaviour fall within a single, syncretic frame of reference; and kinship forms the base line from which this frame of reference is projected. This is a consequence of the syncretic structure of Tale society, based as it is on genealogical connexion. The alinement of individuals and groups for all social purposes follows genealogical lines; with few exceptions, social relations always have a genealogical coefficient. And because they have a common foundation in the genealogical structure of the society, Tale institutions interlock with one another in a consistent scheme. For the same reason Tale social relations do not fall into distinct categories with only adventitious connexions between them. Economic relations serve jural, political, and religious ends as well; political relations are at the same time religious relations; jural rights and duties are aspects of economic, religious, and political bonds.

The extent to which the idiom of kinship dominates Tale thought about human affairs is shown by the tendency of the people to explain conduct that conforms to the norms by appealing to kinship. The late Chief of Tongo, for example, justified his conciliatory tactics with the Gɔlibdaana, in spite of the latter's provocations, on the grounds of their ties of cognatic and affinal kinship. On the other hand, departure from normal standards of conduct is apt to be ascribed to personal idiosyncrasies. Thus when Zayahkpɛmɔre fought with his older brother over the division of their late father's land, the elders of his lineage ascribed it to his violent temper and lack of intelligence. In keeping with this idiom of thought, a gross breach of kinship duty is the prototype of the Tale notion of sin.

Cognatic and Agnatic Kinship

It is essential to distinguish two kinds of genealogical ties among the Tallensi. There are, firstly, cognatic ties, that is, ties of actual or assumed physical consanguinity and of the social relations entailed by them, which link person to person or an individual to a lineage or one lineage to another in a specifically defined and particular bond. Such ties may be traced through males only, through females only, or through both males and females. Secondly, there are lineage ties, social relations based on the tie of common agnatic descent.

Cognatic kinship and agnatic kinship have different, in some situations even opposed, functions in Tale collective life. The distinction turns on the principle that lineage ties always unite people in or relate them to corporate groups serving common interests and held together by common values, whereas cognates do not necessarily form corporate groups. Cognates have mutual bonds of sentiment and reciprocal obligations, but not necessarily common interests. All the members of a given lineage have the same agnatic kin and therefore identical lineage ties; but only identical siblings—that is, brothers or sisters by the same parents—have the same cognatic kin.[1] By automatically making him a member of maximal lineage and clan, his agnatic descent fits the individual into the constituted framework of Tale society. It is this that gives him his political status in the society. It gives him also a special field of defined social relations with clear contours. Cognatic kinship creates a number of contingent social ties for the individual, valid for him only. Unlike lineage ties, they differ in quality; they multiply in the course of his lifetime; in theory their range is indeterminate, since there is no limit to the reckoning of cognatic kinship. Tallensi often discover cognates of whom they were previously ignorant, in the most unexpected places in their own country, even in their own clan. But it is extremely rare for anyone to discover a hitherto unknown agnate, even in these days of relatively great mobility.

The Tallensi maintain, and genealogies of individuals bear this out, that if enough were known of the genealogical relationships of the people of adjacent settlements, they would all be found to be related to one another. In the clan itself, under the surface of its strict patrilineal organization, the filaments of cognatic kinship bind individuals together by special personal bonds which operate independently of lineage ties. This complex and unlimited ramification of cognatic kinship gives these relations great fluidity, in contrast to the comparative fixity of lineage relations. Individuals are often connected by multiple cognatic ties which are differentially effective in different situations; and, as will be clearer later, cognatic ties make breaches in the barriers of lineage and clan exclusiveness, thus extending widely the flow of social relations.

The domestic family is the matrix of all the genealogical ties of the individual, the contemporary mechanism for ever spinning new threads of kinship, and the focal field of social relations based on consanguinity. In it we can observe the working of the nuclear patterns of kinship and the formation of the ideas and values which steer the individual in all his genealogical relationships. In the domestic family we get the sharpest picture of the interaction between cognatic kinship and agnatic or lineage ties. We have there the elementary ties of cognatic kinship linking parent to child and sibling to sibling, and we have also the agnatic tie which

[1] These are the kinsfolk whom Rivers called a man's *kindred*; vide *Kinship and Social Organization*, p. 80. I am avoiding this term as it is best used to refer to a defined social unit in Rivers's sense. Sibship among the Teutons and Celts was reckoned bilaterally on this principle, cf. Vinogradoff, P., *Outlines of Historical Jurisprudence*, vol. i, ch. viii. But the kindred as a defined social unit does not exist among the Tallensi.

sets apart the males as the nucleus of the lineage. We can see the centrifugal, sundering force of matrilateral kinship counterbalancing the centripetal, uniting pull of patriliny. In the context of family life we can see the play of conflict and compromise in the working out of the primary equilibrium of Tale social organization, due to the interaction of these two sectors of social life.

Through his primary relations of consanguinity in the domestic family the individual is linked to agnates in other families and to cognates in other families and clans. There is, however, one significant difference between intra-familial and extra-familial bonds of kinship. Unlike the latter, the former are necessarily ambivalent, each relationship containing within itself both an agnatic and a cognatic component. In a joint family of three generations, for example, a child's relationship with his father differs from his relationship with his grandfather or his mother. Though these are all cognatic relationships, the tension and latent rivalry in the relationship of father and son stand in marked contrast to the comradeship of grandfather and grandson. On the other hand, grandfather, father, and son belong to the same lineage segment; they are united by a common interest in patrimonial land and in the product of their joint labour, by a common ancestor cult, by rights and duties vested in that lineage in relation to like segments of a greater lineage, and by their common concern for the continuity of their line. These are part of the whole complex of common interests and values that mobilize corporate action and maintain corporate solidarity in the maximal lineage and clan of which they form a segment. The men of a joint family may be thrown into conflict with one another on account of their cognatic relationships, but they act in union and on behalf of one another and of the whole unit in virtue of their lineage ties.

There is another paradox in the structure of the Tale family that is of importance for our inquiry. Consanguineous relationships arise out of parenthood; but parenthood presupposes marriage, a union of a man and a woman who are, by definition, not kin. The bonds of kinship are rooted in a bond the very essence of which is the absence of kinship. Hence comes the ambivalence inherent in intra-familial cognatic relations. Hence comes, also, another category of social relations, both in the family and between members of different families and clans, relations of affinity. There are two axes, as it were, in the structure of the family, the axis of kinship and that of marriage.

Before we discuss kinship in the domestic family more fully, we must consider a few matters of more general import. For the constellation of ties and cleavages that makes up the focal field of kinship is conditioned by the formative principles and values that shape the greater society into which the domestic family fits and which it helps to knit together. All person-to-person relations in the family are biased by the values attached to patrilineal descent and maternal origin in the total social structure.

The Generic Concept of Kinship

Among the Tallensi the generic concept of kinship, *dɔyam*, subsumes all kinds and degrees of genealogical relationship, however remote, through one or more progenitors or progenetrices. But its primary reference is to procreation. One might perhaps translate it by the word 'generation' in its etymological sense. Its root, the verb *dɔy*—to bear or beget a child—signifies both the male and the female function in procreation. *Dɔyam*, the abstract noun, describes the process, or the act, or the physiological capacity, of bringing a child into the world, as well as the ties thus created. The logic behind this generalized concept of kinship is plain. Every genealogical relationship goes back, eventually, to one pair of parents. Both in fact and in Tale kinship theory the parent-child bond is the nodal bond of kinship.

Though the Tallensi see every genealogical relationship as a tie of physical consanguinity, this is not the thing that matters most. What matters most is the social relations entailed by consanguinity. A genealogical tie between two people or two genealogically defined units comes into action in the palpable facts of economic life, jural relations, moral values, ceremonial duties, and ritual ideas and performances. Genealogical ties very often have economic or political utility and are sustained by powerful moral and religious sanctions. But behind all this lies a general notion which the natives themselves do not need to formulate but which is implicit in all their kinship behaviour. A great deal of Tale kinship custom is specific. In ceremonial situations different categories of kin often behave in prescribed ways which sharply distinguish them from one another. At a funeral ceremony, for example, one can tell at once, from the kind of gifts they bear and the attitudes they display, whether a party of mourners are relatives-in-law (*deenam*), clansmen (*yidɛm*), or sisters' children (*ahɔs*), of the bereaved. But in the routine of ordinary life the intercourse of kinsfolk has no such formal precision, and is often indistinguishable from the intercourse of friends, neighbours, or other associates. Not even the native, attuned as he is to the fine nuances of his cultural idiom, could tell whether two women working and chatting amicably together are co-wives, mother and daughter, or mother-in-law and daughter-in-law. The general notion we have mentioned corresponds to this indeterminate and elastic manifestation of kinship.

The Tallensi indicate it most clearly in connexion with the rules governing a proper marriage. They draw a sharp distinction between *dɔyam*, kinship, and *deen*, in-lawship. The crux of the rule of clan exogamy and of the collateral prohibition of marriage with consanguineous kin of any degree (and the natives do not distinguish these two classes of restrictions) is the principle that *dɔyam* and *deen* are irreconcilably contradictory. They must not be 'mixed' (*gyɛt*).

A striking illustration of this antithesis occurred at a sacrifice that Diŋkaha made to one of his ancestors. An ambitious and none too scrupulous braggart of considerable intelligence and drive, Diŋkaha had been very useful to me and had made the most of his connexion with me. One of the objects of this ceremony was to show off his friendship with me to his clansmen, and his prestige among them to me. It was, therefore, a specially lavish occasion. In the middle of the ceremony Diŋkaha's father-in-law called in. The old man was respectfully received and ushered into his daughter's rooms. Diŋkaha finished the sacrifice and began to distribute the meat. Various members of his lineage and clan received the portions due to them. And then, intoxicated with conceit at having his white friend in his house and at the obvious appreciation of his stock, in consequence, in the eyes of his clansmen, a rash impulse overcame him. Holding up a goat's foreleg—one of the ritually prescribed portions that should be reserved for those entitled by birth to share in the sacrifice—he launched out into a speech, the gist of which was that he desired his father-in-law to accept it in order to mark this special occasion. A sombre look came upon the old man's face. He was visibly shocked. Speaking gravely but curtly, he refused the gift. *Deenam*, he said, do not sacrifice together; it is an unheard-of thing; he could not accept the gift. Diŋkaha retired in discomfiture behind a smoke-screen of apologies.

Marriage implies the absence of kinship ties between the parties; kinship, the impossibility of marriage. Kinship ties exist in their own right; *deen* is an artificial alliance of a contractual nature. The parties to a marriage deliberately and voluntarily enter into a bond, the bride's guardian permitting her to marry in return for a promise on the part of the bridegroom's guardian to pay him four head of cattle. Kinship ties are not voluntary and are automatically binding. The parties to a marriage are bound by rights and duties which did not exist before. Kinship automatically entails moral, jural, and ritual bonds, whereas there is an avowed element of mutual coercion, and therefore potential tension, in the relations of in-laws. They rely upon a special, impartial jural instrument, the bride-price, for the adjustment of their rival claims on the woman.

Tallensi think of *deen* as a relationship for ever fraught with the possibility of conflict over these claims. Nearly all their litigation nowadays, like much inter-clan fighting in former days, concerns bride-price debts or the rival claims over a woman or her children of father-in-law and son-in-law. Such quarrels are incompatible with kinship. They would cut to pieces the solidarity of kinsfolk—that is why, say the Tallensi, kinsfolk do not marry. *Dɔyam*, in short, presupposes some degree of identification of the parties concerned, mutual or common interests, and especially a bond of amity that excludes strife which might fix a permanent gulf between them.

These norms of kinship the Tallensi regard as axiomatic, one might say as the *a priori* moral premisses of their social behaviour. Behind the utility of kinship in practical life and the jural and ritual sanctions that buttress kinship ties stands the notion of kinship as the rock-bottom category of social relations, inviolable in its own right. The root of this notion lies in the bond between parent and child and it reflects the fact that genealogical relationship is the binding medium of Tale social structure. The Tallensi are outspoken sceptics about human nature. They take it for granted that the ideal norms of kinship will often be violated. They know well, however, that they are usually effective and cannot be destroyed by the transgressions of individuals; for these, in the end, always bring their own revenge and are compensated for in the total flow of collective life. In any case, the lapses of individuals, and the fact that strong sanctions exist to check them, do not diminish the absolute, *a priori* character of kinship.

It is worth noting that economic reciprocity—which is a conspicuous element in kinship, especially among close kin—and jural rights and duties have a much less direct connexion with this fundamental assumption of kinship than religious bonds have. This is connected with the important place of ancestor worship in Tale society. To trace genealogical relationship it is necessary to recollect common ancestors; and if these have religious value, ritual allegiance to a common ancestor or ancestress inevitably forms an intrinsic feature of kinship ties and their most powerful sanction. The more distant a genealogical tie is, the more does it become a matter of moral and ritual, rather than of jural or economic, relations. We shall see this in more detail when we come to compare social relations within the domestic family with the relations of kinship outside the domestic family.

Two Classes of Kinship Relations

Any relation of kinship belongs to one of two classes. If people say 'We are *dɔyam*', the basic analogy they have in mind is that of siblings. Two men who are cognatically related to the same lineage—e.g. two men who have a common maternal uncle's lineage (*ahɔb yir*) or whose fathers or grandfathers had a common maternal uncle's lineage—describe themselves thus. They visualize their relationship primarily as one of common though independent religious allegiance to a particular line of common ancestors, in sacrifices to whom they may both partake. By the operation of the lineage principle two lineages might consider themselves to be related in such a manner. Kɔnbamɛŋ and Pudiniba, two young men of the same clan but of different sections of the clan, were good friends. When I asked them how their friendship had arisen, they resorted, characteristically, to the idiom of kinship. Being members of the same clan is not a sufficient reason for so personal a relationship as friendship. The reason they adduced was that they were both sister's sons (*ahɔs*) of the same Tɛnzugu clan. This had brought them together. Similarly, there is a much closer bond between Ziŋgan biis and Tambil biis, two of the five segments of Bɔɣayiedɔt yidɛm of Tongo, than between either of these segments and the other three segments, because their founding ancestors were sister's sons of the same clan.[1]

The other and more important class of kinship ties presupposes the analogy of the parent–child relationship. When a person says of another '*n-dɔɣume*—I have begotten (born) him', or, speaking of lineages, '*ti dɔɣabame*—We (my lineage) have begotten (born) them (their lineage)', what is meant is that the latter can trace a line of descent to the former or to the former's lineage. A man refers to a sister's son (*ahəŋ*) or to a classificatory *ahəŋ* in these terms. When I was staying at Kpata'ar, my servants received unusually generous hospitality and were obviously much more at ease than they had been at some places we had previously visited. I was several times told in explanation (on one occasion by some Kpata'ar children) that my two local boys were *dɔɣa* by the Kpata'ar na'ab's lineage. The father of one and the paternal grandfather of the other had been sister's sons of Kpata'ar. Again, two lineages can be related in this way, as, for instance, Naɣasaa yidɛm of Kpata'ar and Dmanpiog yidɛm of Gbeog are. The most important feature of such a relationship to the natives is that the lineage or individual of the senior generation sacrifices to their or his ancestors on behalf of the lineage or individual of the junior generation.

The idiom of kinship has such a dominant place in Tale thought that all social relations implying mutual or common interests tend to be assimilated to those of kinship. This happens, as has been shown in our previous volume, with ties of local contiguity and of politico-ritual interdependence between lineages and clans.

The Native Theory of Conception

The Tallensi, we have said, take cognizance of a very wide range of genealogical relationships, and they regard all such relationships as based on the physical fact of consanguinity. The starting-point for this lies in their notions about the physiology of conception. In their view man and woman have equally vital roles in the act of conception. Hence kinship through one's mother, and, consequently, through her ascendants, counts equally with—though admittedly less influentially than, and differently from—kinship through one's father and paternal line.

Dɔyam is the power of procreation. In women it is connected with menstruation, the external signs and periodicity of which are known to everybody, and the nature of which man, woman, or child readily refers to without the slightest squeamishness. A girl is said to be fit for child-bearing (*u saɣa dɔyam* [or *dɔyabu*]) when her monthly courses become established, her breasts develop, and her body takes on womanly

[1] Cf. *Dynamics of Clanship*, pp. 211 ff.

contours. Before a woman menstruates (*lu sie*, lit. fall from the waist), and after she ceases altogether to menstruate, she cannot bear children. When a woman has monthly periods she is capable of conception; when she is pregnant her periods stop. Thus menstruation, say the Tallensi, is a condition like pregnancy (*sie a puur*). It is the sign of capacity for child-bearing.

A man's *dɔyam* becomes fruitful some time after puberty (*u solɔme*, verb), the main sign of which is the emergence of pubic hair. At first, when the adolescent boy begins to have nocturnal emissions, his powers of procreation are not yet mature. It is only after some time, when he is completely *sol*, that he becomes capable of procreation. For procreation depends not on the sexual fluids ejaculated in the act of coitus by both man and woman, but on an active principle, as it were, in these fluids, the *ŋaamis*. The natives cannot explain more precisely what the *ŋaamis* is or how it works. What they maintain, emphatically, is that conception, both among men and among animals, cannot occur without sexual congress, and that it depends on the mingling (*gerɔm*) of the male sexual fluid with the female sexual fluid, or rather on the happy conjunction of their respective procreative essences (*ŋaamis*). Thus the function of the male is as essential as that of the female in procreation, and every child knows this.

Much evidence could be quoted in proof of this. Tallensi know that a male's procreative potency resides in the testicles (*lana*), and they castrate small livestock which they want to prevent from breeding. The suspension of sex relations with a wife who has a nursing child is not a ritual matter, subject to mystical sanctions, but a practical necessity in order to prevent the woman from conceiving again too soon. Its observance is a question of conscience and self-control and few men get through life without a lapse. Some, I was told by one of my most trustworthy informants, practise *coitus interruptus* in order to avoid impregnating a nursing wife. Some men believe in a 'safe period'. I once heard a theory of this kind stated by a man to a couple of friends. His very modern-sounding theory was that the 'safe period' follows shortly after menstruation, since menstruation is a sort of pregnancy, and a pregnant woman cannot conceive again. But the clearest indication of the role attributed by the Tallensi to sexual conjugation in procreation was given in a conversation I listened to at the Chief of Tongo's house. The chief and the elders were talking about the White Fathers at Bolɔga. Garbled ideas about their doctrines have reached many Tallensi. Jesus was mentioned. One man said that the Fathers claimed that His mother conceived Him without knowing a man. A vigorous argument followed. Most of the men were openly sceptical, saying that it was quite impossible. But one or two had a deeper respect for the white man. True, they admitted, black people cannot have children without sex relations; but perhaps the white man, with his wondrous powers and knowledge, has a medicine which enables women to conceive without the participation of a male.

The notion of a procreative essence as distinct from the sexual fluid, however vaguely formulated it is, is of importance. Tallensi distinguish between sexual vigour or desire and the power of procreation. They know that people who are sterile (*kundɔyar*) lack the latter but are not necessarily deficient in the former. Na'abzɔ, gossip said, was sterile because in his wild young days as a soldier he had lived with a Dagban woman who had maliciously caused him by some magical means to 'pour away all his power of begetting (*kpaa u dɔyam waabi bah*)' in excessive intercourse with her. The uncharitable believed that he was impotent to boot, but others were prepared to give him the benefit of the doubt.

The Tallensi regard *dɔyam* as, above all, a very precious human function, quite apart from the pleasures of sex. Thus, when Zikihib's young wife was left a grass widow for three years by her vagabond husband and had a child by a lover, it was unanimously condoned. Was she, it was argued, to cast away her powers of child-bearing for nothing (*zaŋ u dɔyam bah wari*) just because she had a faithless husband and was herself too devoted to her children by him to run off with another man?

Lastly, the notion of the *ŋaamis* is the point at which mystical beliefs enter into the theory of conception. The obvious physiological facts of parenthood are summed up in the maxim, 'A man and a woman unite to procreate a child'. But behind plain physiology lies a mystery. Sometimes a man sleeps with his wife on a single occasion and she becomes pregnant (*u ŋɔya puur*—lit. she seizes a belly). At other times a man has relations with his wife regularly for months and she fails to conceive. Thus conception depends, in the last resort, on Heaven (*Naawun*), the Final Cause by which the Tallensi rationalize chance and which they invoke when empirical or less recondite mystical explanations fail. There is an essential mystical factor in procreation; and if a man or a woman fails to beget or bear a child, appeals can be made to the ancestor spirits and other mystical powers that intervene directly in human destiny. That is why a barren woman in her heart of hearts never gives up hope of having a child as long as she is still of child-bearing age, though the Tallensi know that barrenness is often a fact of nature beyond cure by either empirical or mystical agencies.

The Significance of Paternity and Patriliny

A person's genealogical ties are fixed by his parentage. Among the Tallensi these are the ties that plot the trajectory of the individual's life. The rights and duties that are critical for his role and status in society all stem, in the last resort, from the fact of birth. A person cannot divest himself, or be divested, of the bonds created by his birth and yet remain a member of the society; nor can he fully and unconditionally acquire these bonds except by birth. No other ties can wholly supersede them in linking person to person and affiliating individuals to defined social groups.

We have noted, however, that not all genealogical ties have an equal value. Though a person acquires significant social ties through both parents, his agnatic relationships have an outstanding importance; and this is particularly so for a man. For not only is patrilineal descent the vertebral principle of Tale social organization and the vehicle of the continuity and stability of the social structure, but men hold the reins of authority, direct economic life, control the political organization, and are supreme in religious and ceremonial thought and action. From his father a man derives his rights to inherit land and other property, his clan membership and the political rights and ritual obligations that go with it, and his ritual relations with his most important ancestors. A woman does not inherit land or other property of value, nor does she succeed to political or ritual office. But clan membership and the concomitant totemic observances,[1] as well as her ritual allegiance to her patrilineal ancestors, mean a great deal for her social destiny and for her children. In short, paternity is the predominant side of parentage in this conspicuously patriarchal society.

Like many other primitive societies, the Tallensi recognize a distinction between physiological paternity and jural paternity—between *genitor* and *pater*, as Radcliffe-Brown puts it. However, the Tallensi feel very strongly that a person's physiological father is his or her right jural father. The assumption is that all the social attributes that come to one from one's father should come from a father who both begot one and recognizes one as his legitimate offspring. Thus there is an inevitable tendency for conflict to arise if a person's physiological and jural paternity do not coincide. Such a person tends to be penalized in respect of his social status, for jural paternity by itself cannot altogether take the place of physiological cum jural paternity.

The conflict is least in the case of an adulterine child, who is always accepted as the rightful child of its mother's husband. No difficulties at all arise in the case of a daughter, who marries out of the lineage as soon as she is nubile. An adulterine son has complete and unreserved filial status. He has full rights of inheritance, of succession, and of ritual access to his putative patrilineal ancestors. Nevertheless, the blot on the scutcheon is not without effect. The story of Sayɔbazaa's first-born son, Kologo, illustrates this.

Some years before my first visit to Tongo, Kologo had left his father to go and farm near Datɔk. There seemed to be no adequate motive for this in his case. But when Sayɔbazaa died, in 1936, and Kologo as chief mourner had to be summoned for the mortuary rites, I was able to piece together how it had occurred, from guarded hints and veiled comments

[1] Cf. *Dynamics of Clanship*, ch. ix.

made by other members of the family and by one of Sayəbazaa's maternal kinsmen. Kologo, it appeared, was an adulterine child. Sayəbazaa could never forget this, though it was not a thing that was ever mentioned in public. A man of strong principles, inclined in any case to keep a firm hand on his children, Sayəbazaa was often over-severe with Kologo. The tension admitted by custom to exist between a man and his first-born son was exacerbated. At length Kologo deliberately violated—or so Sayəbazaa said—the Namoo taboos of a first-born son; and Sayəbazaa thereupon cursed him and expelled him from the house. It was evident from the remarks which gave the clue to the story that the seed of discord here was Kologo's physical paternity, though it did not affect his rights to inherit his father's property and ancestral shrines.

This kind of psychological friction is said not to occur in the special case of a child begotten in permitted extra-marital intercourse, which the Tallensi do not regard as adultery (*pɔyambon*). A man who is sterile or impotent may allow his wife to conceive by another man. The proper way to do this is for him to inform the elders of his lineage first. With their blessing and consent he may give his wife permission to find a lover wherever she wishes—'*u gɔma, nye puur, ɔn nye Moog ni Zaŋbiog ɔn nyɛbma*—let her walk about to get a belly; if she meets a Mossi man or a Hausa man (i.e. any passer-by) let her copulate'—is the traditional formula with which he sets her free to be promiscuous, if she chooses, in order to become pregnant. Sensible men and women prefer a more reputable procedure, however. Either the husband asks a friend or kinsman not of his own clan to deputize for him sexually, or he lets the wife choose one of her own distant clan-brothers as a lover. This man is then formally deputed (*galəh*) to be the woman's lover by being presented to the lineage elders, who sacrifice a fowl on his behalf to the lineage ancestors, with an explanation of the circumstances and pleas for a blessing on the affair. The arrangement, though formal, is strictly private, for no man willingly admits to sterility or sexual incapacity; and when, as inevitably happens, it leaks out, public opinion is sympathetic rather than contemptuous. Tallensi say that such cases of begetting a child by proxy do not occur very often.

While I was in Taleland, Baŋam-Teroog's junior wife had a child by a deputed lover. Teroog was an old man, shrivelled and half-blind with age. He once begged me for medicine to restore his fertility, but admitted with regret that he was probably too old for procreation. He deputed his closest friend and distant sister's son, Naabdiya, to beget a child for him. The liaison continued throughout the woman's pregnancy, but ceased as soon as her child was born. I often saw Teroog with this baby, fondling and caressing it with a tenderness that showed more eloquently than words that he regarded it as his own child. Naabdiya, for his part, though his relations with Teroog were as cordial as ever, took no more interest in the infant than any man might take in his friend's children. Tale sentiment takes no cognizance of physical paternity in this situation. No kinship tie is recognized between the physiological father and the child he was deputed to beget. One might almost describe it as, from their point of view, a kind of artificial insemination.

The case of an unmarried woman's child (*yi-yeem-bii*) is different. It is brought up as the foster-child of her father or brother. If it is a girl, no difficulties occur, as she will eventually marry and Tale kinship ideas permit *her* children to regard her mother's lineage as their mother's brother's lineage (*ahɔb yir*). She will even be allowed to marry into her mother's clan provided it is a different major segment of the clan. Several instances of this are on record; for no stigma attaches to anybody concerned, since an illegitimate child is not a true clan member.

An illegitimate boy's circumstances are not so easy. The evidence of two cases I was acquainted with amply confirms conventional opinion on this subject. Such a boy will grow up to all intents and purposes as a child of his mother's father's or brother's family and as a full member of the clan. He will be treated exactly like other sons of the family, whom he will call his brothers. His quasi-father will, for example, provide the cattle and take the responsibility for his marriage, as would not be done for a legitimate sister's son (*ahɔŋ*) growing up in his maternal uncle's (*ahɔb*) home. But he has two fundamental disabilities, which nothing can overcome and which pass, by the principle of the corporate identity of the lineage, to his agnatic male descendants. He has no right to inherit his quasi-father's patrimonial estate, though he may be permitted to do so if there are no other heirs; and he has no right to sacrifice directly to his spirit, or consequently, to the lineage ancestors. He cannot, therefore, succeed to the custody of lineage ancestors' shrines or hold an office vested in the lineage. The tie of true agnatic descent, which alone confers these rights, cannot be fabricated.

An illegitimate boy's status in the lineage is in fact, therefore, inferior to that of his quasi-brothers. He is always liable to a certain amount of covert contempt, though good manners forbid the mention of his irregular descent in the normal course of events. But if he gets involved in a quarrel with his quasi-siblings or quasi-clansmen, even as a child, they might well taunt him as an interloper (*zaŋkuomər*). His lot may be harder, if he has an intractable character, than that of a sister's son (*ahɔŋ*) living with his mother's brother (*ahɔb*); for the latter has a home of his own to fall back upon, where he is entitled, by right of legitimate descent, to his patrimonial inheritance, protection, and communion in the ancestor cult. In no circumstances, however, can an illegitimate son be deprived of those rights that belong to him. His quasi-father's home is his home, his mother's clan his clan. From him may spring an accessory lineage of the clan. In theory, incidentally, he may marry a daughter of a different major segment of his adoptive clan, but I know of no case, in recent years, of this having occurred. Public sentiment would not be sympathetic to it, since he is felt to be so closely connected with the clan.

It sometimes happens that a woman who has an illegitimate child takes it with her when she gets married, and the child is brought up in her husband's house. Eŋwala's illegitimate son, Kumahe, grew up thus under the care of her husband, Yɛanbɔrəgya. The boy and his stepfather were greatly attached to each other. Kumahe farmed with Yɛanbɔrəgya like his own sons, and was treated like a son in the ordinary affairs of the household. When he began courting a daughter of his stepfather's clan, Yɛanbɔrəgya gave him fatherly support and counsel. But when Kumahe's prospective parents-in-law asked for an advance payment on the bride-price, Yɛanbɔrəgya neither provided it nor took responsibility for it. For Kumahe had not acquired filial status in Yɛanbɔrəgya's lineage, and the responsibility for the payment of bride-price on his behalf rested with his jural guardian, his mother's brother. Kumahe belongs to his mother's clan, and both he, his stepfather, and his mother's brother told me, at different times, that he would undoubtedly return one day to live amongst this clan.

The status of a male slave (*da'abər*) in former times was similar, though in some respects less advantageous. The Tallensi seem to have kept few slaves.[1] It is said that a man usually bought a male slave if he lacked a son to help him with his farming and to support him in his old age. Slaves were never natives of Taleland but hapless strangers from other parts of the Northern Territories found wandering in the country. Having no kinsfolk in Taleland to protect them they fell a prey to anyone who chanced to encounter them. Their only security lay in the taboo that made it obligatory for them to be handed over to chiefs, who alone had the ritual status entitling men to sell fellow men. To fit them into the social structure they were incorporated into the family and lineage of their owners by being placed under the spiritual guardianship of one of their owner's lineage ancestors' shrines. This gave a slave a quasi-filial status of the same kind, with the same rights and disabilities, as an illegitimate son's.

In his social relations with his quasi-paternal family and clan a slave was indistinguishable from an illegitimate member of the group. In a quarrel he might be abused as a slave—'a bought thing (*bonda'abər*)'—and his quasi-clansmen would be inclined to regard him with a kind of patronizing contempt. But his owner would take up the cudgels for him as energetically as for one of his own sons if he were wantonly

---

[1] When they are questioned on the subject, men of 50–60 can usually quote one or two slaves they knew of in their childhood, never more. The impression I got from talks with many people was that there were never more than five or six male slaves living at any one time in Tongo, and correspondingly fewer in smaller settlements.

insulted or molested; for it was held to be both good policy and a moral duty to treat a slave no differently from a son. As the ward of the lineage ancestors, he had a place and a moral status in the lineage; but, Tallensi say, he was bound to harbour some resentment at his invidious social position, and would certainly try to abscond if he were ill-used.

These ideas are as active as ever among the Tallensi; for a few ex-slaves still survive, and there are one or two sons, grandsons, and remoter agnatic descendants of slaves in many settlements, who, by the lineage principle, retain their ancestors' social status in a much attenuated form. These people have exactly the same place in society that they would have occupied in former times. To judge by their participation in social activities, both profane and ceremonial, there is no obvious distinction between them and other members of the clan. They are as loyal and patriotic members of the clan as any other members of it. Wɔla of Zoo always took a leading part in the public affairs and ceremonial activities of Zoo. I was surprised to discover accidentally that he was an ex-slave. I was told on excellent authority that he is still often teased about his slave status, but that he takes it in good part, saying that since the coming of the white man a slave is as good a man as his neighbour. Usually no one would so affront a man and his quasi-relatives as to refer pointedly to his slave status or descent if he did not provoke it by offensive conduct. Wrongly to accuse a person of slave descent, if only by implication, is a deadly insult. And even those of whom it is true never voluntarily betray it. Not everyone has Wɔla's aggressive sense of humour, and good manners require that tact and discretion be exercised in such delicate matters of social standing.

Analogously, a slave girl's (*da'abpɔk*) status resembled that of an illegitimate daughter. She was taken in marriage like any other girl, so her children had no disabilities in respect of their patrilineal connexions. They regarded their mother's quasi-paternal kin as their maternal uncle's lineage. But I have records of cases in which the descendants of a slave woman have sought out her true paternal kin in a distant land in order to establish correct ritual ties with them.

All the men with whom I discussed the question affirmed without hesitation that it would be disgraceful and immoral to treat a slave, or an illegitimate son or brother, differently from true agnatic kin. But they all emphasized, nevertheless, that a slave or an illegitimate son cannot possibly become a son or a brother in the full sense of these terms. He can be to you *in loco filii* or *fratris* but not *filius* or *frater*, since he cannot sacrifice directly to his quasi-father's spirit or inherit, as of right, his patrimony. The principle at issue is that physical father and social father, *genitor* and *pater*, must be the same person. The vicissitudes of marriage illustrate the same point.

It often happens that a young woman becomes the bride of one man, is later married to another man, by whom she conceives or has a child, and finally returns to settle down with her first husband. The second husband (or his heir) then has the right, at any time during its life, to redeem his begotten child by paying over to the woman's father a proportion of the bride-price equal to one cow. Whether he has or has not completed the formalities of marriage is immaterial. His right rests upon the fact of his acknowledged paternity. Tallensi attach so much importance to having children that they generally make every effort to assert this right. But often enough, through poverty, parsimony, or mere indifference, the child may be left to grow up under the care of its stepfather. There is no difficulty in the case of a girl. When she marries, her stepfather receives one cow out of her bride-price, the cow of rearing (*ughug naah*), in recompense for the effort and expense of rearing her; her true father, or his heir, receives the remaining three head of cattle, one of which he hands over to his erstwhile father-in-law (or his heir) as the redemption payment for his daughter; and the girl's children regard her physical father's lineage, now formally established as her jural father's lineage, as their mother's paternal lineage.

The case of a boy is, again, more complicated. He may be accepted as his stepfather's own child, as if he were an adulterine child. In theory he cannot be excluded from any filial rights in this man's house. In practice his position is anomalous, both in his own estimation and in the eyes of his stepbrothers. The feeling exists that he is a member of his stepfather's clan on sufferance; sometimes a crisis develops when he tries to assert his rights of inheritance. In any case, Tallensi declare, when a boy in this position grows to manhood he usually endeavours, sooner or later, to return to his true paternal home (*kul u ba yiri*). I came across two or three instances of men who grew up with a stepfather and eventually returned to their true agnatic clan. One of them was quite an old man when he did so.

A man has an unconditional right to do this and must be accepted into his father's lineage and clan. He can assert his filial status without any reservations both in religious and in secular matters. To attempt to exclude him would be contrary to the Tale view that any addition to the numbers of a settlement is valuable in itself. What is more important, it would be a violation of the fundamental norms of kinship and therefore an offence against the ancestors, specifically against the new-comer's father and forefathers. Tallensi say that in fact no one would dream of rejecting a son who comes home in this way. The old man I have referred to not only superseded a 'brother' in the inheritance of his father's estate, but was elected tendaana over the heads of men who had dwelt in their natal settlement all their lives. The new-comer's jural status must, however, be regularized in the normal way. Either his father or his father's heir, or, if for some reason he is unable to do so, the man himself, must pay over to his mother's father's heirs the cow of redemption.

The Ritual Coefficient of Patriliny

All these cases of irregular paternity bring out a point of central importance in native thought. As we shall see in more detail later, the bonds of physical consanguinity and the concomitant social ties created by parenthood are *ipso facto* spiritual and moral bonds. They have a ritual coefficient in which the natives see their deepest meaning and value. One's bonds with one's lineage imply a ritual bond with one's patrilineal ancestors and other mystical forces associated with the existence and well-being of the lineage. They are the chief mystical powers governing the life of the individual. Legitimate paternity is a *sine qua non* for a right relationship with one's agnatic ancestor spirits who watch over one's whole life from the moment of birth. There is a spiritual hiatus between an illegitimate son or a slave's son and his adoptive lineage ancestors. Being only indirectly under their tutelage, and unable to gain direct contact with them by offering sacrifices himself, he cannot use them to master the vicissitudes and frustrations of life as freely as a true scion of their line. Also, as we have seen, the ancestor spirits are the principal sanction enforcing a man's rights to full filial status in his physical father's lineage. As we have observed, political and ritual office can be held only by men who are legitimate members of the lineage in which these offices are vested; and the sanction for this lies in the key functions of these offices in the cult of the ancestors and of the other mystical powers coupled with the lineage.

All social relations in which agnatic descent has a decisive function have this ritual coefficient. Legitimate paternity is bound up with a man's exclusive rights over his wife's reproductive powers, conferred on him by marriage. A child's legitimate paternity is jeopardized if it is conceived or born in a situation in which its father's marital rights do not prevail. Hence, sexual intercourse between a man and his wife (and by extension between any man of the husband's medial lineage and a woman of the wife's medial lineage) at her paternal home is rigorously tabooed; it is a ritual 'pollution of the room (*sayam dug*)'—i.e. an outrage against the lineage identity—of the girl's father; for a woman has the status of a daughter in her father's house, where she comes under her father's authority and the tutelage of his ancestors.

In keeping with this, a child must not be born in its mother's father's, or brother's house. Its ties with its maternal kin must not be confounded with its bonds with its paternal kin. These represent opposed forces in its social world, and matrilateral kinship ties must not be allowed to become a threat to lineage ties. A woman bears a child to her husband, an additional member of his lineage and clan. When she conceives, it is the right and duty of her husband and his family to care for her. His ancestor spirits must guard her and the unborn child. In the perilous hour of childbirth she must be cared for by her husband and his family, and watched over by his ancestors. If she or the child dies in childbirth the responsibility falls on her husband. A child should be born under its father's roof, literally into the lineage to which it comes as a profit (ɲoor) and a responsibility, and under the auspices of its patrilineal ancestors, the spiritual arbiters of its destiny, to whom it will later in life bring sacrifices. Its life will depend on these ancestors, one of whom will immediately demand to be made its spiritual guardian, charged with preserving its life (mar u ɲɔvɔr).

Not only should a child be born under its father's roof, but it should, ideally, be reared, or at least be brought through the first dangerous months of infancy, in its father's house. Circumstances occasionally compel a child to be entrusted to the care of its mother's family, and the Tallensi are practical enough to accept this necessity with equanimity. But they are extremely reluctant to let a young infant pass out of the direct tutelage of its paternal kin and ancestors even for a short while. Thus strong objection is raised if a young wife takes her infant and goes to stay at her parents' house for some time. Here, again, practical necessity may leave no alternative, but there is always a feeling of uneasiness, as can be seen from the following case. When Nindɔyat of Zubiuŋ died, his youngest wife went home to her father's house at Tɔŋ-Seug, about a quarter of a mile from her late husband's house, taking her infant of some six months with her. Nindɔyat's brother and prospective heir tried to prevent her going, but she was not well, and they had to admit that she would be better cared for by her mother than by her co-wives. So they allowed her to go. A couple of weeks later, however, the baby fell ill, and though the young mother was staying only a few minutes' walk from her late husband's house, she returned to it immediately. 'She came running back home', her late husband's brother told me, 'because the child was ill. Its (dead) father had not agreed for it to be taken away (that is, the dead father, now a spirit, had mystically caused the child's illness as a sign of his displeasure). And supposing the child were to die at its maternal uncle's house? Should we not say that they had caused the death of our child?' The proper ritual measures to cure the child, without which practical leech-craft could not avail, could only be taken by its father or his representative in its father's house. The young mother believed this as firmly as her late husband's heir.

For all these reasons it is a taboo (kihɔr) for a child to be born in its mother's father's house. His ancestor spirits cannot watch over mother and child, for they do not 'own (so)' the child. It is, therefore, dangerous for the child's health and chances of survival. Of course, such a thing may, and sometimes does happen by accident. Then the child's father must, whenever he can afford it, erase the pollution by the ceremony of 'removing the blood (vaa ziem)' of the birth from his father-in-law's house. He sends a sheep and beer to his father-in-law as a placation gift. Accepting the gift, the old man calls on his ancestors to bless his son-in-law and to forgive the offence. The beer is drunk by the elders of the father-in-law's clan segment. This ceremony should be performed before the child is old enough to visit its maternal grandparents. For if the child visits its mother's father's house before the pollution is erased and sets eyes—as inevitably it must—on the midden heap, where its placenta is buried, it will die. Instances are known of men who, defying convention and the ancestor spirits, have taken daughters from their husbands, owing to non-payment of bride-price, just before they were due to bear. Decent folk regard such behaviour as little short of monstrous, for it places mother and child in great danger, bereft as they are of the care and spiritual guardianship of the child's paternal kin and ancestors. It is for this reason, Tallensi say, that it is a taboo to demand a girl's bride-price while she is pregnant. Many a man wins a respite from his father-in-law's importunity on account of his wife's pregnancy.

The Significance of Maternal Parentage and the Uterine Line

The Tallensi, as we have seen, insist on the equal importance of both parents in the procreation of a child. Though patrilineal descent is overwhelmingly dominant in the jural, economic, and ritual constitution of Tale society, it would be surprising if maternal origin had no institutional function in Tale social organization and ideology. In fact, as has been shown in our analysis of the lineage system,[1] the two principles of patrilineal descent and maternal origin always work together. The two ideas are inseparable in native thought and run like a cry and its echo through the whole social structure. Whenever I have discussed these matters with informants they have generally begun by enumerating all the things that make 'paternal parentage (*ba dɔyam*)' the most important fact of one's life, and have usually concluded by pointing out that, of course, 'maternal parentage (*ma dɔyam*)' is also of the greatest importance, though in a different way.

One indication of the sociological significance of maternal origin is the quality of the bond between mother's brother (*ahɔb*) and sister's son (*ahɔŋ*), either of the first degree or in a classificatory sense.[2] A person's own maternal uncle and maternal grandfather (*yaab*), and their inner lineage (*dug*), impinge directly and frequently on his life. The maternal uncle's home is a person's second home. He has a quasi-filial status there; and in addition to close bonds of sentiment with his uncle and his uncle's close kin, he has specific ceremonial rights and duties in relation to them. Though he has no property, succession, or inheritance rights in his uncle's home, a man has special material privileges there, which give expression to the notion of his quasi-filial status. They show that he is equated with a son in sentiment while

[1] See *Dynamics of Clanship*, ch. iii.
[2] Cf. ch. xi, below.

strictly differentiated from a son in jural terms. The kinship tie between sister's son and mother's brother is an important breach in the genealogical fence enclosing the agnatic lineage; it is one of the main gateways of an individual's social relations with members of other clans than his own.

But the recognition accorded to the mother's agnatic kin does not bring out the deeper implications of maternal origin as the complementary of paternal origin. These implications are contained in the concept *soog* (pl. *saarət* or *soorət*). This concept involves the idea of matrilineal descent in contrast to that of patrilineal descent. Both in its range of efficacy, its mode of operation, its jural and ritual value, and its emotional and sentimental connotation, matrilineal descent stands in contrast to patriliny.

For obvious physiological reasons the bond of consanguinity with one's mother is unique and unalterable; and it is a peculiarly personal bond. The fact that one's jural status is not derived from one's mother serves to emphasize the personal nature of this bond. A person's mother may desert his father and leave him to be reared (*ugh*) by another woman; he may feel some resentment over this all his life; but she remains his true mother, 'the mother who bore him (*ma dɔyarug*)'. Nothing can alter this fact or extinguish the kinship ties that arise from it.

We postpone for a later chapter a consideration of the emotional ties of mother and child. The concept *soog* has definite emotional implications; but here we are concerned with its implications for the social structure. *Soog* means a bond of consanguinity which excludes completely any reckoning with lineage affiliation. People who are *saarət* define themselves biologically as 'the offspring of one womb'—or, in the actual phraseology of the natives, 'to have come from one vagina (*yi pɛn yɛni*)'. This is the common way of stating it; occasionally, but far less commonly, one hears people defining themselves as patrilineally related by the corresponding phrase 'to be the children of one penis (*woor yɛni biis*)'.

Saarət, therefore, are uterine kin. Between mother and child there is a uterine bond corresponding to the agnatic bond between father and child; and children of one woman are *saarət*, irrespective of their paternity. A woman may have children by different men of the same clan or of different clans; they are *saarət*, irrespective of their clan affiliations.

Soog is more than the bond of personal kinship between mother and child, and between siblings by the same mother. It is the bond of uterine descent perpetuated through the female line in the same way as the bond of agnatic descent is transmitted through the male line. Uterine siblings are *saarət*; uterine sisters' children are *saarət* (but not uterine brothers' children, for the children of men are not their father's *saarət*); uterine female cousins' children are *saarət*; and so on, theoretically, without limit. In short, people of common uterine descent are socially identified with one another; but they do not form a corporate group.

The social recognition of the uterine line entails not only that *saarət* have defined ways of behaving towards one another, but also that the fact of matrilineal descent is given an institutional embodiment. Matrilineal descent confers distinctive social attributes on people. In this Tale culture follows the rule found in most West African cultures that recognize both lines of descent.[1] The dominant line of descent confers the overtly significant attributes of social personality—jural status, rights of inheritance and succession to property and office, political allegiance, ritual privileges and obligations; and the submerged line confers certain spiritual characteristics. Among the Tallensi it is easy to see that this is a reflex of the fact that the bond of uterine descent is maintained as a purely personal bond. It does not subserve common interests of a material, jural, or ritual kind; it unites individuals only by ties of mutual interest and concern not unlike those that prevail between close collateral kin in our culture. While it constitutes one of the factors that counterpoise the exclusiveness of the agnatic line, it does not create corporate groups competing with the agnatic lineage and clan. Carrying only a spiritual attribute, the uterine tie cannot undermine the jural and politico-ritual solidarity of the patrilineal lineage.

Uterine Kinship and the Notion of Witchcraft

The critical spiritual attribute carried by the *soog* line is the potentiality of being a witch (*sɔi*, pl. *soob*—a term evidently cognate with *soog*). This potentiality adheres only to the female line and defines that line in social terms. 'This is my *soog*' a person usually says when introducing a uterine relative. 'If he (or she) flies magically (*aɣat*) I, too, fly magically; if he sees magically (*nye*) I, too, see magically.' The potentiality of being a witch is hereditary in the female line. A woman's son and daughter may both become witches if she is a witch. If a person is accused of being a witch, all his or her *saarət* are automatically suspect of this inborn mystical vice. His agnatic kin are not implicated, not even his own father or his half-siblings by the same father. These are the points Tallensi invariably stress, both among themselves and in answer to an inquirer, if they are asked to define the meaning of *soog*.

It is significant that witchcraft occupies a minor place in Tale mystical thought and ritual action, and that is one reason why the Tallensi make no secret of its hereditary transmission in the female line. They

[1] Cf., e.g., R. S. Rattray, *Ashanti*; C. D. Forde, 'Kinship in Umor—Double Unilateral Organization in a Semi-Bantu Society', *American Anthropologist*, xli, 1939.

PLATE I

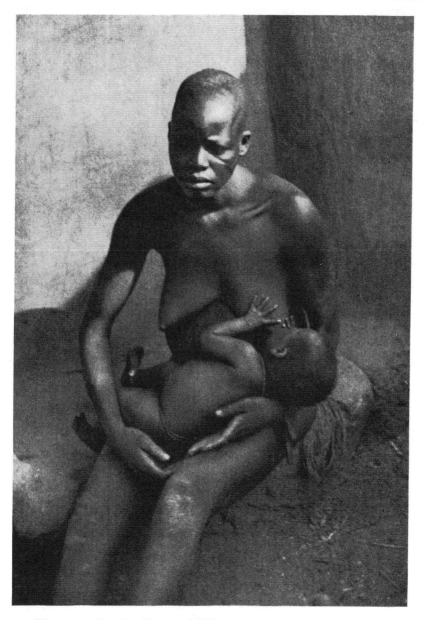

The relationship of mother and child is the root of the uterine (*soog*) tie

PLATE 2

a. The domestic family is the matrix of kinship. A family party out lifting ground-nuts on the home farm. Their homestead is in the background. From right to left: the head of the family, his infant daughter, his adult son, the latter's wife and baby, the family head's wife and daughter

b. A domestic sacrifice: cleaning and apportioning the meat of the goat at the conclusion of the sacrifice. Baŋan-Teroog, his senior wife, and his junior wife's two children. The old woman is holding a chicken ready for the next sacrifice

have no clear notion of witchcraft, no detailed theories of its mode of operation, and no institutionalized means of combating or sterilizing it. A witch (*sɔi*) is supposed to fly about (*u ayarəme*) at night in the guise of a ball of fire; she—for the Tallensi tend to think of a witch as a woman, though they say that men may be witches too—is supposed to be clairvoyant, to 'see (*nye*)' hidden things. She can recognize fellow witches, foresee death coming to a particular person, prophesy an epidemic, and so forth; she may be beneficent, able to impart luck to a person in a mysterious way, or maleficent, killing people by eating (*ɔb*) their souls (*sii*). This is the sum of Tale ideas about the nature of witches. Actually, these qualities make up what is mainly an imaginary stereotype. One never hears of particular individuals being credited with the socially useful qualities or being suspected of possessing the anti-social qualities attributed to witches. Witchcraft is only attributed to people *ex post facto*, when an event occurs for which an explanation in terms of witchcraft is sought.

Witchcraft is something on the fringe of Tale mystical thought and ritual values. I have more than once heard elders of the most conservative way of thinking, to whom the native scheme of ritual values is the most important thing in life, declare roundly that there is no such thing as a witch. Though the Tallensi do not put it into clear words, they obviously feel that the idea of witchcraft is a mixture of superstition and folk-lore, and not a part of the system of mystical and ritual values that really matters for the conduct of life. Of course, superstition and folk-lore are not wholly negligible. Circumstances occur, now and then, in which people fall back on the idea of a witch's occult aggression in order to cope with anxieties and frustrations that are normally neutralized through the agency of the ancestor cult; and then a particular person may be accused of being a witch. Significantly, in every case that has come to my notice, some dating back twenty or thirty years and all of them together numbering less than ten, the accused has been a woman. Most accusations of this sort are in the first instance made by women against co-wives, and are symptomatic of the tensions inherent in the joint family.

An accusation of being a witch is the private affair of the accused's husband and his maximal lineage, her paternal family, and those of her *saarət* who are in touch with her. In former days, if the accusation was confirmed by a diviner, the accused might insist on undergoing the arrow ordeal (*kuh sɔ-peema*), or be compelled to do so by her husband's lineage and her *saarət* in order to prove her innocence. She had to stab herself with a poisoned arrow in public at the same time as a branch of a *keŋkaŋ* (Ficus) tree was plucked; and if she were guilty, it was believed that she would die before the branch withered. But it is characteristic of the Tale attitude to witches that a person who died thus was accorded a proper funeral—unlike, for example, a person who dies of small-pox—and that the decision was not accepted as conclusive by her *saarət* whom it directly implicated. A proven witch's uterine kin, her children in particular, felt the shame for a time, but they were not publicly stigmatized or penalized. Even the husband of an apparently guilty woman would, judging by what happens nowadays, very often continue privately to believe in her innocence; and if he admitted her guilt would not allow this to influence his relations with his children by her.

The public attitude to a witch nowadays is illustrated by the following case which occurred during my stay among the Tallensi. A young man from Yinduuri went to visit a kinsman at Moyaduur. Arriving at his kinsman's house, he was offered some cold porridge by an old woman of the house who happened to be the only person at home. Now, cold porridge is not a dish to offer to a guest. The poorest native would blush with shame if he had nothing better to put before a visitor. But in this instance the young man was weary and hungry after a long tramp. His kinsman was not at home to offer him more seemly hospitality and the old woman had nothing else. So he accepted it gladly.

Later in the day, on his way home, the youth was suddenly taken ill with what soon proved to be acute dysentery. He at once thought of the old woman's cold porridge and told his family of this when he reached home. Next day he died. Thereupon his father accused the old woman of having bewitched the youth through the medium of the cold porridge, and so caused his death. Her unconventional hospitality and the sequence of events seemed to leave no doubt about her guilt. There was, it is true, no obvious motive, but this was not taken into consideration. Indeed, as one man remarked, the youth was himself partly to blame, for no self-respecting adult would eat cold porridge at someone else's house. However, the old woman was sent for and the matter submitted to divination. As the dead youth's clansmen had no doubt about her guilt, it is not to be wondered at that the diviner declared her to have bewitched him. In vain she protested her innocence. The head of the youth's maximal lineage told all his people to mock (*wool*) her with a derisive chant. Neighbouring clans took up the chant, as she passed on her way home, and some weeks later it was made the theme of one of the dance songs of the Gɔlib Festival. 'Wherever she goes', my informants said, 'men, women, and children will look askance at her and jeer at her for being a witch. Shame and grief will dog her, and she will pine away and die.' It was for fear of this kind of public ostracism that anyone accused of being a witch in the old days insisted on undergoing the arrow ordeal.

The main reason why witchcraft is of minor significance in Tale mystical thought is because the elaborate ancestor cult and the Earth cult deal adequately with most social and psychological tensions in terms consistent with the total social structure. The idea of witchcraft is not easily reconcilable with the structure of Tale society, dominated as it is by the patrilineal principle. As we know,[1] the residential unit is based on the agnatic lineage and the local community as a whole is based on lineage grouping. Most corporate and co-operative activities depend on lineage ties. The notion of maleficent secret malice involved in the idea of witchcraft is incompatible with the structure of the localized lineage. The occurrence of witchcraft within a lineage would poison the mutual confidence of agnates, disrupt their corporate relationships, and so throw social life into confusion. As it is, the pegging of witchcraft to the uterine line serves to circumvent any danger it might be to the community. An accusation of witchcraft does not implicate the lineage. It is an individual matter, and other individuals on whom it might be expected to throw suspicion are scattered through various lineages and clans. They may protest, but they have no means of taking organized action in defence of their reputation. In any case, an accusation of witchcraft has a very limited range of reaction. Other lineages and families than those injured by the alleged witch do not feel the injury, and even if they harbour uterine kin of the accused person, self-interest prompts them to disregard the implications of the accusation. The folk-lore of witchcraft provides loopholes for such adaptations of logic to social realities. Some say, for example, that a person only becomes a bad witch if his or her mother gives him or her 'witch's medicine' to eat in infancy.

The hereditary transmission of the capacity of being a witch is not connected with the blood (*ziem*), according to Tale physiological ideas. Both parents transmit their blood to their offspring, as can be seen from the fact that children may resemble either parent in looks. It is solely a matter of the eye (*nif*, pl. *nini*)—not the physical eye but the inner, clairvoyant eye of the witch.

Uterine Kinship and the Notion of Tyuk

The social definition of uterine descent in terms of the notion of witchcraft is consistent with its functions in the structure of Tale society. The meaning of *soog* to the native is neatly symbolized in this notion. And this is true, also, of the only other attribute of social personality that is held to follow the uterine connexion. This is summed up in the concept of *tyuk*.

A person through whose words or actions fighting that leads to the slaying of a man or men is instigated bears a particular kind of mystical responsibility. The slaying of a man gives rise to a chain of mystical blood-guilt, and the person who bears the guilt of instigation may have been an unwitting agent and unaware of his guilt. Supposing, for example, I summon a man from another settlement to come and see me about something, and on his way home he meets a man to whom he owes a debt. Supposing the two men have an argument which ends in

[1] *Dynamics of Clanship*, ch. x.

blows and my visitor gets killed by accident. Then the slayer will bear one kind of mystical blood-guilt and I will bear the *tyuk* guilt. I may not realize this; indeed, it may not be discovered until, on the occasion of my death, the diviner reveals that my ancestor spirits caused my death in retribution for my unpurged *tyuk* guilt. This was the case with Siiyɛlib of Tongo. When he died it was revealed through divination that he had borne the *tyuk* guilt for the punitive expedition against the Hill Talis twenty-five years previously. He had lodged a complaint against a Yinduuri man with the District Commissioner, and the white man's attempt to bring the Yinduuri man to book had led to the first brush with the Hill Talis. Other incidents followed, but the real reason why the white man launched a punitive attack on the Hill Talis a year or so later was because he had been enraged by the insults and defiance of the people of Yinduuri when he went to arrest the abductor of Siiyɛlib's wife and child. The test of historical accuracy would have been quite irrelevant in this context. Siiyɛlib's clansmen were interpreting the facts subjectively, in accordance with the native system of moral values and mystical beliefs, so as to fit his death logically to the morally and ritually significant events of his social biography.

A person who bears *tyuk* guilt must be ritually cleansed—'to wash *tyuk* (*su tyuk*)' is the technical expression—or else he and his family will be dogged by sickness, death, and other disasters. After the cleansing rites, the medicinal roots used are wrapped tightly in the skin of a species of civet cat (*tyuk*—hence the general term for this complex of ideas and actions) and the bundle is lashed securely to a rafter of the man's room. It must never be disturbed; if it is, quarrelling and fighting break out. A strong wind shaking the rafters of the room is enough to stir up strife. *Tyuk* once incurred remains a taint for ever; for it is really the evocation of a latent proclivity (so one must interpret the ideas of the natives on this subject) that goes with the uterine line. When a man undergoes the *tyuk* cleansing rites he summons all his *saarət* who are known to him to come and 'eat' the medicine with him, for this dangerous proclivity once evoked in one of them involves them all.

The concept of *tyuk* guilt and its connexion with the uterine line is less explicit than that of witchcraft. There is no idea of its being a potentiality transmitted by birth from mother to child. Even more than witchcraft it is a *post hoc* inference; but the natives do not explicitly attach a *propter hoc* interpretation to it. Uterine kin do not share their *soog*'s *tyuk* guilt; they are, as it were, mystically contaminated by it, by reason of their *soog* tie. As one informant put it, *tyuk* is 'contagious to (*de lɔŋəra*)' *saarət* like a disease, or it 'kindles (*de ta'agəra*)' *saarət* like a spreading fire. If a man has incurred and washed *tyuk* then the most trivial argument in which he happens to be involved is often in danger of becoming a real quarrel; and his *saarət* also become hot-tempered, or, perhaps, become prone to give vent to hot temper

It is analogous to the way in which a man's agnatic descendants become liable for his sins, though it is not so rigorous and consequential in action as the responsibility for sins and delicts that adheres to the male line. *Tyuk* is connected primarily with males; though it is of minor significance in the social definition of uterine kinship, compared with witchcraft, it obviously fits in with the principles of Tale social organization in the same way.[1]

Uterine Kinship as a Personal Bond

As we have observed, the fundamental distinction between uterine kinship and agnatic descent is that the former does not give rise to corporate units of social structure. *Soog* is essentially a personal bond, a bond of mutual interest and concern uniting individual to individual. Witchcraft, similarly, is an individual act of mystical aggression due to personal malice against an individual. The model of the relations between *saarǝt* is the affection, devotion, and strong feeling of mutual identification that prevails between parent and child or between full siblings of the same sex. Its keynote is mutual trust as between equals. It is never thought of as a matter of rights and duties but as a matter of sentiment, of spontaneous goodwill and intimate, personal confidence. Hence the term *soog* is often loosely used to refer to someone with whom one has a relationship of a similar sort, or to denote a very close relative of a class of relatives, whether or not they are true *saarǝt*. An intimate and trusted friend is like your *soog*, the Tallensi say. Two daughters of the same lineage, but of unrelated mothers, married into a single joint family feel themselves to be particularly closely related and identified with each other by contrast with their conjugal family, and thus speak of each other as 'my *soog*'. The children of two men who were uterine kin, keeping up the friendship of their fathers, talk of themselves as *saarǝt*. Two men of the same lineage, whether they are close or distant agnates, who have a common maternal uncle's lineage (*ahǝb yiri*)—i.e. whose mothers' brothers belong to a single segment of a maximal lineage—feel a bond of personal kinship distinguishing their relationship with each other from their relationships with their co-members of the lineage. In contexts where they wish to emphasize their personal bonds in contrast to their common membership of the lineage they might describe each other as 'my *soog*'. And I once heard a man refer to his son-in-law as 'my *soog* son-in-law (*n-deem-soog*)'. This is a contradiction in terms, for marriage being prohibited between kin of any degree, a man cannot be both a son-in-law and a *soog*. But the speaker explained that he was using this term in order to distinguish

---

[1] There is an interesting psychological problem here, but it lies outside our present scope. *Tyuk* and witchcraft might be regarded as the male and female aspects, respectively, of deep-seated vindictive impulses connected with the mother.

this son-in-law from his other sons-in-law, both because this young man was the husband of his own daughter, whereas the others were the husbands of his dead brothers' daughters, and because this son-in-law was as devoted to him as his own sons. Tallensi often say that a man's own children are virtually his *saarət*, though not technically so. There is no confusion in the native mind about these usages of the concept of *soog*; they understand and explain clearly that these are metaphorical usages.

The feeling of close, personal intimacy in the relationship of uterine kin is best brought out in the native attitude about sexual relations between *saarət*. It is incestuous if the couple know they are *saarət*, however distant their uterine connexion. It is like incest between own brother and sister, and is viewed in the same way as the latter. Tallensi think of it with disgust rather than horror. Sexual desire for a known *soog* relative is so utterly inconsistent with the general attitude of uterine kin towards each other that it is unthinkable in a decent person. It is a taboo (*kihər*) which normal people take for granted. There are no ritual or jural sanctions against incest with a *soog*, and Tallensi would say that there is no need for them. At no point are the relations of uterine kin subject to sanctions; 'I will not refuse him, I will not deny him anything', says the native of a *soog*, thinking of this as an axiomatic feature of *soog* kinship.

Marriage between *saarət* is, of course, forbidden, and the elders of the lineages concerned would never allow it if the couple are known to be uterine kin. But sometimes, owing to the devious ramifications of uterine kinship, a married couple discover that they are distant *saarət*. If there are no children, or the elders of the girl's lineage want a pretext for taking her from her husband, they might insist on the dissolution of the marriage. If a child has been born, or the couple refuse to part for any other reason, their kinship must be ritually severed. The rite is very simple. The essential act consists of the husband and wife grasping a calabash with one hand each and wrenching it in halves. This symbolizes the splitting (*bɔk*) of their kinship.

It is not uncommon for a man to have one or more *saarət* (other than his siblings) among the members of his own clan. They may be the sons of one mother by different fathers, or the sons of sisters, or of more distantly related uterine kinswomen who married into the same clan. In such cases one can see how the loyalties based on uterine kinship are distinguished from the ties of lineage membership. Yikpɛmdaan and Tinta'aləm of Tɔŋ-Kuorəg, the two senior elders of Kuorəg section, are *saarət*, but members of different segments of the section. Tinta'aləm's children and brothers' children speak of Yikpɛmdaan as their father (*ba*); Yikpɛmdaan and Tinta'aləm speak of each other as brothers, since their mothers were full sisters. Their mutual affection and attachment, going back to the childhood of Yikpɛmdaan, when he lived for a time with Tinta'aləm, are well known. Tinta'aləm never undertakes anything of importance without consulting Yikpɛmdaan; Yikpɛmdaan need never be in want of a sheep or goat to sacrifice if there are sheep and goats in Tinta'aləm's house. If any member of the lineage segment of which Tinta'aləm is the head gets into difficulty, he goes at once to Yikpɛmdaan for counsel and help.

A more telling case is that of Lɔyani and Gai. They belong to different segments of Zubiuŋ-Yakɔra.[1] Many years ago Gai quarrelled with the elders of the maximal lineage over the succession to the lineage *bɔyar*. The Yakɔra Tɛndaana of the time took an oath binding all the people of Yakɔra to have nothing to do with Gai in jural and ritual matters until he apologized and a ritual reconciliation was made. Gai and his family keep aloof from all corporate activities of Zubiuŋ-Yakɔra. He has obstinately rejected several indirect advances made to him suggesting a reconciliation. One day there was a funeral at Gai's house, and I called to see how a man who is virtually ostracized by his clan would manage an affair that is usually a corporate activity of the whole clan. Finding no other Yakɔra people at the funeral, I went round to Lɔyani's house afterwards. We discussed Gai and his affairs; and Lɔyani, with that blunt candour that has won him general esteem, told me the whole story. Gai's conduct, Lɔyani concluded, was specially distressing to him. 'For', said he, with a trace of bitterness, 'Gai is my *soog*. I should be the one to go to his help immediately and to support him in all his troubles. But if I did, would not the people of Zubiuŋ say that I was breaking faith? Would I not be rejecting the oath of the late (Yakɔra) Tɛndaana? And so I can do nothing.'

In this case Lɔyani's position of influence and responsibility in the maximal lineage compels him to put the interests of lineage unity before those of his *soog*, and Gai's obduracy makes it more difficult for him to compromise. The case of Ɔndieso and Nɛna'ab, who are also *saarət* belonging to different segments of the same maximal lineage, is more usual. They 'borrow (*pɛŋ*)' things from each other on the same principle as do members of an expanded family. Normally, if a man borrows something from a member of a lineage segment other than his own, it is a debt that must be repaid in due course. Eight or nine years ago, Ɔndieso borrowed a goat from Nɛna'ab's son. No request was ever made for repayment; but about three years later, Nɛna'ab borrowed three shillings from Ɔndieso; and this was tacitly understood, by both, to have cancelled the debt of the goat. In 1936 an ancient quarrel between Ɔndieso's segment and Nɛna'ab's segment that had been dormant for years flared up again owing to a dispute over the inheritance of a widow. For some months the two segments were completely estranged, the more so as the head of Nɛna'ab's segment had taken the dispute to the chief and so brought the slur of publicity on the head of Ɔndieso's segment. Just then there was a death in Nɛna'ab's family;

[1] Cf. *Dynamics of Clanship*, ch. vi, passim.

and Ɔndieso was one of the first to come to the help of his *soog* in his sorrow. The other members of Ɔndieso's segment demonstratively remained away.

Other ties of matrilateral kinship also create bonds of personal attachment between members of the same maximal lineage, but none is so effective as that of uterine kinship.

The Dispersion of Uterine Kin

The majority of a person's uterine kin are, however, dispersed among other clans than his own. This is a natural result of the rule of clan exogamy. But Tallensi, as we shall see later,[1] tend to marry into nearby clans rather than into distant clans. A woman of clan A marries into the adjacent clan B; her daughters marry into the next clans C and D; their daughters marry into clans E and F; and so the process goes on. The result is, firstly, that with the passage of the generations the uterine line becomes more and more dispersed; and secondly, that any person's genealogically nearest uterine kin are also, generally, his spatially nearest uterine kin. In practice, it is these near *saarət* whom he knows and knows of; it is they who are concerned in witchcraft accusations or *tyuk* guilt. His more distant *saarət*—distant in both the genealogical sense and in residence—are often unknown to him. The main reason for this is that uterine kinship remains effective only through personal contact. The children of sisters know one another because their mothers have kept in touch, visited one another, and often helped one another all their lives. Similarly, the uterine grandchildren of sisters know one another, if they live near one another, because their mothers have kept in touch, though not so faithfully as true siblings. Often these contacts are maintained into the fourth generation of a woman's uterine descendants; rarely beyond the fourth generation; and a person does not, as a rule, know all his or her *saarət* whose link with him or her is a common great-grandmother. Some of them will, as likely as not, be Gɔrisi or Namnam and he will not even know of their existence.

In principle, however, uterine kinship is never extinguished, and it often happens that people of different clans, who are strangers to one another, discover by chance that they are distant *saarət*. Supposing, for instance, a man proposes to make an important sacrifice to a lineage ancestor. His agnatic co-descendants of this ancestor are bound to be present; but he will also send to tell the cognatic descendants through women of that ancestor and some of them will come. Two men of different clans may be present who now discover, for the first time, that they are cognatically related through the lineage of their host. They trace out their genealogical connexion (*tumh dɔyam*) and find that they are distant *saarət*. I have seen this happen more than once, and the delight of the men concerned was a vivid testimony to the meaning

[1] Cf. Ch. XI.

of *soog* kinship to the Tallensi. Each of them has found a new friend who will be to him as a brother. If he has business in his *soog*'s clan he will be able to go there with an easy mind; for he will be assured of an hospitable welcome in his *soog*'s house and of his *soog*'s assistance in his suit. Moreover, through this *soog* he will be introduced to other distant *saarət* unknown to him but known to his *soog*.

Saarət discover one another in other ways too. One evening I met Banɔrəg's wife coming from my boys' quarters. She told me that she had taken some food to one of the boys, Ayɛltiga, a native of Zuarungu, who, she had just learnt, was her *soog*. She had been to see her maternal grandmother's sister's son, at Gbambibug (she herself is a Sakpee woman), and he had told her that Ayɛltiga was their common *soog*. So she had hastened home to call on her newly found *soog* and had cooked a meal for him to show him the hospitality due from a *soog*. She told me this with many expressions of pleasure.

The following genealogy shows the connexion between Banɔrəg's wife and Ayɛltiga. It is typical of the genealogical range within which uterine kinship is usually effective.

```
                    Ŋkoog ○ = △ Sii
                    ┌───────────┴───────────┐
    Wakii △ = ○ Sii                    Sii ○ = △ Gbambibug
           │                                 │
    Sakpee △ = ○ Wakii                Gbambibug ○ = △ Zuarungu
           │                                       │
    Tongo △ = ○ Sakpee                      △ Zuarungu
    (Banɔrəg)                                (Ayɛltiga)
```

(Clan name of each person beside the sex symbol;
personal names in parenthesis)

As this genealogy shows, the uterine line can be thought of as 'travelling' from clan to clan with the generations; and that is how the natives visualize it. 'Our mother' (the progenitrix of the line), said Banɔrəg's wife 'went forth from Ŋkoog (*yi Ŋkoog na*) and married into Sii; and then his (Ayɛltiga's) grandmother (*ma kpeem*) married Gbambibug and my grandmother married Wakii; and then his mother (*ma*) married Zuarungu and my mother married Sakpee.' The *soog* line is visualized as a continuous entity. *Saarət* often refer to each other by kinship terms, but in a very loose way. A person is inclined to speak of a *soog* as, for instance, 'my elder sibling', simply because he or she is senior in age, though possibly junior in generation. More commonly a *soog* is simply 'my *soog*'; and if it is a woman, she tends to be identified with the uterine line as a whole and is described as 'mother (*ma*)', irrespective of her generation status, especially if she is older than the speaker. A relationship similar to that of parent and child often exists between *saarət* who differ considerably in age.

42   KINSHIP AND THE LINEAGE SYSTEM

The usual range of effective uterine kinship is a good illustration of the correlation between spatial relationships and genealogical relationships in the social space of the individual. The physical range of the individual's social contacts and communication with others is, as we have already noted, a function of his range of social relations, which is determined principally by his genealogical connexions. In the days before the establishment of the British peace, matrilateral, and especially uterine kinship, played a very important part in enabling people to travel outside their normal range of social contacts, and so to build up social relations with members of clans usually inaccessible to their own clansmen. A story will illustrate how this occurred.

When the Gorogo-Yikpɛmdaana was a young man of 17 or 18, sometime during the first decade of this century, a food shortage approaching famine, such as periodically swept the country, descended on the Tallensi. He decided to make a journey to Gbimis, in Mampurugu, across the White Volta, in order to barter some livestock for grain. But such a journey was full of peril. A Talǝŋ wandering in Mampurugu would be set upon and killed or taken as a slave by any armed Mamprusi who encountered him. So he went, first, to a *soog* at Pwalagu. This man escorted him across the river to another *soog* living in a small village there, and this *soog* conducted him to Gbimis. Under the safe conduct of his Mampuru *saarǝt* he was able to carry out his project. In later years he often made this trip to Mampurugu to buy things for resale in the small markets of Taleland.

Though people can travel where they will in freedom and security nowadays, it is still usual for anyone having business of a ritual or jural kind with a distant or unfamiliar clan to follow the web of uterine kinship thither. The route is much curtailed, but the principle remains. If Banǝrǝg's wife's brother, a Sakpee man, has such business at Bongo, he will probably go to his *saarǝt* at Zuarungu, stay the night with them, go on next morning to a *soog* at Yaraga, and find out from him or her if they have a *soog* at Bongo with whom he could stay and who will guide him and act as his spokesman with *his* clansmen.

In the same way uterine kin assist one another in economic matters. A man who loses time in his farming programme through illness will often ask a *soog* from a neighbouring settlement to come and do a day's hoeing for him where he would not ask for such help from a clansman. Again, crops do not ripen at the same time throughout Taleland. There may be an interval of several days or several weeks between the harvest at Sii and the harvest at Datɔk. It is the custom, at harvest time, especially at the time of the early millet harvest after the hungry months, for people living in areas that have a late harvest to 'beg (*soh*)' gifts of grain from relatives living in early harvesting areas. Later, when the early harvesting settlements have exhausted their supplies, people will go to kinsfolk in later harvesting areas to beg for grain to tide them over. Such reciprocal gifts pass between kinsmen of all categories. But the giving is specially generous and cordial between *soog* kin.

In keeping with the unrestricted range of cognatic kinship among the Tallensi, the close ties of kinship between male *saarǝt* are extended to their children and sometimes to their grandchildren. With men whose fathers were *saarǝt*, whether they belong to the same clan or not, the formal ties of kinship are often mellowed by the affection and trust of a friendship like that of their fathers. This is rarer with grandsons of male *saarǝt*, but not unknown. I have seen a man break down with grief over the death of a clansman who was his father's *soog*'s son. He would have felt no sense of personal loss at all if this extra bond had not existed between him and his dead clansman. Again, there was Tiezien of Kpata'ar's lifelong friendship with his father's *soog*'s son at Zuarungu— a friendship which would not normally have arisen between a Talǝŋ and a Gorǝŋ living eight miles apart.

A link of uterine kinship is often used to define the relations of individuals who are not themselves directly related by kinship. A typical case that shows how far the classificatory principle can be pressed, if there is a *soog* link in the chain of relationships connecting two people, is the following. Zaawɔmya of Bunkiuk began courting the young widow of a Wakii man. But in the course of making inquiries he discovered that the girl's late husband's father's mother and his own mother had been distant *saarǝt*. Zaawɔmya concluded, therefore, that the girl's late husband's father would have stood to him in the relationship of an 'older brother' (*bier*), since he would have called the latter's mother his 'mother' (*ma*). Hence the girl's husband would have been his 'son' (*bii*) and the girl herself his 'daughter-in-law' (*sampɔya*). 'Well just think of it', he said to me, when he told me the story, 'how can a man marry his daughter-in-law? So I gave it up.' When Mansami, Ɔmara's own father's brother's son ran away with the wife of Ɔmara's father's *soog*'s son at Ɖkoog, there was a bitter quarrel between them. Ɔmara accused Mansami of disgracing his (Ɔmara's) kinship ties and ordered him either to give up the girl or leave the homestead. Mansami, obstinately insisting that he and the girl's husband were not related, made this the pretext for keeping her and went off to stay with his mother's brother. Such roundabout connexions through a *soog* link are often exploited for ulterior motives. A common trick of fathers who object to a daughter's marrying a particular man is to allege a remote kinship tie of this sort between the girl and her suitor. The latter and his family head may be sceptical of the alleged evidence for this but they can do nothing about it.

CHAPTER III
THE HOMESTEAD AND THE JOINT FAMILY

Homestead and Family—a Single Social Entity

PHYSICALLY a Tale settlement is an aggregation of homesteads irregularly distributed at varying distances from one another.[1] A homestead is the domicile of a domestic family. The edifice of pile and thatch, and its occupants, constitute a single entity. There is no word for either apart from the other. The native concept, *yir* (pl. *yɛa*), a house, means primarily the joint family as a coherent social unit residing in its own dwelling. An unoccupied homestead is a dead shell, left to crumble into ruins.

When a homestead is abandoned it becomes a *daboog* (pl. *dabaar*), a word applied both to an empty homestead in any stage of decay and to the site of a former homestead, and carrying two main and complementary implications that spring directly from the dominance of the lineage principle in Tale social values. *Daboog* stands for something good and worthy of praise when it refers to the site of a person's father's or grandfather's homestead, or, by extension, to the site or locality of an ancestor's homestead. A *daboog* in this sense is a symbol of the origins and a portent of the good fortune of an existing lineage; it is an object of personal attachment and religious reverence; though vacant it is not dead; the spirits of the ancestors still abide there, and it may be reoccupied some day; it is a symbol of the living continuity of a line of descent. *Daboog* can also be used to describe the site of a former human habitation left deserted and forlorn through the extinction of a line of descent. No ancestor spirits dwell there; it is an accursed spot, a monument of human sin, and a symbol of the most terrible mystical retribution that can befall a Talǝŋ. A curse one sometimes hears uttered when a grave injury has been suffered at the hands of an unknown person is: 'May his house lie in ruins and tobacco be grown there (*K'u yir doon daboog ka ba ɛŋ taba waal nɛŋha*).' A ruined homestead provides an exceptionally fertile patch of soil, suitable for growing tobacco. If a man's line of descent is extinguished, there will be no one to claim ownership of his *daboog*, and anyone who wishes will come and plant tobacco there.

A homestead is always built for a particular family. From the day when the site is chosen it is the scene of human labour, of organized co-operation, and of religious and moral preoccupations. It must be lived in from the laying of the foundations, lest evil mystical agencies desecrate it. Ancestor shrines are immediately installed in it; for the spirits of a man's fathers and forefathers abide in his house, presiding

[1] Cf. *Dynamics of Clanship*, ch. x.

over its destinies just as they controlled its social and economic activities in their lifetime.

A new homestead is erected for preference on the site of a man's father's or other patrilineal ancestor's *daboog*. Such a site is consecrated through having been the scene of human residence in the past, and through the abiding association with it of the ancestors who formerly lived there. If a man builds on virgin land, the site must not only be technically prepared for habitation, it must also be ritually won for human ends. Hence the tendaana under whose ritual jurisdiction the spot falls must first consecrate it, and the new dwelling must be magically protected against those vague personifications of irrational maleficence, mystically dangerous stones (*kubeet*) and trees (*tebees*). So complete is the identification of the family with its dwelling, that if persistent misfortune dogs the family after its removal to a new homestead, and all other ritual measures seem to have failed, the onus is finally thrown on the homestead itself. 'The house has not accepted them (*yir la pu diebame*)', the diviners discover. The whole complex of mystical agencies which endow the house with its moral value for the family is against them.

In the single homestead, as in the settlement of which it is the elementary cell and the structural epitome, Tale social organization has three fundamental aspects—material, associational, and moral. They represent the three major kinds of interests and ends that govern Tale social life. And though all forms of social relations among the Tallensi always have these three classes of components, they do not always work in harmony with one another.

In the homestead, as in the settlement, social relations move in two planes: the plane of lineage relations, in which the canon of agnatic descent dominates corporate action and directs individual conduct, and the plane of domestic relations, in which the bonds of marriage and parenthood, and the bilateral ties of kinship in the narrowest sense, control the behaviour of people towards one another. The persons who form a unit in one plane fall into separate, opposed units in the other. Husband and wife belong to mutually exclusive lineages; brothers by the same father but different mothers belong to separate matricentral segments of the family and are nuclei of independent conjugal families.

The Ideas and Values embodied in the Homestead

It is far truer of the Taləŋ than of the modern Englishman to say that his home is his castle, though not as literally as Cardinall imagines. The natives of these parts, he declares, build their homesteads solidly and a bow-shot apart in order the better to defend them against hostile neighbours.[1] This romantic explanation, however, has

[1] Cardinall, A. W., *Natives of the Northern Territories of the Gold Coast*, pp. 2, 14.

no foundation in fact. The climate, the kind of raw material which is plentifully at hand, the economic system, and the social organization of the natives rather than the alleged lawlessness of former times, determine their mode of house-building. In any case, homesteads very often stand closer than fifty paces together, the distance at which a mediocre shot can hit a tree—though I have seen an arrow carry four times that distance.

A Talǝŋ's home is his castle in the psychological rather than the material sense. It is the centre and fount of his major interests, his dominant purposes, his deepest emotional attachments, and his whole scheme of values; it is his shelter, his storehouse, the stage of his life's drama. The Tallensi, unlike many African peoples, have no age sets or initiation schools. A person grows up and receives his entire education at home. If he practises a craft, such as leatherwork, or is a diviner, his home is his workshop or consulting place.

As an adult, all his economic enterprise issues from his home and is devoted primarily to its upkeep. Unless he is one of the few *nouveaux riches* of to-day he keeps all his material possessions there, and houses all his livestock within its walls. His sex life, in maturity, is centred there. His children, the supreme object of his aspirations, are born and grow up in his home under his care and control. He worships his immediate forbears there. His personal destiny, past, present, and future, revolves about his home, its stages perpetuated in the many shrines and other ritual objects that are housed in it. He receives his friends and relatives at home, and dispenses hospitality there; and if he has nothing to do would as lief recline under the shade tree at his own gateway as go making calls on others. Even the young men who like gallivanting about the markets spend much of their leisure at home.

The quintessence of his home, to a Talǝŋ, resides in his children, and above all his sons, the vehicles of his immortality. That is the essential meaning of *mar yiri*, 'to have a house'. Ask any native what happens to a man who does not adequately expiate a sacrilege such as murder. '*U yiri ŋmaarǝme*—his house will fall to pieces,' is the answer, given with emphatic and solemn conviction, and often with circumstantial illustrations from experience or hearsay. A parent curses an insubordinate child, a chief or tɛndaana curses a clansman who has grossly insulted him, '*u ku nye yiri*—he will not see (i.e. have) a house', that is, he will die without offspring to perpetuate his line and to sacrifice to his spirit; and this is an extremely serious matter. It never fails to bring the culprit to heel with humble apologies. On the other hand, '*i na nye yiri*—you will have a house', is the most propitious blessing a diviner can convey to a man from his ancestor spirits.

Patrilocal residence and the tendency for the lineage to be localized give a man's domestic life greater continuity than a woman's. His natal family and his conjugal family are both strung on the same lineage. The latter grows directly out of the former and very often occupies the same dwelling as, or one close to that of, the former. For a woman marriage signifies a sharp break. As wife and mother she generally lives in a different, even if familiarly close, clan settlement from that of her birth. A man, living all his life side by side with the other members of his lineage, participating in the hierarchy of the corporate units that make up the lineage system, identifying himself with all its members through their common jural, economic, and ceremonial interests, makes an easy, self-evident, and gradual transition from the status of a minor (*tarəm*) under his father's control to that of a father and head of a household. The change in status and social role from that of a daughter and member of one lineage to that of a wife and mother in the settlement of another is more drastic and complex. A woman has no rights in or ties with the community[1] in which she spends the greatest part of her life, exercises her heaviest responsibilities, achieves her most cherished fulfilment, and acquires her strongest emotional attachments, except through her family by marriage, her husband, and her children. Thus a woman's life is fraught with many possibilities of conflict between the loyalties and sentiments towards her natal lineage and those which she gradually builds up in relation to her husband's lineage.

The effect of all this is to make the home of even greater importance for a woman than for a man. Her conjugal home is the supreme and almost the sole domain of her labour and life. Her children are the very hub of her existence. She is first and foremost a housewife and mother, toiling devotedly in the care of her children, in attending to her husband's needs, in giving her contribution of labour and skill to the economy of the household, and in the numerous household tasks that call for daily attention.

The Architecture of the Homestead in Relation to the Structure of the Domestic Family

Tale homesteads are solidly constructed of pile (puddled mud, *tan*), and they are built to last. Erecting the circular walls tier by tier, plastering them, roofing the rooms, stamping the floors, adding the small contrivances and the decorations that increase the comfort and attraction of the homestead, are all tasks requiring considerable skill, care, and co-operation. They are not the work of specialists, though some men and women have more skill in them than others, and many people have such poor skill that they never undertake them. The conventional division of labour involves both sexes equally in the building of a homestead. Building and thatching is men's work; plastering, drawing the crude lines and geometrical designs that

---

[1] She may, and usually does, have cognatic kinsfolk there, but her ties with them are valid only for the particular individuals.

decorate the walls, and stamping the floors into smooth, hard surfaces are all women's work. According to its size and the number of workers available, from the commencement to the final touches, it takes from three weeks to two months of intermittent but often strenuous labour to build a homestead. This falls chiefly on its future occupants. All the members of the family, including the children, lend a hand. But co-members of the owner's clan, especially of his own local segment and their wives, as well as kinsmen, affines, and friends, lend their services too, and this involves considerable expenditure of foodstuffs to reward them.

Again, substantial as they are, Tale houses are not impervious to the weather, with its drastic alternation of great heat and drought and heavy rains. After a couple of years the soaking rains of July and August begin to wear the walls away, rot the thatch, and pit the floors. A man who wants to keep his homestead in trim condition must do some repairs every dry season. New rooms may be added from time to time, if the family grows in numbers, or old rooms allowed to fall in if it diminishes. With such alterations and repairs, a homestead may stand for a generation. In the older settlements many sites have been occupied for two or three generations continuously, the homesteads having been completely rebuilt, bit by bit, several times during this period.

Building a new homestead is an outstanding event in the life of its owner and a matter of public attention. It always marks a significant change in a man's status—his economic and jural emancipation from minority, or his attainment of eldership high up in the lineage hierarchy. Hence it requires moral sanction and ritual precautions. As we have seen, it also mobilizes all the basic social ties a man has. The house itself, embodying the labour and care of himself, his family, and many of his relatives by blood and marriage, stands as a monument to the efficacy of these social ties.

We can see why the Tale homestead, looked at merely from the architectural aspect, is the material projection of the social relations that make up the domestic family. All Tale homesteads have the same architectural pattern, just as all Tale domestic families have the same basic structure. Only in one point of style and construction do Tale homesteads differ in type, and this is not a question of taste. The Tallensi have two kinds of roofs, a conical thatched roof lashed on to a frame of rafters, and a flat roof of beaten pile supported on a ceiling of strong rafters. The thatch roof is the easier to make and the most common. But nearly every thatched homestead has at least one flat-roofed room (*pii*), as a matter both of convention and of utility. It is the scene of many activities in the dry season. Men, women, and children sit or sprawl on the roof to rest, to chat, or when they are busy with some sedentary task such as sewing or spinning. Grain, vegetables, and edible leaves are spread out to dry there. On

PLATE 3

a. Interior of a woman's *Dug*. The rooms from right to left are: a store-room (*Da'ŋboog*), a dry season kitchen (*Da'aŋ*), and a small *Dakir* for the woman's young son and daughter-in-law. The woman's own sleeping-room (*Dakir*) is farther to the right, not visible. Note how clean and bare the *Dɛndɔŋo* is and note, also, the bundles of dry guinea-corn stalks on top of the open kitchen. These have been saved for fuel in the rainy season

b. The homestead of a maximal lineage head, the Gbizug Tɛndaana. Note the ancestor shrines in front of the gateway (X)

PLATE 4

a. The central granary in the homestead of an elder. Note the array of ancestor shrines on the granary. The granary is about 10 ft. high and 5 ft. in diameter at the base

b. In the *Dɛndɔŋo* of the senior woman of the family. The infant children of several wives of the family left in the care of one of them. (This is the homestead of the head of a medial lineage. Note the lineage *bɔyar* against the wall on the left, part of it supported on a tree-stump and part on the floor in shallow pottery dishes)

sultry nights the head of the house often makes up his bed there. When his grain is ripening on the home farm he climbs on to the *pii* every morning to survey it, and often stands there to keep an eye open for stray animals likely to spoil it. There is always an ancestor shrine or two on the flat roof, as it is the appropriate place for a *yin* shrine in the earliest stage of its evolution; and it is from the flat roof that the alarm call, *yaahi! yaahi!* is broadcast when a death occurs or something untoward happens for which the immediate assistance of neighbours is needed.

But some homesteads must be flat-roofed throughout, though the cost in time and labour is great. For this is a taboo (*kihɔr*) of the Earth in some places. Almost all the senior tɛndaanas are therefore obliged to have all their rooms flat-roofed; and at Wakii and Tɛnzugu all houses within the acknowledged precincts of the principal Earth shrines (*tɔŋgbana*) of these places must be flat-roofed throughout. This affects the design and construction of the homestead in many details, but not in its basic pattern.

A homestead reveals much to the instructed eye. Its appearance and condition often betray the character, capabilities, social position, and experience of the owner and his wife or wives. The Gɔlibdaana of Tɛnzugu and the Yikpɛmdaana of Gorogo each have a large rectangular room of sun-dried bricks, built for them by boys trained at the White Fathers' Mission at Bolɔga, and used as sanctum, private storeroom, and personal sleeping-quarters. They are both wealthy, ambitious, upstart headmen, whose political and economic privileges are wholly dependent on the white man's rule. Hence, though themselves illiterate and of the generation that reached maturity before British rule became established, they are 'progressives', alert to useful or merely pretentious innovations that add to their prestige or bolster up their self-assurance. The Tɔŋraana, or, to go outside Taleland, the Nangodi na'aba, wealthy men too in virtue of their political role under the British Administration, but deriving their authority from the native social structure, do not require adventitious props to their prestige. Their private rooms are built in native style, with the useful addition of a rough plank door fastened with a padlock. A plank door is a rarity in Taleland, and very hard to come by. If a room in a commoner's homestead is fitted with one, it may be inferred that some member of the family has been abroad a good deal or has close connexions with people who are or have been in Ashanti, in the Colony, or in European service.

Most Tallensi take great pride in the appearance of their homesteads. A dilapidated homestead indicates that its owner is poor or infirm or lazy, and therefore unable to provide the foodstuffs to recompense relatives who might be asked to help him repair it. A good-for-nothing like Yɛlnaar of Tɔŋ-Puhug has a tumbledown dwelling which his neighbours point to with scorn. A man of more self-respect would be ashamed of it and exert himself to the utmost to have it repaired. But a poor man who has the energy and can himself build and thatch, or has a son or sons skilled in these crafts, will generally keep his homestead in a satisfactory condition. On the other hand, even men who own cattle and sheep are apt to wait until the thatch is rotted through and the walls collapse before undertaking essential repairs. The ingrained thrift of the natives, fostered by their narrow margin of sufficiency in food-supplies, induces them often to submit to discomfort which would tax less hardy folk to breaking-point rather than expend food and other resources to alleviate it.

Indoors, Tale homesteads are usually surprisingly tidy. A good housewife sees that her quarters are swept every morning. Litter indoors is a sign that the mistress of those rooms is a lazy or a sick woman, or one too harassed by family cares or poverty to look after her home properly. A good housewife has her floors regravelled and beaten almost every year to keep them hard and smooth.

But individual idiosyncrasies do not affect the layout of a homestead; for apart from minor variations this depends wholly on the constitution of the domestic unit. The layout of a homestead is an index to the structure of the domestic family occupying it.

The simplest domestic and procreative unit is the elementary family—a man, his wife, and their young children—occupying their own homestead. Often the man's mother (*ma*), either his own mother (*ma dɔyarug*—the mother [of] bearing), or a surviving co-wife (*nentaa*) of his mother lives with him. The whole group constitutes one household, that is, a single economic unit all the members of which are mutually dependent on one another for the production of their common food-supply and the satisfaction of most other wants. Essentially this is a matter of pooling labour and skill, of utilizing land in common, of drawing on the food, livestock, and to some extent monetary resources built up by joint effort, for the benefit of any member of the unit, and of mutual assistance from any private resources that the members may have.

A good example of a domestic family of this kind is that of Ɔndieso of Tɔŋ-Guŋ, a man in the late thirties whose homestead stands on the border of Tɔŋ-Dekpieŋ and Gbizug. Outside his homestead, 10 or 12 yards from the gateway, stands the usual shade tree. Ɔndieso's tree is also, like almost all shade trees, an ancestor shrine. Between it and the gateway is a bare space, with the midden heap (*tampɔyar*) on one side and a large, round, flat-topped ancestor shrine built of pile on the other. It is the shrine of his late father's *Yin*. One or more ancestor shrines stand thus at the entrance to every homestead. 'Ɔn nso yirla—it owns the house', the natives say, meaning by this a spiritual and not material ascendancy in the affairs of the family. It stands outside, at the entrance, as a spiritual sentry guarding the welfare of the house.

If the head of the house is still junior in status in the lineage hierarchy, as Ɔndieso is, it will be the shrine dedicated to his father's Destiny (*yin*), or it may be his father's divining (*bakologo*) shrine. The house is still under the spiritual jurisdiction of Ɔndieso's dead father, though he himself now owns it in the temporal sense. A man of greater social maturity, with grown children and higher lineage status, would very likely have his own *yin* or *bakologo* shrine at his gateway. His house is established; it is no longer the fulfilment of his father's destiny, as is the house of a young man, though it may still be known by his father's or grandfather's name. For as long as a homestead remains standing it is known by the name of the man who first built it.

A bird's-eye view would show a homestead as covering a roughly circular or oval area (Figs. 2*a* and 2*b*). The space in front of the gateway (*zanɔne*—at the gateway) belongs pre-eminently to the menfolk. The public phases of funeral and mortuary ceremonies, which are corporate concerns of the lineage and are conducted by the men, take place there. When anything touching the rights, duties, or interests of the head of the family in his capacity as a member of a particular lineage calls for consultation with fellow members of the lineage, the *zanɔne* is the gathering place. It is the proper place for him to receive greetings, condolences, or congratulations, and to conduct formal negotiations in a matter such as the payment of bride-price owed to him or by him. In the dry season he often rests there, beneath the shade tree, during the sweltering afternoon, chatting with a friend or fondling an infant left in his charge while its mother is busy indoors. Women of the house come and go freely, and often sit or lounge about in front of the gateway; but when 'an affair of the men (*buraas yɛl*)' is in progress they keep away.

The gateway (*zanɔr*) always faces west to south-west, 'where the sun sets (*nintaŋ nluut*)'. This is a convention never broken by the Tallensi, though they have neither a naturalistic explanation nor a mystical rationalization for it, and it is not subject to mystical sanctions.[1]

The gateway is a V-shaped opening, about a foot wide at the base and 3 to 4 feet wide on top, between two round pillars (*meelaŋ*) forming part of the wall of the house. Large irregularly spaced holes are made in these pillars for short logs to be inserted at night as cross-bars against which a heavy, hollow board (*bɛluŋ*), cut from a tree-trunk, or a bundle of poles can be leaned to close the gateway. Tallensi say that they build the gateway thus in order to bar it the more securely against the

---

[1] As the rain-bearing winds blow from the south-east, and the tornadoes that begin and end the rainy season come from an easterly direction, it is possible that the placing of the doorway on the western side of the house is an adaptation to this feature of the climate. Anyone who has experienced the discomfort of a tornado whirling straight into a room, or of a heavy rain, in this region will appreciate the usefulness of placing the only entrance into a homestead on the lee side. But no native has ever given me this obvious explanation, though this may be due to inadequate inquiries on my part.

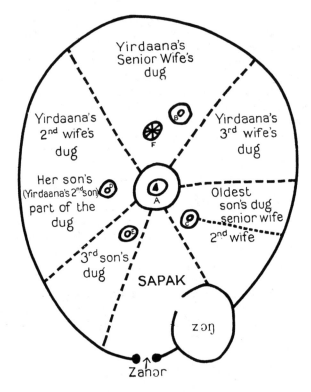

Fig. 2a. Diagram (not to scale) showing the layout of the different *dugɔt* in a large joint family homestead. The head of the homestead (*yirdaana*) has three living wives and three married sons, one with two wives.

        A — Principal granary (*buur tenta'ar*) of the *yirdaana*
        B — Small granary belonging to *yirdaana*
        C — Oldest son's private small granary
        D — Second son's private small granary
        E — Third son's private small granary
        F — *Yirdaana's Yin* shrine

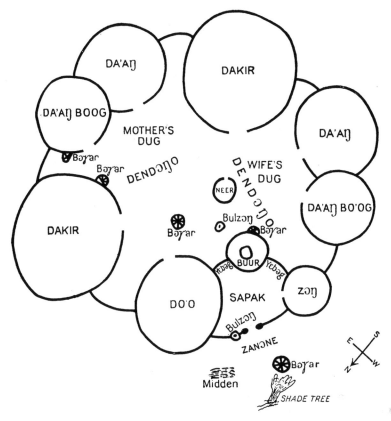

Fig. 2b. Diagram of Ɔndieso's homestead, showing the layout of the quarters and the rooms. (Scale: 1:45 approx.)

Glossary

Bɔyar	Ancestor shrine
Buur	Granary
Bulzɔŋ	Shelter for hens
Da'aŋ	Unroofed dry-season kitchen
Da'aŋboog	Storeroom and wet-season kitchen
Dakir	Sleeping-room
Do'o	Room for adolescent boys
Dɛndɔŋo	Open courtyard
Sapak	Livestock yard
Zanɔne	Open space at the gateway where the men foregather
Zɔŋ	The homestead head's special room
Neer	Grinding-room
Yɛbəg	Low dividing wall

ingress of wild animals—in particular, the ubiquitous and thievish hyena, which prowls the settlements at night in search of offal and unprotected small stock—and the egress of their own livestock. Every gateway in Taleland must be barred at night, except that of the Chief of Tongo. This is a strict rule, and it is one of the conventions defining the social personality of the Chief of Tongo. It is also a sign of the privacy of the domestic unit in respect of the intimate life of its members.

Entering the *zanɔr* of a homestead, the visitor finds himself in the *sapak* or *nayaŋ*, the cattle-yard. It is the dirtiest and most insanitary spot in the homestead, its undressed surface being strewn with rubbish and with the dung or droppings of livestock, if the owner has any. One often sees human excrement in a corner, for young children and sick people defecate there at night. Ɔndieso is a very poor man, even by Tale standards, as the sagging roofs and dilapidated walls of his homestead lead one to suspect, possessing neither cattle nor sheep nor goats, and but a handful of poultry. Hence his *sapak* is very small, less than a dozen square yards in area. Ɔndieso's neighbour, the Gbizug tɛndaana, has a large *sapak*, about 80 square yards in area; but he has cattle, sheep, goats, and a couple of donkeys, not to speak of many fowls and guinea-fowls.

From the *sapak* one can see how the cylindrical rooms are laid out and distributed in the roughly circular or oval area occupied by the homestead. The first room, usually on the right as one enters through the *zanɔr*, is the *zɔŋ*. It is the only room with a doorway in the *sapak*, and it has a special significance in the structure of the house. It is the room *par excellence* of the head of the house (*yirdaana*), fittingly placed between the open space before the *zanɔr*, with which his public activities are associated, and the *sapak*, which shelters his most valuable possessions, his livestock. Cattle, sheep, and goats constitute material wealth, the repository of labour and thrift; but they mean much more than that to the Talǝŋ. They are pre-eminently the property of men, associated with men's major interests. They are the medium by means of which wives are acquired, and thus posterity assured. They are also the principal objects of sacrifice, by means of which the natives maintain their relations with their ancestor spirits and other mystical powers. In bad weather the *zɔŋ* itself is used to shelter the livestock. Inside the *zɔŋ*, along the wall, little cubicles are made for the *yirdaana*'s fowls to nest in. A man of substance often has a double *zɔŋ*, consisting of two chambers with a low doorway in the partition wall. The rear chamber is used as a stall for young calves or sheep, and the front chamber, communicating with the *sapak*, as a stall for a milch-cow or a donkey, for the night.

The *zɔŋ* is identified with the *yirdaana*'s status and social personality. It is a bare room, for a man does not keep valuable possessions, weapons, or implements there. This is due partly to the values associated with it, partly to its use as a stall for livestock, and partly to its being an outside room from which things might easily be stolen. A young man like Ɔndieso has nothing but a couple of unimportant medicine horns stuck into the thatch, a log to sit on, and a few odds and ends in his rather tumbledown *zɔŋ*; for he makes little use of it. Yet the house would be incomplete without a *zɔŋ*; for the *zɔŋ* is the sanctuary of the *yirdaana*'s lineage ancestor spirits. It is no profanation, in Tale eyes, to fold livestock there. The mundane and the mystical are complementary in Tale thought. Because the ancestor spirits abide there, a diviner holds his consultations in his *zɔŋ*. Among the Talis the lineage-shrine (*bɔyar*) always rests inside or against the outer wall of the lineage head's *zɔŋ*; the Namoos generally keep such a shrine in an inside room or courtyard. Even if the other rooms of his homestead are thatched, a tɛndaana's *zɔŋ* must have a flat roof, because the spirits of his predecessors dwell there and the lineage *bɔyar* and indoor shrines dedicated to the Earth are in it. The investiture of a tɛndaana culminates in his ritual induction into the *zɔŋ*, which is the final test of his acceptability to the ancestors and the Earth. A chief has a special *zɔŋ* (*zanto'o*), which is not only the sanctuary of the spirits of former chiefs but his council-chamber and the room in which he performs the rites that bless the community during the Great Festivals.

To an elder of great seniority in the lineage hierarchy his *zɔŋ* has a deeper value than to a man of junior status. A person's status is most conspicuously proclaimed at his or her death, when his or her social personality has to be cancelled by rite and ceremony. When a man of subordinate status in the lineage, a man who is not yet the master of his own house, or a young woman, dies, he or she is carried to the grave through a hole broken in the wall of the homestead for this purpose. But the head of a house, or an old woman, is carried out through a hole specially cut in the outside wall of the *zɔŋ*. '*Ti Talis tɛbhɔm nla*—This is the [great] honour of us, the Tallensi', an informant explained to me. The conventional idea of one who deserves it is that of a man or woman who leaves children and grandchildren to perpetuate his or her line and to celebrate his or her decease. When his homestead is being rebuilt, an old man often tells his sons, half-jocularly but with more than a hint of earnestness: 'Hurry up with the roofing of the *zɔŋ*. I might die, and I don't wish to be carried out through the gateway because the *zɔŋ* is unfinished.' 'May Heaven permit me to attain to lying in the *zɔŋ*, when I die, and forfend the breaking of the wall for me to be carried out' a young man once exclaimed fervently when he was talking about the funeral of a worthy elder. The last rites by which a dead person is finally aggregated to the ancestor spirits take place in the *zɔŋ*.

The *zɔŋ*, the *sapak*, and the *zanɔr* stand for the ideological and jural dominance of the male line of descent. Together, and in particular the *zɔŋ*, they symbolize the continuity of the lineage of which the master of that house is but one member, a link in a process to which he makes his greatest contribution as a father and head of a house. Hence the *zɔŋ* of a lineage head, being the sanctuary of all the lineage ancestors, is regarded as the *zɔŋ* of the whole lineage, and his *zanɔr* as the *zanɔr* of the lineage. When the Hill Talis were forcibly expelled in 1910–11 and their homesteads demolished, the heads of the maximal lineages later came back by stealth to rebuild a small part of their *zɔŋ* walls, for they could not appropriately sacrifice to their lineage ancestors elsewhere than in the lineage *zɔŋ*. If a woman commits adultery, she sins against her husband's lineage ancestors, thus imperilling the health and welfare of her husband and children. An adulteress, that is to say, transgresses the rights over her reproductive powers vested absolutely in her husband's lineage. Thus, if a woman is suspected of adultery she is subjected to the ordeal of entering (*kpe*) the lineage *zɔŋ* or *zanɔr*. She must face the ancestors directly, for she has committed an outrage against the lineage principle the absolute value of which is symbolized in and safeguarded by the ancestor spirits.[1] If she is guilty and does not confess, she will get ill and perhaps die. Women are terrified of this ordeal, which rarely fails to produce a confession.

Though they come and go freely in the *sapak* and *zɔŋ* in the ordinary course of domestic life, the women and children belong specifically to the domestic quarters proper. These lie behind a low wall (*yɛbɔg*) a yard or so in height and about the same in length, at the back of the *sapak*. This wall usually runs between the back of a kitchen or storeroom and a large bullet-shaped chamber from 7 to 10 feet high and 6 to 10 feet in diameter at the base. This is the granary (*buur*). One suffices for a small family like Ɔndieso's. A wealthier man with a more numerous household may have one principal granary and one or more smaller ones. A granary has only one opening, at the top, covered with a lid of tightly plaited thatch like an enormous hat.

In the granary, again, Tale architecture embodies a fundamental element in the structure of the domestic unit. A bird's-eye view of a Tale homestead would show the principal granary as standing roughly in the centre of the circle of rooms, rising like a beacon between that section of the homestead which in use, thought, and feeling is the domain of the men, and that section which forms the living-quarters and is ruled by the women. The granary is the pivot on which the smooth working of the domestic unit turns. It holds the millet and guinea corn which provide the staple food of the natives. Without this, life cannot be satisfactorily sustained from one harvest to the next, and the household cannot exist, let alone keep its unity. What a sufficiency of food means to the Tallensi has been described in our previous

---

[1] This is the complementary notion to that of 'polluting the room' described above, p. 28.

volume.[1] The granary symbolizes all the sentiments and ideas, the apprehensions and joys which the struggle for food evokes in Taleland. It stands for the security of the domestic unit in this struggle. In the organization of the household its importance comes from the fact that it is the focus of the economic cohesion and stability of the domestic group. Into it goes the product of the joint labour of the household, from it comes their sustenance. In filling the granary and in the consumption of its contents, the labour of men, women, and children is equally essential, and the rights of all equally valid. When a joint family splits up, the commonest pretext is friction over grain supplies. The family which hives off does so on the ground that it needs its own, independent food-supply. 'They have each his own granary (*ba mara ba buur baʼbuur*)', is the formula summing up the economic relations of brothers occupying a single homestead but having separate households.

The granary belongs to the head of the house, the *yirdaana*. No one may enter it without his authorization, least of all his wife. A devoted and trusted wife may be allowed to descend (*sig*) into it to issue the grain (*loo ki*) for cooking if there is no suitable male within reach—Tale conventions are not rigidly complied with if doing so involves excessive and absurd inconvenience. But it would be scandalous if she did so on her own initiative. The contents of the granary are formally the property of the head of the household, to be distributed at his discretion. There is no other place in the homestead which is so rigorously private to him. Besides the grain for current consumption, he stores the seed for next year's crop there. He hides a particularly cherished object, or money which he wants to conceal from other members of the family, in his granary, secure in the knowledge that no one will dare to tamper with it there.

The *zɔŋ* enshrines—in both the physical and the ideal sense of this concept—the notion of the continuity of the lineage; the *buur* stands for the social personality of the *yirdaana*, as the centre of an independent domestic family, its economic fulcrum, its jural and ritual head, controller and representative. The position of the granary in the architectural pattern of the homestead corresponds to that of the head of the house in the structure of the family, as the unique link between its parts and the source of its unity.

Tallensi say that a man's soul (*sii*) is in his granary. Using the same phrase one says of a person, '*n süg mbɛ u ni*—my soul is in [drawn towards] him', meaning that one feels a special affinity with him. Among the Namoos the identification of a man with his granary is symbolized explicitly in the taboos that his first-born children have to observe.[2] A man's granary, his cap and tunic, his bow and quiver,

---

[1] Cf. *Dynamics of Clanship*, ch. xi. Also M. and S. L. Fortes, 'Food in the Domestic Economy of the Tallensi', *Africa*, ix. 2, 1937.

[2] Cf. *Dynamics of Clanship*, ch. v.

are the emblems of his individuality. They participate in it, for they are imbued with his body 'dirt (*dayət*)'—a concept which has a physiological facet, meaning the exuviae adhering to a man's garments, quiver, or other objects constantly handled by him, and a mystical facet implying the quintessence of his individuality. The Talis also acknowledge this complex association between a man and his granary and other intimate possessions, expressing it in analogous customs, in the routine of family life and in their ideals of family relations.

To enter the living-quarters of a homestead one climbs over the low dividing wall (*yɛbəg*) at the back of the *sapak* by means of a step (*bimbimər*) and descends, by a similar step on the other side, into an irregular courtyard (*dɛndɔŋo*, pl. *dɛndɔna*) of beaten gravel, which is surrounded by a number of rooms. According to the wealth, rank, or status of the *yirdaana* this *dɛndɔŋo* varies in size from about 20 to about 6 square yards.

This *dɛndɔŋo* belongs to the principal woman (*dugdaana*) of the house. The *dɛndɔna* of junior wives are smaller. In Ɔndieso's house the senior woman is his mother's surviving co-wife, whom he calls his 'younger mother' (*mapit*, lit. 'mother's younger sister'), and who has remained with him since the death of his father. Her rooms occupy roughly the left half of the homestead, facing inwards from the *sapak*. From this *dɛndɔŋo*, turning right between a small room beside the granary and a larger room straight ahead, one enters a similar *dɛndɔŋo* in the middle of another set of rooms, those of Ɔndieso's wife. These take up roughly the right half of the homestead, facing inwards. The *yirdaana*'s mother's (own mother, or proxy-mother) rooms always occupy the position of honour in the centre of the arc; his senior wife's (*poyakpeem*) rooms lie on the right-hand side of these; his second wife's, or his younger brother's senior wife's rooms lie on the left, looking inwards. The rooms of the other wives of the head of the family or of his brothers are distributed as convenience dictates. For example, wives who are clan sisters will usually have adjoining quarters; wives who get on badly will be put in well-separated rooms. If none of a man's father's widows is living with him, and he has more than one wife, his senior wife occupies the central group of rooms, his second wife those on her right, and so forth. Generally the women's apartments all communicate with one another. But if a woman has a quarrelsome disposition or gets on badly with her co-wives for any other reason, her quarters will be separated from those of the next-door wife by a low party wall, to prevent undue trespassing by her co-wives or their children.

A woman's apartments make up a self-contained section in the homestead. This is her *dug* (pl. *dugət*). Basically *dug* means a single room, but it is extended to mean the single set of rooms belonging to one wife. In the Tale family every woman with children is entitled to her own *dug*. Women guard this right jealously, and if a man has not built separate quarters for his wife by the time that she has had her first child, she will become very discontented. A young wife sometimes runs off to her father's home because she thinks she ought to have her own *dug* and her husband has been dilatory about it; and she will refuse to return until he convinces her of his intention to build her *dug* immediately. The observance of this rule is an essential element in the structure of the domestic family. It is indispensable for the satisfactory working of the domestic economy and for the mutual adjustment of person to person. A wife's separate quarters stand for her relative autonomy as wife, mother and housekeeper, *vis-à-vis* the other women of the family.

As the head of the house is *yirdaana*, master of the house, so the senior woman of the house—his mother, or senior wife—is the *dugdaana*, the mistress of the rooms. Every woman is the *dugdaana* of her own apartments, but the mistress of the principal *dug* is the *dugdaana* of the whole house.

In a polygynous family, or what might be called a multicellular family, the senior *dugdaana* has more authority in domestic affairs, and more esteem in the eyes of the public than the other women of the household have. Whether she is the *yirdaana*'s mother or his senior wife, she is the central pillar of his domestic establishment, honorifically more than actively in the case of the former, actively as well as honorifically in the case of the latter.

One sign of this is that most of the ancestor and medicine shrines that are kept indoors rest in the *dɛndɔŋo* and rooms of the senior woman. They include a man's personal shrines, as well as those of which he is custodian as head of a lineage segment. Sacrifice is offered to these shrines in this *dɛndɔŋo*, the women and children of the family often taking part. A man's ancestors keep watch and ward both indoors and out over the things, the place, and the people most precious to him.

When a person dies he or she must not only be gathered to the ancestors, but must subsequently be ritually brought back, as a spirit, into the living quarters, the veritable home. The expression '*Kpeehu la dugni*—bring him [her] into the *dug*', used for this as well as the customary rites, make this clear.

The intimate domestic life of a family goes on mainly in the *dɛndɔŋo*. Meals are often cooked and always eaten there. Food is never cooked outside the homestead except for ritual or ceremonial purposes. A woman does much of her domestic work in her *dɛndɔŋo*. Her babies learn to crawl and to take their first steps there. She entertains guests and relatives, and receives her daughter's suitors there. When the crops are harvested they are spread out to dry in the *dɛndɔŋo* before being stored. A man often sits about in his wife's *dɛndɔŋo* when he has a leisurely manual task in hand. Youths and girls come to dance there when an elderly person's funeral is celebrated. And on pleasant nights, after a satisfying meal, men, women, and children sit there conversing or gossiping or asking riddles.

A woman is entitled to have at least three rooms in her *dug*, a sleeping-room (*dakir*) a dry-season kitchen (*da'aŋ*) and a storeroom (*da'aŋboog*). Men of substance often allow their older wives a fourth room (*boog*), which always has a flat mud roof and serves as an extra storeroom and a guest-room, or as a room in which a daughter-in-law can be temporarily accommodated, or where the *yirdaana* can sit and talk to his visitors in the rainy season.

The *dakir* is the largest room, usually 10 to 12 feet in diameter.[1] Here the woman sleeps with her young children; here her husband comes to her at night; here she is confined when she bears him a child; here she keeps her sleeping-mats and her few personal treasures; and here, if she is his senior wife, her husband's best cloth or tunic, his bow and quiver, and other personal belongings. Her husband and children have free access to her *dakir*. Other members of the family must generally ask her permission to enter it or a family quarrel will result. To enter a *dakir* one crawls through an arched doorway, 2 to 3 feet high and about the same in width. Inside darkness reigns, relieved only by the glimmer of light that enters under the eaves and through the doorway, or a small aperture high up in the wall.

A stretch of wall 2 or 3 feet long forms a shallow recess between the *dakir* and the unroofed dry-season kitchen (*da'aŋ*). Here one generally sees a bundle of firewood stacked in a corner, or, in the right season, a heap of shea nuts. The *da'aŋ* itself is horseshoe-shaped and smaller than a *dakir*—from 4 to 8 feet across the shorter axis and 6 to 9 feet across the longer axis. The doorway is usually about 4 feet high, so that one can go in and out easily, as domestic tasks require. As it is for use in dry weather only, it is open to the sky. After the harvest, millet and guinea-corn stalks are spread on top, partly as a shield from the sun but chiefly as a reserve of firewood. The cooking-hearth (*ɔɔrǝg*), the water-pots (*kɔwoor*), the cooking-pots and dishes (*dɔyat* and *laas*), the stirring-stick (*vugǝr*), and ladles (*bies*), lying about in none too orderly a fashion, show well the uses to which this room is put.

Adjoining the *da'aŋ* is the larger, roofed *da'aŋboog*, the storeroom and larder. This room often has a doorway leading into the *da'aŋ* and not into the *dɛnḍɔŋo*, for the greater convenience of the housewife. Here the housewife keeps her stocks of foodstuffs—her dried vegetables and condiments, the odd piece of dried fish or meat she has hoarded, a pot of millet, perhaps, which she acquired by her own efforts, and so forth—as well as the utensils she is not using, and any bulky articles belonging to her or other members of the family. Here she also cooks in the wet season. At a pinch it may be used as a sleeping-room for a visitor

---

[1] The diameters of a room are always discrepant, it may be by an inch or two or by as much as a foot, so that its base is never a perfect circle. The natives themselves do not notice this as it is due to their crude method of marking out the circle for the base with the foot.

THE HOMESTEAD AND THE JOINT FAMILY 61

or adolescent son. The *da'aŋ* and *da'aŋboog* also serve as a sort of drawing-room. A guest who must be treated with respect is invited to step round to the kitchen to have his meal there in private, a suitor is told to go round to the girl's mother's kitchen to plead his suit with her.

The *da'aŋ* and *da'aŋboog* are the counterpart in the social sphere of a woman of the *zɔŋ*, cattle yard (*sapak*), and granary (*buur*) in that of a man. They mark off the economic field reserved for her and the social sphere in which she is supreme. Etiquette and convention show this, and, as in the case of the *zɔŋ* and the *buur*, ritual notions give expression to it and put the seal of mystical value on it. Women do not have ancestor shrines of their own. But in her storeroom an old woman keeps her *zaalaŋ*. This is a long rope net, holding a neat pile of polished calabash dishes (*ŋman*) of all sizes which she has accumulated during her married life. One of these is her *kumpiog*, 'basket of death'. It is the symbol of her mortal existence.[1] When she dies it stands in her *dɛndɔŋo* and is eventually taken, with the most meticulous ceremonial care, to her eldest surviving daughter. In this room also she keeps her main storage pot (*dɔk*). It is to her what a man's granary is to him. One sign of this is the rule that her first-born daughter may never, in the mother's lifetime, open it. She does so ritually when her mother's funeral is completed.[2]

Lastly, there is the grinding-room (*neer*), a vastly important item in the organization of the domestic economy, and in the personal relations of the women of a family with one another. It is always a small, low room, 3 or 4 feet in diameter, with a doorway barely large enough to admit a person on hands and knees. A hole under the eaves, the size of a soup plate, lets in a glimmer of light. A waist-high table built of mud, in the hollow surface of which two nether grindstones are embedded, takes up most of the interior. In a small homestead like Ɔndieso's one *neer* is enough, and his mother and wife share it, though the older woman seldom has occasion to use it as her daughter-in-law does most of the cooking for the family. If there are several women in a household, more than one grinding-room is needed. One reason for this is purely mechanical. Grinding the grain for the main meal, in the evening, takes at least an hour, in the period of plenty. The women and girls do this at any time of the day, but prefer to do it in the afternoon. Thus more than one woman may want to use the *neer* at the same time. But there is another reason as well. Co-wives are apt to squabble over the use of the grinding-room, especially if they do not get on harmoni-

---

[1] The calabash is the commonest domestic utensil and it symbolizes a woman in many contexts. For instance, when a man's wife bears a child he will send to tell her parents; and the messenger reports, with the euphemism the Tallensi always resort to on such occasions, that the woman has born 'a calabash' (*ŋman*) if it is a girl, or a 'staff' (*duor*) if it is a boy—the staff being a hunting-weapon carried by men.

[2] Cf. Ch. VIII below.

ously, for it is connected with that precise equality of grain rations to which co-wives are entitled and about which they are extremely touchy. To obviate these squabbles, which sometimes kindle suppressed antagonisms into serious quarrels, a man usually provides a separate grinding-room for a wife with a fractious disposition.

In a large and well-ordered house there is a great deal of free and easy communication between the different *dugɔt*. Children in particular go about freely from one woman's quarters (*dug*) to another's, since they are related to all by actual or derived filial ties. The men, too, are free of all the *dugɔt*, for the women are all either their 'mothers' (*manam*)—own mothers, or fathers' other wives, their wives (*pɔyaba*)—own wives or brothers' wives, or daughters-in-law (*sampɔyaba*)—own sons' or brothers' sons' wives. Men and their children, members of the same lineage, are the 'owners' of the homestead. They have determinate rights, duties, and sentiments towards all the women. The women are more circumspect, especially about the *dug* of a co-wife (*nentaa*) or husband's mother (*daŋaampɔk*) if their personal relations are not too cordial; for their social inter-relations are indirect and contingent on their marital ties, unless, as sometimes happens, they belong to the same or to linked clans and have, in consequence, a direct bond of solidarity. In spite of this, the general impression left by a visit to a large house is one of friendly co-operation unsullied by jealous distinctions.

The natives themselves have no illusions on this score. They do not take it for granted that all the women of a family will get on well with one another. They recognize clearly that the spatial differentiation of each *dug* in a house corresponds to its structural differentiation; and with this goes a certain degree of domestic privacy and a differentiation of sentiment and of emotional attachments that may become a source of friction. The *dug* (that is, a woman and her children by one man) constitutes the irreducible unit of Tale social structure, both jurally and morally, held together by the strongest social and emotional bonds conceivable to the Tallensi. The *dug* is the Talǝŋ's conceptual model of infrangible solidarity, and his emotional symbol of unstinted nourishment, of complete security, and of parental devotion. It is the prototype, also, of the closely integrated matri-segment within the formally unified patrilineal lineage, as has been shown in our previous volume.[1]

In general, as the foregoing suggests, a man has no room of his own. He keeps his personal belongings in his wife's *dug* and eats and sleeps there, or in his various wives' rooms in turn, if he has more than one. Chiefs, old men, and rich men sometimes have rooms of their own, usually in their senior wives' *dɛndɔna*, where they keep their more bulky personal belongings and to which they can retire if they want privacy. The Gɔlibdaana and the Gorogo Yikpɛmdaana, as we have seen, make an exaggerated display of their private rooms. But as a matter of fact,

---
[1] Cf. *Dynamics of Clanship*, ch. xii.

vanity apart, they do require ample storage-room for the large quantities of clothes, the saddlery and trappings of their horses, the innumerable odds and ends of European origin, and many articles of native production which they have accumulated by purchase or gift. Their good fortune is exceptional. Others content themselves with small and modest private rooms. Leatherworkers and blacksmiths also often have private rooms where they keep their tools and the materials of their craft.

No special provision is made for young children or girls. They live in their mothers' rooms. An unmarried young man usually has a special room of his own, essentially a sleeping-room (*doo*), in his mother's *dug*; and if there are several adolescent boys in a family a *doo* may be built for them in one of the women's *dugɔt*.

The construction of the dwelling-house shows graphically the division of the domestic family into two complementary spheres. On the one hand, we have the sphere in which the patricentral *yir* predominates; on the other, that in which the matricentral *dug* has priority. It is the line of cleavage between descent from the father (*ba dɔyam*) and descent from the mother (*ma dɔyam*), principles which are antithetical in form but complementary in function in the domestic organization. Maternal origin supplies the canon of differentiation within the family, paternal descent the principle of integration. In the polygynous joint family, which is the natives' ideal domestic unit, the constituent *dugɔt* are relatively autonomous in relation to one another, and in certain respects even mutually opposed. The *yir* combines them into a single integral unit, but they are not swallowed up; they retain their specific identity according to maternal origin. The *yir*, then, is the complementary factor to the *dug*; it is also the synthesis of a group of *dugɔt* at a higher level of organization. This, as has been shown in our previous book, is both the structural model and the social matrix of the lineage system.

The Developmental Cycle of the Joint Family

We have found it convenient to fix our analysis of the Tale homestead by reference to the simplest kind of independent domestic unit. But the elementary family, as we have already remarked, is neither the ideal nor the most common type of independent domestic unit in Taleland; for the typical substratum of a domestic group is not the individual breadwinner but an effective minimal lineage.[1] The domestic group grows, changes, and dissolves with the growth cycle of this lineage, and a particular elementary family is only an episode in this cycle. The structure of the Tale family cannot be divorced from its existence in time. We have to examine it as a process. At any given time we find domestic families at every stage of development in a Tale community.

[1] Cf. p. 9 above for a definition of this unit. A full analysis of its constitution is given in *Dynamics of Clanship*, ch. xii.

The characteristic domestic family of the Tallensi is the agnatic joint family, and other forms of domestic group appear as phases in the growth cycle of a joint family. In a random sample of sixty-one domestic families from Tongo and the settlements adjacent to it, recorded in 1934, forty-one, or about two-thirds of these, were joint families.[1] A joint family consists of two or more close agnates, members of a single effective minimal lineage in all but exceptional cases, and often comprising all the members of a particular effective minimal lineage, together with their wives, children, and other dependants, if any,

[1] This sample of 61 domestic families which is cited throughout this chapter, includes domestic families from 5 clans, but the majority are from Tongo. A similar sample taken in the Sie district gave approximately the same results. As has been mentioned, about two-thirds of these families were joint families. The remainder were either elementary families (i.e. consisting of a man, his wife or wives, and his young children) which had been parts of joint families 5 or 10 years previously and would probably become joint families again in a decade or so; or they were joint families augmented by one or two close agnates of the family head and their dependants, or by other kinsmen. Such an augmented joint family functions in the same way as a joint family in the narrow sense. Thus if the time factor is taken into account all Tale domestic families can be described as joint families.

The composition of the joint family can be regarded from a slightly different angle, which supplements what has just been said. Considering the family from the point of view of the relationship of the head to the other male members, our sample breaks up as follows:

11 elementary families (1 man, wife or wives, occasionally his mother, and his young children).
22 families in which the head was the father of the other adult male(s).
25 families in which the head was the older brother of one or more of the other adult males.
3 families in which the head was the grandfather of one or all the other adult males.

The commonest type, it will be seen, is the joint family presided over by either a 'father' or the senior amongst a group of brothers.

The mean number of persons (men, women, and children) per domestic family of our sample is 10·4, distributed as follows:

Number of persons per family

	1–5	6–10	11–15	16–20	21–5	Total
Frequency	8	28	17	4	4	61

The mean number of adult males (i.e. over 18, approximately) per family is 2·6; of wives, including widows of deceased members, 3·4; of minors, including adolescent daughters, 4·4. The frequency distributions are as follows:

Number per family

Frequency of	0	1	2	3	4	5	6	7	8	9	10	11	12	Total
Adult males	0	10	25	13	7	4	0	2	..	..	..	..	..	61
Wives	0	6	16	14	13	4	3	3	0	2	..	..	..	61
Minors	2	4	11	9	11	8	4	4	1	3	2	1	1	61

occupying a single homestead. All the men of a joint family are therefore related to one another through a common father or grandfather or, infrequently, great-grandfather. A joint family may consist of two or more brothers (full or half-brothers or paternal cousins), with their wives and children, and perhaps an old mother; or a man and some or all of his married sons with their wives and children, together with unmarried sons and other dependants; or an old man, some or all of his married sons and grandsons, with their wives and children and other dependants —'sons' and 'grandsons' in the last two classes being understood in the native classificatory sense as including both own and deceased brothers' sons and grandsons. Joint families of the last-mentioned class are not very common. Here and there one meets a joint family combining features of two classes or having a rather wider range of agnates or other male kin; but these are unusual.

A joint family is obviously a composite unit. If the subordinate families constituting it are taken separately, some or all may be monogynous, elementary families; but one or more of the male members may have more than one wife, and there will thus be subordinate polygynous families within the joint family. For though a Taləŋ starts his career as a family man with only one wife, his aim and ideal, throughout his life, is to have as many wives as he can afford. Actually, judging by the previously quoted sample,[1] the incidence of polygyny among the

---

[1] The following table sets out the relevant figures:

Table showing the Distribution of Wives of 146 Men over 18 Years of Age, belonging to 61 Domestic Families

	Married men						Single men	
Estimated age of men	Number of wives					Total men	Un-married	Widowers or deserted
	1	2	3	4	5			
18–30	32	3	..	..	..	35	18	17
31–45	21	13	3	2	..	39	(most	(most
46 and over	14	14	3	5	1	37	under 30)	over 30)
Totals	67	30	6	7	1	111	18	17
							35	

Percentages						Total 146 men	
Of whole sample	46	20·5	4·1	4·8	0·7	76% married	24% single
Of married men	60·4	27	5·4	6·3	0·9		

The table shows the distribution of effective wives, i.e. wives who fulfil both the sexual and the economic duties due from a wife, or, in a few cases, at least the economic duties. There were 9 non-effective wives, in addition, in this group: 3 incapacitated by leprosy or other chronic disease; 1 senile; 3 elderly women nominally inherited by their late husbands' younger brothers but

Tallensi is only about 40 per 100 married men and two out of three polygynists have only two wives. The modal number of wives is one.

Moreover, plurality of wives is mainly the privilege of older men, because they have both more resources and a longer marital history than the young men. Three-quarters of the married men under 45 have only one wife each.

A joint family is an organized economic and jural unit forming a single household under the authority of the oldest by age or generation of the group of agnates upon which it is based. Its component families are its segments, ordered and articulated in conformity with the lineage relations binding this group of men to one another. This appears in the layout of the homestead. The head of the joint family is the hub of the whole house, as we have seen, and each wife has her own quarters. It is shown, for example, in the fact that a young married son with no children, or only one or two infant children, generally occupies one of the rooms in his mother's *dug*, or, if his mother is dead, in the senior *dugdaana*'s *dug*; for his conjugal family counts, as yet, only as a segment of this *dug* in the social and economic organization of the house.

Taken over a long enough period, the joint family is seen to be a transitory unit. As the younger male members grow up, marry, and have children of their own, inner tensions begin to assert themselves and a tendency to split up appears. If fission does not occur in the lifetime of the head of the joint family, it is almost invariably precipitated by his death. Some or all of the component families then set up in their own independent homesteads, though it may be some years before complete dispersion supervenes. Thus it happens that an elementary family, which was at one time a part of a joint family, comes to occupy its own

residing with grown-up sons; 2 inherited wives who had not yet joined the menage of their new husbands and were unlikely to do so for a considerable time, if at all. Seven of these non-effective wives were the wives of men in the 46 *plus* group. If these are reckoned as well, the distribution is altered somewhat in favour of the polygynists. There would then, for instance, be 3 men with 5 wives each.

In addition to the 111 married men, this sample of domestic families includes 35 single men, 18 of whom, mostly young men, had never been properly married, and 17 of whom were single at the time of the census, owing to the death or desertion of their wives.

Estimates of age given here and elsewhere in this book are very approximate. The difficulties of guessing the age of Africans in societies where chronological age is taken no notice of are well known. In making the above estimates I took the Tong Hills Expedition of 1911 as a base-line. From what I was told of the appearance, size, and activities of a person at the time of that well-remembered event, a guess could be made at his or her probable age in 1934. If one person's approximate age was established in this way, others who were agreed to be his or her contemporaries could be put into the same age-group. For example, the age-group 18–30 includes a number of men who said they were babes in arms in 1911, and the age-group 46 *plus* includes all those who were young married men in 1911.

homestead accompanied often by the family head's old mother. This is the usual history of the independent elementary family in Taleland; and about 1 in 8 of the domestic families of our sample have this constitution. Often, however, when a man secedes from the joint family he already has more than one wife, though his children are all still under marriageable age. Polygynous domestic families of this class occur in about the same proportion—1 in 8—in the sample. And thus the cycle begins again. As the children grow up and marry, each fraction of the dismembered joint family evolves into a new joint family, or at least has the possibility of doing so.

A joint family splits up—into family segments, be it noted, not into a number of dispersed individuals—if it has existed long enough to have reached an advanced stage of internal differentiation; but during its existence it is a remarkably cohesive unit. The fissiparous tendencies inherent in its structure are kept well in check until the pressure of economic needs, psychological friction, or a radical alteration in the constellation of the social relations, such as occurs when the family head dies, makes them irresistible. The split follows the lines of cleavage inherent in the structure of the effective minimal lineage on which a particular joint family is founded, and it takes place by stages.

We shall study the process of fission in the joint family later. Here only the results concern us. The simplest split occurs when the oldest son of the family head 'goes out on his own (*yi u kɔkɔ*)',[1] or 'cuts his own gateway (*bit u zanɔr*)' in the family homestead, during his father's lifetime. He thus sets up an independent household, though perhaps living in a semi-detached part of the paternal homestead. But when the old man dies, he frequently returns to the parental home, and the joint family is reconstituted under his authority.

Permanent fission usually occurs between brothers (full, or half-brothers, or paternal cousins), or by the secession of the family head's deceased brother's sons. It begins, and may persist until the family head's death, as a purely economic division. Thus two full (*soog*) brothers—the older being the family head—may decide to farm independently because the growing economic wants of their respective families no longer permit them to maintain a common household. The bond of full brotherhood (*soog*) inhibits further fission altogether, or until such time as both men have adult children. Until then they generally continue to occupy the same homestead, using a single common gateway, cattle-yard (*sapak*), and *zɔŋ*. Their respective sections of the

---

[1] The intra-family tensions which lead to the 'going out' of the eldest son will be discussed later. They are rationalized, and the secession of the eldest son is given a mystical sanction by the taboo which, among the Namoos, forbids a man ever meeting his first-born adult son face to face in his gateway after the latter has a family of adolescent children. Non-Namoos do not have the taboo, but the beliefs expressed in it are as strong among them as among the Namoos. Cf. below, Ch. VIII.

homestead, called their *dugɔt* by contraposition with the common *yir*, will be separated by a party wall with a ladder on either side, giving access for essential communication without a detour via the *sapak* but preventing trespass by their respective families. Each man is the head of his own, relatively independent, household, working its particular fields and having its own granary; but the older brother has authority over the whole *yir* in jural and ritual matters, exercises general supervision over the affairs of all its members, and, above all, controls the utilization of the patrimonial land and cattle and is the titular owner of all heritable, non-personal property of all its members. Pumaan and Zaŋ are full brothers sharing a house in this manner.

Two half-brothers, or two first cousins (*sunzɔp*-brothers) whose fathers were full brothers (*saarət*) sometimes share a homestead thus, if they get on cordially, especially while the children of both or either are still too young for productive labour. Thus Naabdiya and Barimoda are half-brothers who occupy a single homestead with one gateway in this manner.

In time, however, the combined effects of economic needs, structural cleavages, and personal tensions lead to a further stage of separation. It takes longest, as we have noted, with full brothers whose genealogical equivalence,[1] mutual identification, and reciprocal affection are greatest, and occurs most readily with cousins, between whom the corresponding cleavages are more explicit. The younger man cuts another gateway for himself (*bit u zanɔr*), and henceforth has his own *zɔŋ* and *sapak*. The homestead now really consists of two separate, semi-detached dwellings, each occupied by one domestic family and household.

An example of this is Katiŋoo yiri at Zoo. This homestead is occupied by the three grandsons—Saandi, Ku'ɔni, and Ɔmara—of Katiŋoo, who died about a generation ago. Each of these men, who are all over 45, is the head of a joint family with grown-up children. Their lineage relationship is as follows:

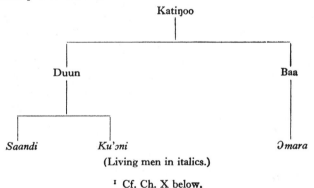

(Living men in italics.)

[1] Cf. Ch. X below.

This house illustrates an advanced stage of segmentation, involving a split between two full brothers (*saarət*) on the one hand, and between paternal cousins (*sunzɔp*) on the other. The three domestic families occupy three separate sections of the common *yir*, divided from one another by walls of the same height as the outer walls of the homestead, each with its own gateway, *zɔŋ*, and *sapak*, and communicating internally by means of ladders. They are described as the component *dugət* of the common *yir*. Saandi, the oldest of the three 'brothers' (*sunzɔp*), and head of the lineage of Katiŋoo biis, occupies the central section. Economically the three domestic families are wholly independent of one another, but Saandi exercises a certain degree of jural and ritual authority over the whole *yir*. As its spatial configuration implies, such a unit has less domestic solidarity than, for example, that of Pumaan and Zaŋ

Finally comes the stage of complete spatial segregation of the domestic families derived from segments of a single joint family. This occurs often between the families of half-brothers, and invariably, in due course, between the families of cousins. Thus Kurug and Lɛbhtiis of Tɔŋ-Puhug occupy separate homesteads, 100 yards or so apart, with their respective domestic families.[1] These homesteads were built by their fathers, Yin and Naandɔmər, who were half-brothers and decided to separate after the death of *their* father, Zupibig. It may happen also in a family like Naabdiya's, when the head of the homestead dies and is succeeded by his younger brother or half-brother. Then his oldest son, if he is a man of mature years with a growing family, may in due course move out to set up on his own with his family and younger siblings.

In this way a joint family evolves into an *expanded* family in the course of a generation or so. An *expanded* family generally forms a close local group. The heads of the several joint families comprising it are all members of one lineage segment of a low order, expanded from what was an effective minimal segment one or two generations before. They have intimate social and personal ties and their families, *pari passu*, have closer intercourse with one another and stronger mutual loyalties than any of them has with other neighbouring families. They retain, in an attenuated degree, many of the intimacies and conventions that normally prevail in the joint family. Their relations to one another are analogous to those of the *dugət* of a joint family, but the lineage of the family heads operates more formally as the basis of their cohesion than in the case of a group of families sharing a common residence. When such a group of domestic families is described collectively as a *yir* and severally as *dugət*, these terms refer to the lineage relationship of their male members. For there is no specific term for the expanded family, nor has it a precise social definition. It exists in the conduct of its

[1] Cf. *Dynamics of Clanship*, p. 193.

members to one another, not as a demarcated social unit. It is the widest field of domestic relations for any joint family.

It is evident that the domestic families that make up a settlement at any given time exhibit various degrees of internal differentiation. It depends mainly on the length of time the particular domestic family has been in existence. At one extreme we find families like that of Baripɛta, a man of about 35, who in 1934 had one wife and one infant. With him lived also one of his late father's widows and his young unmarried full brother. We might describe this as a young family. It constitutes a single economic and jural unit.

At the other extreme is the family of a man like Yinyɛla, whose age in 1934 could not have been less than 75. His household comprised his adult sons (all of them married or old enough to have wives, and the oldest a man of about 40 with adolescent children), his three young children, varying in age from about 11 to 2 years, and his deceased brother's son with his wife and children. He had had many wives, three of whom were still surviving, two elderly women and one a young woman whom he had married six or seven years before. This joint family had reached such an advanced stage of internal differentiation that the competing interests of its component families (the family segments) were becoming difficult to keep in check. The common resources of the household did not satisfy all the wants of Yinyɛla's brother's son's and his own eldest son's families; and these two men began to cultivate supplementary farms for their own use. Yinyɛla's domestic family was, in fact, on the verge of breaking up, though it was still an economic and jural unit under his authority. Had he not died in 1937 his brother's son would have moved out and his eldest son would have 'cut his own gateway (*bit u zanɔr*)'. In between these extremes are families like that of Naɣabil of Kpata'ar, representing a stage of development to which a simple family like Baripɛta's may attain in a decade or so. Naɣabil has four wives. His children range in age from about 17 to infancy. His mother and younger full-brother (*pit-soog*) with his wife and child live with him. In twenty years, if all survive, this family will resemble that of Yinyɛla in 1934.

Broadly speaking, families of the first and third kinds are those of men under middle age, who have but little voice in the jural and ceremonial affairs of the community, and families of the second kind are those of the elders (*kpeem*, pl. *kpɛm*) and near-elders (*kpeemtaɣalis*), men past middle age, who have the dominant role in controlling and organizing social life. About half the domestic families in a settlement belong to each of these two broad divisions. In the highly differentiated joint families which have been in existence for a considerable time, the age range of the *ɣirdaana*'s children and grandchildren often runs from middle age to infancy. For a man goes on taking new wives, if he can, as long as his reproductive powers last. Old men are notoriously desirous of having, and are indulgent to, a young wife (*pɔyabil*), not only for sexual motives but also, and mainly, in order to have a strong young woman about the house to administer those creature comforts to which they are said to become more and more addicted as they grow older. Thus siblings by the same father (*ba ukɔla biis*) may differ in age by as much as a generation. A man's younger half-brother or sister may be younger than his own children though senior to them in generation. This has important effects on the lineage organization.

The custom of the levirate introduces a component of some significance in the constitution of the joint family. In the 61 domestic families of our sample there were 111 married men, and no less than 21—more than one in five—had one or more inherited wives. An inherited wife usually brings her young children by her first husband (if she has any) with her. They grow up side by side with her children by her second husband, who is responsible for their support. Tale kinship ideas make this a simple and self-evident arrangement; but it means, nevertheless, a division within what is normally the most compact and cohesive element of the domestic family, the matricentral *dug*, in accordance with the different paternity of the children. Generally a widow of childbearing age marries a close agnate of her deceased husband—his brother or first cousin—who is, therefore, a close classificatory father of her children. This makes it easy for them to regard her second husband with some of the devotion and affection due from children to their own father, especially if they are still very young. Still, this is a weak place in the cohesion of a family, at which a split easily occurs; for no man, say the Tallensi, can wholly take the place of one's true father. If a widow marries a distant agnate of her late husband, the latter's heir may demand the custody of his children when they are old enough to do without a mother's care. This splits the *dug*. But it also creates compensatory bonds of uterine (*soog*) kinship between her sons belonging to different lineage segments.

Sometimes a man's dependants include a deceased brother's children whose mother has died or married out of the family. Such children are, for all practical purposes, his own children, but the sons frequently secede when they have children. Much less commonly, a man may have an orphaned sister's son (*ahaŋ*) living with him in as intimate a relationship, ostensibly, as if he were his son or brother. Actually, both jural and sentimental reservations hedge round a sister's son's position in the family, for his descent bars him, in the last resort, from ever acquiring real filial status.[1] It is significant that in the old settlements extremely few cases of this kind occur, and it is always assumed that the nephew will eventually return to his natal settlement—though he does not always do so. In the new settlements, where personal kinship ties largely replace lineage ties as the basis of local aggregation, not only sororal

[1] Cf. Ch. XI below.

nephews but more distant cognatic and even affinal kin frequently live with a kinsman until they can set up in their own homesteads.

Sometimes, too, an unmarried sister's child (*tau-bii*) may grow up and live in its uncle's family. It may be an illegitimate child (*yi yeem bii*—a maiden's child), or one whose mother's bride-price was not paid, and who therefore belongs to her father unless or until it is redeemed (*pɔhɔg*) by the payment of a cow by its genitor or his heir. A sister's child is to all intents and purposes a child of the family. But not being of the true agnatic line, it is subject to certain jural disabilities which have no consequence for a girl but handicap a boy, as we have previously seen.

The domestic families of chiefs and headmen are unusual only in respect of size. Their newly won riches enable chiefs and headmen to acquire numerous wives and to maintain households that appear enormous in the eyes of the ordinary man. A petty headman may have ten or more wives. The late Chief of Tongo, a chief of modest means compared with some of his peers in Taleland, had more than thirty. The Gɔlibdaana of Tɛnzugu has at least eighty. The Chief of Datoko is reputed to have a hundred, but he denies this and claims to have only a modest fifty. Except that their domestic economy and organization is more complex and that there is at times more friction between the womenfolk, these hypertrophied joint families have the same pattern of organization as those of ordinary folk.

It is noteworthy that this pattern has not been disturbed by the social changes which have, in recent years, followed the subjection of the Northern Territories of the Gold Coast to European political, economic, and cultural influences. Family disorganization has barely begun to appear in Taleland. There is hardly a domestic family in the country—not one in our sample—which has wholly escaped the effects of these contact influences. One or more of their members is or has been abroad in Mampurugu, Ashanti, or the Colony, for longer or shorter periods of time, farming, working for wages, or trading. But the number of men abroad, at any given time, for very long periods is relatively small[1] compared with other parts of West and Southern Africa, and their absence has little effect on the structure of the residual family. Their labour is lost to the family, but as they are no longer a drain on its resources this does not upset its internal economy. Similarly, as they are mostly young men[2] with little or no responsibility for the management of family

---

[1] Estimates based on my own census material and on Nominal Rolls drawn up by Administrative Officers for tax collection show that an average of just under 7 per cent. of the adult male population of Taleland were away from home and not likely to return in the immediate future, in the years 1936 to 1939. This estimate may be compared with the 60–80 per cent. of able-bodied adult males absent from tribal reserves in Northern Rhodesia and Nyassaland quoted by Lord Hailey, *African Survey*, p. 701.

[2] Reliable information on the ages of these absentees cannot be obtained. But from personal contact with many of them, both on their return home and

affairs, their absence does not disturb jural or ritual relations centred in the family. It is like a tree which remains a tree morphologically and physiologically even if some of its minor branches have been lopped off.

The foregoing is true of the great majority of Tale families. The structure of the normal family can still be accurately described without reference to contact influence, in spite of the fact that a few families can be found in every settlement which have been badly mutilated by the prolonged absence abroad of their male members. Admittedly the norms of family relations have not remained completely insulated from these influences. With the ease of modern communications and the openings for work abroad, young people have incentives and opportunities which their fathers never had for resisting the authority of their elders and for breaking away from the family for a longer or shorter time. But as yet these new incentives and opportunities appear only as modifying factors in the play of the culturally defined family relations. They do not represent a conflicting set of norms, creating divisions within Tale society. For instance, a young man who is still jurally a minor cannot at will leave the domestic family to which he belongs by birth and set up an independent household. He can do so only in compliance with the moral rules and social conventions that regulate the fission of families. In fact, the motive to break away will only arise when certain standard changes take place in the composition of the domestic unit to which he belongs, or when he reaches a stage of social maturity which precipitates certain standard tensions between him and the head of the unit. The alternative for a young man who, in these days, hankers after independence is to leave the community until such time as he is prepared to settle down. He has to seek work abroad, in Ashanti or the Colony, or in the service of the white man nearer home. He is assured of a cordial welcome home whenever he decides to return, whether it be for a few weeks only or permanently. But if he makes up his mind to settle down at home it can only be within the existing social framework, and this means complying with the norms of family organization. There is no other way by which he can get married or acquire a house site or farm-land in his natal settlement, let alone play his part in community affairs. Hitherto these norms have been so well maintained that no returned emigrant has been known to flout them.

Summing up, we see that the Tale domestic system has three morphological strata. It consists of a segmentary economic formation—households of different dimensions and degrees of economic self-sufficiency—embraced within a segmentary jural and ceremonial formation—domestic units not necessarily congruent with households grouped under family heads—and this again contained within a system of residential grouping in which the changes of phase in domestic structure are crystallized.

in places like Kumasi, I can say with certainty that the great majority are under 30.

A domestic unit is most clearly identified by the fact that it has a single common gateway. Though the three domains of domestic organization are not absolutely congruent, the commonest residential unit is the single household, which is also a single though not necessarily completely independent jural and ceremonial unit.[1]

We have been considering the typical development of the joint family as a process of successive fission and dispersion. But the contrary process of reintegration also plays an important part in this development. The changes in the composition of the joint or expanded family that lead to changes in the status and social roles of its senior male members cause it to split up in the circumstances that have been indicated, but they lead to a fusion of independent units in other circumstances. The decisive factors are jural status in the lineage, with which go rights over patrimonial land, and economic capacity.

Let us take a sample case. When Katiŋoo died (see genealogy, p. 68) his eldest son Duun became head of the effective minimal lineage and joint family and inherited the patrimonial farm-land. Duun and his full brother Baa continued to occupy their father's homestead, using only one gateway. After a while—four or five years, perhaps—Baa asked to be allowed to farm for himself as his children were growing up. He still occupied the same homestead as Duun, but his quarters were separated from those of Duun by a high party wall (*bɛŋər*), he had his own granary, farmed for himself, and was solely responsible for supplying the food and other wants of his wives and children. The domestic family now consisted of two households.

[1] The following table shows this clearly:

Table showing the Distribution of Domestic Families (= Gateways) and Households (= Units of Food Economy) in relation to Homesteads

Domestic families per homestead	1	2	3	4	5	6	7	8	Totals
No. of homesteads	34	5	4	0	1	0	0	0	44
No. of domestic families	34	10	12	0	5	0	0	0	61
Households per homestead	1	2	3	4	5	6	7	8	Totals
No. of homesteads	25	11	4	2	0	1	0	1	44
No. of households	25	22	12	8	0	6	0	8	81

(Mean number of persons: per homestead, 14·5; per domestic family, 10·4.)

The 61 domestic families of our sample occupy 44 homesteads. On the average there are 1·4 gateways (i.e. 1·4 domestic families) per homestead; but more than half of the 61 families occupy their own homesteads, with one gateway apiece. There are 81 households in the sample group, an average of 1·9 households per homestead and 1·3 households per domestic family. But nearly a third of these households are single domestic families dwelling in their own homesteads.

Five or six years passed and Duun died. Baa was now head of the lineage and family. The patrimonial land passed to him. For a short time Duun's two sons, Saandi and Ku'ɔni, continued to occupy their late father's section of the homestead and farmed in partnership, independently of Baa. But they soon decided to move out. They went to build at Gbambee, on their late father's bush farm. At first they shared a homestead and farmed together. Then Ku'ɔni began to farm for himself and, a little later, wished to have his own gateway. At this stage the expanded family sprung from Katiŋoo consisted of two homesteads, one at Zoo, occupied by Baa and his sons with their families, who together made up a single household, and the other at Gbambee, consisting of two semi-detached parts occupied by Saandi and Ku'ɔni respectively, with their families, and constituting two separate households.

A little later Ku'ɔni separated altogether from Saandi and went to build his homestead at Zoo on a piece of land that had been their father's personal farm. This site proved to be mystically unpropitious and soon Ku'ɔni moved again. This time he returned to his father's (and grandfather's) original home (*daboog*) and built semi-detached quarters for himself adjoining Katiŋoo's old homestead, still occupied by Baa. He remained economically independent of Baa; but both he and Saandi were still under Baa's jural and ritual jurisdiction, as his brother's sons. A process of partial reintegration had, however, occurred.

Then Baa died and Saandi became head of the lineage and heir to the patrimonial land. So he moved back to Zoo, where he built semi-detached quarters for himself adjoining the group's original home. This happened quite recently; and the distribution of Katiŋoo yir is as we have described on p. 69. Saandi, Ku'ɔni, and Baa's son Ɔmara have each their separate, semi-detached quarters and their separate gateways; they are economically independent of each other; but jural and ritual jurisdiction over the unit is in Saandi's hands.

But this is not the end of the story. If Saandi were to die suddenly, none of his sons would be old enough to farm for himself and support Saandi's widows and children. So they would all join Ku'ɔni's household, and remain in his custody—the widows as his wives (unless they remarried other men, when they would fade out of the picture altogether), the children as his children—until Saandi's oldest boy was old enough to set up an independent household. The process of gradual dispersion would then start again. If, Saandi being dead, Ɔmara were also to die suddenly, leaving no son old enough to support his household, his children would also join Ku'ɔni, and thus all the branches of Katiŋoo's family would be reconstituted into a single unit for the time being. The whole cycle would take from twenty to thirty years.

Our illustration has been in part hypothetical so as not to confuse the reader with too many genealogies. But this is not a fanciful case. A dozen family histories that have followed the pattern outlined above

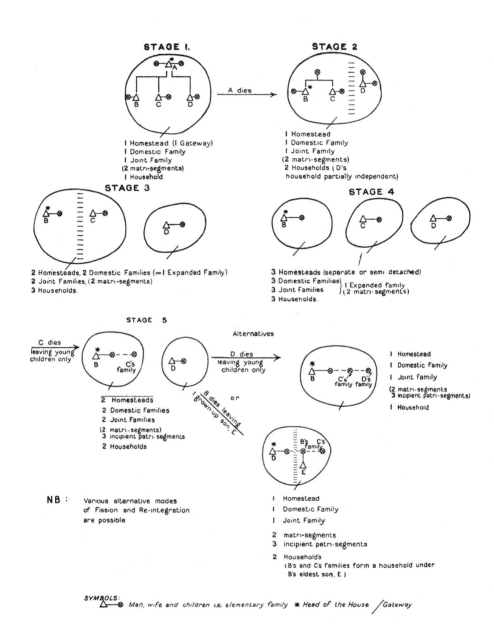

FIG. 3. Diagram showing the developmental cycle of the Joint Family.

could be cited. Such a history explains why Tiezien of Kpata'ar, for instance, has the sons of two of his late brothers living and working with him; and why Yinworəb of Tɔŋ-Kuorəg has both a brother's widows and young children, and his own young half-brothers, as members of his household.

We shall consider the main factors that determine this cycle of development in a later chapter. We shall see that economic needs and structural cleavages are chiefly responsible for fission in the joint family and religious and jural sanctions for the reintegration of an expanded family.

CHAPTER IV

HUSBAND AND WIFE IN THE STRUCTURE OF THE FAMILY

The General and the Particular in the Pattern of Domestic Relations

IT is clear from Chapter II that *dɔyam*, the fact of birth, the event that fixes one's descent immutably, takes precedence over all other conditions governing the social relations and the social roles of a Talɔŋ. This principle comes out in all departments of Tale social life, and nowhere so plainly as in the organization of domestic life. We turn, therefore, to examine the working of kinship in the domestic family, which we have called the focal field of kinship.

It is important to bear in mind that kinship relations in the family group are inter-articulated in a single configuration, dominated by the *patria potestas* of the male head of the family. The relations of father and child are coloured by the relations of mother and child that coexist with them, and the relations of mother and child acquire a special accent in the context of the relations between co-wives. Particular domestic relationships appear in their true light only when they are considered as part of the total pattern. The polarity of *dug* and *yir* moulds them all; all play a part in the balance of centripetal and centrifugal forces in the structure of the family. All, moreover, are subject to the pull and pressure of genealogical connexions and groupings outside the family circle.

The natives are very conscious of this, and take it into account in the management of their lives. They say, for instance, that a woman's parents continue to have great influence over her for some years after her marriage and that is why her husband must keep on the good side of his parents-in-law. 'Don't you know what in-lawship means?' said Bayankura, somewhat lugubriously, when I found him hard at work helping to rebuild his father-in-law's homestead. Again, Tiezien's family believed that he was much under the influence of his senior wife, Tanzoo. So when by various pretexts he caused both of his late brother's sons to lose the young wives they had recently taken, they ascribed it morosely to Tanzoo's jealousy of their mother, Tiezien's second wife.

We shall not attempt a full-dress study of Tale family life; here we are concerned only with the structurally significant norms. In a society as homogeneous and economically undifferentiated as that of the Tallensi, people of the same sex, age, and social standing tend to have the same life history; and organized units such as the lineage and the family tend to have a stereotyped structure and development. The common denominators of action stand out.

Yet it is a constantly reiterated assumption of the natives that no two people are absolutely alike. Peculiarities of personality and character, they say (and observation bears them out), qualify all social relationships. People conform to the norms but each in the light of his own experiences, his special circumstances, his personal idiosyncrasies. The same sort of events, the same kind of person-to-person relations, make up the life of every family; but they are combined in a unique way in the history of a particular family. They give a distinctive tone or atmosphere to the life of that family that can be more easily felt than described. I knew intimately six domestic families which I kept under observation for many months; I knew another dozen or so families fairly well, and spent many hours in yet other homes all over Taleland. I learnt to perceive, but I could never get below the surface of this affective ambient of family life. It is, indeed, difficult to find terms with which to convey the impression of smooth, equable, well-balanced running which a family like that of Ɔmara's makes on an observer, or the contrary impression of strain, or of inadequate co-ordination, which one sees in families like those of Kutɔbis of Tɔŋ-Dekpieng, or of Pumaan of Tɔŋ-Puhug.

Most Tale families seem to go on in a stable and harmonious way; but there are, as we shall see, very many possibilities of friction, some inevitable, some avoidable, which arise out of the cleavages inherent in the structure of the family. How long these forces of dissension remain dormant, or how they are handled when they thrust forward, depends very much on the character of the family head. A tactful and considerate family head like Ɔmara manages to keep a smooth discipline in his family and to maintain amicable relations with his neighbours, whereas an erratic man like Kutɔbis cannot keep his sons in check and is for ever at loggerheads with his nearest agnates. From the point of view of the structurally significant norms, this feature of Tale family life and of Tale kinship in general is important as underlying the elasticity of actual social behaviour within the limits of the norms, and as a dynamic factor in the cycle of changes that a family passes through.

One thing which puts a screen between an inquirer and the inner life of a family is the surprising degree of privacy a family can preserve. It is surprising in the circumstances of Tale social life. One's neighbours are one's nearest lineage kin. The lineage principle compels a man to consult and gain the support of these kin in any matter of importance, and he generally does so in trivial matters too. Men of the same lineage grow up together, play together in childhood, often work together as youths or men, constantly visit one another's homes, identify themselves with one another and act together in corporate affairs. Inevitably they know one another's personal history in detail. And this knowledge is not the mere stuff of gossip, but a real force in the corporate life of the lineage and the community, since the biography of the individual is a thread in the current history of the lineage, tying up with its common interests and solidarity. This applies to women as well, if in a slightly lesser degree. Moreover, close cognates of different clans keep in touch sufficiently to know a great deal about one another's personal life.

In spite of this, domestic privacy is well guarded, for the essential life of the family goes on inside the homestead. There is a basis for this in the rules of residence and in the domestic economy. Residential autonomy is an index of economic autonomy. A household produces almost the whole of the food-supplies it consumes. Its neighbours, however closely related they are, can guess as to the sufficiency but cannot know the exact quantity of a household's food-supplies. Only the head of the household knows this. As we have seen, a major factor of differentiation between and within domestic units is the organization of food production and consumption. One can see this any evening when the chief meal of the day is eaten. It is prepared by the women and consumed by all the members of the household producing the grain. Meals are not regularly shared between separate households, even within the same domestic unit. The correct thing is for a person to take his usual meals at home amidst his own family. Most Tallensi would starve rather than deliberately scrounge (*bimh*) a meal off a kinsman who farms separately, even if the latter lives in the same homestead. Tallensi would think it a disgrace if their children made a habit of going to feed with neighbours, as is the custom in some primitive societies. A hungry child comes to its mother for food; it will not go to a neighbouring homestead in the hope of getting something to eat.

The etiquette of social intercourse indicates as clearly the degree to which domestic privacy is taken for granted. A visitor always announces himself at the gateway. A kinsman, neighbour, or friend calls out, informally, the name of the person he wishes to see, a stranger calls out *gafarra* ('excuse me'), and waits to be asked in. At night the family is usually gathered together inside its own homestead. In fine weather, especially if the moon is bright, men, women, and children spread themselves out in the senior woman's *dɛndɔŋo*, relaxing after the evening meal. If it is a large family a visitor will find them sprawling at ease in what seems a completely higgledy-piggledy huddle. The infants sleep in their mothers' arms, the smaller children doze on the hard gravel floor, the older children chatter in twos and threes, the grown-ups and the young men and girls talk of the day's happenings, yarn and gossip, or play at riddles. Generally, several different conversations go on at the same time. There may be visitors, a neighbour come on some business or suitors come courting one of the girls. A visitor can be seen in entire privacy. He or she is taken into one of the rooms, and no one would be so lacking in manners as to intrude. A young man visits his sweetheart thus in her own home, and is entertained by her in complete privacy. Other members of the family know all about it, of course, but the sweethearts need not fear being disturbed.

Within the joint family, though its members maintain a very intimate association with one another, make free of one anothers' possessions, and go freely in and out of every woman's quarters, each woman and her children are ensured a certain amount of privacy in their own *dug*. Husband and wife form a precisely distinguished unit. They have complete privacy in their sexual relations and a great deal of privacy in other relations. It would be the grossest breach of manners for anyone but their own infant child to intrude on a man and his wife in their own sleeping-room.

In their own home, therefore, a family has much privacy. A man can confide in his wife or his son things that he does not want others to know about—things about his debts, his property, or his ritual possessions. He can talk over with them problems concerning the household or matters of public import. There are ritual activities, such as sacrifices to a medicine shrine, in which only a man and his sons or the members of the joint family share. Sometimes such domestic secrets have to be divulged, especially after a man's death. It may be necessary to clear up a question of a debt he owed or to carry out special rites for one of his medicine shrines. But until then they are usually faithfully guarded. The Taləŋa can keep his own counsel if need be.

The Significance of Marriage[1]

As the preceding chapters suggest, Tale domestic relations do not remain perpetually fixed. They change and develop with the years. At one time the ties of economic co-operation, of reciprocal sentiment and mutual loyalties, of reciprocal and shared rights and duties, are uppermost; at another the underlying cleavages and competing interests push through. This appears very clearly in the relations of husband and wife, the central pillar of the domestic organization. We shall discuss the marital relationship in some detail, for it is a nodal relationship in Tale social life. It is not only the starting-point of the family, but the starting-point of the kinship ties that run across and between genealogically independent clans and lineages. Through marriage the mutually exclusive corporate units of Tale society become interlaced with one another.

The Tallensi regard marriage as the normal state of life for every adult. They cannot conceive of anyone voluntarily refraining from marriage throughout life. There is something wrong, by native standards, with men and women who never marry; and they are few. In the whole of Tongo I knew only five men who had never been married and who would, according to common belief, never marry. One was obviously mentally defective; another was an invert; two were said to be so ugly that no woman would accept them, but both were also definitely unbalanced and eccentric; and the last was a gentle old man, who, it was

[1] A preliminary account of Tale marriage customs is given in my pamphlet, *Marriage Law among the Tallensi*, Government Press, Gold Coast, 1935.

said, had never had the enterprise to find a wife. I heard of no woman who had never married. Deformities which do not wholly incapacitate a person or arouse repulsion are not a bar to marriage. The blind, the deaf, and the lame find spouses if they are otherwise able-bodied and presentable.

Tallensi attach immense importance to marriage, not only because it is the sole means to the most ardently desired of all ends, the procreation of legitimate children, but also because no man or woman can adequately satisfy all his or her wants or lead a normal social life, after reaching maturity, without a spouse. Sooner or later a man must have a wife and a woman a husband. Hence 'finding a wife (*pɔya booga*)' is the most urgent preoccupation of unmarried men, apart from getting a living. Among unmarried young men it is an obsession, the most absorbing pursuit of their leisure and an interminable topic of conversation. A girl's life is entirely directed towards marriage from childhood onwards.

It is a common thing to find a group of men discussing the relative importance of farms and wives, the two basic practical interests of the natives. They seldom fail to come down to the fundamentals. I have heard an elder sum it up somewhat in this fashion: 'If you don't farm you will have no food; and if you have no food you die. Then what is the use of a wife without food? But if you have no wife you will have no children and your life is wasted.' In the end, however, it is usually agreed that farming is the more important, for the man who lives long enough will not lack a wife and without food one cannot support a family.

Land and wives have many features in common, as their juxtaposition in native thought shows. Both stand for the fulfilment of fundamental social needs. Both come under the jurisdiction of the lineage, though they are of direct service to individuals. But there are certain differences which show the special importance of wives. There is no intense competition for the possession of land. Owing to technical and economic limitations there is no inducement to accumulate land. Wealth—that is, property acquired by saving, or in exchange for surplus grain or cash—consists pre-eminently of livestock; and the use to which livestock is principally put is in acquiring wives, performing sacrifices, celebrating funerals, and, to a much lesser extent, competing for certain politico-ritual offices. Such wealth is, therefore, really equivalent to provision for delayed consumption or special forms of consumption arising out of ritual obligations or differences in status.[1] It has no durable productive value. Compared with livestock, the purchase of farm-land is insignificant

---

[1] But Tale standards of wealth are extremely low. Except for a handful of chiefs and headmen—who have herds of cattle numbering from 20 to 50, and, in at least one case, apparently, over 100, as well as numbers of small stock—a man with a dozen sheep, a few goats, and three or four head of cattle is considered to be wealthy (*bondaan*).

as a form of investment, if such it can be called. Indeed, over most of Taleland the buying and selling of farm-land is ritually prohibited.[1] Occasionally disputes arise between the heirs when farm-lands pass by inheritance. But these rare quarrels are considered to be despicable and are ascribed to idiosyncrasies of character. In any case they are quarrels over the apportionment of joint property and there is always the chance that the man who has come off worst will later inherit the very land he was deprived of.

It is the exact contrary with wives. They form the chief object of competition both between individuals and between corporate groups. This is explicitly admitted in the conventions ruling the abduction of wives and marriage with another man's ex-wife.[2] The prohibition against abducting the wife (or marrying an ex-wife) of a clansman, kinsman, or member of a locally contiguous clan admits the fact that such acts are the most prolific source of strife, leading, in the old days, to bloodshed at times. The corollary that it is permissible, nay, commendable, to abduct the wife of a member of a distant, unrelated clan is an expression of the idea that geographically distant and genealogically unconnected clans have no direct common interests.

Competition for wives always was and still is the chief source of conflict between individuals and groups in Taleland. More than 90 per cent. of all cases brought to chiefs' courts nowadays are concerned with wives, and they are always triangular affairs with two men competing for the woman or her offspring. The reason for this competitive attitude about wives in a society almost devoid of durable goods of great productive or prestige value and possessing few prestige-conferring offices is not difficult to see, as has been previously indicated. Wives are the sole means of attaining the supreme end of life for the natives, the perpetuation and increase of a man's lineage. Like land, which is a common interest to the whole nuclear and often inner lineage, wives are of common interest to all the members of their husbands' lineages (not only their inner lineages, but even their maximal lineages and clans), for all of whom the perpetuation of their line of descent is of transcendent importance. This idea, which is expressed in the principle of the levirate, lies behind many of the institutions we shall be considering in this chapter.

Tallensi maintain that marriageable young women have become much scarcer than a generation ago. They blame the chiefs and headmen, whose new-found wealth enables them to have large harems, thus robbing young men of possible wives. Tallensi say that girls naturally prefer to marry young men, who are more congenial to them sexually and socially, rather than old men, however prosperous or exalted they may be. But a girl cannot easily resist an offer of marriage from a chief

[1] Cf. *Dynamics of Clanship*, ch. xi.
[2] Ibid., ch. iv.

or headman or important elder, backed as it often is by lavish gifts to her parents, security of the bride-price, and the attraction of his wealth and power or status. Few parents would hesitate to force their daughter to accept such an offer. Chiefs and headmen do in fact have an excessive number of wives. The five biggest chiefs and headmen of the Tongo district had between them about 160 wives of all ages in 1936. Their predecessors of a generation ago would have had perhaps 30 between them, at the utmost. The extra 130 wives they have means that probably 100 other men have been cheated of wives. This has no doubt diminished the chances of early marriage for a proportion of young men, but not so greatly as the men assert. All the evidence of Tale domestic institutions and of Tale genealogies goes to show that wives were always highly prized because they were always at a premium.[1] In consequence, no unmarried girl or woman of child-bearing age lacks suitors, and no wife of child-bearing age need endure an intolerable marriage. She can always find another husband. That women take advantage of their scarcity value is what one would expect; but they do so to a smaller extent than one anticipates. This is due partly to the strength and stability of the patrilineal lineage system, expressed in inter-personal relations in the power of the *patria potestas*, and partly to the great value women set upon wifehood and motherhood. Life is a failure to a Tale woman who never becomes a wife and mother.

The Stability of Marriage

In consequence, partly, of the scarcity value of wives, but more, no doubt, of the conflict of loyalties and interests which has to be overcome, marriage tends to be unstable in the initial stages. A young man rarely settles down permanently with his first bride, and young women generally treat their first marriage as an experiment unless the husband is a much older man to whom they have been married by formal negotiation. In the course of collecting census material I noted the marriages of over a hundred men. There is not one man over the age of 30, approximately (excluding a few physically or psychologically abnormal men), who has failed to experience one or more unsuccessful and usually short-lived marriages. Most men of 30 to 40 can give a history of five

---

[1] I have no demographic evidence suggesting that there was formerly or is now a marked deficiency of marriageable women as compared with men in Taleland. My own crude demographic inquiries suggest a sex ratio of about unity among the Tallensi. Polygynous marriage, therefore, inevitably means competition for wives, even though women are usually married by the age of 16 or 17, as near as one can guess, and men rarely succeed in finding a wife before the age of about 25. The natives maintain that the age of marriage for girls has been decreasing rapidly since the coming of the white man (cf. my paper, 'A Note on Fertility among the Tallensi of the Gold Coast', *Sociological Review*, xxv, 1943, 3-4).

or six abortive—or rather, to translate the native attitude into our own terms, experimental—marriages. Men of over 50 say, with a laugh, that they cannot remember all the women they have married who left them after a short time. Women are more discreet about their marital history; but observation leads to the conclusion that between 50 and 60 per cent. of all married women have had more than one husband.[1]

A marriage breaks up either through the action of one of the spouses, generally the woman, or through that of the wife's guardian. The Tallensi have no formal procedure for divorce. If a man wishes to get rid of a wife (which happens very seldom) he generally does so by withholding the bride-price, so that her guardian eventually recalls her, or he makes her life so uncomfortable that she deserts him. If a woman decides to leave a husband, she simply absconds. She may do so because she dislikes him, or because he does not feed her well enough, or neglects her sexually or otherwise, or, natives say, out of mere caprice. All women, according to the men, are fickle and gullible; a plausible suitor can seduce any woman. So if a young wife goes to visit her parents and stays longer than two or three days, her husband, be he an ardent young man or a sober greybeard, hurries off to fetch her, usually in considerable dudgeon, for fear that she may be abducted by another man.

Despite these initial pitfalls of marriage, families do get established and remain stable. Though the idea of marriage as a lifelong and irrevocable bond does not exist among the Tallensi, many couples do settle down for life, and many other couples remain united for a long enough stretch of years to produce one or more children.

Many complicated circumstances have an influence on this. Naturally, the jural formalities must be properly complied with. That is to say,

[1] Many of these experimental marriages are not marriages at all, according to the strict letter of custom, since they are sometimes dissolved before placation gifts have been made and often before any instalment of the bride-price has been paid. Some last only a few weeks. But they are always called marriages; for it is a fact that many marriages that begin in exactly this way do turn out to be stable in the end. Counting as 'wives' only those for whom bride-price was paid and who bore children to their husbands, I found, among a randomly chosen group of 20 men over 45, approximately, that only 2 had had 1 wife each; only 3 had had 2 wives each; the remaining 15 (= 75 per cent.) had all had more than 2 wives each. Altogether, these 20 men had had 71 wives (average 3·5 wives each); they had lost 21 (average 1 each) by death; and at the time of the census they had 45 wives (average 2·25 each). But most of them claimed to have 'married' from 10 to 20 times and were able to give a fairly complete history of these abortive 'marriages'.

Among a randomly chosen group of 20 women of child-bearing age—who were therefore not yet at the end of their matrimonial careers—6 (= 30 per cent.) had had only one husband each; 7 (= 35 per cent.) had had only 2 husbands each; the remaining 7 (= 35 per cent.) had had more than 2 husbands each, 4 of them having had more than 3 husbands each. Apart from the propensity to choose a final husband by trial and error, the custom of the levirate helps to increase the number of husbands a woman may have in her lifetime.

the bridegroom's guardian must send the placation gift (*lu sendaan*) to the bride's guardian, and must pay a proportion of the bride-price acceptable to the latter. A wife is usually espoused (*sol*) by paying the bride-price of four head of cattle or their equivalent in instalments over a number of years. If he does not fulfil these jural requirements, a man has no rights to and over his wife. On the other hand, women frequently desert husbands who have paid a part or, occasionally, even the whole bride-price. In such a case an honourable man may feel bound to compel his daughter to return to her husband, but if the girl refuses obstinately he may have to yield to her. Often, however, a father prefers his daughter to find another husband from whom he claims the bride-price that has to be refunded to the first husband. And it is not uncommon for men to instigate a daughter to leave her lawful husband for another man, or to take a daughter away from her husband and give her to another man as a means of raising what we should call ready cash or its equivalent—for instance, a cow to repay a pressing debt, or to buy grain for the household. Thus, observance of the jural proprieties gives a husband a weapon with which he can try to assert his rights to and over his wife. It does not give him an absolute guarantee of these rights nor does it ensure the stability of the marriage.

A girl's parents, and especially her father, can make or mar a marriage. Young people may wed without their fathers' consent, but they cannot remain legitimately married without it. If a man objects to a son-in-law he usually succeeds in exercising his right to take his daughter away, though cases are numerous in which the woman has persistently returned to the rejected husband, who has had to be accepted in the end. By contrast, if a father has himself chosen or likes his daughter's husband, he is a strong ally. He can force the girl, beating her if necessary, to stay with her husband, though here again fathers have been known to fail with obdurate daughters. Generally, however, the strength of paternal authority makes a father's command irresistible; for he might curse an intractable daughter, and this is greatly dreaded.

Again, a woman will not stay with a husband who does not pay at least a portion of the bride-price. It is an insult to her, placing her on the level of a casual lover and exposing her to the taunts of her co-wives of the lineage. Pukiehət's wife was taken from him five times because he could not pay anything towards her bride-price; every time she came back. At length her guardian brought a case against Pukiehət. The chief put it to her that Pukiehət was, in effect, treating both her and her guardian with contempt. Sadly she admitted this and agreed to leave him if he did not meet the debt at once. Pukiehət saw he was in danger of losing his wife. He was a poor man; but he set to work energetically and managed to raise the equivalent of two cows, which was enough to satisfy his father-in-law.

Even a fruitful marriage, the strongest of all bonds between husband

and wife, may suffer shipwreck. Many women leave a husband or are taken from him after bearing one child to him. Only after a woman has borne two or three living children to a man does this bond become a really effective force in maintaining the marriage.

The real foundation of a lasting marriage is not custom or jural or ritual sanctions, but a satisfactory relationship between the married pair; and this is a complex tissue woven of many strands, changing and strengthening with the years. It has elements that can be translated into terms of reciprocal rights, duties, and services. But it is essentially a moral and personal bond, a question of the mutual adjustment of roles and persons in pursuit of the interests married partners have in one another and in common, and the purposes they share. The sexual bond is of vital importance in this relationship.

The personality of a spouse is important. A lazy man who neglects to provide for his wife sufficiently, a harsh man who strikes her at the least provocation, a man who through sickness, impotence, or lack of consideration does not or will not give her sexual satisfaction, yet holds her jealously to her marital fidelity; any such man may find it hard to keep a wife. A lazy woman, a disobedient woman, a woman with a hasty temper or one who is a confirmed gadabout, is likely to have several husbands before she finally settles down. A barren woman, too, with her growing sense of frustration as the years pass, tends to become restless and to drift from husband to husband. Such a one is Gɛlima, Naabdiya's elderly sister, who has tried no fewer than eighteen husbands and has been compelled to seek a haven for her declining years in her brother's home. Barrenness is one of the reasons for which a man may decide to get rid of a wife, but often enough a barren wife who is a good worker and has a tractable disposition gains her husband's devotion and remains with him. Occasionally a wife proves to be a petty thief, who filches the supplies of other women of the household or stores put aside by the men. She will get short shrift, and will be sent back in disgrace, formally, by the head of her husband's *dug*; for such a person is bound to cause endless disturbance in the family. A woman accused of witchcraft by a co-wife may be dealt with similarly, it is said, but in the few cases I have heard of the husbands have not divorced the women. Lastly, no man will tolerate a wife who suffers from nocturnal enuresis, however attractive or proficient she may be. To urinate on the sleeping-mat during sleep is a grave mystical offence endangering the life of the husband; hence, a woman suffering from this complaint is formally sent back to her parents.

The Wife's Ties with Her Paternal Family and Lineage

These accidents of personality affect only a minority of marriages. The constant social factors that steer the course of every marriage are of greater significance to us, and must be examined more fully. When a woman marries she does not forfeit her status as a daughter of her natal lineage (pɔyayabəlǝg) or lose her personal ties with her parents and siblings. We have discussed this, in its broader aspects, in our previous volume[1] and confine ourselves here to family ties. Throughout her life she keeps in close touch with her parents and siblings and other members of her clan, especially her close agnates. If, as is common, other daughters of her clan have married into her husband's clan, these will be the classificatory co-wives with whom she has most contact and to whom she gives and from whom she receives most help, kindness, and support. She visits her natal settlement, as well as her sisters married elsewhere, regularly, and is often visited by members of her parental family. She not only has emotional bonds with her natal family that time never erases, but she also retains certain privileges, which have almost the force of rights, in it and in her natal clan, as we have shown in our previous volume. Her natal family and clan also have claims on her all her life. This is strongly marked in the first two or three years of marriage, before motherhood, habit, and an increasing share in its routine have knit her firmly into her conjugal family.

In the early years of marriage a woman seldom lets an opportunity of visiting her natal family go by. She calls in to see how they are on her way to or from market. Now and then she comes to stay a few days. If she is ill she will generally come to stay with her mother, who will tend her much more carefully than her co-wives or in-laws. When Tɔŋ-Yikpɛmdaan's daughter developed an asthmatic complaint she stayed with her parents for nearly a year. When Da'amo'o's wife went down with guinea-worm she took her three-months-old baby and went to her father's house until she was cured, though it is considered a risky thing to take so young an infant out of its father's house. At sowing or harvest time a man often sends for a young married daughter who has no child to come and help. At all times a married daughter is informed, and sometimes sent for, if there is serious sickness in her parental home. She must be sent for if a member of her parental family dies; and she will go even if it means leaving a tiny infant in the care of a co-wife for a day or two.

On this matter Tallensi are extremely sensitive, for death is the great test of all social ties among them. All relatives of the dead, and especially the principal mourners—parents, spouses, children, siblings—have defined ritual observances, ritual duties, and practical tasks in mortuary and funeral ceremonies. A death often comes as a shock to these close relatives, and especially the death of a parent or sibling to a married daughter of the family. Her mother-in-law or husband will break the news gently to her with a tactful periphrasis. But she must be told and sent for, else she—and, backing her up, her conjugal family—would be deeply offended. On her part, not to go when thus summoned would

[1] *Dynamics of Clanship*, ch. ix.

be a grievous sin against her parents and her ancestors, sure to bring misfortune on her and her children.

I was the unsuspecting witness of the strength of a woman's filial devotion, brought out by the crisis of death, at Sawɔŋba's burial ceremony. Sawɔŋba's daughter married a Tɛnzugu man against her father's wish. To add insult to injury, when Sawɔŋba sent messengers to demand a cow of the bride-price, his son-in-law turned them away with contempt. As the girl refused to leave her husband, Sawɔŋba cursed her, and, being a leper who knew he had not long to live, expressly forbade her to come to his funeral. She was not told of his death, but heard of it indirectly. On the day of the burial, during one of the major rites, there was a sudden commotion in the crowd around the gateway. A young woman dashed forward, making for the homestead. I could see the strained and agitated look on her face as she passed me. But at once one of Sawɔŋba's classificatory sons darted forward, seized her, and dragged her back to the tree where the elders sat. For a minute or two nothing but a wildly shouting mob could be seen under the tree. Then the girl struggled out, sobbing aloud, her body covered with bruises where she had been beaten by her enraged brothers and clansmen. Followed by execrations, she was escorted by one of the elders to where her husband and a party of his lineage kin were waiting. Only the fear of bloodshed, which would make the affair into that much-dreaded thing, a 'case for the white man (*nasaara yɛl*)', had restrained them from interfering. Sawɔŋba's sons and lineage kin did not see the pathos of their sister's action. They were thoroughly incensed, and called it an insult. Had her husband wished to behave properly, he would have sent an elder of his lineage to beg Sawɔŋba's pardon while he was still alive, or, at any rate, to beg the head of Sawɔŋba's medial lineage to intercede with his sons when he heard of Sawɔŋba's death.

These bonds of a woman with her parental family play an important part in Tale domestic economy. After the harvest there is always a great coming and going of daughters to and from their parental homes. And no man would let his daughter or sister depart, at this time, without a gift of a well-filled basket of grain. This is one way in which a woman builds up her own private resources out of which she provides little luxuries, utensils, and clothes for herself and by means of which she often tides the family over a lean period. This is a privilege, but it has almost the force of a right. Occasionally an elderly woman without a son, or, as sometimes happens nowadays, with her only son away for long in Ashanti or the Colony, is left without proper support in her husband's home. She can then go back to her father's home and is entitled to her sustenance as of right. The services a woman's husband renders to her father, now and then, in the early years of marriage, the interest she has in her brother's children, the importance attached to kinship ties with the mother's brother and his lineage, are all evidence of the imperishability of a woman's ties with her parental family.

Last but not least, a woman continues all her life to be under the care of her patrilineal ancestors. She must observe their totemic taboos. One of them is her spirit guardian (*sɛyər*), to whom her husband will have to send animals on her behalf as sacrifices on critical occasions such as her first confinement, and from whose tutelage she must be ritually released on death. Whenever an important sacrifice to these ancestors takes place in her paternal home she is told, and has the right to participate and to receive a definite share of the sacrificial meat. She has duties to these lineage ancestors too. Thus whenever a shrine of a lineage founder passes to a new lineage head, a daughter of the lineage is selected by divination to fetch it to its new home. Her good or ill fortune as wife and mother depends very much on that occult arbiter of life which the Tallensi conceive of as a personal Predestined Fate (*Nuor Yin*); and this is associated with one's patrilineal ancestors. If a woman's children die one after another she is being dogged by an evil Predestiny; and only her paternal kin can perform the ritual of exorcising it. Finally, when she dies, though she is buried by her husband's lineage according to their rites, and her spirit is aggregated to those of their ancestors, since it is her sons who will sacrifice to and worship her spirit, her paternal kin also perform a short and symbolic funeral ceremony for her. Thus she is 'brought home (*mar kul*)' to be received amongst her paternal ancestors, and the cycle of her life is completed.

The Opposition between the Kinship Ties and the Marital Ties of Spouses, and its Resolution

All her life a woman is subject to the pull of her patrilateral kinship ties. As a wife, however, she must submit more and more to the contrary pull of her marital ties. Her husband is even more strongly ruled by his ties with his natal family and patrilineal kin. Many of the chances and changes of marriage come down to the question of how the partners adjust themselves to the opposing loyalties and interests associated with their divergent kinship ties. A marriage reaches stability when the partners achieve common interests and mutual bonds strong enough to hold them together in the face of their respective patrilateral kinship ties. That is why the birth of children plays such a vital part in stabilizing a marriage.

Marriage, then, is in one aspect a unique relationship between one man and one woman; in this context, peculiarities of personality influence the fate of a particular marriage. In another aspect, or more accurately, perhaps, at the other end of the scale of marriage relations, it is a union between a man and a woman who represent and remain members of two mutually exclusive corporate groups. That is why the lineages of husband and wife are implicated in the marriage and have a lasting interest in its course and in the offspring that come from it. Tale speech and etiquette reveal this, and the classificatory extension of affinal kinship depends on this. Thus if your friend's son or daughter has recently married, you do not ask him 'Whom did he (she) marry?', but 'Where (i.e. which clan) did he (she) marry?', and 'A child of whose house (i.e. what segment of the clan) did he (she) marry?'. We shall take up this thread again at a later stage of our analysis. At present we are concerned with the consequences for the relations of husband and wife of their divergent lineage ties.

The tension due to these opposing sets of social ties appears most acutely in the early stages of marriage, obviously as a result of the fact that marriage is an alliance between two genealogically independent corporate units with rival interests in the protagonists. Every marriage in which the husband is a young man begins as a struggle, carried on with many wiles, stratagems, pretexts, and even threats of or recourse to force. Firstly, the suitor has to compete with other young men whom his would-be bride and in-laws often play off astutely against him. The largest part of his courtship consists in winning over the girl's parents with frequent presents and soft words. To elope with her he must buy the secret connivance of her mother or brother, for her father will always stand out for a negotiated marriage. This is not only an acknowledgement of the father's right to dispose of his daughter's hand, but a guarantee of the consent of the bridegroom's guardian and lineage elders and hence of the payment of the bride-price on demand. It is a defeat for the bridegroom, who has to bow to the will of his father-in-law.

The real struggle begins, however, only after a man succeeds in carrying off his bride by elopement. If the elders on both sides tacitly accept the match as a good one, it becomes a matter of mere formality; but all the conventions of the jural transactions necessary to make a legitimate marriage are couched in the idiom of a struggle between hostile groups. That is why they must take place through an intermediary, the *pɔyasama*, a clansman of the bridegroom and a cognatic kinsman of the bride, bound to hold an even balance between the two parties by reason of his kinship with both.[1] But often enough the struggle turns into a genuine and sometimes acrimonious battle for the girl which may go on for weeks or months. It is then that the lack of a constituted legal system in Tale political organization makes itself felt. The girl's father resorts to all sorts of devices to coerce her abductors. He may use ritual pretexts, exploit ties of cognatic kinship with the abductors' lineage or clan, even, in extremity, threaten to kill himself on their doorstep, or, in the old days, to stir up war against their clan. I have been present at several violent altercations between a party of men

[1] Cf. pp. 317–18 below.

come to demand a runaway daughter and her would-be husband's lineage elders. The young man will hide the girl with friends, or use other stratagems to keep her, backed up for the time being, and chiefly for form's sake, by his lineage elders. But later he may have a struggle with the head of his nuclear lineage if he is opposed to the marriage. It is not until the formal placation gift (*sɛndaan*) is sent to the girl's father with his consent and that of his lineage elders, that a truce comes, and not until the first instalment of the bride-price is paid that a promise of peace appears—which may not be for months, or even for a couple of years.

The placation gift and the bride-price provide an objective instrument by means of which the two lineage segments which are the parties to a marriage can balance their divergent interests in and opposing rights over the woman. It is the instrument that separates the woman from her natal family—or rather, it separates her role as wife from her role as daughter, her subordination to her husband from her subjection to her father, so that the conflict between these roles is kept in check.

That is the meaning of the rule I once heard summed up in the maxim: 'A woman must not be at her father's house when they (her husband's people) send the placation gifts. That is a taboo.' The young man who said this was protesting at the breach of this rule forced upon him by the unscrupulous action of one of the leading elders of his clan. The rule applies both to the placation gift and to the bride-price.

A newly wed wife, therefore, often finds herself torn between her desire to be with her husband and her loyalty and sense of duty to her parents, enhanced as this is by her respect for parental authority. Tallensi realize that she must be weaned from her attachment to her parents. Thus for the first month or two of marriage a young wife is not allowed to visit her parents, lest, as the natives say, her longing for her mother should get the better of her and she should refuse to return to her husband. Even after some years of marriage men object to young wives paying prolonged visits to their parents without good cause, as we have seen. I have often been amused at the mood of bristling suspicion which comes over a man left a grass-widower for a week or two, though he has probably consented to his wife's going on a visit and may have other wives at home. It must be admitted, however, that wives run off with other men often enough after such visits to give grounds for the taunt of innate frivolity and fickleness that men throw up against the whole of the opposite sex. A woman in her father's house assumes, for the time being, the social personality of a daughter; and it is as if she is prone, then, to doff her wifehood and with it her sense of duty to her husband. Tallensi say that, if a man falls out with his father-in-law, his wife will take her husband's part when she is with him, but will side with her father at her parental home. Only after several years of marriage, with children pledging her to marital fidelity and an established relationship binding her to her husband, is she most likely to solve the conflict between these antithetic bonds in favour of her conjugal family.

Tallensi say that a woman is like a stranger or guest (both ideas are contained in the native word *saan*) in her husband's house during the first year or two of marriage. Standing outside the intimate life and vital concerns of the family, she cannot yet be relied upon. Gradually she grows accustomed (*maləm*) to her conjugal family; and after some years, when she has several children, she becomes so far absorbed into the family that full trust can be reposed in her and she takes a full and self-confident part in family affairs.

It needs little observation to see how apt is this description of the gradual absorption of women into their husbands' families. On a visit to a homestead to which a newly wedded wife has just been added, one can easily observe the 'shyness (*valəm*)', as the Tallensi call it, of the new wife (*pɔya*) and her husband (*sɛt*) towards each other. This goes farther than formal etiquette. Good manners require that a woman should always show respect to her husband in public. She walks behind him if they have to go anywhere together on a ceremonial occasion. She stoops or kneels whenever she offers him food or drink. But this behaviour is customary for a woman with all adult males other than her own children. It is a sign of the general attitude of respect due from women to men in a society so dominated in public social relations by the patriarchal principle. The 'shyness' of a newly married wife comes out in other ways. She tries to keep out of her husband's way as much as possible during the day, busying herself zealously with the household tasks given to her by her mother-in-law. She is submissive to all his requests. She speaks to him only when she is spoken to. She takes no initiative in anything.

This attitude is even more marked in her behaviour towards her parents-in-law (*daŋaam*, pl. *daŋaanam*), to whom she is bound to show formal deference at all times, and to her adult brothers-in-law, with whom she must always be circumspect because of the incest barrier which we shall discuss later. It often comes into her private relations with her husband if he is much older than she is. She will flirt and be more companionable with a young husband, in private, natives say; for he is probably like herself a *tarəm*, junior, under authority, and connubial joys mean so much to him that he comes down to an equal footing with his wife for their sake.

The Relationships of a Wife with her Relatives-in-law

A woman does not avoid any of her relatives-in-law or her husband, nor are her relations with them regulated by strict prescription. She maintains a general attitude of deference, modesty, and complaisance towards them. A well-behaved young wife is industrious and obedient in helping her mother-in-law with her domestic work, and she will be self-effacing and deferential towards her father-in-law, her husband,

and his adult brothers. The only relaxation of this attitude occurs with her sisters-in-law (*pɔyakie*, pl. *pɔyakies*). With them, often her equals in years and her companions in work, she can laugh and play and joke. Like herself, they are already, or are fated to be, married out of their natal families to 'strangers'. This is a bond of fellowship superadded to that of sex and often age. But they also belong to the opposite camp. Identifying themselves with their brothers and their lineage, they sometimes speak of her as 'our wife (*ti pɔya*)', and she sometimes refers to them as 'my husbands (*n-sɛrib*)'. They will take the side of their brother if she comes into conflict with her husband or deserts him. Her relationship with them is typical of the ambivalence that underlies the joking relationship among the Tallensi.

In the first year or so of marriage a woman tries to avoid having to address her male in-laws and her husband directly in public. If they address her it will be in a somewhat formal and courteous way, her husband and his brothers using her clan name, her father-in-law addressing her as 'mother (*ma*)'. She is most at home—but in a very deferential manner—with her mother-in-law, in whose rooms and under whose care she lives, whose domestic duties she largely takes over, and who also addresses her as 'mother (*ma*)'. To any member of the family she speaks of her father-in-law as 'father (*ba*)' and of her mother-in-law as 'mother (*ma*)', and she addresses the latter by this term. Outside the family a woman speaks of her husband as 'my husband (*n-sɛt*)'; of his brothers as 'my older' or 'my younger husband (*n-sɛt-bier*, or *n-sɛt-pit*)'; and of his parents as 'my father (mother)-in-law (*n-daŋaamdoog*, masc.— *n daŋaampɔk*, fem.)'. Her husband speaks of her as 'my wife (*mpɔya*)'; his brothers as 'my older or younger brother's wife (*m-bier* or *m-pit pɔya*)', or in some situations as 'our (i.e. the lineage's) wife'; her parents-in-law as *sampɔya*.

The status of a woman in her conjugal family is most sharply focused in her relations with her parents-in-law. For it is they who form the axis around which the family revolves. Its unity, its independence, the management of its material affairs, and the maintenance of its well-being all reside in them. Though the general impression one receives of a woman's relationship with her parents-in-law is one of affability and ease, it is potentially anomalous, particularly in the early years. As their son's wife she is in the position of a daughter to them. She will give valuable and indispensable service in the economy of the household. She will produce children to augment the family and the lineage. But, as she herself knows and feels, she is an intruder. She is made to feel this in the early years of marriage even if, as so often happens, she belongs to an adjacent clan, and was personally well known to her conjugal family before marriage. For marriage creates entirely new associations between individuals and families. If she was married by elopement she knows that she is on trial, perhaps the object of a hidden struggle between her husband and her father-in-law. Though she is in the position of a daughter to her parents-in-law, she cannot feel for them nor they for her the love and devotion that moderate the strictness of parental authority and give a tone of easy-going friendliness to the normal intercourse of parents and children. One side of the parent-child relationship, the authority of parents over their children, looms foremost for her. The cleavage between successive generations and the tension that holds them apart, are underlined at the expense of the mutual devotion and identification of parents and children.

Parents-in-law, for their part, have ambivalent feelings towards their daughter-in-law. Behind their ostensible pride and pleasure in their son's marriage lurks the shadow of resentment. A man realizes that his son's marriage is the first step in his eventual emancipation. It is the seed from which grow responsibilities and interests that compete with those he owes to his natal family and threaten his loyalties to them. A woman sees in her son's marriage a sign that her reproductive life is over. Tallensi hold that it is improper, and to some extent mystically dangerous, for mother-in-law and daughter-in-law to bear at the same time. Hence parents often, though covertly, try to prevent a first son marrying young, or else, in self-defence, display exaggerated conceit at a son's early marriage. Only the coming of grandchildren, coinciding as it does with the habituation of the daughter-in-law to her conjugal family, and itself a distinction inspiring great pride and joy in the grandparents, compensates for the renunciations implicitly required of a man's parents when he takes a wife.

Inevitably, therefore, there is an element of tension in the relations of parents-in-law and daughter-in-law. The fact that the daughter-in-law is under the power of her husband's family, particularly of her father-in-law, and that they are formally, if not openly, opposed to her paternal family, to which, however, she is still attached by the strongest ties of duty and sentiment, may add to the strain. It may be quite superficial in a well-regulated family or in the case of an approved marriage, apparent only in the conventions of speech and etiquette. In an ill-managed family, or if there is opposition to the marriage, it often comes out openly. Parents-in-law complain of their daughter-in-law's manners or actions, or mother-in-law and daughter-in-law have petty squabbles. As time passes the strain is mitigated with the gradual absorption of the daughter-in-law into her conjugal family. It is never wholly erased. Even in so well organized a family as Ɔmara's, there was a standing feud between his younger wives and his mother. The old woman, half-sunk in the hebetude of senility, complained ceaselessly of the neglect of her daughters-in-law; and they often quarrelled with her vehemently on account of what they regarded as her exorbitant demands on their firewood, their labour, and their food-supply.

The conventions of behaviour followed by parents-in-law and daughter-in-law towards one another, and the terminology of address associated with them, put a protective fence between parents-in-law and daughter-in-law. 'My mother', or 'my father', in this context means 'a person to whom I owe punctilious respect'. The relation is one of reciprocal respect, because it is based on something in the nature of a contract. The daughter-in-law's attitude is an exaggeration of one aspect of filial respect towards the parents. This aspect is more prominent in kinship relations outside the focal field and in ceremonial relations patterned on, but structurally different from, true parent-child relations, than in the latter. It is reminiscent of the behaviour of his clansmen to a chief or tendaana on formal occasions, when his symbolic position as father (*ba*) of the clan is most apparent.

Naturally the barrier between father-in-law and daughter-in-law is stricter than between mother-in-law and daughter-in-law owing to the difference of sex, though it is not obvious to an outsider. Once she is accepted, a man usually treats his daughter-in-law with kindness and affability. In public he treats her with a familiar friendliness, in the same way as if she were his daughter. But whereas he scolds his daughter without hesitation, he does not scold or criticize his daughter-in-law directly. It would offend and hurt her, and upset their amicable relations. The barrier between them—and this applies in a lesser degree to the mother-in-law too—can be maintained only on the basis of mutual courtesy and affability. Where the barrier is most sharply emphasized is not in their public intercourse but in their relations as members of opposite sexes. For a man to have sexual relations with, or even sit on the same mat as, his daughter-in-law is a sin of the first magnitude. '*Dɛn n-kih pam!* (that is an extreme taboo)', say the natives, with every sign of repugnance. It is a sin that can never be wholly atoned for. Sooner or later the culprits will be slain by the ancestor spirits; for, like incest with a father's wife of which it is the counterpart, it destroys irreparably the moral and religious bonds of father and son. I heard of an old man who died some years ago who used to have his daughters-in-law sit on his lap, and 'play' with them. This, my informants said scoffingly, was just the ill manners of an old dotard. But Gunyaam's seduction of his daughter-in-law was revealed to me with bated breath. It was no wonder, my informant said, that he died soon after, and that misfortunes crowded on his family.

The relations of daughter-in-law to parents-in-law are well summed up in the statement always made by Tallensi if they are asked for an explanation of the terminology of address used between these relatives. They say: 'We stand in awe of them (parents-in-law or daughters-in-law)', (*ti zootbame*, lit. 'we fear them').[1]

---

[1] This terminology of address is of considerable theoretical interest. Rattray (op. cit., p. 6) attributes the custom of addressing a daughter-in-law as 'mother' (customary also amongst the Gɔrisi, Namnam, and other peoples adjacent to

The Relationship of Husband and Wife

The closest bonds a woman has with any member of the family into which she marries are her bonds with her husband. Habit, economic co-operation, and the jural authority of husband over wife bring them closer and closer together as the years pass. But these mutual interests are insufficient by themselves. The true cement of their union is the birth of children. Children give the union its *raison d'être*. They become the focus of the common interests, common pride, and common devotion of the partners, without which their economic co-operation or the other satisfactions they get from marriage would be meaningless. As we have already seen, one thing Tallensi never tire of stressing is that the object of marriage is to have children. When she has borne two or three living children to him a woman will be most unwilling to leave her husband, however hard her life with him may be.

The arrival of children not only forges closer the emotional bonds of husband and wife, but it also unites them socially in a firmer compact.

the Tallensi) to the 'horror of a father having intercourse with a son's wife'. He does not take into account the fact that mother-in-law and daughter-in-law also address each other reciprocally as 'mother'. As is mentioned above, the Tallensi themselves have no complete explanation for this usage, and this applies to the neighbouring 'tribes'. Many informants amplified the conventional formula 'We fear them' by pointing out that it was a degree of respect similar to that due to a mother. As we shall see later, the respect due to one's mother is almost a sacrosanct norm. The natives do not explicitly associate the mode of address with the horror of incest between father-in-law and daughter-in-law, but they do stress the latter in discussing the relationship of father-in-law and daughter-in-law. We shall see later that incest with a daughter-in-law is coupled with incest with one's mother as among the most serious kinship sins conceivable to the Tallensi. Rattray's inference, therefore, probably isolates one element in the usage, but it is a suppressed element. The incest barrier is a factor of importance in the relations of father-in-law and daughter-in-law in very many patrilineal African societies. Logically, however, it would seem to be more in keeping with the relationship of parent-in-law and daughter-in-law for the former to address the latter as his or her daughter, as is customary in a number of African societies. Here, however, a combination of circumstances arising out of the lineage principle comes into the picture. A daughter-in-law is not under her parents-in-law's authority and control in the same sense as their daughter is. She is not a substitute daughter, but their son's wife and a potential mother of their grandchildren of the same lineage. She is a stranger in theory, standing outside the scheme of lineage loyalties and sanctions, yet at the same time the one person on whom the whole future of the lineage depends. Again no Tallensi ever suggested that a daughter-in-law is called 'mother' by her parents-in-law because she is a future mother of lineage members. It is rather her ambiguous position as a stranger tied to the lineage that is uppermost in their thought. Her being addressed as 'mother' by her parents-in-law may be a means of stressing this and of over-emphasizing the respect due to her from them, the usage being a metaphoric derivation from the mode of address used to one's mother and, by extension, in an honorific sense to old women in general. In short, this usage aptly symbolizes the tensions in the relations of parents-in-law and daughter-in-law, in respect to which the latter is almost on an equal footing with the former.

In the joint family it marks them off as a separate and potentially independent family segment. A mother of two children usually has her own quarters, or her own part of her mother-in-law's *dug*, if her husband's mother is one of several wives of her father-in-law. She is a *dugdaana*, mistress of her rooms, in a small way, with some freedom of action where its affairs are concerned. She begins to regard the work that falls to her share, not merely as her contribution to the economy of the household, but more as serving the needs of her children and husband. He, for his part, begins to think of the future in terms of his wife and children. He may still accept a position of dependence on his father or older brother as a matter of course; but the separate needs of his wife and children are recognized in the allocation of food-supplies. He makes an effort to extend his private farm plot in order to grow a little food to tide his own family segment over lean periods. It may be many years before he achieves independence, but his aspirations towards it have a definite channel and a clear objective.

The greater intimacy of husband and wife, after several years of marriage, is shown in their greater familiarity with each other in public. The woman does not hesitate to address her husband by his name or title, and he may use a nickname for her. By the time a woman has grown old with her husband she is on terms of comradeship and equality with him, for she now identifies herself completely with his interests. An old couple often show great devotion to and affection for each other. The man often has such confidence in his wife that he will discuss all his affairs with her, and she can exercise considerable influence on his decisions in family matters, though the last word still rests with him. Though she still shows deference to him in public, she no longer keeps in the background. She speaks her mind freely to him and before him. Often when I have talked to men about domestic organization, kinship, marriage, children, or even their private religious and magical shrines, their wives of senior standing have stopped to join in the conversation. I have seen a lineage head's senior wife listen to a group of lineage elders thresh out a domestic squabble and give her opinion without restraint. A suitor always tries to gain the favour of a girl's mother; for, though she lacks authority to give him the girl, she can sometimes be persuaded to connive at an elopement, or at least to say a good word for him with her husband, and this may sway the balance in his favour.

Nevertheless, it is a basic assumption of the Tallensi that a wife never ceases entirely to be a 'stranger' in her husband's clan. For she never, as we have learnt, loses the social identity conferred on her by birth as a member of a different clan. She does not adopt her husband's totemic taboos; and though her health and fertility, being essential for the satisfactory performance of her wifely role, come under the guardianship of his ancestors, she does not participate in the cult of his lineage ancestors. When she attends the sacrifices made to domestic shrines by the joint family head, she does so as a privileged spectator. She has this privilege because her welfare is bound up with that of her husband and children, and theirs with hers. She remains outside the religious and moral solidarity of her husband's clan and maximal lineage, and, indeed, has only a contingent interest in the solidarity of his minimal lineage. It is noteworthy that women, both daughters and wives, are excluded from the esoteric ritual activities in which the moral sanctions of the unity and continuity of lineage and clan are embodied. In religious, jural, and political matters—all of which are closely interconnected—Tale women have the status of minors. This exclusion is most stringent in the case of the Earth cult and the cult of the lineage *bɔyar*. But the segregation is not so rigid as to keep women in entire ignorance of or wholly disinterested in these male monopolies. Their welfare depends upon the propitious outcome of these activities as much as that of their menfolk. They see, hear, and discuss among themselves and with their menfolk ritual affairs and jural actions that concern their husbands' lineages of which, indeed, wives and children often form the main subject. They grind the flour, brew the beer, and witness the preparations for esoteric religious rites. They see the public and semi-public phases of big religious ceremonies and overhear the endless consultations and discussions between the men which these ceremonies always produce.

A wife, therefore, can be in sympathy with the interests and can respect the values that rule the actions of her husband and her sons as members of their agnatic descent group, while being herself excluded from an effective public role in relation to them. But a cleavage remains. Thus in a conflict between her husband's clan and her father's clan she might very well take the side of the latter, not openly, it is true, but covertly. How strongly the natives feel this was shown at the divination ceremony following the death of Siiyɛlib of Tɔŋ-Seug. This divination was so cryptic and involved that I could make no sense of it. Fortunately I was able to get an explanation from one of my most trustworthy informants, a close agnate of the dead man. Siiyɛlib's death, it appeared, was a mystical retribution for a grave sin he had committed many years before. He had been one of the instigators of the white man's attack on the Hill Talis, and was an accessory, therefore, to the slaughter of many men. Now there were several Talis present at the funeral—kinsmen, affines, and, last but not least, wives of the dead man and his close agnates. If Siiyɛlib's sin were publicly brought out in the divination it would stir up all their hostile feelings. They would feel resentful towards Siiyɛlib's surviving agnates on account of his complicity in the destruction of their fathers and grandfathers. And this would produce strife between the men of Seug and their Talis wives, their Talis cognates, and their Talis affines.

The social and psychological cleavage which underlies all the relations of husband and wife is the structural kernel around which the basic dichotomy of *dug* and *yir* crystallizes. The comradeship which grows up gradually between husband and wife with the lapse of time is the obverse, paradoxical as it may seem, of a process of gradual emancipation of the wife. As her children grow up, the centre of gravity of her life shifts more and more to them and away from her husband. If she has a grown-up son, her interests and emotions become centred more and more on him and his family by marriage. They constitute her *dug*, in which she is secure, honoured, and titularly, if not effectively, supreme. It is her son and grandson who will honour her spirit and commemorate her in worship after her death. Her son has become the effective breadwinner, and she looks to him for sustenance. If a young woman loses her husband, her grief is aggravated because she realizes that she has lost the head and pivot of her young family and must face uprooting and readjustment to a new partner. An old woman mourns the death of her husband greatly, too, but her grief is mitigated, if she has a son, by her feeling of security and of fulfilment. The death of an adult son, especially an only son, is an irreparable tragedy to her.

Thus it happens that a woman who has been twice married often lives, in her old age, with the oldest son of her first marriage, rather than with her husband. This was the case with Tiezien's old wife, Naaho; and the reason Tiezien and Naaho's son, Nyaaŋzum, gave for this brings out a point of the first importance. Laughing, they said, 'She is no use any longer as a wife, she can't cook; and she has no vulva now (*u le ka pɛn yaha*)—that is, her reproductive powers are finished. And they laid special stress on the last point.

A woman attains her fullest freedom in the family when she ceases to have sexual value, that is, from the native point of view, when she ceases to be reproductive.

The Sexual Relationship in Marriage

The sexual relationship is the corner-stone of Tale marriage. At first sight this is puzzling to the observer, for the Tallensi have a thoroughly matter-of-fact attitude about sex. They regard sex as a normal and natural appetite. Any aspect of the generative functions can be discussed without circumlocution in the presence of men, women, or children. A young woman, or a girl, may show signs of shyness or coyness, but no one ever shows any real embarrassment. Bawdy or salacious talk about sex is common amongst men; very rarely does it verge on the obscene. The Tallensi take it for granted that children will indulge in sexual play, and attach no value to prenuptial chastity. In the ritual of the Arrow Medicine (*Peentee*) for protection in war, the services of a virgin boy and virgin girl are required. These children are bound to the medicine by a taboo of chastity in early childhood; but they are released as soon as they approach puberty; for by that time, the natives say, they cannot be expected to resist sexual temptation. Tallensi say that prenuptial love affairs between adolescents have diminished since the coming of the white man, owing to increasing scarcity of marriageable girls and the consequent decline in the age of marriage for them. Premarital motherhood, on the other hand, they regard with a certain amount of scorn. It suggests a weakness of character, but it is not so disgraceful as to spoil the girl's chances of marriage.

The norms of kinship and marriage indirectly lead to prenuptial love affairs and adultery occurring mostly between distantly related members of the same clan. Such amours, whether casual or lasting, are not considered to be incestuous. That the parties are members of the same clan does not arouse public disapprobation, nor does it bring down ritual penalties on their heads or set jural sanctions in motion against them. This makes it seem the more inappropriate to pick out the sexual tie as the corner-stone of marriage. For, as we have previously indicated, the social relations of affinity arising out of marriage are always sharply contrasted with those of kinship; and if sex relations are the essential thing in marriage they must surely be incompatible with kinship. The paradox is resolved if we take into account certain principles of kinship that will be elucidated later. It is of interest here as evidence of the distinction, characteristic of Tale ideas about sex, which the natives draw clearly between sexual relations as a mode of sensual gratification and sexual intercourse in marriage.

Tallensi often cite the maxim 'Copulation and marriage are not the same thing (*Pɛn nyɛbɔg ni pɔyadir, ba. ka bu kɔ'la*)'. But they also say, 'We marry for the sake of copulation'; always adding, however, 'and for the sake of children'. The sexual motive, in short, is considered to be fundamental to marriage, both for men and for women; but it is fundamental as the means to the supreme end of marriage, the procreation of children.

The Economic and Property Relations of Spouses

The significance of sex in marriage will be clearer if we consider first the economic and property relations of husband and wife. By marriage a woman is transferred from her father's authority to that of her husband, and, consequently, to that of anyone under whose authority he comes. Explaining this, Tallensi say, 'A man owns (*so*) his wife. Has he not bought (*da*) her?' This does not mean that a wife is regarded as a chattel. In fact no man would dare to say in his wife's presence that he bought her, except in jest, in an outburst of violent anger, or deliberately to insult her. The concept 'own' here means that a man has authority over and is responsible for his wife. He 'owns' her working power, in the first place. She must perform the indispensable domestic tasks connected with the preparation of food for the household, the provision of water-supplies, the care of the home and of the children, and so forth. She must help him with the sowing and the harvesting of his crops, which cannot be done without the assistance of women. He can command other services from her. For instance, nowadays he can send her to buy grain for him in distant markets and sell it for him in the home market; and he can ask for many little services that make life more comfortable for him. A man has a right to these services; but it is a right limited by the principle of reciprocity.[1] In return a man is bound to protect and care for his wife, in particular to provide her with a home, with food, and with curative treatment if she is ill.

There is an obvious material basis for the economic reciprocity of husband and wife. Primarily it is a function of the system of economic co-operation, by means of which the household satisfies its material wants. The head of the family owns the land and the livestock from which all draw their sustenance. The men do the heavy work of farming and care for the livestock. The women perform the tasks already mentioned. Within this subsistence unit the rule of reciprocity of economic rights and duties governs the economic relations of parent and child, of brother and brother, as well as those of husband and wife. For it is an application of the wider principle that all those who pool their labour in the common task of providing food and shelter for the household are entitled, severally, to a just share in the product of their common labour.

The authority of husband over wife in the matter of economic duties and services is tempered, also, by a principle that really follows as a logical corollary upon the principle just stated. The products of individual industry and enterprise belong to the individual, subject to the nominal over-right of anyone who has authority over him or her, in particular, of the head of the family. The rule applies to all property relations between the members of the family. Thus, as soon as a wife acquires a *dug* of her own she begins to have a certain degree of economic autonomy, and this increases with the passage of time, as her children become more and more able to do without her regular care. She has her own vegetable plot allocated to her by her husband. She often has a ground-nut plot of her own, which she cultivates herself. She has her small private store of grain, obtained by gift from her father or brothers or other kinsmen. Her vegetables, her ground-nuts, and her grain do not go into the pool of family resources. They do, however, serve to supplement these resources; for it is a woman's duty to provide the vegetable food, and it would be unthinkable for her not to use other supplies she may possess to feed her children and her husband in time of scarcity. But if her private supplies are not required for this purpose she can dispose of them as she pleases. She can exchange them for money or goods, or use them to give hospitality to her own kin or guests. The same rule holds for such things as shea fruit and shea butter, which it is a woman's duty to provide for the household. Thus, it is common for women to barter surplus shea nuts for household utensils, and these

[1] Cf. p. 213 below.

THE STRUCTURE OF THE FAMILY

are entirely their own property. A woman owns the sleeping-mats she makes. A potteress is in the same position as a blacksmith or leather-worker. She keeps the money or natural products for which she exchanges her pots. Nowadays many women who live near a market carry on a regular or intermittent petty trade in cooked food. Sometimes, borrowing the small capital (two or three shillings is sufficient) with which to start, they keep the profits of their trade. It is not uncommon for women to own livestock, mainly poultry but often sheep and goats, and occasionally a cow. They may be obtained by gift or purchase, in the case of small stock, or by exchanging the natural increase of small stock for more valuable stock. A woman's sheep, goat, or cow will be herded with the family livestock, but her 'ownership' (*solǝm*, from *so*, to own) remains secure.

A woman's clothing, and her household utensils, most of which she provides for herself, belong to her solely. They are distributed, on her death, to her daughters, daughters-in-law, and sisters. Any money or livestock she may possess passes to her sons on her death, these being what might be called consumers' capital goods, the appropriate owners of which are men. They remain, therefore, in her *dug*, and do not accrete to the patrimonial property of her husband's effective minimal lineage. But it is an accepted principle that her husband has an over-right to them in her lifetime. For, as the natives put it, 'How can a man own his wife and not own the products of her labour?'

There is a quibble in this statement, the concept 'own' being used first in the sense of 'to have authority over', and secondly to mean 'having full rights of disposal over'—rights *in personam* being equated with rights *in rem*, to speak in lawyer's language.[1] And the Tallensi are not blind to this. Theoretically a man is entitled to utilize his wife's property as he wishes. In practice, he would not dare to do so without her consent, and the transaction is looked upon as a loan (*samǝr*). True, like all loans within the domestic family, it is not subject to book-keeping. But just as the woman feels morally bound to put her possessions at her husband's disposal if he is in difficulties, so her husband feels in honour bound to repay her in time, and generously, if he has any self-respect. Similarly, if a woman contracts a debt without her husband's knowledge and explicit permission he cannot be held liable. But no 'man of sense' would publicly repudiate his wife's debt. He reserves his reproaches for the privacy of the home. Significantly, a man does not, as a rule, settle his wife's debt. He will try to temporize with the creditor—an art in which the Tallensi are past masters—until his wife succeeds in finding the wherewithal to satisfy him. Or, if the husband cannot avoid paying the debt, he considers this as an advance

---

[1] Cf. Radcliffe-Brown, A. R., 'Patrilineal and Matrilineal Succession', *Iowa Law Review*, xx. 2, Jan. 1935, for an illuminating discussion of the anthropological relevance of these legal concepts.

which, it is tacitly understood, his wife will one day make good. Often such debts between spouses are straightened out by mutual borrowings, tacitly understood to cancel one another. Very often, however, a man has to cajole his wife with definite promises to repay before she will lend him her property. But the natives are emphatic about one point: that all such transactions belong to the give and take of marital co-operation and solidarity. It is one of the ways in which a woman stands by her husband and a man by his wife.

The Husband's Authority over his Wife

As might well be expected, these rights and duties of spouse to spouse do not rest on anything in the nature of a formal compact. There is no jural machinery or sanction by means of which a husband or wife can be compelled to perform his or her duties to his or her partner. A man can, and sometimes does, chastise his wife for incorrigible laziness, disobedience, or a misdemeanour detrimental to the unity of the family. He does it usually in a fit of anger or exasperation, as one would strike a child, and not as a deliberate punishment. For though Tallensi think that such disciplinary measures are right and necessary sometimes (women being kittle cattle, who will not always listen to reason), they consider them to be a regrettable and undignified necessity not entirely in keeping with the relationship of marriage, and at bottom repugnant to a self-respecting man. That is why when a quarrel between husband and wife ends in blows, neighbours hearing the commotion rush in to separate the pair and calm the enraged husband. 'I often scold my wives', said a Tale friend to me, after a heated argument with one of them, 'but I have never, as I sit here, lifted a hand to them. How could I thrash my wife, seeing that she gave up her father and her mother to come and marry me?' To beat a wife, in short, shows a poor appreciation of her.

Women admit the right of a man to strike his wife, and they see it as a feature of the authority over her conferred on him by marriage. But in fact, cases of wife-beating are far from common. Judging by the cases I have heard of, they are least likely to occur at the two extremes of the marriage cycle. A young man fears that he may lose his wife if he beats her; an older man, as the statement quoted above shows, with a wife of long standing, feels that it is incompatible with their mutual trust and comradeship.

A woman will not, as a rule, bear a grudge for blows struck under provocation. But if she is excessively, or, in her opinion, unjustifiably thrashed, she will run away from her husband. She may go off with another man; or she may return to her father or brother, who, if he is a self-respecting man, will take her part and refuse to give her up until her husband apologizes and promises better behaviour in future. In any case, it is a troublesome affair for the husband. It is worth noting, also, that in her conjugal family only a woman's husband has the right to strike her. Her parents-in-law, for instance, despite their authority over her, would not do so. If anything, they would try to restrain their son from beating her. Only her husband has that combination of authority and intimacy in relation to her which permits the use of physical force upon her.

But flight is not the only weapon a woman has in order to maintain her rights and privileges in her conjugal family. Once she is fairly free from the leading strings of her mother-in-law, she is the mistress of her time and energies. It is an accepted axiom of married life, which no man questions, that a wife is free to dispose of her time as she pleases, provided she does not hamper the essential economic activities of the household, or neglect her children, or remain away from home for unwarrantable periods or at times—e.g. during the Great Festivals—when all the members of the family should be together. The routine of domestic tasks, over which men have no control, is a strong line of defence against the interference of men in their wives' disposal of their time. But differences of opinion on this matter are a common cause of squabbles between husband and wife. A young woman dresses up to go to market; her husband objects, saying that other men will be paying court to her there, or that the children will be left hungry all day; she insists; and a heated argument ensues. Nine times out of ten the woman has her way. Occasionally the husband succeeds in stopping her, by persuasion or by force. It is only at sowing or harvest time, or when, for instance, preparations for an important ceremony are in hand, that a man has full control over his wife's time.

At all times a wife's freedom to arrange her work and her leisure as best suits her may subject her husband to inconvenience. If, at the end of the day, she is too preoccupied or too tired to cook, he can but grumble and go hungry. And if he annoys her she can make a point of being too busy to attend to some want of his or too tired to cook the evening meal. This, men say frankly, is one of the strongest arguments in favour of keeping on good terms with one's wife.

Tallensi regard these utilitarian rights and duties, services and attentions of husband and wife towards each other as a most important feature of marriage. But it is clear that they do not constitute the unique relationship that distinguishes the marriage tie from other social ties of the Tallensi. Thus a woman performs much the same utilitarian services as daughter in her natal home, and as mother, wife, and daughter-in-law in her conjugal home. They are but a part of the whole configuration of co-operation, mutual help, reciprocal services, etiquette, and mutual tolerance that keep the wheels of family life running smoothly. And it is clear, also, that they imply the existence of common interests that create a sense of mutual moral obligation.

This underlying bond of mutual moral obligation is the basic sanction of reciprocity and co-operation in the domestic family. In the case of husband and wife, the man is more his wife's physical and spiritual protector than her lord and master. Baŋ of Zubiuŋ-Yakɔra and Nindɔyat of Zubiuŋ-Kpaɣarayaɣar had a complicated dispute over an ancient cattle debt. It culminated in blows when Nindɔyat tried to lay hands on Baŋ's wife. That, declared Baŋ, he would not stand for.

A man is responsible for ensuring the beneficence of the ancestor spirits and other mystical powers towards his wife; and that he does this out of a sense of moral duty is evident when his wife gets ill. I well remember two particularly pathetic cases. Baripɛta, a handsome, industrious, intelligent, and popular young man, had one young wife. Shortly after the birth of their child, she was stricken with leprosy. The Tallensi are generally prepared to admit that this disease is incurable by their magico-medical methods. They say that it is contagious to the sufferer's young children. The bodily corruption of the disease disgusts them, and they say that lepers are difficult to live with as they become bitter and vindictive. Baripɛta knew all this as well as anybody else. His wife had become an economic and social burden instead of a helpmate. Yet he continued to cherish her, and, poor though he was, to try treatment after treatment for her, at the cost of many fowls and goats and pence. It is true that a jural principle was involved. As she had contracted the disease in his home under his care, he was responsible for her. He could not return her to her father, for instance. But it was plain from his behaviour and talk that he continued to care for her, with even greater consideration than usual, not out of submission to a customary jural rule but out of a feeling of immediate duty towards and concern for her.

It was the same with Ɔmara. His senior wife fell a victim to leprosy when her eldest children had already reached adulthood. He went to great expense in trying to get her cured. Explaining this to me, he said that, firstly, a sick person's nearest relatives never give up hope of a cure, and secondly, he was her husband, therefore he must try his utmost to save her. If he gave up she would be mortally hurt and might pine away. It was his duty to her and to her children.

The Sexual Relationship as the Corner-stone of Marriage

The moral bond of husband and wife is founded on their sexual relationship, conceived as the means to the end of reproduction. It is this that makes the sexual relationship the corner-stone of marriage.

The simplest proof of the significance of the sexual relationship is the fact that a marriage is not properly consummated until coitus takes place between the partners. This is seen most clearly when a widow remarries. She may be given in marriage to one of her deceased husband's brothers by the head of his effective minimal lineage, or she may be claimed by her deceased husband's brother, and may acquiesce, to begin with. If she has sexual relations with her new husband she becomes his wife, whether or not the formalities of remarriage are completed. If she succeeds in avoiding intercourse with him she is not his wife, and may sleep with any other man without fear of being accused of adultery. Cases of this kind are common. A particularly instructive case was that of a wife whom Pal-Zɔŋ inherited from his dead brother. As she was pregnant at the time, he did not attempt to sleep with her. She miscarried, but continued to put him off with excuses. The reason for this soon became apparent. An agnatic cousin ('brother' in native terminology) of Zɔŋ's was living with him, who, being half blind, spent most of the day at home. This gave him the opportunity of ingratiating himself with the woman, and he became her lover. Though Zɔŋ was indignant at the humiliation put upon him, and obviously burning with jealousy, he could do nothing about the affair. For it was not incest, as Zɔŋ's marriage with the woman had never been consummated.

It follows from this rule that a woman cannot refuse to cohabit with her husband. It sometimes happens that a girl is given in marriage by her father to a man whom she does not like, and that she takes up this line of resistance. The husband then has the right to thrash her or to use other forms of force in order to make her yield. The story of how Baŋɛlib consummated his first marriage is a somewhat ribald instance of this rule. The girl literally fought him off for days. Then one morning, as she was crawling out of their sleeping-room, his brother seized her by the neck and held her as in a vice, caught in the narrow doorway. She was helpless, and Baŋɛlib, who had purposely stayed in the room, 'mounted her from behind', in the words of one of his brothers who told me the story. Another man I knew, in the same plight, sent to inform his father-in-law. The old man arrived at cockcrow next day in a towering rage and laid an ultimatum before his daughter. He was not going to eat or drink or budge from the door of her room until her husband told him that the marriage was consummated. The girl, weeping with humiliation, yielded immediately to this heartless form of third degree. Tallensi say that if a man has connexion with his wife for the first time in such circumstances she is at once impregnated—a bit of folk-lore that shows how marital cohabitation is felt to be essentially the means to procreation rather than to gratification.

Reciprocally, a man cannot refuse to cohabit with his wife. If he does, she will quarrel bitterly with him and leave him; and she will have the support of her father or guardian in this action. A polygynist must divide his sexual attentions equally among his wives, or else the neglected wives will quarrel with him and with their co-wives. Indeed, men say, somewhat cynically, that more family quarrels arise because of the jealousy (ŋuur) of co-wives over the sexual attentions of their common husband than for any other cause. Though a woman cannot prevent her husband from having a clandestine lover, she will resent it as a slight on her sexual attractions if she finds out, and make life uncomfortable for him in revenge.

We have previously said that the Tallensi have no institutionalized procedure for divorce. This needs to be qualified. A very drastic procedure to which we have referred in our earlier book[1] exists by which a man can get rid of an objectionable wife. It is usually described as 'blowing (on)' (*pɛbh*) a wife, for it consists in the man's blowing ashes over his wife. By this action he expels her utterly from his house with all her brood. He casts her off and disowns her children; and he forfeits the bride-price. Everybody knows of this custom, and it is held to be entirely licit for any husband. The origins of attached lineages[2] are often attributed to clan sisters who were allegedly divorced in this way. But it is impossible to get a record of a single case that has occurred within the last forty or fifty years, or, indeed, within living memory. Though natives say that a man could, if he wished, 'blow on' his wife if she angered him continuously, or if she were dissolute, or were objectionable in any way, in fact her delinquencies would have to be of so grave a nature as to imperil his life and the welfare of the family for a man to cut through his marriage ties irrevocably at such enormous sacrifice.

The example of such a misdemeanour always quoted is concerned with their sexual relations. It is a taboo (*kihər*) for a woman to deny her husband's sexual rights over her. She would do so, by implication, if she were to kick him over in the act of coitus.[3] This is a sin of such gravity that the marriage must be dissolved at once or else disaster will come upon both partners. For it means that husband and wife have fallen out so badly with each other that they have come into sexual conflict.

This is implied, also, in a more symbolic way, if the disagreements between husband and wife come to a head in her attacking him with her stirring-stick (*vugər*) and his retaliating with his bow (*tap*). The stirring-stick, an indispensable implement for cooking porridge, is one of the emblems of femininity, and the bow, the principal weapon of the chase and of warfare, the chief emblem of manhood in Tale custom and ritual. Men are by convention excluded from the kitchen; women, both by convention and by ritual injunction, from the chase, and from contact with its magical and mechanical appurtenances when they are being used for hunting. One of the very rare occasions on which sexual continence is ritually enjoined on men is when they are poisoning arrows for hunting or war. Thus, a fight between husband and wife with bow and stirring-stick is a fight in terms of their opposed sexuality, a repudiation of the fundamental bond of marriage. It is a sin, and the couple will die if they do not immediately sever their marital relationship completely.

---

[1] *Dynamics of Clanship*, ch. iv. [2] Ibid., p. 51.
[3] The point lies in the postures adopted by the Tallensi in coitus. As in many other primitive cultures, the woman lies on her back, and the man squats on his haunches between her thighs. She can, therefore, easily push him over with a kick, the natives say.

Tallensi speak of these two sins against the marriage bond with genuine horror. During my second tour in Taleland, Maankye and his wife died within a few days of each other. Men of the family told me that this was the retribution justly visited on them for having fought with stirring-stick and bow but refusing to part. Such breaches of the marital bond might conceivably provoke a man to 'blow on' his wife, but I have never heard of an actual case. More probably she would be handed over to the lineage elders, to be sent back by them to her father.

Incidentally, the prohibition against keeping a wife who wets the sleeping-mat at night obviously belongs to this class of offences against the marriage bond, though, being involuntary, it is less heinous than the others. The real mystical danger to the husband is that a black ant might crawl through the woman's urine and then sting him. To disgust at the physical fouling of the nuptial bed in this infantile manner, so out of keeping with adulthood, is added fear of the magical consequences of the sexual maladjustment represented by the condition. But here again, in the few cases I know of, the woman was returned to her father through the elders of the husband's lineage.

It should be added that a wife's refusal to allow her husband to have coitus with her on a particular occasion is not regarded as a denial of his rights. This is one of the ways in which a woman gets her own back if she is vexed with her husband. And it would be very uncouth for the man to try to force her to yield to him. 'He coaxes her, until she at last gives him the vagina (*zaŋ pɛn tiu*)', my men friends told me.

The Sexual Rights of the Husband and the Corporate Interests of his Clan

A man has exclusive sexual rights over his wife, as we have said. If any other man has relations with her this is either incestuous or adulterous, and a serious wrong against the husband himself and his effective minimal lineage, section, or clan, according to the structural relations of the husband's and the seducer's effective minimal lineage, section, or clan.

To appreciate the significance of this we must recollect that a woman marries an individual, but marries *into* a lineage and clan. Men, and even women and children, of a clan or lineage speak of the wives of its members as 'our wives (*ti pɔyaba*)'. If a man sees the wife of a clansman trying to sneak away in flight from her husband, he will take it on himself to bring her back home by force if necessary. If a man's wife is seduced or abducted by a member of another clan, any of his clansmen will take reprisals, if they get a chance, by seducing or abducting the wife of a member of the offending clan. There were many fights in the old days, as we have learnt, between clans because the wife of one clan was abducted by a member of the other.

This corporate interest of the husband's lineage and clan in his wife, implying, on the surface, a diffused 'ownership' of the woman, is most precisely shown in the joint leviratic rights of clansmen.[1] It is, however, not far in the background of all the relations of a woman with her husband's clansmen, individually or collectively. For it is the commonest and most commonplace expression of the corporate unity and solidarity of the agnatic descent group. And it is not an undifferentiated collective interest or right, but very clearly differentiated in accordance with the segmentation of the lineage.

The crux of this differentiation is the sexual relationship of husband and wife. As his sexual partner a woman is the wife of her husband in a rigorous sense that distinguishes him from all his clansmen, both in relation to herself and in relation to her paternal lineage and clan. Unlike the other reciprocal rights and duties of matrimony, those that pertain to sex are unconditionally binding on the spouses and strictly reserved to them. A man's authority over his wife in other respects is often shared with others—his parents, for instance. His sexual rights over her cannot be shared. In the economic management of the household a woman has some freedom of action; she has none in her sexual relationship with her husband. Nor is a husband sexually free, in the same way, for instance, as he is free to dispose of property acquired by his own efforts. Though he is nominally free to indulge in extramarital liaisons, he can in fact only do so clandestinely and at the risk of friction with a jealous wife. Sexual relations are licit in wedlock; outside marriage they are illicit, especially for a woman; before marriage no social cognizance is taken of them if they do not involve adultery or incest. Love affairs between distant members of the same clan come into this category of tolerated illicit sex relations, hence their irrelevance to the function of sex in marriage.

This is a consequence of the stress Tallensi lay on legitimate parenthood, for which marriage is a *sine qua non.* Tallensi express contempt for the Gɔrisi who, it is notorious, often constrain a daughter to 'sit at home and bear children' to augment her father's family. Though Tallensi do not approve of a girl's bearing a child before marriage, no moral stigma attaches to her. She has no difficulty in finding a husband, if she is physically and mentally normal. Her illegitimate child (*yi-yeem-bii*) is welcomed by her parental family, especially if it is a daughter. For instance, Pa'anbɔbis has a sister, now a staid elderly woman and mother of a legitimate family, who had an illegitimate daughter in her youth. This girl was married off by Pa'anbɔbis's father, who was entitled to her bride-price. She bore a daughter and was then taken away from her husband because he failed to pay the bride-price. When she married again her daughter remained behind as a 'child' of the family, and Pa'anbɔbis will receive her bride-price. People said he was a lucky man.

[1] Cf. *Dynamics of Clanship*, ch. iv.

His family had had a windfall of two daughters in half a generation and that meant eight cows.

Yet the Tallensi believe emphatically that a girl can only realize her womanhood to the full by bearing legitimate children. For this she must marry; and marriage means having only one husband at a time. It is as her husband's sexual mate that a woman is most sharply separated from her natal family; it is her husband's exclusive rights over her reproductive powers that definitively makes them husband and wife.

This proposition applies also to the husband's field of social relations. Within the region of family and kinship ties where generation differences are socially recognized, sexual relations may occur only between married partners. Sexual intercourse between a man and a woman of the family who is not his wife is incest. The Tallensi have no name for this act. They say, simply, 'It is tabooed (*de kihme*)'; and they look on it with unanimous revulsion. Translating their ideas into our cultural idiom, we should say that they regard any form of incest as an unnatural act.[1]

Incest, to a Talɛŋa, includes sex relations with a sister or daughter, that is, a woman of one's own lineage: with a mother, the wife of one's own or classificatory father; with a brother's wife; and with a son's wife. Such acts of misconduct are considered incestuous if they occur within the limits of the expanded family—that is, the family group based on the inner lineage (the narrow *dug*). The natives stress this, putting the emphasis on the fact that the narrow *dug* is the smallest lineage segment with a common ancestor shrine (*bɔyar*). Such acts are, also, often regarded as incestuous within the limits of the family cluster based on the medial lineage, particularly if this lineage has a narrow span.

Incest occurs occasionally in every Tale community. Such an act soon leaks out, and is remembered with contempt for many years. I have discussed such cases with many informants, and was able, also, to witness the public reaction to two cases that occurred during my field work.[2]

There are no penal sanctions against any form of incest, nor are the culprits believed to be subject to automatic mystical retribution. Incest is so incompatible with the pattern of co-operation and the structure of disciplinary and affective relations in the family that this itself serves to banish it from the field of family relationships. Though incest taboos are never deliberately inculcated, the habits, attitudes, and organization of family life (to put the native expressions into sociological language) create internal barriers against incest, in the normal person. This applies particularly to incest with a sister or daughter, whether it is a single impulsive act or a more lasting liaison. Tallensi explain that a normal

---

[1] A preliminary analysis of this subject was given in my paper, 'Kinship, Incest, and Exogamy in the Northern Territories of the Gold Coast', in *Custom is King: Essays presented to R. R. Marett*, 1936.

[2] Cf. *Dynamics of Clanship*, ch. xii.

man does not even have sexual desire for a sister or a daughter. This is the standard, conscious, sexual attitude to a sister and it is in keeping with the conscious attitude about incest with a sister or daughter. Such an act is spoken of as tabooed (*kih*), but it is neither a crime nor a sin. It is simply despicable conduct that the culprits ought to be ashamed of as unworthy of grown persons. Even children talk of copulation with a sibling as something beneath contempt, though, in fact, it is common knowledge that up to the age of about 8 or 9 boys often try to have sexual intercourse with a small girl playmate in their play and for the most part playmates are close lineage siblings. Adults reprove the children if they discover them in this kind of play, but dismiss it as due to childish irresponsibility.[1] This, indeed, is the essence of the general attitude towards incest with a sister or daughter. It is disreputable, because it does not conform to the accepted standards of responsible adult conduct. Only in the case of incest with a full (*soog*) sister is there a feeling of horror. It is felt to be unlucky in a vague way. She is the person of the opposite sex with whom a man is most fully identified. What is more important, she perpetuates their mother's uterine line and therefore stands for the indestructibility of the unique bond between mother and child. Sexual intercourse with her would be almost like incest with one's own mother; and this feeling is extended to distant female uterine kin (*saarət*) as well.

Incest with a mother, a brother's wife, or a daughter-in-law is in a different class of reprehensible acts. It is a taboo for a man even to sit on the sleeping-mat of a woman related to him in any of these ways (and thus, we may presume, symbolically betraying a wish to seduce her). To have intercourse with her is a very grievous sin. It is utterly repugnant to Tale morality.

Incest with one's own mother the natives regard as a thing of such monstrous iniquity that it is ridiculous to conceive of anyone who is not mentally deranged committing it. Incest with a father's wife, other than one's own mother, or a brother's or son's wife is almost as heinous a sin and is regarded with little less horror; but it is known to happen sometimes. In one of the cases that occurred during my stay in Taleland, a man raped his father's elderly wife (his own dead mother's co-wife), whom he called '*ma-pit* (younger mother)'; in the other, a notoriously dissolute young man seduced his father's brother's wife, whom he would also describe as '*ma-pit*'. Both were publicly derided in the songs sung during the dances of the Great Festivals. One of the songs about the second man went as follows:

> Badiemaal (his name) you who rape vaginas, Oh!
> Bakyɛlbanɔya (the woman) is a slut.
> Zimbil-Badiemaal is a dog.

[1] Cf. my *Social and Psychological Aspects of Education in Taleland*, Memorandum XVII, International African Institute, 1938.

PLATE 5

b. Homeward bound from a visit to her father's house, where she has received a gift of some millet and other foodstuffs

a. A senior wife (*pɔγakpeem*) in her *dendɔŋo* sorting newly harvested millet. With her are one of her daughter's children and the small son of a co-wife

PLATE 6

a. Kinship *versus* affinal relationships: sons-in-law, sitting in the customary posture of respect, on the right, come to offer condolences to their father-in-law's family and lineage on the occasion of a death

b. A husband goes to inform his parents-in-law of the birth of his wife's first child. He carries a hen as a gift and a thick stick of Shea wood on which four notches have been cut, which shows that the baby is a girl

Badiemaal, is this how you behave?
Zimbil-Badiemaal will never inherit the (lineage) bɔyar;
Why did you copulate with Naaho's wife?

Badiemaal, pɛnzierug, woo-oo!
Bakyɛlbanɔya a bumbarəŋ.
Zimbil-Badiemaal, u a baa.

Badiemaal, i ɛŋa ŋwala?
Zimbil-Badiemaal ku vaa bɔyar;
I nyɛb Naah pɔya bo?

It was widely held that both of these men would take the first opportunity to get out of Taleland.

The Tallensi explain that such acts are so severely reprobated because they cause deep and irreconcilable 'enmity' (*diuŋ*) between father and son, brother and brother, and this is a mortal blow to the solidarity of the family and the lineage. They arouse the wrath of the ancestors. If the injured father, brother, or son does not bring the matter up before the elders of his medial lineage or maximal lineage, he will be struck down by the ancestors. If he does, he must be ritually reconciled with his offending son, brother, or father. But in spite of such a formal reconciliation, 'the enmity remains within'. The sinner will never be able to offer sacrifice to his injured father with a clear conscience, or an injured son to the spirit of his father who so grievously sinned and offended him; nor may two brothers between whom this bitter inner discord prevails sacrifice together. Therefore, as the scornful song about Badiemaal declares, the sinner cannot, with a clear conscience, inherit the shrines common to the lineage; and since a man's sins spiritually taint his children and children's children, the sinner's whole line of agnatic descendants will be virtually outcast from the moral unity of the lineage, even if they are allowed to participate formally in the cult of its ancestors. Again, a man who has seduced his brother's wife cannot inherit her after his death, for he has broken the bond of brotherhood. The incestuous sexual act is sinful because it disrupts the moral relationship of father and son or brother and brother, and thus undermines the solidarity of the lineage at its core. There is a magical deterrent as well, which reflects this. If two men have sexual relations with the same woman and one of them gets ill, the other may not see him; it would cause him to sink and perhaps die; and to shun a sick parent, sibling, or child is the very negation of family solidarity.

A man's 'fathers', 'brothers', and 'sons' within the limits of the nuclear lineage are the men who have the most direct interest in his wife, especially in her reproductive powers. They will all be concerned in, and one or other of them will be responsible for, the payment of her brideprice. His children mean almost as much to them as to him. They replenish the lineage. They are under the ritual and jural authority of his own or proxy father, during the latter's lifetime, and may pass into the ritual and jural custody of one of his 'brothers' on his death. If he dies, a 'brother' will have the first and strongest claim to his widow's hand. Yet these are the men who must most rigorously respect his exclusive sexual rights over his wife and most staunchly defend them against all others. Men of the same nuclear lineage can substitute for one another in all relationships of filiation; for these are the relationships that constitute them a corporate unit. They dare not usurp one another's role in the marital relationship; this would bring them into competition with one another. The sexual bond is the heart of the unique person-to-person aspect of marriage, and sexual competition the negation of the tie of common descent and the greatest source of inter-personal and inter-group conflict. Lineage and clan have a corporate interest in a wife of any member of the unit as the mother of future members of the group, and in her offspring. But no member of the unit may have a personal sexual interest in her while her husband is alive.

We can see, now, why sexual relations with a sister or a daughter are so much less reprehensible than incest with a wife of the lineage. Incest with a sister or daughter does not destroy the solidarity of the males of the nuclear lineage for it does not imply rivalry between them. She belongs to all of them equally by birth; she is genealogically and socially identified with them; she and they already have defined rights and duties and sentiments of attachment to one another; as a member of the lineage, she has as great an interest in their solidarity as they have and the physical replenishment and perpetuation of the lineage is of as much concern to her as to them. In relation to her lineage siblings, sexual gratification as a source of pleasure is distinguished from the reproductive function. In terms of the latter she is identified with the lineage as a whole. The common interest a woman's agnates have in her as a woman is in her reproductive powers being placed at the service of another genealogical group in return for the bride-price, and not, as in the case of a wife, in her reproductive powers serving the interests of their own group.[1] If a man desires his sister or daughter sexually it must be a matter of mere lust (kɔrih), a foolish impulse, and not an expression of his desire for progeny as a socially mature adult. The gratification of lust, contemptible as it is in these circumstances, does not shatter the moral unity or injure the common interests of the lineage as does the usurpation of procreative rights over a wife. It does not, like the latter, destroy a father's authority over his son or a son's filial piety towards his father; for though it is a perversion of the social role of father or brother, it is not a usurpation of critical rights.

What has been said of the nuclear lineage applies in only slightly lesser degree to the inner lineage—the widest corporate unit responsibly

[1] Cf. p. 250 below.

concerned with the marriages of its members. Beyond the range of the inner lineage but within that of the medial lineage there is some doubt as to whether intercourse with a woman member is incestuous or not.[1] Feeling varies according to the span of the unit and the number of segments it includes. Beyond the range of the medial lineage it is not uncommon for men to have affairs with women of their own maximal lineage or clan. The attitude towards incest with a sister or daughter is stretched to the point of complete tolerance. Sexual relations with a distant clan-sister (*pɔyayabalǝg*) do not clash with the habits, morals, and organization of family life nor with those of lineage or clan relationships. Indeed, the structure of the society practically compels a man who wants a lover (*gab*) to seek for one among his own clanswomen. Any woman not genealogically related to him is someone he is allowed to marry. His sexual interest in her is an interest in her for the sake of offspring. The Tallensi attach so much importance to marriage that they think it absurd and despicable for a man to desire only a sexual liaison with a woman he can legitimately marry. Owing to this and to their tacit appreciation of the critical function of the sexual relationship in marriage, they have the utmost scorn for anyone who tries to seduce a girl he is courting. One of the strictest points of the etiquette of courtship is that the man must make no sexual advances to the girl; inquiries prove beyond doubt that it is extremely rare for courting couples to break this rule. For, apart from etiquette, it would also be an infringement of the taboo against a man's having sexual intercourse with a woman of his father-in-law's—or potential father-in-law's—clan in the latter's settlement.

A distant clanswoman is in a different position. One cannot marry her, but at the same time she is not so closely identified with one or so familiar as a sister. She is not felt to belong to oneself as one's sister or daughter is. Her genealogical and social identification with one's clan seems to be merely a formal usage and this is enhanced by the knowledge that she will marry out. She is the unmarriageable stranger. One can desire her and enjoy her for sexual gratification without an interest in her reproductive powers and without prejudice to her later legitimate marriage. A girl's clan-brother lover is often the most influential go-between in her courtship. Sexual intercourse with a married clanswoman is, of course, adultery from her husband's point of view. It may create trouble between her husband's inner lineage and her own. The head of her inner lineage will demand apologies from the head of her lover's inner lineage and may insist on a ritual reconciliation. There will also have to be a ritual reconciliation between the adulterer and the woman's husband's lineage. Cases of adultery very often take this form and that is one reason why husbands do not like young wives to stay long at their parents' homes.

[1] Cf. *Dynamics of Clanship*, p. 204.

By contrast, sex relations with the wife of a member of the same lineage or clan outside the range of the inner lineage is a wrong. It is not incest, but the most reprehensible form of adultery. It does not bear the same moral stigma as the corresponding form of incest, nor does it carry religious penalties for the adulterer. Unless the two men concerned have personal cognatic ties, which makes the offence more serious, they are related to each other only as members of related lineage segments. Their personal identity is submerged in the corporate unit, and the offence is interpreted as an injury to the husband's segment by the culprit's segment of a like order. What is a moral and ritual offence in the inner lineage shades over into a misdemeanour or jural injury in the wider lineage. The shift of evaluation is correlated with a change in the intensity though not in the kind of interests involved, and a widening of the span of the unit. The wider lineage has similar but less direct interests in a man's wife than his inner lineage; its unity and solidarity are of the same order as, but less intimate than that of the inner lineage. It has a jural and political unity and solidarity, primarily associated with formal sentiments of amity and mutual loyalty; whereas the cohesion of the inner lineage (based as it is on common economic interests, co-operation and consultation in the everyday affairs of life, contiguous residence, and minimal internal segmentation for jural purposes such as marriage arrangements with other lineages) is primarily moral, and associated with strong emotions of person-to-person amity and loyalty. Thus, beyond the range of the inner lineage, when the customary ritual reconciliation between the segment of the adulterer and the segment of the husband has been completed, the matter is over and done with so far as the public relations of the parties are concerned. No material compensation is made to the husband, and, in the absence of a judicial system, there is no one who can inflict a penalty on the adulterer. The wronged husband may harbour resentment against his wife's seducer; the magical danger inherent in their seeing each other if either is ill remains as a barrier between them; but the corporate unity of the lineage and clan to which they both belong is restored.

Still, adultery with the wife of a clansman or of a member of a linked maximal lineage[1] (to which the same rules apply) creates dissension in the corporate body. It violates the principle that all men of the clan have a formally equal interest in the wife of a fellow member. It leaves behind rankling animosity that hinders united action. For these reasons it usually arouses an outburst of anger against the wrongdoer. Public opinion is a strong sanction against it therefore. Though cases are far from common, they occur more frequently than the corresponding form of incest. I was able to obtain details of a few cases that occurred immediately before and during my stay in Taleland. In one case the husband and his brothers were so outraged that they fell upon the offender in his

[1] Cf. *Dynamics of Clanship*, ch. vi.

homestead, thrashed him soundly, and destroyed many of his personal belongings. This is typical of the anger stirred up by adultery within the clan. Such action would not be taken against a man who committed incest with a father's or brother's wife, though he might be sent to Coventry for a time. For this kind of incest is, at bottom, a question of conscience. The public reaction with regard to it is of no consequence compared with the vileness of the sin and the wrath of the ancestors.

If a man's wife is seduced by a member of another clan, this is also adultery, as has been mentioned, and a wrong against the husband's clan. If the two clans have local or structural ties, the breach must be mended by the prescribed ritual reconciliation. If they have no such ties, no redress is available to the injured husband's clan. He and his clansmen will try to 'cancel the debt (*kɛrəg samər*)' by seducing the wife of a member of the clan that has wronged him, when any of them gets a chance of doing so.

A man's exclusive sexual rights over his wife are secured, also, by mystical sanctions to which the woman is subject. If she has sexual relations with any man other than her husband she commits a grave sin. It is, as the natives say, 'dirt' (*dayət*), mystical defilement. It may bring sickness or death on the woman's husband or children or even on herslf, for it is a serious affront to her husband's ancestors. As we have noted before, adultery (*pɔyamboɔn*, lit. woman-thing) in a wife is regarded with revulsion not unmixed with real dread. The woman has committed something not far short of sacrilege, for she has flouted the rights of her husband's lineage over her reproductive powers. Hence she cannot be admitted to his home again until she confesses before the shrine of the lineage ancestors, the symbolic incarnation of the lineage itself. The threat to the life of the lineage is felt to be so grave that among the Hill Talis an adulteress is forced to confess at the External Bɔyar,[1] the supreme ancestor shrine. Men do not hesitate to use the most callous third-degree methods, short of physical maltreatment, to exact a confession from a wayward wife.

Lastly, a man's wife continues to belong to him sexually after his death until his final funeral ceremonies have been made. Apart from a few ritual observances in sign of mourning, which do not embarrass her greatly, a widow is free to go about her normal life in the interval between her husband's death and his final obsequies. But she is subject to one iron taboo: she may not have sexual relations. It is a much graver sin than during her husband's lifetime, endangering not only her children and herself but her husband's spiritual status. A dead man whose wife has *kaa gaba*, broken the mourning of widowhood, as this misdemeanour is called, cannot have descendants given to him as spiritual wards, for his spiritual status is smirched. It is for this reason that, when

[1] Cf. *Dynamics of Clanship*, ch. vii.

a man dies leaving young wives without infants his funeral ceremonies are hurried on. Tallensi do not believe that young widows without infants will remain chaste for long out of a sense of duty or for fear of mystical penalties. A man's widow, in short, remains his wife, sexually bound to him, as long as his social personality continues to be recognized. Death alone does not expunge a man's social personality. The management of his property, his social roles, and all his rights and responsibilities, continue to be exercised by proxy in his name after his death until his funeral ceremonies are finished; for it is by these ritual acts that his social personality is expunged. His property then passes to his heir, his social roles to his successor, and his widow is free to remarry.

The Husband's Relationship with his Affines

The sexual bond of husband and wife is also, as we have noticed, the critical element that discriminates a woman's marital relationship with her husband from her filial relationship with her father or with anyone who takes over his social role. As we have mentioned before, the economic duties and rights of a woman in her conjugal family are not very different from those that she exercises in her natal family before marriage or if she comes to live with the latter at any time. Her jural status as a minor under her husband's or father-in-law's authority corresponds to her jural status in her father's family. It is essentially with respect to her reproductive capacity that her role and status as wife and mother are sharply separated from her role and status as daughter and sister.

This will be clearer if we look first at the general rules and conventions of a son-in-law's relations with his father-in-law's family and lineage.

The term *deema* (pl. *deenam*), affine, correctly used applies to wife's parent and daughter's husband, and to anyone identified with them in a particular situation. It is the self-reciprocal term of address between these relatives, as well as the term of reference for them. I have heard it used as a special gesture of consideration and courtesy by a man to his brother's wife, but this is not usual. For the relationship between affines, in the Tale sense of this term, is not quite the same as that of a woman with her husband's parents and siblings. A man's affines have no authority over him. The tensions connected with common residence are absent. There are no common economic, jural, or ritual interests between affines.

As in all Tale social relations, differences of personality and the flexibility of custom result in variations in the actual behaviour of affines to one another that sometimes obscure the real nature of the relationship. I have seen a man chaff his mother-in-law (*deempɔk*) in a way that would be regarded as excessively familiar by the majority of natives. In a well-established marriage one often finds great friendliness and mutual goodwill between parents-in-law and son-in-law. They visit one another regularly, help one another more than the strict letter of custom requires, and are proud of one another. In particular, this positive element in the relationship of affines becomes attached to the brother-in-law (*dakii*), and it is not uncommon for brothers-in-law to be real friends if they live near one another, or belong to allied clans, and if there are no brideprice debts outstanding. In former days a man would protect an affine belonging to another clan from molestation by his own clansmen, in the same way as he protected a kinsman of another clan. I have seen men show deep grief at the death of a parent-in-law or brother-in-law.

On the other hand, the sense of an underlying divergence or even conflict of interests that is so conspicuous in the early stages of a marriage never wholly vanishes. The intercourse of affines always tends to be coloured by the feeling that they might be at strife at any time. This is what makes *deen*, affinity, the arch symbol of all that is most antithetical to *dɔyam*, consanguinity. A formal distance must be maintained between affines; and the passage of time merely blurs but never obliterates this.

A man must show formal deference to his parents-in-law or their representatives, especially in the early years of marriage, and always in ceremonial situations. When he encounters them, or visits them, he sits down to greet them in the posture of respect—crossed legs (*pɔt nɔba*), bowed and hatless head—adopted before a chief, a high ritual functionary, or an ancestor shrine. He is a 'stranger' in their house and they in his house. He is 'shy' of them, and must be on his best behaviour in their presence. It would be most unmannerly, almost immodest, for father-in-law and son-in-law to eat together. In certain circumstances this attitude is extended to the whole settlement of a father-in-law's clan. For example, one rarely sees a respectable Tongo elder eating bought porridge publicly in the market at Ba'ari or Sii. Partly it is unbecoming for the head of a family, as people might gossip, saying that he had no food at home. But the main reason is that Tongo people marry men and women from Sii and Ba'ari. A Tongo man thinks of these places as the homes of possible or actual affines, and he would feel very ill at ease eating bought porridge publicly in the presence of an affine. When a man's parents-in-law or their representatives come on a visit to his house, he must show them honour (*giem ba*). The officious hospitality showered on a visiting father- or mother-in-law, or anybody representing them, by a son-in-law, and vice versa, makes a totally different impression from the friendly welcome offered to a kinsman from another settlement.

Affines have no axiomatic ties. Their relationship rests on a welldefined jural compact. Their parallel interests in the woman who links them, and in her children, are clearly differentiated. This means that a son-in-law has to make special efforts to keep the goodwill of his parents-in-law, particularly in the early years while he is not quite sure of his wife. If his father-in-law sends for him to help with the hoeing, or with house building, or his mother-in-law requests him to help thatch her rooms, he must respond with alacrity and bring as large a party of his clansmen to assist him as he can manage. In this way a man shows honour to, ingratiates himself with (*giem*), his affines; for these services are not enforceable obligations, and usually cease to be asked for after the marriage has become stabilized. They bear no relation to the bride-price, and are lavishly recompensed. A visiting work-party brought by a son-in-law expects generous hospitality, and the father-in-law, if he is a reputable man, would feel that he had lost dignity if he did not feed and entertain the work-party well. But though these services cannot be enforced, no man would risk offending his parents-in-law by refusing them. These material demonstrations of respect, gratitude, and goodwill are essential for the smooth working of a relationship artificially established by a jural compact. Parents-in-law praise and like an obliging son-in-law, even if he has not paid the bride-price, the natives say.

This is one side of the affinal relationship. It also has an aspect of friendliness and familiarity, as we have seen, which comes out most conspicuously in a man's relations with his siblings-in-law. A man has a joking relationship with his siblings-in-law similar to that of his wife with his sisters and distant clansmen. It goes so far that a man may sleep with an unmarried sister-in-law (*daküpɔk*) who is visiting his house, and is therefore in that situation identified with his wife. A man's siblings-in-law belong to the familiar and friendly generation of his wife. They are identified with her. But they also belong to the potentially hostile lineage of her father, whose heir a brother-in-law will one day be. In very many ways a man's siblings-in-law are sympathetically drawn to him; but their rights in relation to his wife may pit them against him. The convention of joking serves to reconcile these two potentially discordant elements of their relationship. But when the marriage has lasted many years, and the possibility of a conflict of rights disappears, the element of friendliness in the relationship can assert itself without prejudice to its jural aspect. Thus, conventional teasing usually drops out of the intercourse of siblings-in-law of long standing.

The formal distance between affines is further shown in the duties and obligations to which a man is liable on the death of a son-in-law or parent-in-law. On the death of a parent-in-law a man is obliged to attend the mortuary and funeral ceremonies. He should come escorted by a large party of clansmen and their wives, and the mourning party should wear their finest clothes and be led by drummers and musicians. A son-in-law should provide the gravestone for a parent-in-law. He should distribute money freely to the grave-diggers, to the drummers, singers, and musicians, whose raucous noise stimulates the crowd and adds prestige to the occasion, to the widows, to the old women tending the corpse, and to the girls dancing extravagantly in honour of the dead.[1]

A son in-law should help to dig the grave and to carry the corpse to the grave, or depute a clansman to do these tasks on his behalf. These duties are undertaken readily and with pride, as a rule, whether or not a man has been on good terms with his deceased parent-in-law, though there are no sanctions for enforcing them. Men perform them as a mark of respect to their affines, both to the dead and the living, and it would be a serious affront, causing friction with his living in-laws and deep resentment on the part of his wife, if they were neglected. In addition, there is the incentive of personal satisfaction, for they give a grand opportunity for self-display. The mourning party he brings, his largesse, and the conspicuous assistance he gives at the burial, are all means of showing off his personal importance and his excellence as a son-in-law.

A son-in-law is obliged also to send certain food contributions of prescribed kind and quantity to the funeral of a parent-in-law. Small contributions accompany the mourning party. The principal contribution is due on 'the day of sleeping at the funeral (*kogbedaar*)'. This consists of a sheep or goat cut up and ready cooked, together with a large basket of slabs of porridge and a pot of relish. Unlike the duties previously mentioned, these food contributions are 'debts' (*samər*, pl. *sama*)—i.e. obligatory gifts. If a man cannot pay any of them when they are due, he must do so whenever he is able to; and if he omits to do so altogether before his death, his son will have to settle the debt. For here a sanction that operates in many social and religious obligations of the Tallensi comes into play. If a man dies without paying a ceremonial debt of this kind, then, in accordance with the principle of equivalent returns, he must be done by likewise. *His* son cannot accept the same food contribution from *his* son-in-law until the debt is paid; and this is felt as an affront to his spirit. His son would therefore take steps immediately to set the matter right. In fact it appears to be very rare in normal circumstances, for a man to omit these duties altogether during his lifetime.

Conversely, if a man's daughter or his son-in-law dies, he in turn sends a mourning party to represent him and convey his condolences. He is also obliged to send certain customary food gifts. But these are small in quantity; for though they represent a return in kind for what is due from a son-in-law in like circumstances, they are made by a superior to an inferior, by one who has already conferred a benefit that can never be

[1] The currency chiefly used on such occasions consists of cowrie shells (*layapielɔb*, pl. *layapiela*, lit. white money, the original form *layah*, pl. *ligəri*, being nowadays restricted to British currency), now worth only a hundred a penny. A man can be generous for a shilling, and prodigal for half a crown.

fully repaid in the bestowal of his daughter as a wife. A similar sanction to that mentioned in the case of a son-in-law operates here.

If one watches the behaviour of men at the funeral of an affine, one can see that they feel themselves to be under strong constraint. They and their clansmen accompanying them keep together, and when there are no ceremonies or festivities in progress they stay apart from the rest of the crowd. In former days a mourning party of affines always carried arms, and it is said that fighting sometimes broke out at funerals. When Tallensi comment on the ceremonial obligations of affines, they emphasize the feeling of constraint associated with them. One is impressed by the contrast between this attitude and the attitudes associated with the ceremonial obligations that follow on the death of a clansman or cognatic kinsman. It is as if the native feels his ceremonial obligations to an affine to be forced on him from outside, without his choice, whereas he seems to accept his duties and obligations on the death of a kinsman willingly and from within.

It is evident that reciprocity between affines is different in character from that which prevails between people who have a bond of common interests, such as members of the same family. There is not the same free give and take. When gifts or services pass between affines, whether they are prescribed or ostensibly spontaneous, there is a deliberate effort to counterbalance them. A sort of book-keeping occurs. This appears most clearly in the jural formalities of marriage, but it comes out quite plainly in the apparently voluntary services and reciprocal hospitality of son-in-law and father-in-law. The side that benefits feels impelled to make an equivalent return in order not to give the other party grounds for a grudge. And people who flout this convention not only upset their good relations with their affines and so provide pretexts for conflict with them, but also incur the censure of public opinion.

One incident will illustrate this. Banɔrəg asked his son-in-law, a member of an adjacent clan, to come and help him finish the hoeing of his home farm. The young man brought a couple of his clansmen and they worked with zeal from early morning till sunset. Then they went home, politely refusing Banɔrəg's invitation to come home with him for the evening meal. Had they come as a formal hoeing party they would have been entitled to a good meal as a reward at the end of the day. But they had come informally, and their own homes were near enough for them to get back in time for the evening meal. They spoke of their day's work for Banɔrəg as a simple act of courtesy to a father-in-law. As we watched them saunter homewards, Banɔrəg said to me 'Sons-in-law are shy (*deenam mmar vi*). They can't come home with you (their father-in-law) and eat with your children (as if they were your kin)'. But next day Banɔrəg sent a large basket of millet flour to his daughter with orders to cook a generous meal for her husband and his friends. He would feel ashamed, he told me, if he did not 'thank' the young men thus; and besides, people would say he was mean. This attitude does not occur with the true reciprocity that prevails in the domestic family or between near kin.

Sex in the Relationship of Affines

While, therefore, the relations of affines assume the existence of a formal distance between them, they are not encumbered by avoidances or other social barriers that make friendliness impossible or ordinary social intercourse a burden. There is amity as well as opposition in their relationship. In one matter only is there a rigorous barrier between affines. In respect to sex and procreation they are strictly separate. The emphasis is on the deed, not the word; there is no prohibition against talking to or in the presence of an affine about sexual matters.

One aspect of this ban on bringing sex into the relationship of affinity is the native attitude about a sexual offence against an affine. For a man to seduce the wife of an affine is almost as heinous a transgression as intercourse with the wife of a man of one's own expanded family, though it is not regarded as incest; and the offence is nearly as bad if the culprit is a close agnate of the woman's husband's affine or the woman the wife of a close agnate of the affine concerned. It is a grave offence, also, if a man or his close agnate abducts the wife of an affine or his close agnate. There are no explicit mystical sanctions against either of these wrongs, but Tallensi describe them as 'a thing of enormous evil (*yelbiog tenta'ar*)' bound to bring ill fortune on the wrongdoer, and in any case involving such serious social consequences that no man in his senses would descend to them. They think of the possible culprit as being the son-in-law, and they say that the father-in-law would take away his daughter and the bride-price be forfeited. Affines are bound to fall out with one another now and then. Usually apologies proffered through an intermediary lead to their making it up again. But in the case of a sexual offence against a father-in-law, it is quite impossible to beg or receive pardon. For it is a sin; it 'pollutes the room (*sayam dug*)' of the injured man.[1]

'Pollution of the room' in this sense is very rare among the Tallensi. But it is not unknown for a man to abduct the wife of the father- or brother-in-law (true or classificatory) of one of his own clansmen. The elders of both the abductor's medial lineage and the wronged husband's medial lineage are then extremely indignant. The latter demand the return of 'their' wife; and in all the cases I have come across the former see to it at once that the woman is sent back to her husband.

[1] Cf. p. 28 above. *Sayam dug* has the double sense of a mystical defilement of the sleeping-room—the inner sanctuary of family and of reproductive life—and of an irreparable infringement of lineage rights. If the offender is a distant clansman of the true son-in-law, a ritual reconciliation between the two lineages might be allowed after the defilement has been ritually removed.

It is base to seduce an affine's wife, or the wife of his near clansman, anywhere, but it is abominable to do it at the injured man's own house. Strictly speaking, 'polluting the room' refers to the seduction of a father-in-law's wife, or the wife of his close agnate, at his house or in his settlement. If a man's father-in-law or one of the latter's close agnates seduces the son-in-law's wife (of another clan than theirs), or the wife of one of his close agnates, it is generally treated as a particularly reprehensible form of adultery. The son-in-law would not, for example, necessarily divorce his wife on that account. A ritual reconciliation will be made and the matter closed. Tallensi say such offences are extremely rare, and I have never heard of a case.

The offence borders on a sin if it is committed by a son-in-law or someone genealogically identified with him, on the one hand because of his quasi-filial relationship with his father-in-law through his wife, and on the other because of the sex barrier between affines. The striking thing is that it is a particularly heinous case of 'polluting the room' of a father-in-law for the son-in-law to have sexual relations with his own wife at her father's house. The bond which most closely unites a married couple is the relationship that cuts the woman off most completely from her filial relationship with her paternal family. As we have noted before, if her husband has sexual relations with her in her father's house her status as wife and mother is confounded with her status as sister and daughter; her husband's status as son-in-law is confounded with his status as father and husband in his own family. If the husband did not abrogate his marital rights at his wife's father's house, an insoluble conflict would arise both on the jural level and in their emotional relations. So strict is this taboo that it extends to any man of the son-in-law's lineage, and any daughter of the father-in-law's lineage, more particularly within the limits of the medial lineage. A man may not even meet his wife face to face on the path leading from her parental home to his, if she is on her way from her parents' house to her husband's; for this would symbolize a wish to treat her as his wife at her father's house.

An accidental breach of this symbolic taboo can be mended, though not without difficulty, by a ritual reconciliation. A breach of the prohibition against sexual relations between husband and wife at the latter's paternal home (and *yir*, home, in this context includes the whole settlement), or the equivalent offence committed by a close agnate of the husband, is irreparable. The marriage must be broken up, and children borne of it may be taken away by the woman's father. If this is not done, disaster would fall on everybody concerned. The bride-price is forfeited by the offending husband.

Opportunities and temptations to break these taboos often occur, for instance when a young man takes a party of his clansmen to spend a few days with his father-in-law in order to help him with some work. A man's wife generally accompanies him on such occasions. The visitors expect not only to be well fed, but also to be well entertained. They expect their stay to be made pleasant by dancing, feasting, and flirtations with unmarried girls of the host's clan, and many marriages come about as the result of such contacts. Young men going on such parties are more likely to grouse at their treatment if there were not enough girls to flirt with than if they were stingily fed. But it would be a gross breach of hospitality, as well as an irreparable wrong, if any of the visitors seduced any of the girls; and the son-in-law and his wife always sleep in separate rooms.

These parties are extremely common. Towards the end of the dry season, when house-building is in progress, or in the latter half of the rainy season, when hoeing is very active, there are weeks during which a visiting party of in-laws can be found in a large settlement almost every day. Yet the sexual taboos we have mentioned are rarely broken. I was told of a few alleged cases that had occurred. But the only well-authenticated case I heard of was during my second visit to Taleland, when it came up in connexion with a court case over the woman who was concerned. The scorn and disgust with which people spoke of these cases showed how strongly the natives feel about these taboos.

The taboo against a woman's bearing her husband's child in her father's house links on to this complex of ideas. It is also a 'pollution of the room' of the father-in-law, and a very serious matter. For, as we have previously mentioned, it puts the child thus born into an anomalous position which is dangerous to his welfare. But a breach of it happens so often by accident that it does not inspire repugnance. The pollution can easily be removed by the husband's sending a placatory gift, as we have already recorded, to his father-in-law to 'clear away the blood (*vaa ziem*)' of the delivery. At the same time Tallensi do not like this to happen, and a woman near her term is not encouraged to visit her parents. I have known a man to be so angry with a wife who disobediently went to her father's house towards the end of her pregnancy and gave birth there that he refused at first to have her back.

A man also pollutes his father-in-law's room if he vomits (*ti*) in his father-in-law's house. It is unlucky. The son-in-law and his wife 'will not have it well (*ku nye sɔmma*) with them'; but amends can be made in the same way as for the birth of a child in the father-in-law's house. The symbolism is obscure and the natives cannot explain it. Vomiting is normally taken as a symptom of illness. It may be that they feel vomiting in such circumstances to be a sign of rejecting the hospitality of parents-in-law and therefore a sign of inner hostility to them. The context of this taboo suggests, however, that vomiting in a father-in-law's house is connected with the bearing of a child there, the symbolism being taken either from morning sickness or arising indirectly through the association of regurgitated food with the fluids discharged in childbirth.

Finally, the prohibition of sexual relations between father and daughter or brother and sister in the expanded family also links up with this complex. Tallensi say that if a man's daughter becomes pregnant before marriage he will hasten to marry her off as soon as possible, if she does not elope with a suitor of her own accord. A man once told me that people do this for fear that it might be said of them, 'Oh, so-and-so is not marrying his daughter off because he wants to keep her for a wife for himself'. I do not know if this statement accurately represents the way men feel the pressure of public opinion in cases of this sort; but it is an accurate indication of the feeling that a woman's procreative powers are out of place in her father's home and belong properly to her husband's home.

The Adjustment of Co-Wives to One Another

We have still to consider one of the main problems of adjustment that face a woman in her husband's family, her relations with her co-wives (*nentaa*, pl. *nentaas*). These include both her husband's other wives and his brothers' wives. A woman refers to a co-wife as 'younger (or older) sibling of the same sex (*pit* or *bier*)', and addresses her by her clan sobriquet, e.g. Namooga. A woman's children describe her co-wives as 'mother' (*ma*), with the suffix *pit* or *bier* according as she is junior or senior to their own mother, and address her as 'mother of such-and-such a clan', e.g. *ma Namooga*.

Women do not, as a rule, object to their husbands having other wives as well. Indeed, it often happens that a monogamist's wife presses him to marry again so that there should be someone to share the work of the household with her, or even takes the initiative in finding another wife for him. It is quite common for women to bring younger clan sisters, or a brother's daughter, a sister's daughter, or a daughter of a mother's brother's lineage, to live with them with a view to their eventually marrying their husbands or husbands' brothers. From such marriages spring cognatically related matri-segments of a lineage, with a special link through their progenitrices in addition to their agnatic ties.

Through this custom of fetching in (*pie na*) a kinswoman-wife (*poyasoog*) one often finds women related by kinship married into the same joint family or the same expanded family. But this is not a preferential marriage. It is due simply to the inertia of kinship. A woman who wants to bring a girl into her husband's house usually does so because she has need of someone to help her with the care of an infant or because she is ill or elderly and has no daughter or daughter-in-law to relieve her of the heaviest domestic tasks. And she looks naturally to her kinsfolk, upon whom she has claims by right of birth, to provide her with a suitable girl. Again, though the Tallensi do not like two full or half-sisters to marry the same man or to marry into the same joint family, it is not a taboo. A man who particularly likes his son-in-law and his people readily consents to another daughter's marrying into the same joint family; and this cordiality is easily extended to more distant clansmen on both sides. A Tɛnzugu man who has a son-in-law at Zubiuŋ with whom his relations are cordial will be pleased to see another daughter marry this son-in-law or one of his close agnates; and if the son-in-law himself or a member of his medial lineage comes to seek the hand of a daughter of the father-in-law's medial lineage, the men of that lineage would be favourably disposed to the suitor.

Another factor favouring successive marriages with women of the same lineage or clan is the preference of the natives for wives from a nearby rather than a distant clan. A man looking for an additional wife tends to turn his eyes first to the same neighbouring settlements in which he formerly sought a wife, and men of the same lineage tend to seek wives in the same settlements, as we shall find.

When co-wives refer to one another as 'sisters' they are using a kinship term in a metaphorical sense to indicate their social equivalence—that is, their identity of role and status in their conjugal home and settlement. But if they are kin they speak of one another as 'sisters' in a deeper sense. They have a bond of mutual attachment that holds independently of their relations as wives of the same man or the same lineage. As 'sisters' in the kinship sense they help each other more regularly and more altruistically; they share such things as foodstuffs and firewood more readily; they mother each other's children with more devotion and with a greater feeling of common interest in them; they live together more harmoniously, in general, than unrelated co-wives. This is especially true of a woman and a co-wife whom she has 'fetched in' as the term *poyasoog*, literally a *soog* sister wife (that is, a wife who is like a *soog* sister to another wife), suggests. The older woman watches over the younger almost as if she were a younger full sister or her own daughter.

Tallensi take it for granted that co-wives are apt to quarrel. 'Oh yes', both men and women say with a laugh, if they are asked about it, 'co-wives quarrel—but nevertheless they stay on.' The point is that quarrels between co-wives are taken as a matter of course and do not lead to a wife's desertion. These quarrels may be nothing more than the flaring up of frayed tempers; for among the Tallensi, as among ourselves, people who live so intimately together as the members of a family are prone to fall out over trifles. Or they may be real fights, beginning with taunts and insults and ending with blows. Neighbours, usually men of the husband's lineage, hearing the uproar, may rush in to separate the women, if the husband himself or other men of his family are not on the spot to do so. For there is no one among the women of a household with authority to discipline the others. The senior mistress of the home, whether she is the mother or the senior wife of the owner of the house, ranks above the rest of the women, but has no disciplinary authority over them.

According to the natives, quarrels between co-wives are often due to one or other of them having an intractable disposition. Men add that women lack self-control and are very prone to petty jealousy; they are apt to quarrel if they think they are being unfairly treated, if, for instance, one wife seems to receive more than a fair share of her husband's attention. But when actual cases of such quarrels are examined they are seen to be an expression of the tensions springing from the cleavages in the structure of the domestic family. They are temporary disturbances of the balance between the relatively autonomous matri-central *dug* and the inclusive patri-central *yir*. That is why they occur so rarely between women who are related by kinship or clanship, and who therefore think of their *dugət* as subdivisions of a single wider *dug*. Co-wives live in harmony as long as they act in the interests of the common *yir*; dissensions arise between them when they do not accept the paramountcy of the *yir*, and assert their relative autonomy in relation to one another. In the normal run of family life the interests of the common *yir* come first, for the sustenance of the family and the general welfare of all its members depend upon proper co-operation between them, resting on mutual loyalty and goodwill.

The women of the household, both those who are co-wives to one another, and those who are mother-in-law and daughter-in-law, or mother and daughter to one another, usually work together harmoniously to perform their share of the productive labour of agriculture. They work under the direction of the head of the house, and the products of their labour accrue to the common food supply. This is a part of the co-operative economic organization of the household. Thus at sowing or harvest time one often sees a whole family working together in the fields. When a sowing party is at work one sees the men striding vigorously ahead, dibbling the holes with their long heavy dibbles cut from saplings, while the women follow behind, chattering and laughing amicably as they sow the grain. And when the harvest is in full swing, one sees similar cheerful family parties out on the field or homeward bound at dusk in Indian file, the men in front, perhaps carrying their pear-shaped wicker coops in which they have collected a brood of chickens that had been allowed to run in the fields during the day, the women sauntering close behind them, the heavy baskets of grain on their heads, and small boys and girls gambolling in the rear blowing their whistles and shaking their rattles (*kiŋkayah*) of serrated calabash disks.

The independence of the *dug* comes out in the utilization of the food-supply. As the women have to supply the vegetables for cooking the relish which the natives regard as an indispensable accompaniment to their heavy porridge, each woman who has her own *dug* is entitled to a vegetable patch beside the wall of the homestead. Except for the senior woman of the house, who has a slightly larger vegetable patch

PLATE 7

a. A senior wife takes care of her junior co-wives' infants while they are away at the water-hole

b. A pair of devoted co-wives. The younger woman (with her infant) is about 35, the older about 65, their husband over 70. The older woman has a son of about 45

PLATE 8

a. A domestic sacrifice of fowls, guinea-fowls, and beer. The head of the joint family is addressing the shrine, which occupies a recess in his senior wife's *Dug*

b. Ɔmara and his four youngest daughters—each the daughter of a different wife—having a snack at mid-day

than the others, all the women must be allocated more or less equal plots for this purpose. Each woman, with the help of her daughters or a daughter-in-law, collects and stores wild herbs and edible leaves, buys condiments and seasonings like salt, pepper, and locust bean balls, sometimes with the proceeds of her own petty trading in the markets, and collects shea nuts for the preparation of shea butter, the most important source of fat and the most prized emollient in the native cuisine, for the use of her own *dug*. If a man gives a penny or twopence to one wife for the purchase of seasonings, he must, either immediately or on subsequent market days, give some money to his other wives for this purpose. If he obtains some meat, he must either distribute it amongst all his wives or give all of it to his senior wife to use or preserve for the benefit of the whole family. Only a wife in childbed is entitled to have extra luxuries, which it is the duty of her husband to provide.

Though each woman cooks for herself with an eye to the feeding of her own children and her husband, in the first place, co-wives are obliged to share food prepared with grain from the common supply. In times of plenty, if all the wives of a man have cooked a meal, each woman dishes out a portion of porridge and the accompanying relish for her husband, a portion for herself and her child or children eating with her, and a smaller portion for each of her co-wives. The husband should taste all the dishes sent in to him by his wives, and should pass on to the older children who do not eat with their mothers the dishes he does not want for himself. In times of scarcity a man's wives may cook in rotation for the whole family. But if a woman has a private supply of grain, obtained by trade or from her own relatives, she is entitled to use it for feeding her own children and the husband only; she need not give anything to her co-wives or their children.

In the production and utilization of food-supplies, as this brief sketch shows, the common interests of the *yir* are distinctly paramount. Co-wives co-operate most harmoniously, both among themselves and with the other women of the household, in this sphere of family life. In the organization of productive labour and of the domestic economy, and in the conventions regulating mutual help in this sphere, the dependence on one another of all the members of a household for their sustenance is constantly emphasized. But the relative autonomy of the *dug* is never wholly submerged. The women do not pool the products of their individual labour and enterprise. They do not pool their utensils, and family quarrels sometimes arise because one woman or one woman's child has borrowed and damaged a utensil belonging to another. They keep their firewood supplies, the accumulation of which is one of their most arduous tasks, jealously separate; and they do the same with vegetables and seasonings. There is sometimes friction between co-wives over the use of the grinding-room. But it is significant of the balance usually maintained between the centrifugal tendencies of the *dug* and the centripetal pull of the *yir* in the economic sphere that the habit of co-operation and mutual help between the women of the household goes deeper as a rule than their inclination to think of their own *dugɔt* first. Thus there is a great deal of voluntary mutual aid between the women of the household. The things a woman owns she guards jealously; but she will often lend gladly to another woman of the household on the basis of the true reciprocity that prevails in family affairs. A woman who has prepared a new supply of shea butter, for instance, usually gives some to each of the other women of the household, knowing that some day she will receive gifts of a similar kind from them.

It is in the children of a family that the balance between *dug* and *yir* is most precisely embodied. They represent both the differentiation of *dug* from *dug* and the synthesis of all the *dugɔt* in the *yir*, in their most significant aspects. Thus, all the children of a man are formally the children of all his wives, and this might include the children of his brothers too. The women of a family, and especially co-wives, usually help one another a great deal in caring for one another's children. This commences with child-birth. As we have seen, the care of a parturient woman falls largely on her co-wives and other women of the same family. A new-born child is not given the breast at once by its mother but by another nursing mother; and a nursing co-wife would be the first person to be called upon. Later, the infant will often be left in the care of a co-wife for an hour or two or a whole day at a time if its mother has to be away from home. If a woman dies leaving young children, they are reared by her co-wives as a rule. When a girl becomes pregnant for the first time, it is one of her mother's co-wives who has the honour and duty of ceremonially girding her with the matron's perineal band. Co-wives often take pride in and show great devotion to one another's children. This is especially true of a senior wife past the age of child-bearing. Such a woman, identifying herself closely with the husband and being herself no longer engrossed in her own young children, mothers the children of her younger co-wives with zealous devotion.

And yet, as the natives constantly repeat, the relation of mother and child is unique. Its mother's co-wife can never be the same to the child as its own mother. A woman cannot have the same feelings towards her co-wife's child as towards her own child. The lot of an orphan, Tallensi say, even in a household full of women, is always a hard one. An orphan never receives the devoted attention and the selfless love which can be given only by its own mother. It has to depend upon the mercy and the sense of duty of women who are its mothers only in name.

This is the reason why small children left orphans are sometimes sent to live with their maternal grandmothers until they are big enough to fend for themselves. Some months after his mother's death I met Gundaat, a pathetic little chap of about 9. Talking about various things, we got on to the subject of mothers. Gundaat told me, in a tone of resignation that was touching in the circumstances, that he missed his mother dreadfully. When she was alive, he explained, he never went to bed hungry. She always had something for him to eat even in the leanest times. But nowadays he often slept hungry; for his other 'mothers' had their own children to think of; in times of scarcity they would put aside extra food for their own children but not for him. At best he might get the scraps.

The genealogical and social differentiation of a woman and her children from every other woman and her children of the same domestic family is the kernel of the notion of uterine (*soog*) descent. The cultural definition of this notion gets its psychological content, its meaning for the individual, from the relations of mother and child and co-wife to co-wife.

To every woman, therefore, her own children are the most complete incarnation of her own social self, of her autonomy and status in the family, and of the differentiation of her *dug* from those of her co-wives. That is what the concept *soog* means for a mother in relation to her children. Emotionally wrapped up in them as she is, she becomes almost anarchical in her concern for their welfare. There are women who resent it strongly if a co-wife scolds one of their children; and it is quite common for a woman to get into a fury if her child is struck by a co-wife's child, let alone by a co-wife herself. Many quarrels between co-wives begin in this way. That is why children are taught to keep out of their mothers' co-wives' rooms as much as possible and to behave carefully if they go into them.

The ever-present tension between co-wives, reduced to a minimum at most times, occasionally bursts out acutely. This is liable to happen if a child gets ill of a malady that defies all attempts to cure it, the more so if it is an unusual sickness of sudden onset. The distracted mother is likely then to turn on a co-wife (another wife of her husband, or a wife of one of his brothers) whose own children are well and happy and therefore the bitterest reminder of her evil fortune. Being co-wives the women are sure to have had differences and even quarrels in the past. So now the sick child's mother accuses her co-wife of being a witch (*soi*) and of having caused the illness of the child. Infrequent as accusations of witchcraft were in former days and are now, Tallensi say that most of them were made by women against a co-wife owing to the illness or death of a child. This is the more significant in view of the association between witchcraft and uterine descent. An accusation of witchcraft brands a woman and her children equally, but it does not impugn the male line or, consequently, the *yir*.

When hostility between co-wives reaches this pitch it cannot but result in a serious disturbance of the unity and cohesion of the family. Formerly, as we have learnt, the accused woman might have been compelled to undergo the arrow ordeal, or would herself, backed by her paternal kin and more strongly by her uterine kin (*saarǝt*), insist on doing so. If she survived, she and her children and other *soog* kin would never forgive her accuser. There would be chronic friction in the family. If she died, her children and other *soog* kin would still resent the imputation against them and would have a lifelong grievance against her accuser and her children. The accuser would in any case bear the ritual blame, and would be in danger of mystical retribution. Nowadays, to judge by one case that came to my notice, the accused woman and her kin insist on an oath by the *bɔyar*, usually the *bɔyar* of the husband's medial lineage. Both women swear to the justice of their case before the *bɔyar*, and the one who suffers a serious misfortune soonest—a misfortune such as grave sickness or death in her own *dug* of the house—is deemed to be in the wrong. Whatever the outcome, it amounts to one member of the family invoking the *bɔyar* which watches over the welfare of the whole group to injure another member of the unit; and this is a sacrilege, even if it is done in the name of justice. It must be atoned for by sacrifices to which both women and their husband (or husbands) have to contribute. But the *bɔyar* is never wholly appeased; it may still bring misfortune on the family for the sacrilege. And, of course, both women and their *soog* kin might continue to harbour resentment. An accusation of witchcraft, itself the symptom of the conflicts latent in the structure of the polygamous family, breeds endless discord.

But it must be emphasized that such cases are rare. For the most part women rub along pretty well with their co-wives. In this the senior wife (*pɔyakpeem*)—seniority being reckoned according to order of marriage—may exercise a great deal of influence, especially if, as is likely, she is older than the others. Though she has no disciplinary authority over her younger co-wives, she has considerable moral authority over them. As her husband's closest confidante among his wives she knows all the affairs of the family and has its interests close at heart. She stands for the common allegiance of the wives to their husband and the family. A wise and tactful senior wife will keep an eye on the household economy and on the children without seeming to interfere with the liberty of her younger co-wives. Looking up to her with respect and affection, her younger co-wives will accept advice and guidance from her that does much to make the routine of family life smooth and pleasant. The fiction that she is the real mistress of the house (*dugdaana*) and that all the children 'belong' to her in a special sense gives her a formal status that makes this easier. If a suitor calls to see a girl of the family he must pay his respects to the senior wife before he goes to greet the girl's own mother. If a woman's son-in-law sends her gifts of sweet potatoes, yams, and guinea-fowls at the time of the Harvest Festival, she will call all her co-wives proudly to see the gifts, and will distribute some of the tubers among them; but in addition the senior wife will receive a guinea-fowl as a mark of special honour. In such ways is the mistress of the

THE STRUCTURE OF THE FAMILY

house apprised of what is going on in the quarters of the younger women and enabled to exercise benevolent supervision over them.

Her supervision is of special importance when any of the younger women is confined. She sees to it that mother and child are properly attended, that the rites of confinement and of emergence from seclusion are properly performed, that mother and babe are bathed in the prescribed way, and that the mother is given nourishing food. I was passing Ɔmara's homestead one afternoon, about a fortnight after the birth of a child to one of his wives, and called in. The new baby's mother was just coming out of the gateway with an empty water-pot on her head, and I noticed that she was looking far from well. Ɔmara's senior wife, a woman of sterling character, unsoured even by the leprosy that was rapidly getting a hold on her, was sitting outside in the shade. 'Where are you going to?' asked the older woman. 'To the water-hole,' replied her young co-wife. 'Don't go alone,' said the senior wife, 'I'll come with you'; and she rose to accompany the girl. For the first few weeks after the birth of her child a woman must not go about alone outside the homestead. She is still suffering from 'the dreams of a parturient woman (*pɔyarɔyah za'ahug*)'; that is, she is weak and liable to hallucinations or attacks of terror—or, as the natives think of it, to attacks from evil trees and stones—which might drive her mad. That was why the older woman accompanied the young mother. Many such incidents could be quoted in illustration of the concern shown by a senior wife for the welfare of her juniors.

Of course, not all senior wives exercise their role in a wise and unselfish spirit. A woman with an overbearing disposition may make life difficult for her juniors. One result will be that each woman tends to keep strictly to her own *dug* so as to avoid clashing with the senior wife or the other women, and co-operation between co-wives tends to follow the letter of convention rather than the spirit of family unity. Again, there are families in which the senior wife has through age, infirmity, or weakness of character resigned the effective supervision of the household to a younger co-wife, though she still remains the titular senior. But observation shows that on the whole senior wives conform to the pattern we have outlined above. Their position in the family, their responsibilities and privileges, shape them to this pattern.

It must be remembered, also, that the size and stage of development of a family have a great influence on the relations between co-wives. In a family like that of Da'amo'o of Tɔŋ-Dekpieŋ who has but recently set up in his own homestead, there are only three women, two being Da'amo'o's wives and the third his younger brother's wife. They are all young women round about the age of 20, two with an infant each and the other still a maiden (*pɔyasarət*). In such a family the differentiation of *dug* from *dug* is rudimentary. The three girls work in co-operation and live together harmoniously like sisters and with no visible distinction of status or role. In another family of this kind the mistress of the house may be the family head's mother, and then she will exercise the role we have attributed to the senior wife in the preceding pages. In a joint family that has reached an advanced stage of development the women will be related to one another in a more complex scheme. Any particular woman may have one or more close co-wives, the other wife or wives of her husband; there may be, in addition, her co-wives at a remove, the wives of her husband's brothers; her own mother-in-law and perhaps a co-wife of this woman who is her mother-in-law by extension; and possibly daughters of the family. In such a family the wives of one man often feel a strong bond of solidarity in contradistinction to the wives of the other men of the family. The cleavages between the component family segments of the joint family are sharper than those between the wives of one man. As their children increase and get older, the women of each family segment aline themselves more strongly with their husband in his efforts to separate off. They begin to find the communal commissariat irksome and pressure from them often has a decisive influence on their husband's wish to 'go out on his own'.

CHAPTER V

PARENTS AND CHILDREN IN THE FRAMEWORK OF THE LINEAGE

Some General Principles Recapitulated

ALL Tale genealogical connexions go back to the fact of procreation. Hence the relations of parents and children are the focal point of the whole kinship system. Our task here is to investigate the notion of *dɔyam* in its primary social context.

We have emphasized elsewhere that the social structure of the Tallensi is not intelligible if it is stripped of its temporal dimension.[1] The essence of the lineage system is its continuity in time; from this comes its strength and its stability. But it might have been otherwise. Such a system might well, with each generation, grow narrower and more rigid in all its parts, like an endogamous aristocratic caste. Or it might, as has happened with the Tallensi, spread itself more and more widely by continual ramification and so keep its strength without losing suppleness.

How has this come about? The central dynamic factor is the pattern of relations between parents and children, especially between fathers and sons. The continuity of the lineage is a continuity of successive generations, and this has two aspects. There is the straightforward, cumulative continuity of descent, epitomized in the notion of patrilineal descent; and there is the dialectical continuity of the filial generation ousting and replacing the paternal generation. In terms of patrilineal descent, father and son are identified with each other and united by common interests; in terms of the sequence of generations, they are not. Indeed, there comes a time in the lives of father and son when they almost seem to be rivals. In a lesser degree this holds also for mothers and daughters. We shall have a good deal to say on this topic in what follows.

The strength and stability of the Tale social system is in part a result of the institutionalized means the culture offers for the reconciliation of conflicting motifs in the focal field of social relations. They enable a balance to be struck between the common interests of successive patrilineal generations and their divergent interests due to the difference of generation, as well as between the centripetal pull of the agnatic line and the centrifugal drive of matrilateral kinship. The principle of reciprocity is of outstanding importance in this context; and the structural mould that makes these reconciliations possible is the ramifying form of the lineage.

[1] Cf. *Dynamics of Clanship*, ch. iii, and my paper 'Descent in the Social Structure of the Tallensi', *Africa*, July 1944.

It is useful to keep these general principles in mind in considering the details to which we must now give our attention. Putting it broadly, the relations of parents and children can be grouped in three general categories: relations of identification; of opposition or contra-identification; and of reciprocity; and the pattern in each individual case is the product of the interaction of these three categories. Our interest will lie chiefly in the structurally significant norms which give coherence and consistency to the multifarious variety of actual behaviour.

The Importance of 'Rearing'

We know that Tallensi regard the possession of offspring, particularly of sons, as the supreme purpose of life. To live long enough to see one's sons' children—to 'reach grandchildren (*paa yaas*)' as the natives say—is a gift surpassing all material wealth. Tallensi believe that it is better to die in poverty and leave children than to die childless but rich. We have seen, also, that they hold it to be the ideal of normal parenthood for physiological and social parenthood to coincide. This is more than a question of conferring social status by descent. From the native standpoint the important thing is that a child's natural parents are the right people to rear it, educate it, and control it.

Tallensi say that *ughug*, bringing up a child, is as vital a part of parenthood as *dɔyam*, bearing or begetting. There is a proverb, 'Rearing is more important than bearing (*Ughug n-gaat dɔyam*)', often quoted when they comment on the devotion of a person to a proxy or foster-parent. This is socially recognized in the obligation to give a 'cow of rearing (*ughug na'ah*)' to a foster-father out of the bride-price cattle received for a foster-daughter by her natural parent or guardian, and for a foster-son, when he returns to his natal home. It is, to be sure, only a moral obligation, but no self-respecting native would evade it. It is a recompense for the troubles the foster-father had to endure in bringing up the child. Tallensi feel strongly that it is not enough to bring a child into the world; one must also bring it up successfully, and that is the hardest part.

In spite of reshufflings due to widows remarrying and the instability of early marriages, the majority of Tale children grow up with their natural parents. A census taken in 1934 showed that of 170 children estimated to be under 16 selected at random in one settlement, nearly 78 per cent. were living with their own parents. Approximately 20 per cent. were in the care of one natural parent and one proxy parent, and only 2 per cent. were orphans cared for by more distant kin.

Tallensi perceive that the social and personal relationships of a particular parent with his or her children are a result very largely of the way the children are brought up. They stress the influence of individual differences in personality in these relationships. There is always a personal bias in the way people interpret the accepted norms and conform to them. Extreme cases illustrate this best. There is the harsh disciplinarian whose sons fret under his control and often take the first opportunity of running away. Sayɔbazaa was said to have been a man of this kind—puritanical, industrious, and inclined to be overstrict with his children. Four of his sons left him to seek work abroad. He made his daughters marry men he chose for them, and when one of them ran away with another man he whipped her and sent her back to her first husband. At the opposite extreme are men like Guna'ab and Yɛanbɔrigya. They are casual and irresponsible. Guna'ab's sons were often pointed out as an example of bad parental influence. They did not farm but tried to earn a living by trading in chickens; they were reputed to be lazy and extravagant, and showed no respect to their father or his brothers—'just like their father', people said.

Nevertheless, it is a fundamental axiom that the ties of rearing do not wipe out the absolutely binding ties of procreation (*dɔẏam*). Whether a person is reared by his own parents or not, whether he is badly or well brought up, nothing can erase the binding ties between parents and children. It is desirable for children to be brought up by their natural parents because then there will be no contradiction between the ties of *dɔẏam* and the adventitious ties of affection created by upbringing.

By Tale custom, if a woman leaves a husband by whom she has had a child and is properly married to another man, the child lives with her during its infancy. When it is five or six years old it can be claimed by its natural father. This is called 'separating (*pɔhɔg*)' it from its mother. Tallensi think it immoral to separate a child from its mother before it is well able to fend for itself. I once heard a group of elders expostulate angrily with a man for taking his two children, aged about 4 and 7, from their mother who had married another man. The elders said the children would not thrive in the care of another woman; their father was acting out of sheer malice. He would be well advised to leave them with their mother for another three or four years and then claim them. Their prophecy was right, for the children pined away and both died within a year. This is an extreme case. But it is a good illustration of a problem that often arises when men claim the custody of their children from an ex-wife. A compromise between the claims of natural parenthood and jural paternity has to be struck which will not endanger the child's life.

Rights and Duties of Parents

We shall have much to say about the rights and duties of parents and children in this book and it will be useful to list here briefly the most important of them. The central fact is the dominance of the father in all social relations; but this is balanced by the personal equality of the parents in the intimate domestic sphere.

A father's first duty to his children is to provide them with food.

He is not bound to provide them with clothes, but a good father buys a loin-cloth for a small son and may give a daughter money to buy a waistband and the materials for her back-flap (*voog*). He should also allow his adult sons the time and opportunity to work a little for themselves and so earn enough to buy clothes. He may allow them to wear some of his clothes, on special occasions.

It is a father's duty to send for and pay someone who has the necessary medicine to treat his child in illness. He must consult a diviner to find out what the illness is due to and must perform the sacrifices prescribed by the diviner to help in the cure. This is one aspect of the father's responsibility for the general welfare of his children. Great importance is attached by the Tallensi to the father's duty of making sacrifices to the ancestors on behalf of his children.

A father is jurally responsible for his sons and unmarried daughters. This is not particularly significant or onerous until children reach adolescence. Little notice is taken of damage caused by a child. But if it is serious—for example, if small boys allow cattle they are herding to damage crops—the injured party can inflict condign punishment on the culprits. He will also protest to their fathers. A father's responsibility for his children is of chief importance in questions of marriage. Thus a father is responsible (within the limits of his lineage status) for his son's bride-price payments and for any breaches of custom, involving conflict with other lineages or clans, that his child commits. In theory a father is also responsible for a son's debts unless they are of a petty kind. If his son gets mixed up in a fight he must appear with him in court. He must take steps to effect a ritual reconciliation with a lineage or clan to which injury has been caused by his son or daughter.

A father's rights are more comprehensive. He 'owns' (*so*) his children. He has the right and the duty of disciplining them. Hence he has the right to inflict corporal punishment on them. In the old days he could, in theory, sell them into slavery if he wished, and a few cases are known of this having occurred. But such an act, like any action that endangers the child's life, is morally reprehensible. He has the right to pawn (*zien taləma*) a son or daughter in return for a loan, and I know of several such cases that occurred before the coming of British rule. This practice has, however, become almost obsolete since it is feared that the Administrative Officers will prosecute anyone found to have pawned a child. A father has the right to dispose of a daughter in marriage as he pleases and to use her bride-price as he pleases. He can do it in such a way as to make her in effect a pawn for a loan which will later be reckoned as an instalment of her bride-price. Men often give a young daughter of 9 or 10 years and upwards to someone from whom they receive loans. The girl is virtually a pawn (*taləma*), and the understanding is that when she is old enough she will marry a member of the lender's family. If, when the time comes, she refuses to do so, her father may marry her off to someone else and will repay the loan out of her bride-price. A father has the right to take his daughter away from a husband whom he objects to.

A father has full disposal over his son's labour and skill. He also has an over-right over any personal property his son may acquire by his private enterprise. He decides whether his son shall live and farm with him or set up his own household.

A father's rights and duties have no legal sanctions in Tale society. They rest on a moral basis being inherent in the form of economic co-operation and property relations, the jural and ritual customs, and the whole complex of mutual dependence in family and lineage. They are never stated as a formal code by the natives, as we have done here, though explicitly recognized by them.

A mother's rights and duties are less precisely defined. Though they have the same basis and sanctions, at bottom, as paternal rights and duties, this is not so overt in native thought or practice. The affective basis of the relations of mother and child has a different tone to that of the relations of father and child. Hence many of a mother's rights are, in practice, dormant. Thus she is entitled to thrash her children, but it would be considered unbecoming and even unnatural in a mother to do so except under extreme provocation.

A mother has the right to the obedience and the respect of her children. She controls her daughter's work in the domestic sphere in tasks such as cooking, fetching water and firewood, and so on, but not in extra-domestic productive activities. For women's work in agriculture (e.g. harvesting) daughters come under their father's orders. A mother is entitled to assistance from her sons in the cultivation of her private vegetable and ground-nut plots. If her son is married, a mother has the right to leave all her domestic chores to be done by her daughter-in-law. A mother has the right to receive small gifts, such as tobacco and guinea-fowls, from her daughter's suitors. She may accept more substantial gifts, such as money and hoes, and in return pledge herself to help the suitor to elope with her daughter, even if this is contrary to her husband's intentions. If her daughter is married by arrangement, the mother is entitled to certain formal gifts of guinea-fowls and grain from the bridegroom's people. She is entitled to ask for help from her daughter's husband in roofing her rooms and in other tasks that are of concern to herself only. She is entitled to gifts of guinea-fowls and yams or sweet potatoes from her daughters' husbands at the time of the Harvest Festival. But most important of all is a mother's right to be supported by her sons from the time that they become capable of farming. Whether she has a husband or not, she will generally live with a son after she gets past the age of child-bearing.

A mother's chief duties are to care for her children in childhood. She must cook for them and see that they are fed. She must nurse them in illness. She is mainly responsible for their training in habits of cleanliness. She also has to teach her daughters housekeeping skills.

This formal summary is interposed here as a means of orientating our analysis. The reality, we shall find, is not so simple.

Classificatory Parents and Own Parents

Tallensi affirm that no one can wholly take the place of a person's own parents. A child may be brought up by its dead father's brother or dead mother's co-wife. Outwardly there is nothing to distinguish the relationship of such a child, during its pre-adolescent years, to its proxy parent from that of a child living with its natural parent. Men or women point with pride and affection to orphans in their custody as 'my children'. They claim to care for them as conscientiously and devotedly as for their own children. But, the natives say, there is always something lacking; and observation shows that the affective ties of proxy parent and child are much weaker than those of natural parent and child. Sometimes, indeed, there is an acknowledged emotional barrier between them.

One can see this in young children like Gundaat, whose story is told in a previous chapter (p. 130). A young child is more restrained, more formal, with a proxy parent than with a natural parent. Boys seem to be less amenable to proxy parents than to own parents, especially as they approach adulthood. When young men who have been abroad, working in Ashanti or the Colony for a period of years, are questioned about their motives for leaving home, the commonest reason they give is the death of a parent. 'My father (*ba*) died, and my junior father (*ba-pit*) took over the house (*die yir*) and so I went away', is the usual formula. One soon discovers that there was always some tension and often friction between the youth and his father's brother. The youth says that his *ba-pit* did not treat him properly; and when one questions his *ba-pit*, he usually says 'the boy did not respect (*nan*) me'. This is a modern development of what is a deeply ingrained feature of Tale social organization. A man will often continue to live and farm with his own father until the latter's death. I know men of 40 and over who are still living with their own fathers. But very rarely does this happen with a father's brother. A dead man's sons break away from the parental home when a father's brother inherits it as soon as they are able to. In such a case there is usually a convergence of different factors of segmentary differentiation in the lineage. The emotional cleavage serves as the catalyst that directs and accelerates the normal processes of splitting along economic and structural lines of cleavage.

This is the negative aspect of the idea that one's natural parents should be one's social parents, as it appears in the classificatory extension of the parent–child relationship. On the positive side it follows from this conception that all those who are socially identifiable with one's parents and play a part in one's upbringing can, and in certain circumstances must, stand to one in the relation of proxy parents. The rule applies most directly to the men and women of the same domestic unit who are identified with one's parents by generation and by social role—to one's father's brothers (*sunzɔp*), including his full and half-brothers and first cousins on his father's side, who are his prospective successors; and to one's mother's co-wives (*nentaas*). If these men and women all belong to the same household they are directly concerned with the production of food, the provision of shelter, and the satisfaction of the other wants of the unit upon which the physical welfare and growth of a child depends. If the men belong to relatively autonomous economic units but to the same domestic unit, they will nevertheless have a common interest in the family patrimony, to the inheritance of which they all have rights, and a common ritual dependence on the immediate ancestors of the nuclear lineage. The women will sometimes help in caring for one another's children; the men will sometimes help one another in farming and always act as a unit in ritual and jural matters under the authority of the most senior of them. And the ritual care of a child is of as much importance as its physical care. A child will not thrive (*maan*) if it is not under the spiritual wing of its patrilineal ancestors, as we have learnt.

Outside the domestic unit the terms *ba* (father) and *ma* (mother) and the distinctive modes of behaviour correlated with them, are not extended beyond the expanded family (i.e. the family cluster built up on the inner lineage) in normal circumstances. The only exception is in the case of a uterine kinsman or kinswoman of a parent, who is identified with the foundress of the uterine line and is therefore described as a 'father' or 'mother' irrespective of genealogical distance.[1]

Within the clan or maximal lineage it is a cardinal rule that generation differences are not recognized beyond the limits of the inner lineage. 'Begetting does not cross the (inner) lineage—*dɔyam pu yakət dug la*' is the Tale maxim. This is correlated with the structural relations of the inner lineage to lineage segments of higher order. The inner lineage is likely to be the widest segment with a common interest in patrimonial land. In relation to the clan or the maximal lineage it is usually the smallest recognized corporate segment, whose members are significant for the clan only as members of the segment. As will be remembered, it is also the unit within which sexual relations with a co-member's wife are definitely sinful. In short, the inner lineage (and the family cluster which is its residential and familial correlate) marks the limit beyond which a person takes part in corporate activities not in his own right and in his personal capacity but as a member of the

---

[1] Kinship terms without inverted commas stand for the primary meaning of the terms, e.g. (natural) father; those between inverted commas stand for the extended or derived meaning of the term, e.g. (classificatory) 'father'.

segment. Clansmen beyond these limits are no longer concerned with the rearing of a child. They are not directly involved in either the economic or the educational or the ritual responsibility for its passage through life. Hence they all fall into the broad category of clan kin (*yidɛm*) or clan brethren (*mabiis*) irrespective of age or generation, though individuals among them might be addressed by specific kinship terms, in certain situations, as an honorific gesture. Tallensi feel that a mother's brother (*ahɔb*) is a nearer kinsman than a contemporary of one's father of another inner lineage of the same clan; and while it is not uncommon for an orphan to go and live with his *ahɔb*, it is very rare for an orphan to join the household of a clansman of a different inner lineage.

Tale jural and ritual institutions show, and intelligent informants perceive quite clearly, that the emotional elements in the relationship of parent and child are distinct from the jural and moral elements. There are both pragmatic and ritual sanctions for the latter but not for the former. Indeed the emotional elements sometimes serve as a sanction or as a rationalization of conduct in the relations of parents and children. With natural parents the emotional elements and the jural and moral elements of the relationship are completely interfused. With proxy parents the former yield precedence to the latter, and it is often easier to study the jural and moral elements of the relationship with proxy parents than with own parents. The widest range within which the relationship of successive generations is recognized is principally distinguished by ritual and ceremonial customs. We thus get a series beginning with people who will describe each other, if questioned, as 'my own father (mother) (*m-mɛŋ ba (ma)*)' and 'my own child (*m-mɛŋ bii*)', or by some equivalent phrase; stretching to those who refer to each other as *ba-pit* or *ma-pit*, younger father or mother (or if it is a father's older brother or mother's older co-wife, *ba-bier* and *ma-bier*), and *bier*[1] *bii*—child of older sibling of the same sex (or *pit bii*—child of younger sibling of the same sex); and ending with people who say of their classificatory parent or child 'I only call him father (mother, child) (*mbuon u la mba (ma, bii)*)'. There is always a physical difference of generation between own parents and children, generally such a difference between close proxy parents and their siblings' or co-wives' children, but quite often little or no difference of age between classificatory parent and child at the limit of the range. It is quite a common thing to meet

---

[1] *Bier* is the common term for senior by age or generation; but it is a curious point that the usage quoted above is not exclusive. Tallensi also describe a father's older brother as *ba-kpeem* (elder father), and a mother's older co-wife as *ma-kpeem*. But this form is more commonly used to refer to a grandparent. The context makes it clear whether the reference is to a proxy parent or a grandparent. The use of *kpeem* instead of *bier* may be a borrowing from the Gɔris and Namnam, whose dialects are closer to Mole than to Dagbane and who have the dialect variants *kɛma* and *yɛbɔga* for senior and junior.

children of about the same age playing together who are classificatory parent and child. A 9- or 10-year-old will explain that he calls his companion 'father' or 'child' because 'my father begot (*dɔya*)—or was begotten by—his father and calls him child—or father', using the concept *dɔy* in its generalized sense of a recognized relationship of belonging to successive generations.

The decisive tests are in terms of the jural and ritual relations in which kinship comes into action, and not in terms of a count of generations. Thus paternal authority is an aspect of the organization of productive co-operation in the household; it accompanies defined property rights, and entails jural responsibilities in matters like marriages and deaths as well as ritual duties to the ancestors. These are the things that make up a father's social role. Postponing further consideration of this for the present, we may note that, broadly speaking, three zones can be discerned within the limits of the inner lineage. First, that of Ego's natural parents, who exercise the full social roles of parents; second, that of Ego's proxy parents, seldom more distantly related to the natural father than agnatic second cousins (and their wives), and distinguished by the fact that they share and may take over the social roles of the natural parents; and third, that of Ego's classificatory parents, who are most unlikely (for no rigid line of demarcation can be laid down) to take on the true parents' social roles. The authority and responsibility of a classificatory father is of a general nature, and a man is subject to it only in virtue of his lineage membership.

As we shall find later, these principles hold not only for the classificatory extension of parent–child relationships but also for siblings and matrilateral kin. The regulating mechanism is the lineage structure.

We are defining the gradations that can be observed in the tone and emphasis of the parent–child relationship in the broadest terms. We are speaking of norms; and as we have previously remarked, the norms do not always emerge as simply as this in the actual relations of parents and children. They are subject to the distorting influence of many social and personal factors in this as in other departments of Tale life. Da'amo'o, who ran away from home as a boy when his mother died, must have had very little love for his old father, who was, by all accounts, a hard, arrogant, and demanding martinet. Baŋ, on the other hand, who lost his own father in early childhood and grew up under the care of a distant lineage-brother of his father, Tɛndaan Gieŋ, whom his widowed mother married, was deeply attached to the latter.

As in most primitive societies, there are always a number of people whom a Talǝŋ, child or adult, will refer to as his 'father' or 'mother', or 'child', at any given time. But, as has already been suggested, a natural parent or own child is clearly distinguished from others to whom one stands in the same social relationship. It is enough to visit a large domestic family for half an hour, at a time when the whole family is at home, to see this, especially where young children are concerned. With adults the discrimination is not so obvious in the ordinary daily routine as with children. I have seen a babe of six months left in the care of its mother's co-wife, whimper and strain eagerly towards its mother when it saw her arrive at the homestead with a load of firewood in the company of two other women of the household. An older child will run to its own mother for protection, if it is frightened, clutching her knees and thrusting its face between her thighs. A small boy of 3 to 6 years of age will try to follow his own father about wherever he can; and a little girl of this age hangs around her own mother, as she gets on with the household tasks, in a way that would be impossible with her mother's co-wife. On the other side, one can easily notice the difference between the sympathy and often grief of a woman over the illness or death of a co-wife's child and the utter prostration into which a mother falls if such a misfortune strikes her own child. Similarly, a man shows deep concern over the sickness or death of his brother's child. He will abandon a visit he has planned to a relative, give up work for the day, shelve any plans he may have made; for next to a death, nothing is so upsetting to a Tale household as the illness of a child. But this is as nothing compared with his grief over the death, or his distress at the illness of his own child.

This affective discrimination of own parents and own children is the psychological counterpart of the differentiation of descent lines within the lineage and of segments within the family. Sentiment and structural relationships go hand in hand and the ritual superstructure of Tale society mirrors both. This consistency of the total scheme of social relationships means that we can make inferences about aspects of the relationship between parents and children that are not expressed in their ordinary intercourse, from ritual ideas and practices and from the changing pattern of co-operation and association between them. The fact that a man can only sacrifice directly to the spirits of his own parents and to antecedent ancestors through his own parents, and not to or through the spirits of proxy parents, is as important a factor in the unique bond of parent and child as the fact that a child is usually brought up by his own parents.

Structural arrangements and ritual ideas show that, in spite of the precise discrimination of own parents and own children, proxy and classificatory parents do have a parental role even during the lifetime of own parents. They take pride in these children, and speak of them as 'my children'. Everyone who is 'father' or 'mother' to a person must be treated with the respect due to a parent and has some degree of authority over him or her. I recall one day seeing Sinkawol, a young man of about 25, instructing Kyekambɛ, a lively boy of about 12, in a task connected with house-building. They both belonged to the inner lineage of which Nyaaŋzum of Kpata'ar was the head. This lineage presents a remarkable jumble of ages and generations owing to the longevity and protracted fertility of its founder, Kuŋkɔŋki. Because a period of about fifty years elapsed between the birth of Kuŋkɔŋki's first son and the birth of his youngest son, the latter's children are 'fathers' to his older brothers' children some of whom are three or four times their age. That is how Sinkawol came to be the classificatory 'son' of Kyekambɛ. Now and then Sinkawol had to speak sharply to his pupil. I asked if he would hit the boy if he did not obey his instructions. 'Oh no', replied Sinkawol gravely, 'I cannot strike him. He begot me. He is my father. If he were my brother or my son I wouldn't hesitate to clout him.' Kyekambɛ could not exercise authority over Sinkawol owing to his social immaturity and inexperience. But he would take precedence of Sinkawol in matters of inheritance, and when he grew up would be entitled to precede Sinkawol in rights of succession to ritual office, if he wished to.

Proxy and classificatory parents also feel a responsibility for the welfare of their 'brothers'' children. Thus if two brothers have separate households, they are not obliged to assist each other with food in times of shortage; and pride restrains a man from asking for help from a brother who is economically independent of him. I have seen men grow wan with hunger, through living for days on end on nothing but wild herbs; but they would never ask for assistance from their better-off brothers. It is up to the latter to offer a gift of grain voluntarily. And when such a gift is given (it is usually only 3 or 4 lb. of grain, enough for a couple of meals) it is offered as a gift for the children and their mothers. The giver will send a calabashful of grain to his brother's wife, with a message that it is for the children. As the natives always say, 'Your brother's children are your children. You cannot see them growing thin with hunger and let them starve.' A woman, too, will sometimes give food to the children of a co-wife of the same joint family, if the two women get on well together.

A proxy parent's authority over his or her classificatory children during their own parent's life cannot be exactly defined. It depends on the situation in which authority is exercised, on the personalities and economic relationships of the people concerned, and especially on the genealogical closeness of own parent and proxy parent. Ɔmara and Saandi are agnatic first cousins (brothers, in native terms) occupying adjoining semi-detached homesteads. They do not farm together. Saandi has no direct responsibility for feeding Ɔmara's children or for educating them. He is, however, directly interested in their welfare and upbringing. For as the head of the nuclear lineage, he must be consulted, and will have an influential, though not the decisive voice in all matters of a jural or ritual kind affecting Ɔmara's children—such matters, for instance, as the marriage of a son or daughter, or the rites of placing a child under the ritual guardianship of an ancestor. If he sees any of Ɔmara's children misbehaving he can stop them and punish them if necessary. But ordinarily, though he can scold Ɔmara's children, he would cause grave offence to Ɔmara if he were to strike them. When, to quote a case that occurred in a similar structural setting, Pumaan's son threw a stone at Zaŋ's (Pumaan's younger brother's) wife, Zaŋ shouted anathemas at the boy and complained to the neighbours but dared not whip him; that was Pumaan's prerogative. For Zaŋ and Pumaan have separate households and are both sticklers for their rights. By contrast, Boyazie, who lives and farms with his older brother and gets on extremely well with him, can command obedience from and can discipline the latter's children by corporal punishment if need be. But even in such a case a man might hesitate to strike his brother's children if he and his brother were not on terms of the greatest mutual trust. If Saandi asks his brother's son to do an errand or a job for him the boy will usually obey, but he cannot be compelled to do so, as he can by his own father. Co-wives, as we know, are particularly cautious in dealing with one another's children.

There is, however, at any given time, only one man who has full paternal authority over a person, child or adult. In the first instance it is the man who begot him or her; and if this man dies, it is the man who takes on his social role, that is his distinctive rights and duties, by inheritance. The critical rights and duties are those connected with the land and other patrimonial property which the child's father owned or was heir to, and those connected with the cult of the child's father's father. In practice this means the head of the household to which the child belongs, who is also the person who sacrifices to the child's grandfather's spirit; and this limits the range to the child's father's brothers by the same father.

During a child's minority a father's agnatic cousin (brother in native terms) may act *in loco parentis* if the father's nearer male agnates are lacking; but it is a position of trusteeship rather than of full paternal authority. The son will set up an independent household as soon as he is able to farm for himself. He will then take possession of any land which his father acquired by his own efforts and will become the effective owner of, for example, bride-price cattle obtained for his own sister, though he cannot dispose of them without the formal consent of the head of the nuclear lineage. In relation to an adult, a father's cousin (or remoter classificatory 'brother' of the same inner lineage) retains only the ritual and jural attributes of a father; and this chiefly in virtue of being head of the inner or nuclear lineage to which the person belongs. Important as these attributes are, they represent a less direct and personal authority than that of one's own or one's proxy father.

We shall see later that the relations between grandchildren (*yaaŋ*, pl. *yaas*) and grandparents (*yaab-doog* or *ba-kpeem*, masc. *yaab-pɔk* or *ma-kpeem*, fem.) are a foil to those of parents and children. It is convenient here to state the range within which grandparents are acknowledged. On both the mother's side and the father's side grandparents are primarily one's own parent's own parents. The terms are extended to own grandparents' siblings (in particular to a grandfather's brothers) and their wives, but rarely beyond that limit, and never, in my experience, beyond a grandfather's agnatic cousin. This is correlated with the cycle of development of the joint family. By the time a man has grandchildren he is not likely to be still sharing a homestead with his brother, let alone cousin, and his classificatory siblings will have only a formal interest in his grandchildren.

The diagram on p. 148 sums up this discussion of the range of parenthood acknowledged by the Tallensi.

The Significance of 'Having no Father alive'

Clearly the formula 'Begetting does not cross the (inner) lineage' covers a complicated tissue of social relationships. Another aspect of it appears in the significance Tallensi attach to whether or not one's father is alive.

This is a matter of considerable practical importance, more particularly for men, but also for women. A person's status in his clan, and in every segment of it to which he belongs, depends largely on whether 'his father is alive (*u ba bɛ*)' or not (*u ba ka*). It is correlated with the distribution of jural and ritual authority and responsibility in the lineage. During his own father's lifetime a person's status is submerged in that of his father for jural and ritual purposes. He comes directly under his father's authority, as we shall see presently. He attains his first degree of independence only on the death of his own father. This is shown to some extent in every department of his life, but most significantly in the sphere of ritual. A man cannot make sacrifices to his patrilineal ancestors in his own right while his own father is alive. His father does this on his behalf. It is only when his father dies that a man can sacrifice directly to his ancestors; for such sacrifices can only be offered through the medium of his father's spirit.

This marks a very important stage in a man's social maturation, whatever his chronological age may be. Henceforth the responsibility for keeping the goodwill of his ancestors rests directly on his own shoulders. It will be he himself, for instance, not his father, who decides whether a sacrifice demanded by such-and-such an ancestor should be offered at once or postponed. And with this first stage of ritual responsibility usually goes some degree of autonomy in jural and economic matters, as we shall see presently. Nevertheless, no man attains full autonomy within the limits of the lineage system until he is altogether 'fatherless'. While he has a proxy or classificatory father alive he is still to some extent under paternal authority. It is worth

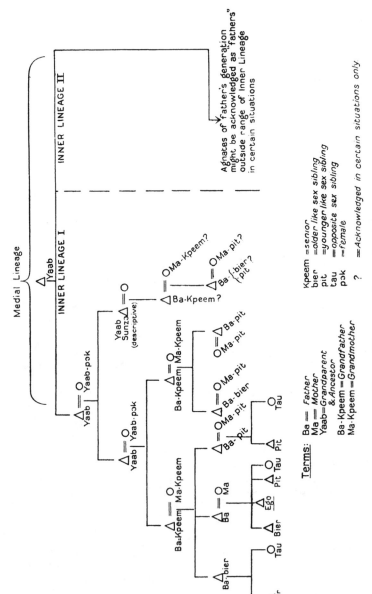

Fig. 4. The range of parenthood.

considering this situation more closely as it will give us a further insight into the working of the classificatory principle.

The simplest and clearest index to it is in certain observances at the funeral of any man of one's father's generation. A man whose 'father' is alive may not perform the principal rites such as the killing of the goat or sheep from which the loin-cover for the corpse will be cut, or the rites of 'entering the *zɔŋ*'; and he may not eat the ceremonial food associated with or consumed in these rites. To infringe these taboos is not only an insult to one's 'father' but a sin, since it is equivalent to wishing him dead. There are men whose proxy or classificatory fathers are alive who know more about ritual matters than their seniors. I have seen such men stand by and direct others in the performance of funeral rites which they themselves are forbidden to carry out. I have seen them raging with exasperation at the incompetence of the old men or women who were carrying out the rites; but they would have been shocked at the suggestion that it would save temper and trouble if they performed the rites themselves.

Again, the application of the notion varies relatively to the dimensions of the lineage involved in a particular situation and the whole constellation of classificatory kinship recognized within it. At one extreme stand matters that concern only the members of the nuclear lineage. That would be the case, for example, if the nuclear lineage assembled to make a sacrifice to its immediate founding ancestor. Thus, to take a lineage we have met in an earlier chapter, if Katiŋoo biis meet to sacrifice to Katiŋoo, only his grandsons and great-grandsons are concerned (see genealogy on p. 68). In such a situation the two patri-segments of Katiŋoo biis (Duun biis and Baa biis) are each formally recognized as a separate unit and the sacrificial meat is divided equally between them. If Ɔmara were dead, the share due to his patri-segment would fall to his sons; and they would, in this context, say that they have no father. They are, in fact, through the eldest son, taking the place of their father in intra-lineage relations; their status is no longer submerged in that of their father. They are thinking in terms of the contraposition of the two component patri-segments of the lineage. Within the limits of the nuclear lineage, the term 'father' (*ba*) means own father and a man whose own father is dead has no father. He speaks of his proxy-fathers (father's brothers and cousins) as his *ba-pirib*, junior fathers, or *ba-biernam*, senior fathers.

The higher the segmentary order of the lineage involved, the wider is the application of this notion. If the situation involves the inner lineage, then the nuclear lineage emerges as the smallest corporate unit recognized. This happens in sacrifices to the founding ancestor of the inner lineage or in certain funeral customs where food contributions are made by the head of the nuclear lineage on behalf of the whole unit. In this case a man whose own father is dead but whose father's brother or father's father's brother's son is still alive would not claim to be fatherless. For, in matters where the nuclear lineage acts as a unit in relation to other like units, he has no independent status. The unit is under the authority of a 'father' and a 'son's' status is submerged in the 'father's'. Similarly, if the lineage involved is a medial lineage, the smallest sub-segments recognized will be its component inner lineages. Then a man will only claim to be fatherless if he has no 'father' alive within the inner lineage to which he belongs. Beyond this range—for example where the unit of corporate action is a maximal lineage in which the smallest sub-segments recognized are the medial lineages—the question usually does not arise. At this range generation differences no longer count.

This is a schematic formulation, for there is always a margin of flexibility depending both on the internal structure of the unit concerned and on such adventitious factors as the personal relations of the men who are involved and the character of the situation. Continuity of person-to-person relationships in the routine affairs of the lineage and family help to keep appropriate kinship distances alive. A describes B as his 'father' because he knows that his natural father C during his lifetime always spoke of B as his 'brother'. But human memory is fallible, and in doubtful cases Tallensi take the line of greatest personal advantage consonant with existing structural arrangements.

We shall understand it better if we consider a few examples of how the notion of being fatherless influences behaviour in practice. At Soog one of the component maximal lineages of the clan comprises two major segments which function as medial lineages in corporate affairs. Each of these segments is represented by its head at ceremonies at the External *Bɔyar* of Soog. When Sɛbəg, the head of one of these segments, died, the most senior remaining member of the unit was his 18-year-old son, Bɔyabil, who therefore succeeded to the headship of the segment. Shortly after Sɛbəg's death an important sacrifice was performed at the External *Bɔyar*. The beer used for the preliminary libations was being shared among the elders and a calabashful was passed to Bɔyabil. The youth shook his head in refusal. 'No, drink,' said one of the elders, 'it is a taboo. You are an elder now, not a child.' Up till then Bɔyabil had been prohibited from drinking this beer, as no one who has a father alive may drink of it.

Another incident on this same occasion was equally revealing. Certain of the fowls slaughtered in sacrifices to an External *Bɔyar* are known as 'tabooed fowls (*nɔkiha*)'. They may not be touched, let alone eaten, by anyone who has a father alive. A man inadvertently handed one of these birds to Diŋkaha's son. Noticing this, Diŋkaha burst into a tirade against the man. 'Do you wish to cause my death or my son's death?' he cried.

In both these instances to be fatherless meant to have no natural

THE FRAMEWORK OF THE LINEAGE

father or proxy father alive. But let us take a more complicated as well as more commonplace case.

Ziŋgan biis form an inner lineage, one of the five inner lineages that together constitute the medial lineage of Bɔyayiedət yiri of Tɔŋ-Guŋ. The genealogy overleaf shows the agnatic relationships of the members of Ziŋgan biis we are concerned with here.

The head of the whole inner lineage is Kutɔbis. He is also the head of one major segment of the lineage, Pa'anbɔbis biis; the head of the other major segment, Zayahna'am biis, is Ɔndieso. Within his own segment of Ziŋgan biis Ɔndieso is master. He farms for himself; he sacrifices directly to his own father's and ancestors' spirits; he owns his sisters' bride-price cattle and can dispose of them as he pleases and is responsible for finding the bride-price for his own wives or his sons' wives. In these matters that concern his nuclear lineage primarily he does not acknowledge Kutɔbis as his 'father'. He looks upon Kutɔbis as only the head of the inner lineage. As such, he must be formally consulted by Ɔndieso in matters that involve jural or ritual relationships with other lineages or clans, such as arise through marriage. Thus, if Ɔndieso's daughter is sought in marriage, it is Kutɔbis who receives the emissary with the placation gifts from the bridegroom and keeps the fowl he brings, thus signifying his formal assent and regularizing the marriage. Nevertheless, it is a purely nominal authority that Kutɔbis exercises. The real decisions rest with Ɔndieso. Again, if Ɔndieso seduces the wife of, say, a Gbeog man, the injured man's lineage head will protest to Kutɔbis and negotiations for the reconciliation rites will be carried out by the latter. He will accept nominal responsibility for Ɔndieso in this matter and will take charge of the arrangements that concern Ziŋgan biis in the reconciliation rites. But the animals required for the rites must be supplied by Ɔndieso himself. To give a third example, Kutɔbis will be summoned at once if there is a death in Ɔndieso's family and will preside over the mortuary and funeral ceremonies. But, again, the animals and foodstuffs that have to be provided by the 'owner of the funeral'—the person actually responsible for its performance—must be supplied by Ɔndieso. Kutɔbis has, in fact, no power directly to order Ɔndieso to do anything; he has no claims, as of right, on Ɔndieso's services or material help; he has no responsibility for Ɔndieso's welfare, apart from the general moral responsibility he has for the welfare of the whole lineage. As the natives say, he 'owns' Ɔndieso 'with the mouth only (*nuoni maa*)'. All this is implied when Ɔndieso says: 'If it is a question of the (inner) lineage only, I have no father (*la a dug pooni maa, nka ba*).' Kutɔbis's relations with him arise from the fact that Kutɔbis is *dug kpeem*, head of the inner lineage, custodian of the founding ancestor's *bɔyar* and of the lineage *zanɔr*. If he were Ɔndieso's classificatory 'brother' or 'grandfather', it would make no difference to their relations. The symbolic expression

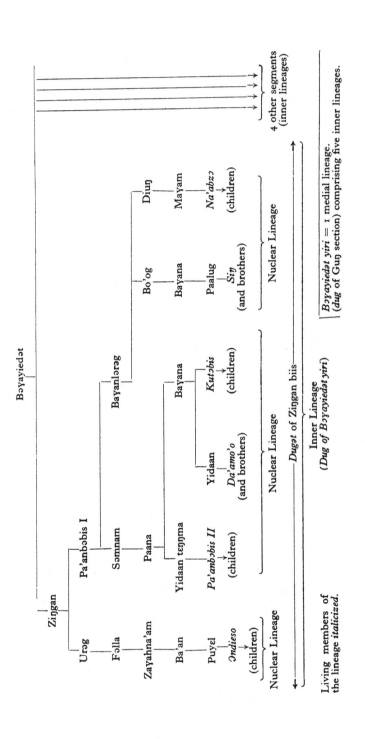

THE FRAMEWORK OF THE LINEAGE

of this is clearest in funeral customs. If Paanbɔbis II, Kutɔbis's brother, were to die, Ɔndieso would take part in all the rites prohibited to men whose fathers are still alive. He would not refrain out of respect for Kutɔbis.

But in matters which involve Ziŋgan biis as a segment of Bɔyayiedət yiri, Ɔndieso acknowledges Kutɔbis as his 'father'. Thus when Bontuya, who belonged to one of the other four inner lineages of Bɔyayiedət biis, died, Ɔndieso went to the funeral as one of the representatives of Ziŋgan biis. He then refused to take part in the rites tabooed to men who have fathers alive, saying that if he did it would be an insult to Kutɔbis.

Ziŋgan biis also appear as a unit in reckoning prohibited degrees of kinship for purposes of marriage. As we have mentioned before, the inner lineage is the widest corporate group that is a jural unit in marriage. A distant 'sister's son' (*ahaŋ*) of Kutɔbis would not be allowed to marry a daughter of Ɔndieso. And this criterion applies also to the inheritance of widows. If Kutɔbis were to die, Ɔndieso could not seek any of his widows in marriage, because they are his classificatory 'mothers'. On the other hand, he could do so if Kutɔbis were his classificatory 'brother' or 'grandfather'. He can court the widow of any member of any of the four other inner lineages of Bɔyayiedət yiri since generation differences are not recognized beyond the boundaries of Ziŋgan yiri.

In spite of the ambiguities lurking in his relationship to Kutɔbis, the predominant affective tone it has for Ɔndieso is that he is a 'son' and will remain a 'child' (*bii*) in public affairs that involve the whole clan as long as Kutɔbis or any of his brothers is alive. Until they are dead there will always be a living if shadowy representative of paternal authority standing between Ɔndieso and his remote ancestors—and that means between him and the world at large, as it impinges on him through the corporate activities of the whole clan. This influences Ɔndieso's attitude to life considerably. He feels that he has not yet reached full social maturity, though he is much more intelligent and better informed than many of the clan elders. One sees and feels this vividly enough in one's intercourse with the natives, but it is not easy to pin down. It came out, for instance, in Ɔndieso's behaviour whenever he accompanied me to the Chief's court. He always took a back seat then, as befits a 'youngster'. It came out also in his attitude to Kutɔbis whom he despised for his uncouth ways and all-round incompetence, but yet deferred to with the modicum of respect that is correct in one's relations with a 'father'.

A man who can say 'I no longer have any fathers' associates himself with the elders, the *kpɛm*, in thought and action even if he is younger in years than some men whom he calls 'sons'. He thinks of himself as a 'father', in particular in relation to the ancestors, as one who has the duty of watching over the welfare of others. It is most marked among the chiefs appointed since the coming of the white man. Unlike their predecessors they were mostly young men when they were appointed, some of them still having their natural fathers alive. But 'a chief', the Tallensi say, 'is the father of his clan. No one can claim fatherhood over a chief' (sɔ pu dɔya na'ab la—literally, no one has begotten a chief). Whatever their individual shortcomings, Tale chiefs have one thing in common, and that is a strong sense of responsibility for the welfare of their own clans.

As usual, this conception has a religious precipitate. It emerges in the status of a man's *Yin* shrine.[1] A man's *Yin* shrine is not fully established until it is ritually 'built' (*me*). Before that it is only a temporary and incomplete entity—even though it has been receiving sacrifices for perhaps twenty years. And usually it is not until a man belongs to the generation of fathers in his inner or medial lineage—that is, attains the status of being 'fatherless' in most social and ritual situations—that he 'builds' his *Yin*. Thus it often happens that a man dies before his *Yin* is built and his son has to carry out this rite. This applies also to the last stage in the development of a man's *Yin*, its removal to the *zanɔne*, the open space before the gateway. His father's *Yin* shrine is taken indoors and his is put in its place. This is a sign that he has reached the climax of his life. He is not only fatherless, but is perhaps the last of the oldest generation of the inner lineage. He has 'built a house (*me yiri*)', that is, has sons and grandsons to carry on the line and can spend what is left to him of his old age in honoured ease.

It must not be thought from the foregoing that Tallensi never extend the term 'father' outside the inner lineage. They speak of all men in the clan or the maximal lineage who belong to the oldest age groups as 'fathers'—and by analogy address any old woman married into the clan as 'mother' and any older clansman as 'older brother'. But these are all courtesy titles. A man will always treat an old man of a different inner lineage to whom he gives the courtesy title of 'father' with respect; but he does not owe him any filial duties or come under his authority directly.

To round off this picture, let us return again to Ziŋgan biis for a moment and consider the case of Da'amo'o (aged about 35). He is Kutɔbis's late older full brother's (*bier-soog*) son. He occupies the same homestead as Kutɔbis, but has his own gateway and is economically independent of Kutɔbis. Kutɔbis is his proxy father. In no circumstances can Da'amo'o claim to be 'fatherless'. He is not fond of Kutɔbis; but he cannot escape from his jural and ritual authority. Kutɔbis succeeded to his late brother's social role in full; hence Da'amo'o is his 'child' in all ritual and jural respects. This comes out in Da'amo'o's attitude to life. When a man in this position is asked about affairs that concern the clan, or even his inner lineage as a whole, he will often reply 'I am a child, I do not know. You must ask my older brothers and my

[1] Cf. p. 227 below.

fathers.' Practically the only sphere in which Da'amo'o can act without first obtaining Kutɔbis's assent is in economic matters that concern his own household alone. He cannot even sacrifice to his own father's spirit without first telling Kutɔbis, though responsibility for making the sacrifice is his and his only.

Da'amo'o's and Ɔndieso's wives had babies about the same time. Ɔndieso went off by himself to consult a diviner in order to find out which of his ancestors was to be the child's spirit guardian; Da'amo'o went with Kutɔbis, who consulted for him. In 1936 Da'amo'o collected a part of his sister's bride-price, consisting of a bull and £2. 10s. He showed it to Kutɔbis, who is the formal 'owner' of income of this sort, and with the latter's permission sent the bull off to his own father-in-law in part payment of his wife's bride-price. He put away the money. But about this time a rash action of Kutɔbis's eldest son brought a long-standing dispute between Ziŋgan biis and another inner lineage of Bɔyayiedɔt yiri to a head. In order to settle it, Kutɔbis, acting on behalf of the inner lineage, had to pay 30s. to the head of the other inner lineage. And as the original dispute and its recrudescence were both occasioned by members of Kutɔbis's nuclear lineage (Pa'ana biis) he had to 'find the money'. He obtained the money from Da'amo'o. Complaining about this to me, Da'amo'o said: 'It is not a debt—Kutɔbis is my father. I cannot ever demand my money from him. But one day my father-in-law will come for another cow for his daughter's bride-price. Then I will go to Kutɔbis and if he has a cow and wants to behave decently he will give it to my father-in-law.' Had Kutɔbis borrowed the money from Ɔndieso it would not have been a claimable debt either; but Ɔndieso would not have given him the money without a definite promise to repay it and without some indication of how Kutɔbis expected to be able to find the money to repay him. These differences between Ɔndieso's relationship with Kutɔbis and Da'amo'o's will be symbolically expressed in their different duties at Kutɔbis's funeral. Ɔndieso will undergo none of the rites of mourning and purification that orphans are subjected to, Da'amo'o is bound to go through all of them.

Our discussion of what it means to a Talǝŋ to have a father alive or not arose from a consideration of the formula 'Kinship does not cross the (inner) lineage'. For the sake of simplicity we have here spoken of lineages as if they were fixed units of structure instead of slowly changing configurations of social relations. In actuality the slowly changing equilibrium of intra-lineage and inter-lineage relations makes itself felt all the time. What is to-day a relatively clearly defined inner lineage will, in ten years' time, perhaps, be in process of splitting up into two inner lineages. Already there are signs of it in the relations of the two segments of Ziŋgan biis and in another generation it may well be that classificatory kinship will cease to be acknowledged between them.

This margin of elasticity in the range of classificatory kinship within the lineage often leads to conflict and it is in these conflicts that the process of fission is often completed. They arise chiefly in connexion with the inheritance of widows and the succession to the lineage *bɔyar* (that is, to the headship of the lineage)—the two situations in which consistency between the corporate unity of the inner lineage and the recognition of generation differences is most severely tested. What happens is that the heads of what were previously regarded as the component segments of an inner lineage advance contradictory claims to the custody of the lineage *bɔyar*. One may claim it on the grounds of seniority of generation—being the classificatory father of the other— while his opponent refuses to admit this and claims seniority by age. It is a conflict between 'seniority of begetting (*dɔyam kpɛmɔt*)' (i.e. by generation) and 'seniority of predestiny' or, as we might say, chance (*Naa-Yin kpɛmɔt*) (i.e. by age). The long-drawn-out quarrel between Yinyɛla and the other elders of Tɔŋ-Puhug turned on a point of this kind. Yinyɛla claimed to be a generation superior to the heads of all the other segments of Lɛbhtiis yiri,[1] but the other elders would not admit the validity of this claim. The genealogical evidence supported Yinyɛla, and the precedents he quoted from the days of his father and grandfather were probably accurate. But that was not the question; the relations of the segments of Lɛbhtiis yiri had changed in the last two generations and, as the elders put it, 'begetting has died out (*dɔyam kpiya*)'.

An earlier stage in the fading out of classificatory kinship appeared in the controversy over Baroog's widows. Nindɔyat's eldest son was discovered to be secretly courting one of the women and Baroog's father immediately raised an outcry. Nindɔyat, he protested, was his 'son' and Baroog's 'brother', hence Nindɔyat's son would be committing incest if he married Baroog's widow, his classificatory mother. But Nindɔyat stood by his son, arguing that they were no longer members of a single inner lineage but of two separate inner lineages. 'We are each our own *dug* (*ti a ti dug ti dug*),' he said. The weight of public opinion in the clan was against him, however, and the woman in the case took fright. But a split in the lineage is inevitable, though it may take a generation to complete.

Change of Status Due to Death of 'Father' Shown in Property Relations

There is more to be said about the social consequences of having or not having a father alive, and we shall revert to the subject later from another point of view. What is so far clear is that a man's social status, particularly in jural and ritual matters, but also in economic affairs, advances step by step with the dying off of his fathers. Strictly speaking, he is not altogether autonomous until he has no more fathers within the range of the inner lineage, but in practice he is free of effective

[1] Cf. *Dynamics of Clanship*, p. 196.

paternal control when he has no more fathers in the nuclear lineage. The death of his own father marks the beginning of what might be called this process of emancipation, though it is not overtly felt to be that by the natives. As previous references have shown, this is usually the thin end of the wedge that in due course splits the joint family economically and eventually gives the sons jural and ritual independence. It is not too much to say that the cycle of fission and reintegration in the joint family, with its co-ordinate processes of ramification in the lineage, is kept in motion by the deaths of fathers. That is one reason why the relations of successive generations are most conspicuously symbolized in funeral rites and ceremonies.

Underlying all changes in status due to the extinction of particular social relationships are changes in property relations which include, for the Tallensi, both rights over people and rights over material objects and economic resources. These rights pass from one generation to the next by inheritance or succession. There are rights over farm-land, the basic capital resource of the natives, and over homesteads; rights of disposal over livestock and other valuables, as well as over services and social bonds that have been created in exchange for valuables; rights over the working power and allegiance of men, women, and children; and last but not least, rights to the custody of ancestor shrines and other religious objects and to the politico-ritual offices that go with some of them.

All these property relations are tied directly to the lineage structure; they are graded and interlocked with one another in conformity with that structure. They fall into two major categories: patrimonial rights and property, for which the Tallensi have a specific term, *faar*; and individual rights and property, for which there is no specific term. Looking at it through native eyes, in terms of the continuity of the lineage and the march of the generations, we can see why this is so. *Faar* belongs to the lineage—it may be only the nuclear lineage or it may be the maximal lineage. All the members of the lineage are potential heirs to it. But the man who is in possession at a given time has complete freedom in using it—though not in disposing of it. On the other hand, individually acquired property and rights belong to the individual. A 'fatherless' man is free to use, dispose of, or destroy his individually acquired property—be it a piece of land, an animal, a garment, money, or whatnot—as he wishes. A man subject to some degree of paternal authority is in theory obliged to be ruled by his 'father' in the use and disposal of his individual property, though in practice he has a very large measure of freedom in this matter. But the crucial point is this. Individual property becomes patrimonial property when, as inevitably happens on the death of the original owner, it is inherited. In this way it comes about that every segment of a lineage tends to have its own transmissible *faar*.

The general rules governing inheritance and succession are simple. Because they are so closely tied up with the lineage structure and come under the strongest sanctions of the ancestor cult, they are seldom, to my knowledge, deliberately violated. But they leave room for adjustments and compromises, to some extent also for arbitrary action bordering on injustice, that seem, on the surface, to contradict them. Inheritance and succession follow the lineage and go from fathers to sons in order of seniority by generation or by age.[1] Within the inner lineage, that is, within the range in which classificatory kinship is recognized, seniority by generation (*dɔyam kpɛmɔt*) takes precedence over seniority by age (*Naa-Yin kpɛmɔt*), beyond that range it is entirely a matter of seniority by age. This is what the maxim 'Kinship does not cross the (inner) lineage' implies. Since a 'son' cannot take precedence over a 'father' in the inner lineage, it follows that a man's next senior 'brother' inherits before his oldest 'son'. But Tallensi say 'A father's property is heritable; a brother's property is not (*Ba bon n-vaagɔt; mabii bon pu vaagɔra*)'. A 'brother' inherits from a 'brother' only what came to the latter from their 'father' (plus what has accrued to it by natural increase or improvement), not what the latter acquired by his own effort. Theoretically all 'brothers' are coheirs and the senior is merely the manager with first pick of the inherited property. It is this which leads to apparent anomalies. Thus when Kurug died his oldest brother Sawɔŋba inherited the *faar* land. But he preferred to stay on in his homestead at Gbambee rather than move back to the lineage *daboog* at Kuorɔg. This homestead and the *faar* land surrounding it therefore remained in the hands of Kurug's sons. When Sawɔŋba died there were no more 'fathers' and the oldest generation of men in the inner lineage were all 'brothers'. Again the heir preferred to stay at Gbambee. If the next heir of Sawɔŋba's branch also refuses to go back to the lineage *daboog*, the chances are that the *faar* land there will cease to be regarded as patrimonial property of the whole inner lineage and will become *de facto* the *faar* of the branch that stayed on at Kuorɔg.

The point of this is that whereas 'brothers' are equal to one another 'fathers' and 'sons' are not. A 'brother' inheriting lineage *faar* is not on the same footing as a 'father'; he cannot exercise all the rights and the authority of a 'father' which belong intrinsically and exclusively to a 'father's' social status, 'because of begetting (*dɔyam la zugu*)'. A proxy father who has no brothers alive is at liberty to use his rights over *faar*

[1] The private property of women is an exception, but it is of relatively small importance in the total economy and its mode of transmission is, in fact, quite consistent with this principle. A woman's household utensils and garments are divided among her daughters and daughters-in-law on her death. Any livestock she has acquired by her own efforts or through her cognatic kin go to her sons and become their joint private property. The reason for this is that livestock, unlike utensils and clothes, can breed and so become *faar*, which is not transmissible by descent from or through women.

in an arbitrary manner and to his personal advantage. If he wishes, he can, for example, pawn *faar* land or consume *faar* cattle in spite of the protests of his 'sons'. They have no redress. Or a father may use his position to distribute parts of the patrimonial land among his sons and proxy sons so that they should all have some good land to work for themselves after his death. The 'son' who inherits cannot cancel such gifts. A 'brother' would arouse fierce opposition from his junior 'brothers' if he attempted to use or dispose of *faar* arbitrarily without their consent. When disputes occur over the division of patrimonial lands or other property that passes by inheritance, it is always amongst a group of 'brothers', never between 'father' and 'sons'.

The difference of emphasis due to difference of generation appears most plainly in the inheritance of rights over people. Tallensi say that 'an older brother (who succeeds to headship of the household or lineage) is like a father (in relation to his juniors) (*Bier yman ni ba la*)'. But they also add that he is nevertheless not a father. An oldest brother, as senior son, steps into the shoes of his 'father' in relation to society at large. He does not acquire paternal status within the lineage *vis-à-vis* his 'brothers'. The rights he exercises over dependants are shared by them. And when he is succeeded by a 'brother' the latter does not assume new rights over these dependants but merely extends his existing rights.

Beyond the range of the inner lineage, where generation differences no longer count, questions of inheritance and succession turn chiefly on rights to the custody of the shrines of founding ancestors. The moral and ritual authority of heads of lineages beyond the range of the inner lineage rests on their custody of these shrines. Sometimes, ritual offices like the tɛndaanaship go with the succession to the custody of maximal lineage shrines; and in many cases this also confers rights to control the use of or to have sole use of certain farm-lands vested in the head of the maximal lineage.

It follows from the foregoing that when a 'father' dies there very often is a wide rearrangement of property relations in the whole hierarchy of lineage segments to which he belonged. To take an actual case, let us return to Ziŋgan biis (p. 152). When Yidaan, the head of the inner lineage, died in 1933 he was succeeded by his brother Kutɔbis as head of the domestic family. As Kutɔbis was oldest by generation in the inner lineage he succeeded to the custody of the lineage *bɔyar* of Ziŋgan.[1] He would not have done so if, say, Ɔndieso had been senior to him by generation, though younger in years.

---

[1] About a generation ago, as is still the case with many lineages of this order, there was a tract of low-lying (*bo'og*) land that went with the *bɔyar*, and the head of the inner lineage automatically had control over it. Any member of the lineage could, however, farm part of it with his nominal permission. After Pa'ana's death this land was divided into three parts, one part going to Ɔndieso's grandfather, another to Bayanlɔrəg's descendants, and the third to Pa'ana's sons.

Kutɔbis also inherited the lineage *bɔyar* of Pa'anbɔbis biis, of which nuclear lineage he and his sons and brother's sons form a segment. Again, this might have gone to the head of the other segment of Pa'anbɔbis biis if he had been senior by generation or age to Kutɔbis. With this *bɔyar* goes some land at the now abandoned site of Pa'anbɔbis's homestead. If on Kutɔbis's death the present head of Bayanlɔrɔg biis, Na'abzɔ, is still alive it will come to him.

Kutɔbis also inherited the ancestral shrines of his immediate forebears Bayana, Pa'ana, and Sɔmnam. With these shrines go several strips of land, especially the large home farm (*saman*) adjoining the homestead, which are the patrimonial property of Sɔmnam's line of descent. On Kutɔbis's death they will be inherited by his younger 'brother' Pa'anbɔbis II. Lastly, Kutɔbis inherited some land which had been allocated to his father Bayana as a private plot and thereafter became the patrimonial property of Bayana's descendants.

He also assumed paternal rights over Yidaan's children. As Yidaan's sons farm independently of him, he cannot command their labour, though they are bound to assist him if he is hard-pressed and asks them to do so. In theory Kutɔbis has the unrestricted right to dispose of his late brother's daughters in marriage, and to use the bride-price paid for any of them as he pleases. Actually, he would not marry off any of the girls without consulting Yidaan's oldest son, Da'amo'o, and would, as we have seen, hand over the bride-price to Da'amo'o. He retains the right, however, to draw on the bride-price of any of Yidaan's daughters in a difficulty calling for payments he cannot meet. We have quoted an instance of this on p. 155. Kutɔbis also nominally inherited what was left of the livestock and clothes Yidaan had amassed,[1] but handed them over to Da'amo'o, retaining only the right to use them in an emergency. As regards Yidaan's widows, the older woman chose to stay on with Da'amo'o, as she was past the age of child-bearing. The younger accepted Kutɔbis as she had a child at the breast. But it was confidently said, by members of the lineage, that she would probably leave him when her child was old enough for her to have another.

Parallel Significance of 'Not having a Mother alive'

On the principle that both parents have an equally indispensable part in the procreation and upbringing of children, whether or not one has a mother alive is also socially recognized. There is a general taboo binding on everybody who has a mother alive. They may not drink water out of an earthenware dish (*laa*); they must always use a calabash (*ŋman*), the normal drinking vessel. This is connected with the ritual use of earthenware dishes as food and drinking-vessels in the purification of

---

[1] This was because Kutɔbis and Yidaan were *saarɔt*, full brothers. As we shall see later, full brothers have a very great degree of social equivalence and are entitled to inherit one another's personal effects in a way that half-brothers are not.

orphans at funerals. The ritual prohibitions falling on 'those who have a father alive', at funerals of old men, also fall on 'those who have a mother alive', at funerals of old women. But owing to the lesser importance of maternal than of agnatic descent in determining social status, whether or not one has a mother alive is of less social importance than whether one has or lacks a 'father'. The range within which classificatory 'mothers' are socially recognized is the same as for 'fathers', since 'mothers' derive their status from their husbands. But it is only the wives of 'fathers' belonging to one's own nuclear lineage who receive the deference due to a 'mother'. Beyond that range it is a voluntary matter whether or not one treats a 'father's' wife with the respect due to a 'mother'. Putting this in another way, a proxy mother is usually one's own mother's co-wife within the limits of, at most, the expanded family, who might or actually did take one's mother's place in bringing one up. It is this which distinguishes a 'mother' who is a 'father's wife' from one's natural mother's uterine sisters and kinswomen, who are also called 'mothers'. In one matter only is the recognition as classificatory 'mothers' of the wives of all 'fathers' of the inner lineage strictly enforced, and that is in regard to incest. This is of special importance when it comes to the inheritance of widows.

To take an example again from Ziŋgan biis, Da'amo'o and Ɔndieso both call Kutɔbis's wives their 'mothers'. They would not be able to marry any of them if Kutɔbis were to die. But if one of the wives dies, Da'amo'o, having lost his own mother, is obliged to go through the rites of mourning as for a mother. Ɔndieso will not. He may have his head shaven as a sign of mourning for her if she was particularly friendly with his family, or was particularly helpful to him, say by taking care of his wife during a difficult confinement. But this would be a voluntary gesture of respect, not a ritual obligation. If they are both present at a funeral of an old woman who is not married into their inner lineage, Da'amo'o will refrain, out of respect for his proxy mothers, from taking part in the rites forbidden to 'those who have mothers alive'. Ɔndieso will not, unless he wants to make a special gesture of respect to Kutɔbis or his wives. The personal relationships of the people concerned are irrelevant within the nuclear lineage. Da'amo'o, in fact, heartily dislikes Kutɔbis's senior wife and has a strong affection for Ɔndieso's proxy mother and his (Da'amo'o's) classificatory mother, Yinduuŋ, who is living with Ɔndieso. But he cannot escape the mourning rites he must undergo if the former dies, and is not obliged to undergo these rites if the latter dies.

The difference in the conventional attitudes towards a proxy mother and a proxy father is also shown in the way Tallensi look at the duty of supporting an aged parent, a subject we shall consider further in Chapter VII.

CHAPTER VI

THE MORAL BASIS OF THE RELATIONSHIP OF PARENT AND CHILD

The Fundamental Axiom of Parenthood

BEFORE we try to unravel further the complex strands that unite parents and children we must elucidate an idea which the Tallensi put forward as the fundamental axiom of parenthood. We have mentioned it already in our analysis of the notion of descent, but we have to examine it now from the point of view of the person-to-person relations of parents and children. It is the axiom, clearly stated by the natives and apparent also in Tale values and usages, that the fact of having begotten or borne a child creates an absolute moral bond between it and its parents. This idea is felt by them to be the real ultimate sanction behind right conduct in the relations of parents and children; and there is a very close agreement between ideals and actualities in this province of Tale social life.

Ignorance of hygiene and medicine, insufficiency of food and clothing, magical ideas, and Tale cultural standards in matters such as cleanliness or ventilation are undoubted handicaps to the child in its struggle to grow up. But sheer, callous neglect of a child by its parents, such as we sometimes hear of in more civilized societies, would be regarded with horror by all Tallensi and is unheard of. Similarly, a person who abandoned an aged parent to destitution would be regarded as a good for nothing (*boŋwari*). It happens occasionally, nowadays, when young men who find life irksome at home can so easily sneak off to foreign parts and stay away for many years. But it is a very rare thing and is universally reviled.

The Tribulations of Parenthood

If one asks a native why parents are and should be devoted to their children; or on what grounds they claim to 'own' (*so*) their children and to be entitled to their services, affection, gratitude, and respect; if one asks a girl who is keeping sullenly indoors, because she has been forcibly recovered from the lover she eloped with and beaten into the bargain, why she submitted passively to her father; or if one asks a young man nursing a bitter grievance against a father who has stopped him from marrying the girl he was courting why he does not defy the old man; if one asks any Talǝŋ, man or woman, such questions as these the answer invariably is, 'It is *dɔyam*'. 'Have you not begotten (or borne) them?' 'Has he not begotten you?' And then, almost always, comes the afterthought which contains the crux of the explanation, '*Dɔyam pu tɔ?*—Is not begetting (bearing) hard?' The phrase sounds trite, especially after one has heard it fifty times. But it is charged with deep emotion for the native to whom it stands for all the tribulations and anxieties connected with the whole task of bringing up a child.

Men say that these tribulations begin with the act of sex itself. Desired though it is for the pleasure it gives, sexual intercourse is debilitating. Ejaculation (*duun duurəm*, a term primarily used for micturition) is a giving up of something vital that is a source of strength and youth. That is why young, unmarried men are so much more vigorous than married men.

Then there is the strain under which a man lives during his wife's pregnancy, particularly if it is a first pregnancy. Pregnancy, the creation of life, must not be brought into contact with death. Hence he, as the father of his wife's coming child, must not take direct part in mortuary or funeral rites. If he is one of the bereaved, the rites he is compelled to undergo are modified so as to eliminate contact with the corpse or objects symbolizing it. No particular evil is thought to follow on a breach of this taboo, which can, in fact, be magically purged if circumstances compel a man to it. But no man would be so callous as to flout the taboo deliberately.

Again, a man must not cut a new bush farm while his wife is pregnant, lest she miscarry. Both are critical events, affectively as well as socially, involving economic readjustments and the assumption of new responsibilities. Preparing a new bush farm absorbs you completely; it is, the natives say, 'a commotion of the heart (*suhkpelǝg*)'. But when your wife is pregnant you 'take heed only of her pregnancy (*i wona u puur la*)'. You cannot give attention, at the same time, to a new and vital economic enterprise like cutting a new bush farm. Apart from a wife's pregnancy only two other critical happenings are so obsessing as to be considered mystically incompatible with making a new bush farm—building a new house, a momentous undertaking, both materially and ritually, which marks an important change in a man's social personality; and taking a new wife, which also involves or portends big readjustments in one's social relations. It is significant that a man who is cutting a new bush farm or building a new house keeps away from funerals outside his own inner lineage since they are both emotionally disturbing and a distraction. All these critical events demand watchfulness and solicitude, for unknown dangers of both a physical and a mystical kind threaten their outcome. A man has to go about consulting diviners. He offers special sacrifices to his ancestors and puts the matter in their particular care.

Another sign of the concern that tempers a man's joy at his wife's pregnancy is the caution he must use in the chase. He must not kill certain mystically dangerous animals, else his wife may miscarry or bear a deformed child.

A man's close relatives are also concerned when his wife is pregnant, especially if it is a first pregnancy. His mother and the older women of the family keep an eye on the girl lest she overstrain herself or break one of the dietary taboos. If his father is alive it is he who visits diviners and appeals to the ancestors.

The woman's paternal family, too, are concerned, especially in a first pregnancy. When they have been informed of it, her father appeals to his ancestors to bless her in her coming ordeal, and her mother and sisters bring her gifts of firewood, as her time approaches. It is also her mother's duty, round about the fourth or fifth month, to send one of her co-wives to 'gird the girl with a perineal band (*suol u voog*)', the garb of a matron; for until she has a child a woman wears no genital covering.

The prohibition against giving or accepting bride-price during a woman's pregnancy expresses this general solicitude too. Bride-price transactions involve tension and possible conflict between her father's people and her husband's; and this is not only distressing to her but dangerous to the unborn child. If, for instance, her father, defying convention and the ancestor spirits, as some men are heartless enough to do, takes her from her husband because the bride-price is not paid, the child's legitimate paternity may be prejudiced, as we have noted before, and its health suffer, or the woman herself have a difficult labour.

The solicitude for a woman with child reaches its peak at her confinement and during the subsequent three or four weeks, until she has regained her strength and resumes her normal activities. Many men have described to me their feelings in the hour of a wife's labour. 'You sit listening to her cries and groans of agony. You can't sleep. Your heart is clenched with fear and pity. You do not know how it will end. Do not women die in childbirth or become ill? Do not children die or get injured at birth?' A man's relief and happiness when his wife has passed safely (*salǝg*) through her confinement is written plainly in his voice and gait. Zaŋ, one of the most morose men I have known, was all smiles and affability on the morning after his wife's confinement. When friends and neighbours congratulate a man on his good luck (*zusɔŋ*, lit. good head) it is as much on account of his wife's safety as on the child's arrival.

During the days of seclusion—three for a boy and four for a girl—and for the next week or so, it is the husband's duty to provide sustaining food and appetizing condiments for his wife. He will go out to fetch large logs for the fire that must be kept going day and night in the woman's room while she and the babe are still weak and liable to catch cold. Every morning he will go out or send someone to collect the leaves and herbs to infuse in the hot water with which mother and child are bathed. And if necessary he will himself carry water from the waterhole or do other services for her comfort that men usually consider to be beneath their dignity.

A confinement also involves extra labour and the dislocation of routine for the womenfolk of the husband's family. The care of the woman and the child falls largely on the other women of the household, though the wives of neighbours belonging to the same expanded family, if they are near, might give some help too.[1] The younger women fetch water and cook for her. One of the experienced old women, her mother-in-law or the wife of a neighbour, usually of one of her husband's fellow members of the same inner lineage, supervises and sees to such matters as the bathing of mother and child and the ritual emergence from seclusion of the mother. When she is getting about again, her mother-in-law or senior co-wives must keep a watch over her to see that she does not over-exert herself or go any distance unaccompanied. For as we have mentioned earlier, a woman after childbirth is nervous and may be driven mad by evil trees and stones if she is alone far from home.

These are some of the things a man thinks of when he says that begetting or bearing a child is hard; but they are only the beginning of a father's tribulations. Talking with men immediately after the birth of a child to them, one feels a secret anxiety behind their obvious joy. Many children die in infancy,[2] the Tallensi say, and how can a man know if this particular child will survive? During the first few months of life a child is extremely vulnerable, both physically and mystically. Medicine to keep out evil trees and stones is carefully daubed over the gateway and over every orifice in the homestead wall, and in a circle round the spot where the child lies. *Nɔya teem* ('mouth medicine'), to protect it against malicious praise is given to it. Lucky omens, whether of a conventional or an unconventional kind, are noted. Then, some days after its birth, the child's father or the head of the joint family visits a diviner to find out which of the lineage ancestors is taking it as a spiritual ward (*sɛyəraan*) to guard its life (*gur u ŋɔvɔr*) and watch over its growth. Only after two to six months from the day of its birth is the child at length allowed out of doors; and then it must be ritually carried out, for the first time, by a clanswoman (*pɔyayabəlɔg*) of the father's clan (i.e. by a 'female father', *bapɔk*, of the child) chosen by divination, so that the ancestors may bless this important step in its development. And this is not the end of the story, for a father's responsibilities for his children never come to an end, as we shall see presently.

[1] Among the Tallensi, as among many patrilineal peoples, the parturient woman's sisters do not assist at the birth of the child. For, as the natives say, it is not their child. The responsibility of assisting at the birth falls on the wives of the lineage to which the child belongs—women who will later be recognized as its proxy and classificatory mothers. It is one of these women, too, who suckles the child for the first two or three days until the mother's milk begins to flow properly. A parturient woman's mother and sisters bring her gifts of foodstuffs and firewood; and her father also sends her a gift of foodstuffs, guinea-fowls, salt, and other condiments, according to his means. They have nothing to do with the care of mother and child during and after the confinement.

[2] Infant mortality is high—probably about 150-200 per 1,000. Cf. my paper 'A Note on Fertility among the Tallensi of the Gold Coast', *Sociological Review*, vol. xxxv, nos. 3 and 4, 1943.

For a woman too, and for any native who is looking at it from the point of view of motherhood, the difficulties of bringing a child into the world centre round pregnancy and labour. Tale women generally seem to take a pregnancy in their stride, especially later pregnancies. They go on with their household tasks until the last minute. Children are sometimes born in the bush, and quite often born outside on the home farm, where the mother has been busy with some task. Miscarriages due to the strain of heavy work such as fetching heavy loads of firewood or going to distant markets to buy grain by the sack, and bringing it home by head carriage are not uncommon among multiparae. Primiparae, as we have seen, are usually watched over by older women, but miscarriages due to overstrain occur among them too. A woman who has had a child is trusted to look after herself.

But in spite of their apparently casual attitude to it, women think of pregnancy as fraught with weariness, discomfort, and anxiety. A woman thinks of the purely physiological discomforts such as the attacks of sickness and giddiness she may suffer. She thinks of the circumspection she must use in her eating and drinking. Very thin gruel, cold left-over porridge, sweet potatoes, too much cold water, are all things which would injure her health and must be avoided; nor may she eat honey, else her babe will be born with a catarrhal snuffle. A woman thinks, also, of the increasing lassitude that makes her household tasks more and more burdensome as her term approaches. She remembers the store of firewood she must gather and the provisions she must lay in for her confinement, though it is hard enough to satisfy the current needs of the household. And at the back of her mind she has always the fear of a miscarriage. She is subject, also, to ritual taboos, the most important being the avoidance of funerals.

Then, of course, there is the act of giving birth (*dɔy*) in the narrow sense. Tale women do not think of it in anticipation with terror or repugnance, but they do associate it with pain and possible complications. The crude midwifery of the old women who assist at a birth, relying in part on magical measures, cannot correct a breech presentation (*tula*) or expel an undescended placenta.

Women always put particular emphasis on the agonies of the hygiene of confinement. Mother and child are subjected to a course of hot baths, douching, and massage which the natives say is extremely painful. A white onlooker finds the process harrowing, to say the least. Water heated to nearly boiling-point is used and medicinal leaves and herbs are infused in it. The infant goes rigid with pain when it is washed in this decoction, and the mother squirms and shrieks as it is sluiced over her body and still tender sexual parts. Massage and oiling with shea butter follow the bath. The treatment is given twice or thrice daily during the days of seclusion and is gradually reduced over the following two or three weeks, fewer baths being given and the temperature of the water lowered. Tallensi think it is essential for the health of the mother and babe, and one important item in it is forcing some of the decoction down the babe's throat. Whether or not it actually has a cleansing or invigorating effect must be left to medical judgement. For the native women it has the double significance of an ordeal, and a prescribed treatment that they would not dream of neglecting.

As we have seen, the care of the child on the ritual side falls on its father. The much more exacting physical care of the child in its parlous passage through infancy is its mother's responsibility. This is stressed when Tallensi insist that it is not on account of a magical taboo but because a child is still partly dependent on the breast until it is about three, that sexual intercourse between a man and his nursing wife is discontinued. They say that a child requires the undivided care of its mother until it can run about and eat solid food by itself, and that it will wilt away through lack of nourishment if she conceives prematurely. Nursing mothers become pregnant only too often through lack of self-control, but this is never condoned by public opinion. The only time a Tale woman tries to induce an abortion is when such an accident happens, for no sacrifice is too great to preserve her living child.

When Tale parents are asked what were the special difficulties they had to overcome in rearing their children, they always mention sickness first. Mothers especially have a great dread of sickness in their children. One does not notice this in the easy-going, placid atmosphere of a well-conducted family when there is no 'sleeplessness' (*gɔgiŋgara*), to use the apt native euphemism for sickness. But one sees it when a child gets ill. Minor ailments throw its mother into a state of anxiety. Serious illness puts her into a panic or prostrates her with grief. She refuses food—which is always regarded by the natives as a sign of severe illness or great emotional distress—and stops all her work. I have seen illness in adolescent or adult children have this effect on women; and the younger the child the more do they suffer.

It is easy to imagine what the death of a child in infancy or childhood means to its mother. A man is expected to control his emotions, but a woman may express her grief freely. A father's grief is palliated, also, by the active role he takes in the ritual by which the emotional shock is neutralized. A woman's part in this ritual is more passive and she feels the blow more acutely in consequence. A mother remains inconsolable for many days and even weeks over the loss of a child.

The way Tallensi think of a mother's grief over the death of her child was brought home to me when Diŋkaha's little girl of about three died after a lingering and horrible illness. He had been devoted to the child and was greatly distressed, but in a few days he had accepted the diviner's verdict philosophically and was his old bouncing self again. His wife, on the other hand, broke down completely. Then, a couple of weeks later, news came that an older child of hers by a former husband, with whom it was living, had also died suddenly. Diŋkaha, greatly concerned for his wife, warned all the members of his family not to say anything to her about it. If she heard of this calamity now, he said, she would surely die. Later on, when she had settled down again he would himself break the news to her.

Incidentally, fathers do not always get over the death of a child, whether an infant or an adult, with ease. It is easier for a young man, the Tallensi say, because he thinks to himself that his wife can still bear children to him. But even young men have been known to abandon themselves to despair. An extreme case was that of Dɔɣayam, who pierced himself with a poisoned arrow when his favourite child died; and the average Talɔŋ, it must be remembered, speaks of suicide with contempt. The grief of a father when a grown-up or adolescent son dies is very moving. When Pumaan's son Kpeemi and Tinta'alɔm's son Suor, both fine young men in the twenties, died, it was as if a shock ran through the whole community. On both occasions the men of the clan gathered in full force to mourn at the bereaved house and the atmosphere of tragedy was felt by all. I cannot forget the picture of Pumaan, as taciturn and dour a man as one could meet anywhere, holding himself tautly, his face ashen, his eyes staring ahead, stoically suppressing his despair as an elder should do. Tɛndaan Teroog, an old man over seventy, made no pretence of stoicism when his eldest and only adult son died leaving a number of wives and children. He simply pined away and followed his son to the grave in a couple of months.

When Tallensi say that it is hard to bring a child into the world, they have in mind more than the physiological facts of birth, and the dangers of infancy and childhood. They think of the whole gamut of social and emotional relations between parents and children arising out of the fact of birth. For a Talɔŋ, as we have seen, does not become altogether independent of his parents until their death—nor, indeed, even after their death. The pragmatic bonds of jural and economic dependence become transformed into the equally strong, nay stronger bonds of ritual dependence on the ancestor spirits of whom the parents are the immediate prototypes and intermediaries. And in many ways the ritual relationships of the Tallensi with the spirits of their parents give a truer insight into the parent–child bond than their visible behaviour towards one another. 'Fear the dead but do not fear the living (*Zom kpiim ka di zo vopa*)', says one of their proverbs which enshrines their feeling that a person is under a far more compelling bond with his parents when they are dead than during their life. We shall return to this presently.

The gist of our analysis is that to the Tallensi parenthood means responsibility that weighs heavily at times. This comes out both in the notion that bearing or begetting a child is hard and in the correlated notion of the importance of rearing. At the same time there is no native, man or woman, who would not insist that a person has lived in vain if he

THE RELATIONSHIP OF PARENT AND CHILD

dies childless, and that children are the greatest source of joy and pride, comfort and support that anybody can have. The Tallensi are much like ourselves in this matter and do not think there is any inconsistency between these two aspects of parenthood. Their whole philosophy of life is like that. Realists as they are, they take it for granted that life has many risks and troubles, but, as they often put it, 'Does anybody desire death on that account?' When I told them that Europeans often refrain deliberately from having children, they were either sceptical or appalled.

The Parent–Child Bond as an Absolute Bond

Tallensi say that the bonds between parent and child can never be obliterated and may not be repudiated. This is a fundamental moral principle and it goes back to the notion that bearing or begetting children is hard. From it follows the duty of filial piety.

You cannot disown your child. 'Even if your child is a good-for-nothing, you have no alternative but to keep him,' said Lɔyani, one of the most intelligent and upright men I knew. 'Have you not suffered to beget him?' he went on. 'How can you reject him? You are always thinking of your children's good, though they are often selfish and think only of their own advantage. Your child may be lazy or ill-behaved. But yet you cannot drive him away, you cannot harass him so that he quits you.'

Many examples could be quoted to illustrate the strength of this ideal. I sacked one of my servants for petty theft. A day or two later an elder who was known to be one of my friends came to intercede for him. He admitted that the man was a thief, but he was very disappointed when I declined to take him back. 'You are his father,' he said, 'and you ought to take him back.' Then, after a short silence, he added gravely, 'You white men! You are not like us. You do not understand the meaning of "to beg forgiveness".'

A better instance is an incident in which Lɔyani himself was concerned some days after he made the comment quoted above. A youth of Lɔyani's clan stole a fowl owned by another member of his own joint family, whom he called his older brother (*bier*). The theft, a despicable thing in any case, was made blacker by the youth's attempt to conceal it; and when it was discovered, the whole clan was agog with it. The culprit's father, in his shame and anger at the disgrace brought upon his family, struck and cursed him saying that he must never again set foot in the house. Thereupon the young man took refuge with Lɔyani, whose son was his friend. Lɔyani himself, like all respectable people, was shocked at the theft. 'Heaven save me from theft,' he said, when he told me the story. 'Death were better than that. It is shameful.' And he went on to describe how everybody scorns and derides a thief. Nevertheless, as soon as the boy arrived Lɔyani went to the elders of the boy's lineage to get them to intercede with the father to withdraw his curse and take his son back. But meanwhile the boy sneaked away and went to his brother in Mampurugu for fear of public ridicule. 'But', said Lɔyani, 'one day he will return and his father will certainly take him back.' It is because a man cannot disown his child that a Tale father always stands by his son in what the natives call *pɔyadir ycla*, marriage affairs, the test occasions of jural responsibility. A man may have strong private objections to his son's marriage and eventually cause it to be dissolved. He may criticize and scold his son for it. But in public he will support the boy if the marriage does not infringe some rule of kinship or convention of social relationships. This, it should be noted, is not the same thing as a man's responsibility for his son's brideprice which rests on a different principle. For the same reason a woman can never be denied refuge in her father's house if she has nowhere else to stay.

A woman, too, cannot disown her child. Indeed Tallensi say that it is unthinkable for a woman, bound as she is to her child by even stronger emotional bonds than a man. It happens, of course, that women desert, or are taken away from one husband to marry another and leave a child behind. But if the child is still too tiny to fend for itself it accompanies its mother until it is old enough to be separated (*pɔhəg*) from her. Tallensi are very critical of a woman who deserts a child when she leaves its father, though not without ulterior motives; for a runaway wife is a loss, whether she leaves children or not. As has been mentioned, they say that in such cases 'Rearing is more important than bearing'. And yet, they say, a woman yearns after her child no matter who has the custody of it. She might easily desert a later husband to return to an earlier husband with whom she has left a child; and if a woman who has been married more than once returns to her first husband, his rights take precedence of all the others' by Tale custom. That is why men object strongly to a wife's attempting to visit or even see a child she has left with a former husband. I have seen a man keep watch on his wife for days lest she make such an attempt. 'Do you know what bearing (a child) means to a woman?' he said, in explanation. In any case, her marital history makes no difference to the *soog* (uterine) tie between a woman and her child and to the social relationships arising out of it. As we have already learnt, there is no surer guarantee that a woman will stay with a husband than if she has two or three children by him. If she has children, a woman who commits adultery almost invariably returns to her husband, risking the wrath of his ancestor spirits and enduring the shame of a semi-public confession. If she has none, she usually runs off with her paramour.

The ideas we have been discussing are not thought to have a ritual sanction where own parents and children are concerned. But with proxy parents, as might be expected, a ritual sanction comes into the picture openly. A man who disowns or ill-treats or in other ways neglects the duties of a 'father' to a dead brother's children, especially minor children, incurs the anger of his paternal ancestors. Human nature being what it is, Tallensi say, it happens all too often that men behave disgracefully to a dead brother's children. Sometimes retribution comes in their lifetime. Sometimes, however, the sanction which re-establishes the moral law only comes into action after their death. Then the diviners who are consulted declare that they have not been 'accepted' (*die*) by the ancestors whom they have gone to join. Their own sons must make ritual amends to set the matter right, and so the moral principles they sinned against are vindicated.

Filial Piety

The counterpart of parental duty and devotion is filial piety. It is regarded by the Tallensi as an equally binding moral principle and an equally strong motive of individual conduct; and they trace it back, also, to the tribulations parents undergo in bringing a child into the world. It is not a formally elaborated doctrine, as among the Chinese, nor a dogma of faith, as among the ancient Hebrews, nor a legal principle, as in ancient Rome, but a diffused norm of conduct. The Tallensi would laugh at the idea of kowtowing to a parent, and their respect for parental authority is far from being blind obedience. For one of the significant characteristics of the relations of parents and children is their ambivalence. In everyday intercourse there is a freedom in these relations, verging on camaraderie. Yet they are full of tensions due to the self-assertion of children against their parents. It is the characteristic picture of the relations between successive generations in a patrilineal society—parents and children bound to one another by the strongest ties of sentiment and interest but latently pitted against one another, particularly in the case of fathers and sons. Filial piety among the Tallensi can be interpreted, in some of its expressions, as a bulwark against the disintegrative effects of these tensions or as a stabilizing mechanism of behaviour the main function of which is to close the gap between parents and children if it threatens to become too large.

We have seen how important it is for a man's status whether or not he has a father alive. If anything, his status is advanced by the death of his nearest fathers, and it is not until he is 'fatherless' within the nuclear lineage that he attains jural autonomy. In this, as in all aspects of the relations of father and son, Tale custom is ambivalent. After a certain stage of social maturity men desire to be free of paternal restraint, and yet they are glad to leave the bigger responsibilities for their lives in the hands of a father. It is not surprising that the affective stress, in Tale thought, is on the blessings of having a father alive.

Speaking conventionally, Tallensi say that one must obey one's father, respect him, work for him, take his side against everybody else—even against one's mother—'*ɔn dɔyi la zugu*—because he begot you'. One's dependence on him increases one's attachment and sense of duty towards him. Dependence on one's father is a good thing, a highly desirable and advantageous state of affairs, and the essence of filial piety is to accept this condition of dependence as the right thing in life. Tallensi say that a man has no cares while his father is alive. He looks after all one's affairs (*maal i yɛla*). He takes charge of the farming, attends to all ritual matters such as sacrifices to the ancestors and the consultation of diviners if one is ill, and assumes responsibility for such things as the payment of bride-price. He takes care of the house (*gur yiri*) both in the physical sense of always staying at home and in the jural and ritual sense of being its responsible head, leaving his sons free to go about as they please. The emphasis is on the father as the one who bears all responsibility for one's welfare in economic, jural, and ritual matters. That is why, the natives say, a man mourns the death of a father, for henceforth he must take on the burden of responsibility for himself. It means the end of protection and security in relation to society at large and to the spirits of the ancestors.

The picture is overdrawn but not inaccurate. The burden of social responsibility does not weigh so heavily as this statement implies. Siŋ and Gbana, both young men in the twenties, managed their households very well. But both often bemoaned their fate in having been left fatherless when still boys. 'If my father were alive I would have had a wife by now', said Siŋ, 'and Na'abzɔ (his proxy father) would not have used my sister's bride-price cattle for his own purposes.' The death of the father often means the uprooting of his sons. 'Now', said Kɛlibsɔ after his father's funeral ceremonies were over, 'we (he and his brothers) shall become poor men. When our father was alive we had a large home farm to cultivate. Now our junior father (*ba-pit*) will take that and we shall have to go and farm our bush farms. Soon the day will come when we shall move out, for who knows how a *ba-pit* will look after you?' I have heard boys of 9 or 10 talk in this way after the death of their father. It is easier for a woman who has her husband's protection. But even she suffers a sad loss in the death of her own father. His heirs, even her own brothers, will never have quite the same intimate and personal interest in her and her children.

There is a direct connexion between this emphasis on the dependence of children on parents and the worship of the ancestors. Nor is the underlying feeling of a hidden antagonism between father and son, of which we shall have more to say presently, altogether incongruous with this overt stress on the security the father symbolizes. The social relations of father and son, at every stage of the latter's development, are always a compromise between the mutual dependence of father and son and the limited dependence enjoyed by the latter.

There is not the same degree of tension between mother and child or even mother and daughter, and hence, perhaps, Tallensi do not have such a definite conventional rationalization of their attitudes towards the mother. They say you respect your mother and cherish her in old age because she bore and fed you. In childhood you were more attached to her than to your father; you ran to her whenever you were tired or hungry or ill and she comforted and fed you; as an adult you realize the importance of 'father's begetting' (*ba-dɔyam*) in jural, ritual, and economic matters such as marriage or landowning, and in crises like sickness or death; but your mother is still honoured as the centre of your domestic arrangements if you are a man, and if you are a woman, she is the one person you can always come to in sickness or trouble, in the certainty of loving attention. Comfort, emotional security, and food—these are the distinguishing qualities of a mother in Tale thought. It corresponds to the more personal character of the bonds between mother and child, by contrast with the jurally and ritually weighted ties with the father.

Tallensi say that one must respect one's living parents; but to one's dead parents one owes reverence and submission in surpassing degree. That is what the proverb 'Fear the dead and do not fear the living' means to them.[1] One can defy a living parent sometimes and rely on being forgiven; one cannot defy a dead parent. One can live without the help of a living parent, if necessary, but not without the mystical protection of one's dead parents.

In the religious practice of the Tallensi the ancestors exercise their powers without compunction. They punish and slay as arbitrarily as they bless. Every dry season men return to rebuild their parental homes which have been allowed to lie in decay for many years. They come from Mampurugu, from outlying parts of Taleland, or from Ashanti and the Colony. Some have been away for years. Pal of Zubiuŋ had a prosperous farm in Mampurugu, where he had gone to settle on being discharged from the regiment after the war of 1914–18. During his fifteen years in Mampurugu he had become fairly wealthy, with five wives, a horse, several head of cattle, and a quantity of good clothes. Dɛma of Tɛnzugu, who joined the regiment as far back as 1912 and had lived in Ashanti as a trader since his discharge after the war, was obviously a man of considerable wealth by Tale standards. Both returned to rebuild their fathers' homesteads in 1935–6. They told the same story. Wives and children had died; there had been repeated bouts of sickness in the family; other misfortunes had piled up over the years; and all, as the diviners declared, because they had 'rejected (*zayah*) their fathers (*banam*)' by remaining in foreign parts. It did not matter much while there were older brothers at home to 'give water (*zaŋ kuom ti*)', that is, make sacrifices, to the ancestral shrines. But

---
[1] The verb *zo*, to fear, has a wide range of meaning and here it means to show respect towards, to revere, to stand in awe of.

when they were left as heads of their lineage segments they had to come home. Their fathers' spirits would have killed them if they had not done so. Dɛma is frankly happy to be home again amongst his own people after his wanderings. Pal, who is dependent on farming for his living, still speaks with a tinge of regret of the fine farm he had to abandon in Mampurugu. But he feels that he had no option, and there is even an element of pride in his submission to the *force majeure* of his dead father, since he is now the head of his lineage segment. It was the same with Na'abzɔ, Kayar, Yinworəb, Baŋgam-Teroog, and many others, too numerous to mention, who returned home after years abroad in order to 'give water' to their fathers.

While the whole ancestor cult is an elaborate expression of filial piety towards the dead parents, one of the commonest ways in which the observer comes across it is in the practice of leechcraft. Almost every native owns some 'roots (ŋaya)' for the treatment of sickness, and the therapeutic value of the roots lies not so much in their physical properties as in the fact that their owner is able, by right of ownership, to mobilize magical virtue in their support. As a preliminary to the curative rites the owner of the roots always calls upon his or her ancestors for a blessing, and this opens with the phrase 'My father, I shall call you (first). You have no concern with this matter, but I call on you (to help me) for the sake of begetting, because you begot me (*Mba, n-na mbuola nyɛni. Nyɛn baha ka dɛni, ka mbuoli la dɔyam la zug, nyɛn dɔyəm la zugu*).'

Naturally the ritual aspect of filial piety is of greater importance for a man than for a woman, considered in terms of their social personalities and with regard to the father; for he stands for the lineage and clan, with all that membership of these units implies, for the land and other patrimonial property, and for the ancestral home (*daboog*). But it is important for a woman, too, and in relation to the mother as well. A woman is the spiritual ward (*sɛyəraan*) of one of her paternal forbears and remains under that ancestor's or ancestress's guardianship all her life. And it is through her father that she maintains good ritual relations with her ancestor guardian—either through sacrifices made by her father on her behalf or through the intermediation of her father's spirit when he is dead. Moreover, her father's spirit is of great importance to her children. It is significant that if a male line dies out a female survivor takes on the duty of sacrificing to the lineage shrines, which she can only approach through her father's spirit.

A man's mother's spirit is of as much importance for him as an individual as his father's. He has a shrine dedicated to her and other shrines dedicated to ancestors of hers. A mother's shrine is often the first after his *Yin* shrine to be dedicated by a man and is always felt to be more peculiarly his own than a father's shrine, which is heritable by half-brothers. A man would not return from abroad because of the demands of his dead mother's spirit; she is not tied to the lineage home in the same way as a father's spirit is and can be 'given water' more easily wherever the man happens to be. Nevertheless, his welfare and that of his dependants rests as much on his maintaining good relations with her spirit as with his father's spirit.

Filial piety among the Tallensi is a great deal more than a customary injunction to honour and respect one's parents. Psychologically it is a very complex sentiment. Even during their lifetime parents have quasi-mystical attributes, as we shall see more clearly when we consider the relations of parents and first-born children, and these dominate the sentiment. A parent can bless or curse a child. A parent's curse, in particular, is greatly dreaded, as we have previously noted, and, in consequence, only resorted to in case of gross affront or unforgivable defiance on the part of a child. If a parent expresses or merely feels resentment against a child, that is equivalent to a curse which may cause it illness or other harm. Thus one element in the sentiment of filial piety is respect for the blessing and fear of the curse of a parent. That is why, men say, it is sometimes embarrassing to have an old mother in one's house, though one is bound to keep her, both in duty and out of affection. For old women become completely egoistic. All they think of is having enough to eat and being comfortable, and if they are crossed they are apt to curse anybody incontinently.

In a large joint family one often finds a young man with a growing family of his own torn between his devotion to his father and his desire to be economically independent so as to provide for his wife and children more satisfactorily. He cannot go out to farm on his own without his father's blessing and consent else his venture will surely fail. He begins to drop hints or makes a tentative approach to his father. But if the latter shows displeasure he retreats at once. I have seen this happen more than once. When Tɔyalbɛrɔgu wanted to go out to farm on his own, his father Naabdiya reproached him, saying that *he* had not deserted *his* father as Tɔyalbɛrɔgu now wished to desert *him*. Tɔyalbɛrɔgu apologized and withdrew. But, as Naabdiya told me, 'I still had resentment in my heart and he still secretly cherished his plan'. A couple of weeks later Tɔyalbɛrɔgu developed a large boil in the armpit. In panic he begged an elder to ask Naabdiya to forgive him and formally withdraw his implicit curse, which, he was certain, was the cause of the boil. It was the same with Yinyɛla's son Duun. Though as an eldest son he felt entitled to start farming on his own, he dared not ask that hard old man's permission for fear that it might arouse his resentment.

It is an interesting point that when a young man who has been living and farming with his dead father's brother, for example, sets up in his own homestead, the pretext for the separation is often not an economic one. It is commonly recognized that the young man moves out because he needs more land and freedom to provide for his family by himself.

But if the father's brother does not take the initiative of pointing out to his 'son' that he would be better off on his own, the latter cannot do so. It would be like suggesting that his proxy father is not treating him as fairly as his own father. The usual course of events is that something goes wrong with the young man's affairs. It may be a trivial mishap, such as a hen being caught by a hyena, or something more serious, such as the sickness of wife or child. The young man goes with his proxy father to consult a diviner; and the diviner declares that the trouble was caused by the young man's own father, because the young man has not yet built his own homestead. The dead father lets it be known that he wants to go directly to his son's own house to accept sacrifices and not have to go to his brother's house as a mere guest. Thus the dictates of filial piety are subtly and doubly fulfilled.

Filial piety, as these examples show, is the psychological bridge between the relations of parents and children in life and in the ritual relationships of the living with the ancestors. All the ancestors are projections of the parents, different manifestations of the images Tale culture draws of certain aspects of the parents that do not appear in conventional, overt behaviour. This is clear, also, from the element of reverence that enters into the sentiment of filial piety.

Siŋ's father and Na'abzɔ were the sons of two brothers. When Siŋ's father died, Na'abzɔ married his widow and took charge of the children. But Na'abzɔ is a notoriously cantankerous person. So Siŋ took his younger brothers and mother and set up in his own homestead as soon as he was old enough. In jural and ritual matters, however, Na'abzɔ is still his 'father'. Passing Siŋ's house one day with an elder I heard sounds of violent quarrelling between him and Na'abzɔ. Na'abzɔ stood on the flat roof of a room in his house hurling abuse at Siŋ, who replied angrily, but politely, from his gateway 50 yards away. My companion and I turned aside to talk to Siŋ. It appeared that Na'abzɔ had as usual been nagging Siŋ and his brothers unreasonably. He demanded that they should leave their own farm-work to come and hoe his farm. When Siŋ asked for his help, which was indispensable, in an important ritual matter, he had refused out of petty spite; and now he had upset Siŋ's sister's marriage by arbitrary and inconsiderate demands on her husband. I asked Siŋ, 'Why don't you take hold of Na'abzɔ and thrash him? That should stop him.' He looked at me in dismay and said, 'No, no. I couldn't do that. It is forbidden. He is my father. He begot me.' My companion, almost as shocked, chimed in, 'No, you can't strike your father, you can't strike your mother. They have borne (*dɔya*) you. He who strikes his father or his mother is a good-for-nothing.' He went on to say that everybody knew what sort of a person Na'abzɔ was, but Siŋ must be patient. It would all come right. For would not Na'abzɔ die one day and Siŋ inherit all his property? Similar comments were made by everybody I met about Dɛŋkumis's brother's son, Dmaarɔb. The young man was a lazy spendthrift and there was constant trouble between the two. One day Dɛŋkumis forcibly stopped him from beating his wife and he turned and struck Dɛŋkumis. There was an uproar, for other men of the lineage set upon Dmaarɔb with sticks and fists. Next day Dɛŋkumis, followed by all the men of his lineage segment, dragged the delinquent to the chief. As it was a *dugni yɛl*, an affair of the inner lineage, the chief dealt with it as head of the clan. Trembling with anger and contempt he read the youth an excoriating homily on how a person ought to behave to his parents. Dɛŋkumis, ended the chief, had been too patient with the worthless scamp just because he was his brother's son. Let him beware. Another action of this kind, and Dɛŋkumis would be commanded to throw him out of his house.

Another story deserves recording as an example of the working of filial piety. Kuŋaaŋba was born when his father was an old man. At that time a famine swept the country. A distant clansman of his father seized his mother and her babe to sell them into slavery and recoup himself for a debt owed to him by Kuŋaaŋba's father. But the woman managed to escape. When the famine was over she returned home to find her husband dead and his brother Gɔlime at the head of the household. Gɔlime, however, disregarding the rule that whoever inherits a man's property and status must take over his duties and liabilities, at first refused to have her back. She was like a corpse that had come to life again, he said. But his own wife, with an independence of spirit that Tale women often show, threatened to leave him if he did not take her co-wife and the child back, so he gave in. In due course Kuŋaaŋba's mother remarried one of her late husband's classificatory brothers, under whose care the boy grew up. Jurally and ritually Gɔlime remained his 'father'. Then Kuŋaaŋba went to work for the white man at Kumasi. He returned with a quantity of clothes, a bag of salt, and three or four pounds in cash. He found Gɔlime, now an old man in decline, left almost destitute, as his own sons, whom he had always treated with severity, had both run away to the Colony. Kuŋaaŋba at once took the old man to his own house. He gave him a cloth to wear, bought a supply of grain for him, and left him some money when he himself departed for another spell of work abroad. Thereafter Kuŋaaŋba took care of Gɔlime as if he were his own father until the end of his life. 'For', said Kuŋaaŋba, as he concluded his simple tale, 'was he not my father? What did it matter that he had treated me badly in my childhood, since I am still alive and healthy? I couldn't leave my father to die of starvation just because his own sons were wastrels.' I asked Kuŋaaŋba if Gɔlime had ever expressed remorse for having neglected his duty to him in his childhood. 'No,' was the answer, 'he would not do that. He would keep it to himself but his heart would be sore (*u suh ndum*). And now that he is dead he will (as a spirit) do good to me.' It was true, commented an elder who had listened to the story; a son who had no charity (*ɔn ka sugəru*) would perhaps have done otherwise, but Kuŋaaŋba's way was the right way.

It is on the death of a parent that filial piety is most sharply evoked, just as it is the death of a child that brings out most poignantly a parent's love and devotion. We have referred to this previously. In this matter filial sentiment and ritual sanctions converge.

The supreme act of filial piety sons owe to their parents is the performance of their mortuary and funeral ceremonies. If a man or woman dies leaving no sons then this duty falls upon his or her nearest proxy sons. The initiative and chief responsibility rest with the oldest living son. The burial rites must be carried out immediately; but when and how the funeral ceremony is to be made is for the sons to decide. No one can put pressure on them to hurry on the funeral if they wish to postpone it for several years. It is customary to delay the funeral of an elder, an old woman, or a person holding a ritual office until the third year after his or her death, ostensibly so as to enable the sons to collect the large stock of grain and the livestock required for the ceremony. Meanwhile, in the case of a man the sons exercise the social role of the deceased. If he was a tɛndaana they will perform the duties and exercise the rights of his office, and this may be a motive for delaying his funeral beyond the customary period. The old men who are eligible for the office can object and grumble; they cannot compel a dead man's son to make his father's funeral. The issue lies between the dead man and his sons. If they delay unduly they will incur their father's anger. For until his funeral has been celebrated he dwells between the world of the living and the world of the spirits. As the Tallensi say, his one leg is in the earth (among the spirits) and his other on the surface of the earth (among the living) (*u gbɛr dɛkɔ bɛ teŋni ka gbɛr dɛna bɛ doorni*). He cannot 'join his forefathers (*paag u banam*)' until he has been 'taken back into the house (*kpeeh dugni*)' as a spirit. And the situation is the same with a dead mother, though she is of less jural importance.

The duty of burying a parent and celebrating his or her funeral is the first step in the most exacting of all filial duties, the cult of the dead parents. Native thought and behaviour show that the Tallensi feel it as an inescapable compulsion of conscience, and not as a mere act of propriety. Tallensi are quite matter-of-fact about the corpse (*kum*) of a dead parent. They describe it as the 'slough (*fɔrəŋ*)' of the soul (*sii*). What they are concerned about is the spirit (*kpiim*) of the dead parent. A man cannot rest secure until he has assimilated his father's or mother's spirit into the framework of his life, domesticated it, so to speak, as the expression *kpeeh dugni* shows; and this is the function of the funeral ceremony. For that reason Tallensi want to have the graves of their parents near their dwellings. True, a man's ancestor spirits accompany him wherever he goes, but they are most tangibly present in his house, where he sacrifices to them. It often happens that a man has to be buried in one of the peripheral settlements, or abroad, where he has been living temporarily. Then, if his sons return to the ancestral home, perhaps years after his death, he will one day, through a diviner, order them to exhume (*gurəg*) him and rebury him among his ancestors at the ancestral home (*daboog*). The notion that when a person dies he joins his ancestors (or a woman her husband's ancestors as well as her own), and that his body should therefore lie among their bodies, is a basic idea in Tale religion and an obvious reflex of filial piety.

As the case of Sawɔŋba's daughter, previously quoted (p. 89), shows, daughters are as much bound as sons to mourn the death of a parent. All the children of the deceased must come to the funeral so as to undergo the mourning rites. They are ritually unclean until they have done so and have had their heads ritually shaved (*kuo zug*) in sign of it. Though the ritual uncleanness (*dayət*) of a person who has lost a parent does not interfere with normal life, it is felt to be a psychological burden, for, as we have noted, until a dead person's funeral has been made, his or her social personality is not wholly erased from the real world. I have heard children of 10 or 11 say gravely that they wished their mother's or father's funeral could be made soon so that they could 'shave off the uncleanness (*kuo dayət la bah*)'. The uncleanness adheres primarily to the deceased's own children, but it also affects proxy children who have no living parent (as determined by the criteria of 'fatherlessness' or 'motherlessness') of the same sex as the deceased. One of the ways in which Tallensi demonstrate respect and affection for a classificatory parent such as a father's agnatic cousin or a classificatory father's wife, who has never been a proxy parent to them, is to undergo the chief mourning rites for him or her—provided, of course, the mourner is 'fatherless' or 'motherless' in that situation. When an old man or woman who was the last of the generation of 'fathers' or 'mothers' of the inner lineage dies, the men and women of the lineage to whom he or she is a classificatory parent gather from far and wide for the funeral and all undergo the rites of shaving the head. It is not compulsory for anyone to have the head shaved for a classificatory parent, but it is a pious gesture which at the same time proclaims the solidarity of the lineage. *De mortuis nil nisi bonum* might be a Tale proverb. Old grudges are forgotten—though not necessarily buried for ever—and men and women who have been estranged from their classificatory brothers and sisters or the deceased parent turn up to the funeral to do the proper thing.

Nowadays the death of a parent is one of the strongest sanctions that induce the men who go to work abroad to return home, if only for a while. The absentees may dawdle for weeks or months or even two or three years—for funeral ceremonies can be postponed, as we have noted, for periods up to three, four, or more years—but most of them come home eventually for the rites. Those who delay so long that their relatives at home decide not to wait for them are the exceptions that prove the rule. In a few cases they are men who have struck root in their new environment after many years of living there and find it difficult to get away. Sometimes they find it easier to procrastinate because they originally left home through a quarrel with the deceased parent. But generally they tarry because the deceased is a proxy parent or because they have older brothers at home who will conduct the funeral. Later, perhaps, when the mantle of the lineage headship falls on their shoulders they will return, like Pal and Dɛma, to take over and end their lives in the ancestral home. It is a feature of Tale custom that natural human weaknesses are not unduly penalized by public opinion. As long as he lives a man can always try to make good his derelictions of filial duty. It lies between him and his ancestors. The community is neutral.

At funeral ceremonies of old people one also sees that filial piety includes pride in one's parents. The *koordaana*, owner of the funeral or chief mourner (that is, the deceased's oldest son), and his brothers strain their resources to the utmost to provide a lavish funeral. It is not uncommon for nearly the whole harvest of a household to be consumed in making the beer and providing the cooked food required. In addition, animals must be slaughtered in honour of the dead. A poor man may be able to give his father only a couple of sheep or goats which he has had to borrow for the purpose. On the other hand, when Doohraan, the head of Siiyɛŋ biis of Tongo, died, rich in years and in honour, his sons slaughtered a cow, a donkey, and about a dozen small stock for his spirit; and Sayawuob postponed his mother's funeral for two years so that he should be able to give her a cow. At a big funeral, when the war parade (*dee*) and the whole concourse of clansfolk, kinsfolk, neighbours, and friends of the dead stand milling at the gateway, the oldest son climbs on to the wall to address the crowd. Wearing his ceremonial plumed helmet of straw, with a large red cock in his hand, he looks down haughtily upon the crowd and delivers his harangue. His speech, spun out with all the tricks of rhetoric in the Tale repertoire, is proud almost to the point of arrogance. He is relating the great deeds of his dead father or mother. They may seem trivial, sometimes, to the cold-blooded ethnographer—so and so borrowed five cows and paid them back in two years; so and so was a redoubtable farmer who in one year sold enough grain to buy three cows; another man boldly carried off his wife from under the noses of Mamprusi who had seized her; and this old woman was a potteress who by her own efforts earned the money to buy two cows, and in addition had been faithful to her first and only husband until his death. But it is not the substance so much as the occasion of these funeral panegyrics that matter to the Tallensi. At the end of his speech the son beats the cock (or if he is a rich man it may be a goat) to death on the wall and flings it to the crowd with a challenge that any person who can claim equal achievements should take it. But someone in the crowd always cries out that there is no one who can match these achievements or can claim that his father or mother did so.

This is the most dramatic though not the only expression of pride in one's parents among the Tallensi. They always show off an old parent, own or classificatory, with great pride to a visitor. I have often been led out of my way to shake the hand of a blind and senile old man or old woman who was too bemused with age to understand the long speech with which we were presented to each other. Women and children tell the stranger proudly, 'Don't you know so and so? I am his child.' This pride in one's parents is the reciprocal of their pride and satisfaction in the possession of children. It is so marked with old people in part because the Tallensi honour old age as a sign of good luck (*zusɔŋ*). The death of an old parent is an occasion of rejoicing rather than of lamentation for they say, 'Has he not savoured life to the full? (*U pu di ŋxvɔr sa'ahi*).' At the same time the natives say that the death of an old man is a loss to his sons even though he had long relinquished the management of household affairs to them and had only a titular superiority in the affairs of the community. He may be blind, deaf, and senile, as Doohraan was, but he is still the head of the family and lineage, the hub of their unity, and the intermediary between them and their ancestors. However infirm an old man may be of body or understanding he is regularly told of everything that happens in the house, and his consent is always obtained before anything is done in his name, as everything that pertains to the family or lineage must be.

From all that has been said here it can be seen that filial piety among the Tallensi is by no means a simple and stereotyped attitude. Respect, affection, a feeling of mutual identification, and a sense of dependence, supported by the whole strength of the lineage system and the ancestor cult, are mingled with great freedom in everyday intercourse, as we shall see shortly, and with the strain of latent antagonism. It is an indication of the strength and internal consistency of the social system as a whole that ruptures between father and son are not very common.

Filial piety is a significant element in all Tale genealogical relationships. A person's loyalty to and solidarity with his lineage springs from his relationship with his father, his ties with his matrilateral kin from his relationship with his mother. The founding ancestor of a lineage is visualized as its 'father' and the progenitrix of a lineage segment as its 'mother'.[1] A person identifies himself with his patrilateral kin through first identifying himself with his father, and with his matrilateral kin by extending his identification with his mother. Economic motives, jural rules, and ritual sanctions work on the individual through his sentiments of filial piety.

This can be seen clearly in the interlocking of land tenure, local cohesion, and clan solidarity. The land a man owns in his clan settlement

[1] Cf. *Dynamics of Clanship*, pp. 201 ff.

is usually land that has come to him by inheritance from his father.¹ It is hallowed land because it has come to him thus. This land is the basis of his local and economic ties with his lineage and clan. In psychological terms it stands for the most significant aspects of his own development and of his relationship with his father. It was here that he learnt to farm, working side by side with his father and thus coming to know every inch of it. His father's social personality is for him closely associated with this land, with the homestead which stands on it somewhere, and with the family graves including, in time, those of his parents, that lie there. When he inherits this land it is the principal sign that he has at length stepped into his father's shoes.

The cycle of development through which the nuclear lineage regularly passes shows the working of filial piety very clearly. A typical history is that of Ba'ahug's house. When Ba'ahug inherited the homestead and the home farms of his nuclear lineage, at Tɔŋ-Kuorəg, about thirty years ago, he had living with him his son Saŋbɔŋ and his full brother Zɔŋ. Then Ba'ahug died and his brother Zɔŋ inherited the homestead and the patrimony. In due course Saŋbɔŋ moved out to build his homestead on his own father's part of the patrimonial bush farm at Gbambee, and there he brought up his family. In 1934 Zɔŋ died and Saŋbɔŋ inherited the homestead and patrimony. He remained at Gbambee, however, until 1936. There had been illness and other mishaps in his family, and the diviners declared that his father, who was buried beside the original homestead at Kuorəg, was demanding that he (Saŋbɔŋ) should go back there. So in 1936 he handed over the homestead at Gbambee and some of the land there to his oldest son and returned to take up his abode in the ancestral homestead. For him the cycle of development from the domestically unitary joint family through the phase of its dispersion and back to a phase of unity was completed. The unity would have been more obvious still if he had made his oldest son accompany him to the old homestead, and if his late 'father' Zɔŋ's children had remained with him. Actually Zɔŋ's sons, finding that the land that would now be available for their use was insufficient, decided to move to Biuŋ; and there was no need for Saŋbɔŋ to summon his own oldest son to come and live with him as the homestead at Gbambee is regarded merely as an outpost of the ancestral home. There is this advantage, also, about keeping up the Gbambee outpost, that when Saŋbɔŋ dies Zɔŋ's oldest son will be the heir and will return to resume the ancestral home and lands. This will mean that Saŋbɔŋ's sons will probably have to move out to their father's land at Gbambee, so the homestead might as well be kept up. If Saŋbɔŋ had died at Gbambee before inheriting the ancestral home he would have been brought home to Kuorəg for burial beside his father and forefathers.

In the next generation there will be a new development. For Saŋbɔŋ's

¹ Cf. *Dynamics of Clanship*, ch. xi.

sons their father's home and land has a double location. In terms of their own experience and immediate attachments it is the home and land at Gbambee; in terms of the jural and ritual functions of the lineage it is the home and land at Kuorəg. The oldest of them may go back to Kuorəg when he inherits the patrimony. The younger may prefer to stay at Gbambee when he becomes head of the lineage and leave the Kuorəg homestead and land to the other branch of the lineage. He will be living in what is to him his father's homestead and on what is to him his father's land in the most intimate and personal sense. And when he dies his kinsmen will probably be informed by the diviner consulted on the day he is buried that he desires to be buried at Gbambee and not at Kuorəg. Thenceforth a new home is established for one of the lines of agnatic descent sprung from Saŋgbɔŋ. This branch will still maintain close jural, economic, and religious ties with the other branches of the same segment established at Kuorəg and will act together with those branches in all corporate affairs, but it will be independently localized. Thus filial piety which has drawn Saŋgbɔŋ back into the local orbit of his ancestral lineage, and will keep him there even after death, will be the ostensible incentive that will make one of his sons establish a new home for his posterity at Gbambee.

The following genealogy shows the agnatic relationship of the individuals that have been mentioned:

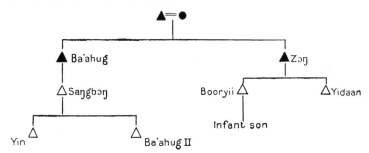

And the table on p. 184 shows the cycle of development of this nuclear lineage as we have sketched it.

The natives are well aware, of course, that these processes of dispersion and reintegration in the nuclear lineage arise directly out of the genealogical cleavages and economic needs of its component segments. But the chief sanction for each defined stage in the process is, in their eyes, filial piety. Objectively, it appears to the anthropologist as a socially accepted rationalization or pretext covering a rearrangement of property and jural relations made necessary by economic needs and the logic of the social structure; subjectively, it is felt by those concerned as an irresistible ritual sanction, crystallized as a command from the father's spirit. It works consistently in the direction of keeping the lineage intact

Date	At Kuorəg	At Gbambee	Elsewhere
c. 1920	Ba'ahug — Zɔŋ Saŋbɔŋ — Booryii		
1933	Zɔŋ Booryii — Yidaan	Saŋbɔŋ Yin — Ba'ahug II	
1936	Saŋbɔŋ Ba'ahug II (and other sons) Booryii — Yidaan and their children	Yin Yin — Ba'ahug II and their children	
19—?	Yin [Yidaan and/or Zɔŋ's grandsons in separate homestead?]	Ba'ahug II (Ba'ahug II establishes new home at Gbambee)	Booryii — Yidaan (At Biuŋ)
19—?			[Zɔŋ's surviving sons and/or grandsons may have a homestead of their own at Kuorəg, or at Gbambee or at Biuŋ]

in relation to its local and spiritual focus. Economic necessity is undoubtedly the chief incentive to fission in the joint family, but the process of reintegration is as much or more the result of ritual and affective forces.

This is the essence of the pull exercised on every Talǝŋ by his father's original home (*daboog* pl. *dabaar*), and on lineages in their corporate existence by the *daboog* of their founding ancestor. We have already recorded several cases of men who returned to rebuild their fathers' homesteads after many years of absence. As these instances show, it often involves an economic loss when a man gives up fertile land in a peripheral settlement to return to one of the ancient settlements where the soil is less productive. There are many men who in their young days farmed at Biuŋ or Gbambee or Datɔk and had many cattle, sheep, and goats then but now have no more than their neighbours. Their explanation is that they had to give up their farms in the peripheral settlements to come and rebuild their fathers' original homesteads, thus exchanging plenty for poverty. This was the story of Sayɔbazaa and Na'ampaahya, of Saandi, Loobuol-Kugǝr, and of Sayawuob, and of many more than need be mentioned here, in addition to those already referred to. It was the religious and affective associations of their ancestral homes that drew the Hill Talis back to the hills in 1936 after twenty-five years of exile, in spite of the economic sacrifice this meant for a great many of them. Down on the plains most of them had all the land they needed immediately around their homesteads. It was fertile land, too, won from the uncultivated bush. They were better off for food than they had been on the hills. But they gladly gave up their temporary homes and farms to return to their exiguous stony patches and strips on their hilltops, the crops of which have to be supplemented by farming bush farms three or four miles away. For all their rationalizations about the better climate and pleasanter surroundings of the hills, the truth was that it was a matter of faith. On the hills they were back among their fathers and forefathers, and this gave them a sense of religious security they had lacked on the plains. It meant, also, that they were back in the right local setting of their clan and lineage relationships.

The return of the Hill Talis to their ancestral homes is a striking case because it involved the building of between 250 and 300 homesteads[1] in two dry seasons and the movement of over 2,000 people. But every dry season, within a settlement, one finds men rebuilding homesteads on the long-deserted sites of their fathers' homesteads. This happens when a man at length succeeds to the position his father held in the lineage structure. So Deemzeet built a new homestead on the site of his own father's homestead when he became head of the section of Puhug at Tongo. Or it may be simply that a man has a series of

[1] A minimum estimate. The total number of homesteads built or rebuilt was probably nearer 500, but I was not able to check this.

misfortunes and learns from a diviner that this is due to his dead father who is angry with him for leaving his *daboog* site derelict. That was the case with Pa'anbɔbis and Mambaŋya.

We have said previously that the sentiments, the rights, and the duties of parent and child to one another are traced back by the natives to the fact of birth; but in actual social usage they are fortified by strong ritual sanctions. Tallensi have these in mind when they say that a father's authority is irresistible because 'he sacrifices for you (to your ancestors)'. Your father 'owns (*so*)' you because he begot (*dɔya*) you; and he sacrifices (*kaab*) on your behalf because he begot you; you can only approach your ancestors through your father while he is alive, and if you do so after his death it is always through the intermediation of his spirit. It all goes back to the fact of birth, but the ritual sanctions are the most important instrument by which a father's authority is maintained, as our discussion has several times shown, particularly in the case of a proxy or classificatory father. Siŋ cannot defy his proxy father Na'abzɔ 'because', as he says, 'he sacrifices for me'; Da'amo'o chafes under the vexations Kutɔbis and his sons frequently put upon him, but he cannot, for the same reason, disregard Kutɔbis's authority over him as his late father's brother. It is very rarely indeed that a man in a paternal position will refuse to sacrifice on behalf of another who is in the position of a 'son' to him; but the fear of this sanction has a restraining influence in cases such as those of Siŋ and Da'amo'o. The whole hierarchy of authority in the lineage rests on this ritual office. Most of the men of Yinyɛla's inner lineage were opposed to his cutting himself off from the rest of Puhug, but they had to 'follow (*dɔl*)' him because he had custody of the lineage *bɔyar* and 'sacrificed for them'.

CHAPTER VII

THE GENETIC DEVELOPMENT OF PARENT-CHILD RELATIONSHIPS

TO complete our analysis of the norms governing the relations of parents and children we must now glance at their development in the course of the child's life. Different themes are dominant at successive periods of the child's physical and social maturation. At first the dominant theme is the love and devotion of the parents; then their authority and responsibility come to the forefront; later the principle of reciprocity emerges as a leading idea; and lastly we see the differentiation and hidden opposition between successive generations on the surface.

Babyhood[1]

Tale babies (*bilie*, pl. *bilies*) are the darlings of the family. Totally naked except for the amulets of their spirit guardians around the neck, they are seldom quite clean. But then, bodily cleanliness is the least of the virtues amongst the Tallensi. Though I have seen babies at the sitting stage (about a year old) left alone in a shady spot for an hour or so, it is more usual for them to be in someone's care at all times of the day. Looking after baby is everybody's job—grandparents, older brothers and sisters (boys are as tender as girls with a baby), mother's co-wives, father, and, most important of all, mother.

Up to the time that it is weaned, which occurs towards the end of its third year, a baby (*bilie*) is mainly in its mother's care. For at least the first year it is wholly dependent on the breast for nourishment. It is given the breast whenever it cries or frets or the mother feels inclined to nurse it. Whenever the mother sits down to rest or has

[1] Tallensi distinguish different stages of infancy according to the feeding-habits and level of physical skill reached by the infant. They never count months or years, but a parent is often able to state roughly how many months or years have elapsed since the birth of the child, working it out, most commonly, by reference to harvest and sowing times or to the Great Festivals. A babe in arms is *bilie*; until it is weaned it is described as 'still suckling (*u na mɔyarme*)'. If it is said to be still suckling but 'eating a little porridge (*u diit sayabo biel-biel*)' one can infer that it is at least 2. The unweaned infant's stage of development is further specified by stating whether it is crawling (*u bɔyarme*) or walking (*u kyɛnme*) or already talking (*u vɔlǝmrǝme*). When the child is weaned it is said to 'have left off milk (*u tuk biihim*)'. Lastly comes the stage, at between 3 and 4 years, when it is said to be old enough to have another immediately following sibling (*u saya nyeer marǝga*)—an idea we shall explain in a later chapter. The subject-matter of this chapter is supplemented by my paper, *Social and Psychological Aspects of Education in Taleland*, cit. supra.

nothing else to do, her babe is at the breast, sucking hungrily or, if it is replete, just playing with the breast with its mouth, its fingers, and its toes. If the mother is away another woman of the household will give the baby medicated water to drink when it cries or will put it to her breast for comfort. It may be any woman of the family, but will usually be a co-wife.

By the age of 18 months a baby's diet is being regularly supplemented with small lumps of porridge, often pre-masticated by its mother. It is gradually and usually painlessly weaned by increasing its solid food (chiefly porridge), until it is eating the same food as the adults. The only time Tale women have to wean a baby abruptly is if they become pregnant through lack of self-control during the nursing period. Tallensi say that this distresses the baby but that harsh measures are not required as a pregnant woman's milk disgusts a baby. They also say that the premature deprivation of its mother's milk prevents the child from thriving. In fact the premature pregnancy of its mother is probably more of a psychological deprivation for the child than a nutritional loss. By the time a child has its milk teeth and is able to run about, at the age of about 3, it gets no more nourishment from the breast. But its mother's breast is still its chief solace. If it is in pain, or frightened, or just tired and peevish, it cuddles into its mother's arms and clings to her breast for consolation, and a younger baby makes this impossible.

The completion of weaning marks the first stage in the child's physical and psychological severance from its mother. It has learnt to do without its mother for hours or days at a stretch. It remains contentedly in the care of an elder sister or other member of the household or even its maternal grandmother, as long as it is well and not hungry. It runs about and plays with other children of the homestead and neighbouring homesteads. It can talk fluently and so communicate its wishes to others. And its independence is increased when its mother becomes pregnant again and it can no longer run to the breast for comfort. Its mother is still the centre of its universe—and will remain so for two or three years more, in the case of a boy, and until marriage, for a girl—but the toddler has begun to glimpse the wider social space into which it is growing. Since it began to crawl it has often been told to 'go to your mother (own mother)', 'go to your mother so-and-so (mother's co-wife)', 'go to your grandfather (or grandmother)', 'go to your father (own father)', 'go to your father so-and-so (father's brother)', 'go to Yin, Tee, Baa (a sibling)' by one or other member of the family. Thus it has learnt to divide the people who come into its social space into 'own mother', 'own father', 'other mothers and other fathers' (who take care of it now and then), and 'other children', those whom it plays with, or eats with, or sees about the house. Own parents stand out clearly to the infant—its mother for obvious reasons, its father, as one man put it, 'because she (his little daughter) is often told and because she sleeps with her mother and sees me in her mother's room'. The other categories are blurred; any adult of the domestic group is described as a 'mother' or 'father'.

During these first three or four years a child's father, though he sees less of it than its mother does, is as loving and indulgent a parent. A baby can do no wrong; for, as Tallensi say, 'it has no sense (*u ka yam*)'. I have seen an infant screaming in a tantrum or nagging tiresomely at its mother while she was too busy with a household task, such as cooking, to attend to it, and its father come in and carry it off to soothe it. What discipline or frustration of impulse a child encounters in this period comes mainly from its mother or a young nursemaid. For example until it can drink by itself, an infant is regularly given a drink (*ŋuh*, causative from *ŋu*, to drink), at least once daily, usually when it is bathed. This is an item of hygiene with a quasi-magical stamp. The fluid may be plain water, unboiled or previously boiled and cooled down; or it may be a decoction of roots (*ŋaya*), the generic term for any vegetable products used in Tale leechcraft and medicine. Its composition is prescribed by the child's spirit guardian (*sɛyər*). After its bath the mother lays the child on her lap facing sideways, holds her cupped hand to its mouth, and pours the drink from a small calabash into the babe's mouth. It splutters and chokes, kicks and screams with rage, but the liquid is poured down its throat relentlessly.

Until they can run about by themselves Tale children are not expected to be house-clean. By the age of 3, however, most of them have learnt to run outside to defecate during the day and to ask to be taken outside in the night. They are still apt to micturate indoors wherever they may happen to be. Tallensi do not inculcate clean habits by direct training or by punishing faults in a child. A child acquires cleanliness by a gradual process of habituation[1] and social maturation as its general self-control, its powers of locomotion and of speech, and its identifications with adults grow. But if a small child, already accustomed to run outside, has an accident indoors, it is likely to be rebuked by one of the adults, most probably its mother or an older sibling.

It is also the mother who stands for the most serious deprivation the child experiences up to the age of weaning, the loss of the breast. There is nothing in their folk-lore or customs suggesting that the Tallensi have anything but the most matter-of-fact attitude towards the female breast. I have seen a man, with that utter lack of squeamishness characteristic of most Tallensi, when treating his brother's wife for inability to nurse her baby, himself suck at her breast in order to test the flow of milk. But there is a custom which hints that the mother's breast is felt to be a special symbol of motherhood. If a woman is very grievously affronted by her grown-up son or daughter, and she takes hold of her breast and says, 'I suffered to bear you and this is how you treat me

---

[1] Described in my *Social and Psychological Aspects of Education in Taleland* as a response to the expectation of normal behaviour.

(*Man daa nye fara dɔyi ki ɛŋɔm la ŋwala*)', this is a curse of the most terrible kind. For that reason, no doubt, none of my informants could quote an instance of a mother actually putting this curse on a child. The symbolism is of interest, however, in view of the stress Tallensi lay on the mother as food-giver in their conventional picture of her.

Childhood

The next three or four years of a child's life are probably its freest and happiest. Its energies are spent in play or in roaming around the immediate neighbourhood of the homestead in the company of slightly older siblings and classificatory siblings. But children of this age delight in being with their parents too. They will hang around their mother in the kitchen and trot around or sit with their father when he is resting under the shade tree. They see and hear everything that is going on in the house and are tolerated at all domestic occasions. In this way, and through their mimetic play, they build up the rudimentary schemas[1] of ideas, manual dexterities, and sentiments out of which grow the skills, interests, and values of later life. Love and indulgence is still the keynote of their parents' and other close relatives' attitude to them. Tallensi say that small children at this stage are still more attached to their mother than to their father because it is she who feeds them. In fact, as we have already mentioned, throughout a Talɔŋ's life he thinks of his mother as the one who gave him food without stint, going hungry herself, if need be, so that her child might be fed.

By the age of 7 or 8 the child's world is becoming much more complex; and the shadow of discipline and authority is creeping over it. Until it reaches the threshold of adolescence, at about 12 to 14 years of age, it still remains free to play for much of its time. But from the age of 7 or so boys and girls are eager to participate in the adult routine of life and they become more and more involved in it. They begin by being given the simplest economic and household tasks such as scaring the birds from the fields of ripening grain, tethering the goats, rounding up the poultry—tasks which children of both sexes perform—or sweeping the house, carrying a tiny pot of water, gathering edible fungi or herbs for the pot, which girls only do. A very common task of both girls and boys at this stage is acting nursemaid to a baby. As this shows, there is very little social differentiation between them as yet.

By the age of about 9 or 10 children begin to adopt the sexual division of labour customary among the Tallensi, and with it the corresponding division of social roles and ideals. Boys start following their older brothers and take their turn at herding their father's cattle if he has any. They are becoming more skilful with the hoe and by the age of about 12 reach a high degree of proficiency. A 12-year-old boy helps his mother

---

[1] Cf. the discussion of this concept in my Memorandum just cited.

to hoe her ground-nut plot and may have a small ground-nut plot of his own. Sometimes he will work short spells with his father on the home farm. He may have a fowl or two of his own and will be trying to breed chickens and guinea-fowl. He is thinking of farming and of the breeding of poultry and livestock in the same terms as his father does. A girl of 9 or 10 is learning from her mother how to cook, how to beat floors and plaster walls, how to carry out all the routine domestic duties of a housewife. She is acquiring the woman's view of life centred on marriage and motherhood.

On the economic side the child's world has become differentiated into two divisions in accordance with the sexual division of labour. It has become correspondingly differentiated on the structural side into a sphere of masculine interests and dominance and a sphere of feminine interests and dominance—overlapping spheres, it is true, but still with differences of major emphasis. At sowing time and harvest time, when a house is being built, a funeral made, or a sacrifice carried out, a boy is with the men, sometimes lending a hand and so acquiring the right ways of doing things, as often as not weaving himself in and out of the activity, together with his friends, in play.

It is striking to see how boys at this stage identify themselves with their fathers in speech, gesture, and behaviour, and this gives a bias to their character for life. Nindɔyat of Zubiuŋ's three boys, from the oldest, aged about 20, to the youngest, aged about 7, had their father's arrogant, vulgar egotism. Ɔmara's three sons, covering about the same age range, were, like their father, quiet, modest, and self-effacing. Samane's two small boys of about 7 or 8, who always followed him about like two pups, had his engaging swagger and blunt self-confidence. And one sees it, also, in the way a small boy will hector his mother—for instance, when the family is out sowing or lifting ground-nuts—in exactly the tone of voice and manner that his father uses. Little girls identify themselves in the same way with their mothers both in the work they do and in their ways of behaving. I used to learn a great deal about the opinions and personal attitudes of men and women from the gossip brought to me by their children. By the age of 8 or 9 a girl feels herself to belong to the women. She talks with disdain of her 5-year-old playmate or sister who still eats fowl and she is full of the women's gossip of babies and pregnancies and marriages.

Up to the age of about 5 a child is allowed much latitude in conforming to the standards and values of Tale culture. By the age of 8 or 9 it is 'acquiring sense (ŋɔya yam)', beginning to understand these standards and values and is expected to conform to them as far as its physical and social maturity permit. Its parents will henceforth assert their authority and exercise discipline to assure this, and thence comes a further social and emotional differentiation of the parents. Properly speaking it is only the father who exercises authority over a child; a mother rules her child through love and solicitude. Tallensi have a maxim. 'If you do not harass your child it will not acquire sense (*Nyεn pu mugh i bii la u ku ŋɔya yam*).' They do not mean by this that to spare the rod is to spoil the child, as I thought when I first heard it, but that a child must be kept in order and made to conform to accepted standards or else it will not learn to conduct itself properly. They think of this as being chiefly a father's task. A mother, they say, will not thrash (*bo*) her child for misbehaving; she will only scold and upbraid (*nuom*) it. A father has the strength of will (*suhkpe'emər*) to thrash his child for misbehaving, and it is his duty to do so.

However, a father does not cease to be tolerant, kindly, and affectionate when his child becomes old enough for discipline. I have never seen a child actually being thrashed by its father, but I have had many accounts of punishments received by children and by men and women in their childhood, and I have often heard children scolded by a father or mother. From what has been said in the early parts of this chapter it can be surmised that Tallensi are very long-suffering with their children. If they punish them it is in anger admitted by the child to be justified. I have heard of children being punished for disobedience, for neglecting or spoiling a task entrusted to them, for yielding to temptation and breaking a food taboo, for stealing a mother's co-wife's ground-nuts, and for other similar faults. They are punished, that is, either for defying the authority of their parents, or for failing to conform to moral or ritual custom or good manners, or for causing economic loss or damage.

In fact Tale children are not often punished. By the time they are considered to be mature enough to deserve punishment for faults they have learnt to accept the control and authority of their parents and seniors as a natural thing and have begun to develop an adult's conscientiousness about the standards and values of their culture. It is noteworthy, for instance, that Tale children are rarely disobedient. Even adults rarely defy a parent's commands. A child of 7 or 8 usually keeps totemic taboos as strictly as an adult.[1] A 9- or 10-year-old has watched sacrifices to the ancestors often enough to have a good idea of what they mean. He knows what a ritual sanction is even if he does not yet understand it. His sense of property is well developed. He distinguishes clearly between *tuum* and *meum*. He knows his father's hen or sheep or cow and his father's brother's, and he can trace the boundaries of his father's farm plots. He has begun to take a responsible part, though but a very small one, in the scheme of domestic organization pivoting around his father. This is the root of his submission to his father's authority.

Two stories illustrate these points very well. When Naabdiya was about 8 years old he was lying on a mat in his mother's *dεndɔŋo* one evening, half asleep, listening to the conversation of his parents. The

[1] Cf. *Dynamics of Clanship*, p. 125.

PLATE 9

a. The tribulations of motherhood: the daily bath and massage of the mother after childbirth

b. The husband's mother and a co-wife of the new mother give her new-born baby its daily bath. The water is so hot that the baby goes rigid with pain

PLATE 10

a. Kinship patterns are not specific in public etiquette or domestic intercourse. An unposed group having a rest in the middle of the day. From left to right: *Kpana Tey*, his daughter-in-law, his grandson, and his youngest child

b. A father eating with his youngest son while his oldest son lounges beside them (Hill Talis)

desire to urinate overcame him and being drowsy he wetted the mat. His father saw this and flew into a rage. 'You, a big lad, and you do this,' he stormed. 'You yourself will wipe the mat with your body'; and he commanded the child to roll in the urine so as to wipe it up. 'I wept', said Naabdiya, 'and I was afraid, but I began to roll in the urine. Then my mother cried out to my father to leave me alone. "Do you want to kill the child? (she cried) I suffered to bear a child and you want to kill him. I myself will wipe it up." But my father did not allow her to do it. A woman's heart is soft because she has borne the child. Thus my father taught me wisdom (*paalǝm yam*).' The moral drawn by Naabdiya needs no comment.

The other story shows the strength of paternal authority and the degree to which a boy of 10 or 11 has become imbued with the values of his culture. The boy is Yindɔl, the first-born son of Zaŋ. In 1936 his father went to Kumasi for some months. Before leaving he put aside a small quantity of grain for the family's needs and gave orders that on no account should anybody go into the granary to take any more grain until his return. The supplies he had put aside were soon exhausted. With the help of small gifts from her kinsfolk his wife managed to scrape a meal every other day for her three children. She herself lived almost entirely off wild vegetables which she cooked to supplement the children's porridge. But though they were practically starving neither she nor Yindɔl would go to the granary, because, as Yindɔl said when he told me of their plight, Zaŋ had forbidden it, and in any case he, as a first-born, could not go into his father's granary. Why did his mother not ask her husband's brother to get her some grain from Zaŋ's granary? I asked. 'Oh no', said the boy, speaking as if he were the head of the house in his father's absence, 'she dare not do that. Besides, we shall need that grain for the farming season.'

But at the same time as the child is learning to take the authority of his father for granted and fitting himself into the configuration of domestic relations, a contrary process is emerging. This process springs from the psychological and social cleavage that underlies the strong ties of duty, affection, and common interest between parents and children, the universal cleavage between successive generations. The structure of the family gives this process its form; and it is expressed through the economic organization and in ritual values. The 12-year-old is becoming differentiated as a person in his or her own right. Indeed, with boys this process commences at an earlier age, and its first sign is a small boy's refusing to sleep in his mother's room. Girls often continue to sleep with their mother until they are approaching puberty, unless there is a grandmother in the house; then they will go to sleep with her when they are about 6 or 7. A boy, however, is ridiculed by his playmates if he still sleeps in his mother's room after the age of 7 or 8. Generally boys of that age sleep with a grandparent or with the older boys in their *doo*, the room specially set aside for the boys of the homestead to sleep in. Tale ideas of propriety come into this. If a woman has children over the age of about 3 sleeping with her and her husband wants to come to her, he will order the children to go and sleep in another room. Older children are said to know that they must leave the room for the night when their father comes to their mother. Tallensi are horrified at the suggestion that children who 'have sense' might witness sexual relations between their parents.

As we have mentioned, a boy of about 12 is generally able to help his mother with the cultivation of her ground-nut plot, the produce of which is entirely at her own disposal. He often has a small ground-nut plot of his own and the produce of it belongs to him. He may, for instance, sell his ground-nuts for a few pence in order to buy himself a loin-cloth. Or he may prefer to keep them; and then he will store them in one of his mother's store-pots. He may have a hen of his own, too, as we have observed, and its eggs, or any chickens he succeeds in breeding from them, belong to him. Now it is very unusual for a boy to be given this first start in animal husbandry by his father. For he already has a share in his father's property. He will contribute to its acquisition by his labour, and he will one day, as the natives always emphasize, inherit it. A boy gets his first hen from his mother or from one of his matrilateral kinsmen, most commonly his maternal grandfather (*yaab*) or uncle (*ahəb*), but sometimes his father's *ahəb* or some other kinsman of that class. This is a quasi-paternal gesture on the part of the maternal uncle knitting his ties with his sister's son more closely. Many a Taləŋ can point with pride to a cow which he bought with the proceeds of selling goats and sheep of his own breeding, the first of which was bought with the money he had saved from selling chickens bred from the hen his uncle gave him. And when the cow gets old he is obliged to take it to his mother's brother to be sacrificed to the latter's lineage *bɔyar* as a thank-offering.

The significant point, here, is that a boy begins to act and feel as a social personality in his own right in economic terms and in opposition to his patrilineal line. His self-differentiation is a function of his matrilateral kinship, correlated with the antithesis between the *dug* and the *yir* in the structure of the joint family. Their childhood attempts at animal husbandry may be the first stage in the economic differentiation of sons of the same man by different mothers; and it is this that leads, at a later stage of the lineage cycle, to their separation. When that time comes it is a common thing for a man to 'beg' (*soh*) land, to build on and farm, from his maternal uncle. The gift of a hen is repeated at a higher economic level in a form appropriate to the nephew's wants and maturity.[1]

The economic self-differentiation of a son is both a sign of his psycho-

[1] Cf. below, Ch. XI.

logical and social self-differentiation from his father and a stimulus to it. Naturally it results in conflict at times.[1] For example, Kpana-Tee took his grandson, a boy of about 14, to live with him because the boy had quarrelled with his father, Kpana-Tee's oldest son, who was farming on his own in one of the peripheral settlements. The youngster had two hens which he had bred from a hen given to him by his *ahɔb*. He wanted to sell one in order to buy a loin-cloth for the Gɔlib Festival. His father said this was extravagance and forbade it. But the boy, supported by his mother, insisted that he could do what he liked with his 'things' (*bon*). This angered his father so much that he thrashed him. Thereupon the boy ran away to his grandfather, who took his part, and told him not to go back home for the present. As a man grows older the chances of such conflicts due to the clash between paternal authority and filial self-determination increase and are only kept in check by the sanctions of filial piety.

The process of incipient self-differentiation at this stage is distinctive of boys. It does not occur with girls before pubescence. Until that stage their relations with their parents continue to have a more childish stamp than is the case with their brothers. Whereas a 10-year-old boy would be ashamed to be found hanging round his mother when she is busy in the kitchen, a 10-year-old girl still enjoys sitting among the infants listening to her father in conversation with other men at the *zanɔne*. One notices that little girls of about this age are more quiet and docile than boys. Attached as they are to their mothers, they do not yet show that diffidence towards their fathers in public which another two or three years will bring. They do not feel the weight of the father's authority yet, beyond the ordinary discipline he exercises over their manners and habits. But there is a rapid change as they get nearer to puberty and at the same time become more proficient in women's work and more absorbed in the social world of the women. A 12-year-old girl shows more respect to her father in public than her brother does. Like her mother she will always stoop or crouch to greet a male visitor of her father's or when she is offering her father food. With her mother she is to all appearances on intimate and friendly, almost sisterly, terms. She may still be sleeping with her mother, especially if the latter is past child-bearing age.

Between the age of about 7 and the beginning of pubescence at about 12 to 14 years of age, the pattern of parent–child relations crystallizes out in the form it will have for the rest of the child's life. Proxy parents and classificatory parents are correctly discriminated and set in proper relation to own parents. Kinship sentiments are finally formed.

[1] But this is not associated with overt signs of 'adolescent instability', nor is there an institutionalized group revolt of adolescents against the generation of the fathers. Cf. my previously cited Memorandum.

Parents and Children in Everyday Intercourse

One of the most interesting things about the relations of parents and children among the Tallensi is their conduct to one another in the intercourse of everyday life. It brings out, incidentally, the distinction always clearly made between own parents and proxy parents. There is a familiarity, almost a camaraderie, between parent and child that makes the observer wonder how the authority of the parent can be as effective, and the respect and obedience of the child as sincere as the evidence of custom and belief show them to be. In this matter the Tallensi resemble us more closely than they do some other primitive peoples. It is most striking in the case of the father. From babyhood up, Tallensi address their father, both own father and classificatory father, by his name. The term *ba* (pl. *banam*), father, is used to refer to one's father or classificatory father but never in addressing him, while he is alive. After his death it is often used in addressing him in prayer as an expression of reverence. It is also used as a term of respect when addressing someone from whom one is begging a favour, or to show particular deference or courtesy, chiefly to old men. A passer-by greeting an old man not closely related to him or her, or a person of rank such as a chief's brother, addresses him as father; a person asking a small boy not closely related to him or her, for a drink, says, 'Bring me the water, oh my father'; a man who has come to intercede with a friend on behalf of the friend's son pleads, 'Desist, oh my father, desist'. Similarly, parents speak of a child as *m-bii*, 'my child', of a son as *n-dawoo* (pl. *dawoos*), 'my son', of a daughter as *m-pɔyawoo* (pl. *pɔyawoos*), 'my daughter', but always address a child by name.

With this mode of address goes great freedom of speech and behaviour towards a father, particularly one's own father. If children are asked about their attitudes to their parents they always say that they do not 'fear' (*zo*—in the sense of 'to stand in awe of') their own father as much as they 'fear' their father's older brother. Children will speak directly to their father, argue with him, contradict him politely, if necessary, laugh with him. No topic of conversation is tabooed or barred by etiquette.[1] No one can tell from the behaviour to each other in ordinary intercourse of a man and his adult son or married daughter that they are parent and child. In fact, the greater the apparent comradeship of a young adult with an old man, the more likely is it that they are own father and child.

One's mother, on the other hand, is never addressed by name but always as '*ma*, mother'; but a mother's co-wife is commonly addressed by the name used for her by her in-laws. There is also more restraint in the manner in which a person speaks to his mother than in his manner

---

[1] Sex matters, for instance, are freely discussed between parents and adult children, subject only to the rules of polite conversation.

of speaking to his father. A boy might order his mother about when the family is out harvesting, for instance, and a girl might argue with her mother as spontaneously as if she were an equal. But the underlying attitude of deference can always be detected.

This undertone of deference is also present in intercourse with the father, only less obviously than in relation to the mother. For instance, if a child is some distance away and its father or mother wants to call it, he or she will shout the child's name. But if a child, even when grown up, wishes to call a parent he will go up to him or her. A boy or a man will borrow his brother's cloth without asking permission. He will not take anything belonging to his father without permission. If two brothers or sisters or a sister and brother are eating together either will start first and both may be dipping their hands into the dish of porridge at the same time. If a child is eating with his parent he will wait for his parent to begin first and to tell him to eat, and will wait for his parent to finish and leave the dish to be 'cleaned out (*veeh*)' by him. In particular, the familiarity between parents and children never goes so far as mutual teasing, as in a joking relationship. If a native is asked about this he frowns and says that it would be most offensive for a son or daughter to tease or joke with (*kooh*) a parent or vice versa. You cannot tease or joke with your parent or your child, the Tallensi say, because you do so with your grandparent or grandchild. We shall return to this presently.

We see, again, that there is an apparent paradox in the relations of Tale parents and children. The natives cannot explain it and are puzzled if they are asked for explanations. But if we take into account the whole complex of parent–child relations an interpretation is possible. What we meet again is that ever-recurring principle of Tale social organization, the conjunction of polar forces, the synthesis of tendencies that work in opposite directions. The sense of continuity between the generations, which is so strong among the Tallensi, has to be reconciled with the sense of divergence due to differences of generation and of interests between them, if the relations of parents and children are to run smoothly. In terms of sentiments and attitudes the authority parents have over their children must be reconciled with their love for them; and children must be able to show respect for their parents, to bow to their control, without ceasing to love them and without foregoing their own independence. Children are the fulfilment of their parents' life— and at the same time felt to be in some way their parents' rivals. Parents suffer and spend themselves to give life to their child. They provide for him and fix his place in society. But he can never escape from their constraint. In all their relations with each other parents and children have to cope with actually or potentially conflicting motives and sentiments as well as with the pull and pressure of divergent social forces.

The familiarity and friendliness between parents and children in their everyday relations is one of the means by which these diverse tendencies are reconciled. The liberty to address his father by name is a reassurance, to the child, of the love and solicitude that lie behind the authority his father exercises over him. Perhaps it is also an expression of the identification of father and child by the lineage principle. And the greater deference in his behaviour towards his mother than towards his father is a sign that he recognizes her control, though she seems to have only love and devotion for him. Familiarity in everyday intercourse compensates for the filial piety due to a parent in the more formal, particularly in the jural and ritual aspects, of parent–child relations. The greater overt freedom with the father compensates for the greater emphasis on respect and dependence in the child's relations with him; the franker signs of deference towards the mother compensate for the greater emphasis on her love for her child as against her authority over him.

Clearly there is a very high degree of consistency between the social images of the parents projected in the cultural norms of the Tallensi and the actual behaviour of children to parents. The mother is thought of as the food-giver. Her love for her children is subject to no limits or laws and her status in relation to them is almost sacrosanct. Her relations with them are based on love tempered with authority. The father is thought of as the source of discipline, the guardian of good conduct. He is strict without being harsh or tyrannous. His role is of special importance in the face of the community at large and in relation to the spiritual powers that govern human life. His relations with his children are based on his authority over them, his responsibility for them, and justice tempered with love.

Adolescence and the Principle of Reciprocity

For a Tale boy the years between about 13 and 20 bring changes in degree rather than in kind in his relations with his parents. There is no affective or social break to mark a transition from childhood to adulthood among the Tallensi. Even among the Hill Talis initiation into the cult of the External Bɔyar is not associated with adolescence; it can take place at any age. A boy's social development is a process of gradual advance along lines laid down in early childhood.[1] As he grows older

[1] Tallensi distinguish the main phases of a boy's development not by chronological age but by two criteria of a broader character, either separately or together, according to the situation. They have a physiological criterion and an economic one. Physiologically they distinguish three major phases, after babyhood, in a boy: (a) when he is still a 'small boy (bumbil)' with undescended testicles, showing, as they put it, only a 'pale scrotum (lanzee)'; (b) Pubescence, denoted by the verb sol, to mature physically, and marked by the testicles descending (lana sigərəme) and the emergence of pubic hair (saŋkpɛruŋ kɔbɔt). They say 'he has matured completely (u sol ba'ahme)' of a boy who has reached puberty and is entering manhood. (c) Lastly comes adulthood, when he is a 'grown man (bonkɔrəg)'. It is by reference to these physiological phases that men often date events in their life. The second criterion is that of advancing economic proficiency. A 'small boy' is capable only of scaring the birds from the newly

he grows more and more proficient in the economic skills he began to acquire in childhood and better versed in the details of his culture. By the time he is 20 or so he knows most of what is known to his people about farming and animal husbandry, hunting and fishing, and building. He is wholly imbued with the values of his culture and has a good working knowledge of its institutions and customs. It is enough to enable him to play his part as a young man in the life of his community, but there is still much to learn which only years of experience and responsibility will give him. He is, however, an active if unimportant participant in corporate activities of the lineage and clan, and in the management of family affairs, with a right to his own opinions. In step with his growing social maturity a boy's field of social relations increases in range and in depth. His father's authority begins to loom larger, but at the same time his father's responsibilities on his behalf also increase and his own self-differentiation advances; and a theme that was of minor effect in their relationship hitherto comes into prominence. This is the principle of reciprocity.

During this period the identification of father and son is greatly deepened. It grows out of the intimacies and co-operation of everyday life. As they work side by side on the farm the father teaches his son farming skills and lore. When he performs a sacrifice at home his son is his assistant, learning from him how to carry out such rites, and what doctrines and beliefs lie behind them. In such situations he learns the names of his ancestors and begins to understand the structure of the lineage system and where he fits into it. He makes the acquaintance of matrilateral and sororal kin who come to take part in rites of this sort. The division between the men of the lineage and the women of the lineage, and the distinction between the father's side of the family and the mother's side become of direct practical relevance to him. Sometimes a man will call his adolescent and adult sons to him and tell them various things they ought to know in case he gets ill or dies. He tells them about his farms and other property, about his debts and those who owe him debts, and, a most important matter, about his ancestor and medicine shrines. In doing this he is, in effect, telling them what he knows of the history and traditions of his lineage and clan. These are matters which a man does not speak about to his daughters or wives. If they learn of them it is only incidentally, through listening to the conversation of the men. Daughters and wives are present at domestic sacrifices to ancestor spirits, but only sons are allowed to share in the cult of a man's private medicine shrines. Most important of all is the responsible

---

sown farms or from the ripening grain; a lad of 7 or 8 can be trusted to take care of sheep (*dɔl pihi*); older boys, up to the age of 14 or 15, are cattle herds (*kiem nigi*) and already help with the hoeing; after the age of pubescence a boy works on the farm side by side with the men—he farms (*u kɔɔrəme*). These phases are also used to date events, often in conjunction with the physiological criterion.

part an adolescent begins to play in the household economy. His work becomes an essential contribution to its welfare and hence he has a voice in its management.

A man who grew up under his own father's direct tutelage and learnt the arts of life from him in this way is said to be one who 'reached' (*paa*) —that is, knew in person—his father. Tallensi perceive that this is a mechanism of primary importance not only for maintaining the cohesion of the family and the lineage, but also for the transmission of their culture to their offspring. A man quoting precedents from the past for instance, in support of a claim to a debt or to a right to succeed to a particular office, bases his argument on the statement, 'I reached my father and saw such and such things', or, 'I reached my father and he told me this or that'. A man well versed in the details of the social structure, of ceremonial activities, or of economic lore, or in the finer points of etiquette, morals, traditions, and beliefs, says proudly, in explanation of his knowledge, 'Did I not reach my father?'; and a common excuse offered for ignorance is that the person concerned 'did not reach his father'.

The identification of father and son becomes of considerable social importance at this stage and henceforth. Thus it is a very common thing for youths of 18 and upwards to represent their fathers in jural and ceremonial affairs that do not demand their fathers' personal presence. If a man is asked by a clansman to act as intermediary (*pɔyasama*) in a marriage transaction, he will often send his son as his deputy. And if the intermediary chosen is a young lad, his father will act for him. So also a man sends his sons with the customary gifts he is obliged to contribute to his father-in-law's or mother-in-law's funeral. Old men always delegate their sons to act for them in political matters and often in jural affairs. In disputes about wives it is a common thing to see a man's son coming to the tribunal as his father's representative to answer for the actions of the brother whom he accompanies. In jural and ceremonial situations the identification of father and son is coextensive with the range of recognized generation differences within the inner lineage.

We have previously remarked that the identification of father and son is a fundamental element in the structure of the lineage. It is also, and more significantly from our present point of view, a fundamental feature of the normal personal relations of father and son. This is seen most simply in the affection and devotion so often found between father and son and in the strength of the sentiments and religious values associated with the father's original home.

The relationship of mother and son also changes during this phase, but again there is no abrupt break. As a boy approaches manhood he becomes more and more absorbed in the activities and interests of men and sees less of his mother in everyday intercourse. But his affection for her remains. He still helps her to cultivate her ground-nut plot, if he has no younger brothers to take this on, and assists her in other ways. Later on, when he marries, his intimacy with his mother will be revived. It is to her *dug* that he brings his wife and in her care that he places the girl.

A girl grows away from her father as she approaches puberty. This is not due to physiological taboos, for there are none connected with a girl's puberty or with menstruation in general. There are no ceremonies to mark a girl's attainment of physiological maturity, nor is there any break in her affective relations with her parents. The only significant break in the steady process of social maturation for a girl is her first marriage. Her growing away from her father is due to the sexual division of labour and the corresponding division of interests in the family. Though there is no barrier to ordinary social intercourse between the sexes in a domestic family, there is the separation of interests and activities that we have mentioned before, and adolescent boys and girls are caught up in it.

A girl of 13 or 14 years and over does not run to her father and cuddle up to him as her 6- or 7-year-old sister might do. She is with her mother and the other women most of the day assisting with the more arduous domestic tasks. She helps to clean the house, to fetch water and collect shea fruit or firewood, to grind the millet, to cook, and to care for the younger children. At harvest time, or when they are beating the floors of their rooms, she does a full day's work with the other women. She is already adept in all these feminine skills and is well versed in all the gossip of the women. A girl of 12 or 13 can be left in charge of the house for a day or two while her mother is away. She goes to market by herself to buy or sell things for her mother; and also, a more important consideration for her personally, to display her charms and flirt with the young men. She accompanies older girls on firewood parties or when they go to dance at funerals.

When a girl approaches puberty her mind is set upon marriage. Tallensi estimate a girl's stage of development before marriage by the appearance of her breasts. Leaving aside betrothal of a girl in childhood, which does not require her consent, a girl is not considered to be mature enough for serious courtship until her breasts are formed (*u biiha n-yi*). She is then called a maiden (*pɔyasarət*). Before that stage, when her breasts are budding (*u biiha m-pukət*), suitors may already be coming to her or soliciting her parents. A girl may be married before she menstruates (*lu sie*), though it is not considered seemly for her husband to sleep with her until she is capable of child-bearing. When her suitors come to her, probably the only person who knows which of them she likes best is her mother; and if she and her lover decide to elope her mother may help them. As we know, the bonds of affection between mother and daughter remain as strong as ever after the latter's marriage and are kept alive by frequent interchange of visits and of gifts. Thus, in the shea fruit season it is a common sight to see a young woman carrying a basket of shea nuts to her mother or fetching one from her mother. Even if a girl marries someone her mother dislikes, this seldom estranges them. If a woman with a young child has to go away for a few days and her mother is near, she usually choose to leave the child with her mother rather than with a co-wife. Thus during pubescence a girl's intimacy and identification with her mother deepens both in terms of her social personality and on the affective level. This is the genetic basis in behaviour and sentiment of the social tie conceptualized in the notion of *soog*.

It must not be thought, though, that a father's affection for his daughter fades away as she approaches marriageable age. Far from it. But it is inevitably biased by the expectation that she will sooner or later leave his household to marry, bear children for another clan, and cease to be a daily care and concern to him. Hence the saying that girl children are of no profit (*ka ŋoori*). Tale women are as proud as their brothers of their paternal ancestry. As we know, they never lose their bonds with their lineage kin; but they come, in time, to identify themselves primarily with their husbands' interests and not with their fathers'. Her divided interests and sentiments bring it about that when a girl reaches womanhood the element of antagonism in her relations with her father may become prominent. I have never seen it overt in relation to the mother.

As we have already recorded, a father's authority over his daughter is most conspicuous in connexion with her marriage, and it is this that often creates conflict between them. This is due largely to the fact that self-differentiation for a woman, both in economic terms and in status, comes through marriage. In principle, as we know, a man can dispose of his daughter's hand as he pleases, resorting to corporal punishment, if need be, to force her to comply with his wishes. Principles and practice often coincide, but, as we have seen, a good father tempers his autocratic rights with consideration for his daughter's wishes and welfare, particularly if, as is frequent, she is supported by her mother.

Usually, however, a man has much affection for a married daughter, and a woman, particularly in the early years of marriage, often remains greatly attached to her father. For instance, Tɔŋ-Yikpɛmdaan, perhaps because he had lost most of his children, was greatly attached to his two married daughters. When one of them was attacked by a mysterious lingering illness he himself went to fetch her home and insisted that she should stay with her mother until she became well again. But a man's attachment to his sons is very much greater as a rule. A man may be greatly distressed at the death of a young married daughter, but it is as nothing compared with his grief over the death of a young adult son. And this applies to women too, though they suffer great grief at the death of a married daughter.

These affective divergencies spring from the different social relations of father and son on the one hand, and father and daughter on the other. Though a woman's ties with her paternal family are never severed, a man's jural responsibilities for his daughter cease with her marriage. He never loses the moral and religious authority of a father, however, or the corresponding ritual responsibilities for her. His curse is as potent as ever. The shrine of her spirit guardian is in his keeping and he sacrifices to it on her behalf when her husband requests him to do so. His chief ritual responsibility arises if she is persecuted by an evil Predestiny (*Yinbe'er*). It is his duty to have the rites of exorcism performed so that she can bear children and fulfil satisfactorily her role as a wife. He is obliged to send ceremonial gifts to the funeral if she or his son-in-law dies; and he must 'fetch her funeral home (*die koor*)' and carry out the rites that bring her spirit back to her ancestral fold when she is dead. He has a very definite social and personal interest in her children too. When a woman bears her first child her husband must send immediately to tell her parents and they demonstrate their continued affection and concern for her and her children by sending her gifts of food and other necessaries as generous as their means allow. A poor man might send only a basket of unthreshed guinea corn or millet and a couple of guinea-fowls, while his wife sends some shea butter, vegetables, and firewood. A rich chief I knew, when his first-born daughter had her first baby sent a procession of his younger wives bearing an assortment of gifts, including a 25-lb. bag of salt, several baskets of grain, a sheep, six guinea-fowls, and various luxury articles. Throughout her life a woman has a right to substantial gifts of grain from her father's house at harvest time, and to a home if she is left homeless. Women make a special point of collecting these gifts of grain at harvest time whether they are in want or not. As Tanzoo, the wife of a well-to-do man with enough grain and to spare, said when she received a large basket of early millet from her brother, 'I should feel ashamed not to fetch this grain. My co-wives would scoff saying I have no brother, no father.' Thus it is a source of pride, a test of family solidarity and, most important, a recurrent demonstration of a right to share in the products of the patrimonial estate which they might have owned if they had been born men.[1] These duties that a man has towards his daughter are the nucleus of his relations with her children. They are socially prescribed and fall upon his heirs when he dies.

From Adolescence to Adulthood

Let us return to the relations of father and son during this phase of the latter's growth and study it more closely. The son is a member of

---

[1] Cf. *Dynamics of Clanship*, p. 178.

his father's household making an essential contribution to its economy by his labour and skill; he is his father's future heir; he will one day sacrifice to his father's spirit; above all, it is through him that his father's agnatic line is socially and physically perpetuated. And yet there is the cleavage of successive generations between them and the self-differentiation of the son which begins in childhood.

From adolescence onwards economic co-operation is the sheet anchor of the relationship between a youth and his father. The guiding principle is the rule that all those who work together to supply the needs of the household are entitled to a just share in the products of their common labour, and its corollary that the fruits of individual labour belong to the individual. But the working of this rule is complicated by the fact that the head of the household owns the land and 'owns' (that is, has authority over and responsibility for) his dependants. Thus a man 'owns' his son's labour and the products of it. Strictly speaking, a son cannot own property of any kind while his father is alive, and a father can dispose of a son's property as he pleases. By this rule a man does not even 'own' his children if his father is alive; and this means proxy father as well as own father. Tallensi assert this rule very emphatically, both in speech and in act, for they hold it to be the crucial sign of a father's authority. Though this authority arises automatically from the fact of begetting, its most concrete expression is found in the economic relations of father and son. When I asked the Chief of Tongo how many cattle he had he replied soberly that he had none; all his cattle belonged to his old father Nakyɛna'ab. Though, in practice, Nakyɛna'ab will not forbid the chief from doing what he pleases with these cattle, the chief never disposes of a cow, either in ritual or by sale or in jural transactions such as the payment of bride-price, without telling his father and obtaining the old man's formal consent.

The Tallensi regard the economic relations, the jural relations, and the moral and ritual relations of father and son as different aspects of the same thing. Each of these categories of relations has a binding force on the other categories. A man 'owns' his son because he begot him; but he sometimes says that he has authority over his son because the latter is dependent on him and that he has responsibilities for his son because the latter works for him. In the same way a son must work for his father as an obligation of filial piety; but his work is also the return he makes for his father's economic support and for the ritual and jural responsibility his father bears on his behalf. Just which factor is emphasized depends on the particular situation. The different elements of this configuration are linked together by the principle of reciprocity. Its essence is the idea that duties imply equivalent rights for the *tarəm*, the junior or inferior person, as well as for the *kpeem*, the senior or superior.

This configuration is not peculiar to the relations of own father and son. It is the general pattern prevailing between the head of a household

PARENT–CHILD RELATIONSHIPS

and any of his dependants—between husband and wife, proxy father and son, older brother and younger brother. And, as we have mentioned before, its elements often stand out more clearly where the consolidating effect of the emotional ties between own parent and own child is absent. They emerge clearly, also, when there is a divergence between a son's (or other dependant's) desire for independence and his father's (or the household head's) claims on his labour and loyalty.

By the time a young man marries he has advanced on the path to economic independence beyond the stage of breeding chickens for himself. He has his own ground-nut plot and generally also his *sensɛyar*. This is a plot of land allocated to him by his father, or the head of the household, where he can grow the ordinary cereal crops. It may be no more than a few hundred square yards or it may be up to an acre in size. The larger his father's home farm (*saman*) is and the fewer his brothers, the larger will a young man's *sensɛyar* be. A man allocates these private plots to his sons with an eye to the future. When, in course of time, the sons (or *their* sons) separate, each will keep the plot given to him by their father as the portion of the patrimonial land that henceforth belongs exclusively to his agnatic descendants.

A young man cultivates his private grain plot and ground-nut plot in the spare time left after he has done the work required of him on his father's farm, which always has the prior claim. There is no hard-and-fast arrangement. Much is left to the young man's own discretion. He knows very well that the first essential is to make sure of the common food-supply. At the same time his father manages to keep a discreet but sharp eye on his economic activities. It is a firm rule of etiquette that no member of a family should go anywhere without informing the head of the family. When a young man goes off to hoe his grain plot or ground-nut plot in the morning he will tell his father, in what seems to be a casual aside, what he is going to do, if he has not already told him the previous day. Then the father will either let him go or he will ask his son to leave it for a day or two until they have finished this or that job on the household farm.

In a well-run family, and at most times, this loose arrangement works perfectly smoothly. But there are times when clashes occur; and there are families in which friction over this issue is common between father and son. For instance, there was the tussle between Naabdiya and his younger son Mosuor. Mosuor wanted to lift his ground-nuts so as to sell them and buy a new cloth for the Giŋgaaŋ Festival. Naabdiya, however, insisted that *his* ground-nuts should be lifted first, before the dry weather hardened the ground and made the task more laborious. Mosuor protested that Naabdiya was being unfair to him; Naabdiya's wife and the other children could help him in the meanwhile; and Mosuor went off to his ground-nut plot. This incensed Naabdiya, who cried out that the boy was flouting his commands, and in his anger he pronounced the ominous words, 'You will see'. In an hour or two Mosuor's temper cooled off and he began to feel uneasy over the enormity of his offence. His father had uttered what amounted to a curse; and before the day was out he had called on one of his father's oldest friends to ask him to go and beg Naabdiya's forgiveness for him.

We have seen in a previous chapter that as a son grows older and his conjugal family increases, his desire for independence grows stronger, owing to the increasing wants of his wife and children. But it is not easy for a son to obtain his father's permission to set up on his own. It may take five or six years of pressure on the son's part before the old man gives way. A son only desires to go out on his own if he has younger brothers who will remain at home to work for his father—there would be no motive if he were the only son. When these younger brothers marry the pressure on the common resources of the household grows and it becomes expedient to disperse temporarily. Economic separation does not remove a son from his father's authority. He can be and often is called upon to help with the work on his father's land; his property still belongs formally to his father. Indeed, any sheep, goats, and cattle he may acquire by his industry or receive for a daughter's bride-price are housed in his father's homestead and not in his.

Nowadays a common form of independent labour and enterprise by young men is to go south for a season or longer. The chief economic stimulus for this is the desire for money to buy clothes or to make certain of the payment of bride-price for a wife. A father is not bound to provide his sons—or any other dependant—with clothes. These young men go in the dry season carrying crates of fowls to sell or seeking 'white man's work'. The youths who go at other times of the year are often stealing away without permission. But in the dry season, when farm work is at a standstill, a man will often give his sons permission to go south until the rains commence. Some men do so very readily in the hope that the boys will bring back money and 'things'. Others are still reluctant to let their sons go off, even for a short while, lest they should be tempted to stay away for a long time. Tallensi say that the freedom of movement of to-day is undermining parental authority. They say that if a man is severe with his sons, as he has every right to be, they simply run away and go south. Hence the men who think that working abroad spoils a youth or who cherish the ideal of keeping the family together all through their life, and therefore try to restrain their sons from going south, have to be tactful in handling them. Observation shows that it is usually the wise and considerate father, the man who manages his family well, who succeeds in restraining his sons from making long sojourns abroad. Where there is much friction between father and son, the son is apt to find a way out by going south; and, as we have mentioned, the likelihood of a son's leaving home is increased if one or both of his own parents are dead and he is living with a proxy parent. As is natural, fathers and sons take different views of this situation. Sons do not think that they are showing a lack of filial loyalty when they go abroad. For, they argue, it is only a temporary absence and the money they earn will eventually accrue, in part at least, to the family exchequer. As has been mentioned previously, no man ever turns away a son who comes home from abroad, whether he brings any goods and money or not; and a son who does bring back 'things' and money is doubly welcome.

We said earlier that a father owns all his son's property. This might seem to contradict what was said about the independent ownership by a son of the livestock he acquires by breeding from a gift hen or by other means. The Tallensi themselves do not admit a contradiction in this. They see it as an instance of the gradation of rights and duties that is distinctive of their whole social organization. A father's over-right entitles him to veto his son's using his own property in ways that seem extravagant; but it would be an injustice rightfully resented by the son if he were stopped from using his fowl or goat or sheep for purposes that public opinion considers legitimate. Thus everybody would agree that a father who forbade a son from using his own fowls and guinea-fowls in his courtship, or from selling his own ground-nuts in order to buy a cloth, would be acting unfairly. The case of Kpana-Tee's grandson (p. 195) illustrates this principle.

The rights of a father and the rights of a son in the son's property are reconciled by the principle of reciprocity. If a man makes use of his son's goat or sheep he should, in due course, make an equivalent return; for example, by using one of his own sheep or goats to do something for the son. This object is immediately achieved if the son's property is used for the son's benefit, as in the payment of bride-price. There is no book-keeping, but in the long run the son should feel that the gains he has received are commensurate with the amount of his own property that has been used up. A proxy father should be more careful in this regard than a man's own father. A proxy father is less concerned about the future of his 'son' than the latter's own father would be and is therefore sometimes inclined to take selfish advantage of his paternal authority. Though they have no alternative but to submit, young men deeply resent unfairness of this sort, whether on the part of their own father or on that of a proxy father; and this may be the first stimulus to their determination to set up on their own.

This is epitomized in one of the reasons Tallensi regularly produce when they are asked why young men secede from their paternal households. They say: 'It is because of hens and eggs.' Every man has at least a hen or two, even if he has nothing else, and, as we know, his hen symbolizes the starting-point of his accumulation of property. But hens lay their eggs anywhere and this gives rise to petty quarrels. Anybody who finds an egg claims it and another member of the family may dispute the claim. But if the head of the family claims an egg no one can gainsay him, so a young man might find himself left without any eggs to breed from. That is why he wishes to be independent. It is a kind of rudimentary myth summing up the economic causes of family fission. The point of interest is the emphasis on the inequitable behaviour of the 'father'. He uses his economic authority to his own advantage without making an equivalent return and thus prevents the 'son' from getting a start on the road of economic independence.

The adjustment of father's rights and son's rights has an added subtlety where cash is concerned. Supposing a young man returns from abroad with four or five pounds in cash that he has saved. According to the letter of custom he should hand all of it over to his father. But money, unlike a cow or a sheep, can be easily concealed and does not require attention; our young man can retain a part of his savings without his father's knowing of it. If it is his own father he may keep only a few shillings, particularly if he has recently been, or is about to be married and the money is wanted to pay his wife's bride-price. If it is his proxy father he will probably hand over only a pound or two, unless, again, the money is required for the bride-price of his wife; and then he will try not to hand over the money until his father-in-law actually demands the bride-price. It is common knowledge that this is the regular practice of young men returning from abroad. Fathers have no power to stop it, though most of them would like to; for up to a point, the young men are within their rights. Have they not 'taken their own legs and gone to get their money' by labour that is always arduous and sometimes dangerous? Again conflicts are inevitable, though as yet not more frequent than over other forms of property. For some men are only too apt to fritter away the money entrusted to them by a dependant before the time comes for it to be used for the benefit of the latter.

As we have mentioned before, one of the heaviest responsibilities a man bears on behalf of his son, or for a dependant standing in the same economic and jural relationship to him, is in 'marriage affairs'. It is the bridegroom's father or proxy father who has to undertake the series of jural actions required from his paternal kin in order to legitimize the union. In marriage by arrangement (*pɔyalak*) it is the bridegroom's father who starts the negotiations and carries them through. The young man himself hardly sees his bride, after his first few courting visits, until she is brought to his home. In marriage by elopement (*pɔyazaŋǝr*) the bridegroom's father's consent is essential for the marriage to be properly concluded. While, as we have already indicated, a father never openly disapproves of a son's marriage, but on the contrary always displays apparent pleasure over it, he can easily cause it to break down by holding back the bride-price.

As we know already, the two significant jural acts in the conclusion of a marriage are the sending of the placation gifts (*lu sɛndaan*) and the

PLATE 11

a. The first-born son of a Namoo is ritually 'shown' his father's granary for the first time on the last day of his father's funeral ceremony

b. The youngest son and the youngest daughter of a dead woman wear the *dooluŋ* during the concluding rites of their mother's funeral

PLATE 12

a. A grandfather with his son's children

b. The effective minimal lineage: the father, his eldest son (working in the distance), his two small sons, and his two grandchildren out on the farm for the day

payment of at least a part of the fixed bride-price of three cows and a bull, or their equivalent. The essential responsibility for the performance of these two acts lies with the bridegroom's father or father's heir, subject to the formal consent of the elders of his inner lineage. Formally, the bride's paternal kin send their invitation to the bridegroom's paternal kin to *lu sɛndaan* through the head of the latter's nuclear or inner lineage, and make their demands for bride-price through the same channels; for no jural act takes place except in the framework of the lineage system. But actually the responsibility for satisfying the bride's kin falls on the bridegroom's father. He must 'find the things'—the fowls and guinea-fowls—for the placation gifts; he must send off the intermediary (*pɔyasama*) who carries them to the bride's family; he must furnish the animals or goods or money to pay the bride-price. 'Is it not his child? (*Pa u büga*)' say the natives, implying that this is a duty arising out of the fact of parenthood. In part it is a specific duty; in part it is an aspect of a general responsibility that a man bears for his son's jural relations. Thus if his son's wife is abducted it is the father who calls on the other members of his inner lineage to stand by him in taking action to recover the wife. If his son has abducted another man's wife the father is directly answerable. Strictly speaking a son cannot contract a debt involving heritable property such as cattle or large sums of money without his father's authorization. Even if the son is a man of substance, a wise creditor will insist that his father's (and also his brothers' of the same nuclear lineage) consent to the transaction be obtained first and made known to him. If this is not done the creditor's chances of recovery are small. It becomes a question of one man's word against another's and Tallensi are past masters in the art of putting off a creditor. The concurrence of the debtor's father and brothers fixes liability for ever, and if the debtor dies before settling the debt his father, or his heir, is liable. These rules do not apply to small sums of money, say a shilling or two, or things of small value such as a hen or a loin-cloth. But petty borrowing and lending rarely takes place between people who are not friends or close kin, and it is thus generally fitted into the scheme of reciprocal aid that obtains between friends and kinsfolk.

In their jural aspect these obligations of a father arise from the fact of 'begetting (*dɔyam*)'; in their economic aspect they are greatly influenced by the principle of reciprocity. Where obligations of such great social consequence are involved, the principle of reciprocity is not limited to particular individuals but it binds their heirs and successors as well owing to the operation of the lineage principle. One or two cases will show how these two aspects are interwoven.

While Tampɔyar was courting his wife he had very little recourse to his proxy father's help. The few shillings he had received from selling ground-nuts and a fowl or two sufficed to provide the occasional penny he gave the girl whenever he saw her in the market and the gifts of tobacco and kola nuts he took to his prospective parents-in-law. He had some guinea-fowls of his own and his proxy father gave him a few more to take as presents to his prospective mother-in-law. Just when he thought the time was ripe to elope with the girl her father warned him not to attempt it as she was under a ritual taboo which prohibited her from marrying in this way. To his chagrin Tampɔyar was therefore compelled to ask his proxy father Kurug to negotiate for the girl's hand. At this point Kurug began to temporize. Marriage by arrangement is an expensive business. Had not Tampɔyar better wait a while until the guinea-fowl chicks were bigger? Tampɔyar's answer was a fit of sulks, a warning to his 'father' that he felt injured. Had he not stayed at home to help with the farming when he could easily have followed some of his contemporaries to Kumasi? Then he would have earned enough to pay the expenses of his marriage himself. Why should he tire himself out in farming if this was the treatment he got in return?

Meanwhile Kurug had been talking to the other men of his inner lineage about the affair. He felt that it was high time Tampɔyar had a wife, and he knew that if the young man were frustrated his work during the coming farming season would suffer. Moreover, he might take it into his head to run away to Kumasi. Kurug's lineage brothers shared his views. Besides, Kurug had enough cattle to pay the bride-price at once if need be and it was his duty to get a wife for the youth. It was his duty as the boy's proxy father; it was a return he owed the boy for the labour he had been contributing for several years to the household economy; it was, also, a return he owed to Tampɔyar's dead father. When the latter died Kurug had inherited his wife and his property as well as his children. Kurug had benefited from this inheritance and must now repay it to the dead man's son. And so he at length agreed to arrange the marriage. He asked one of his neighbours and clansmen, whose grandfather had been a sister's son (*ahɔŋ*) of the bride-to-be's clan, to act as intermediary and began to get together the fowls and guinea-fowls that would be needed for the ceremony by which the bride is given to her future husband's lineage representatives.

Kurug himself provided the bulk of the 'things' required for this ceremony, but Tampɔyar gave a couple of his own guinea-fowls. Kurug provided the basket of millet with which the bride's mother's co-wife was 'seen off home (*beeh*)' when she paid her the customary formal visit shortly after the marriage, and he provided all but one of the fowls and guinea-fowls for the placation gifts, Tampɔyar himself giving one fowl. Lastly, it was Kurug who gave the two cows which Tampɔyar's father-in-law demanded as the first instalment of the bride-price. These were cows to the purchase of which Tampɔyar's labour had contributed; and if Kurug had died before Tampɔyar's marriage, Tampɔyar would have inherited them.

This case, typical of dozens that occur every day among the Tallensi, shows how the motif of duty and the motif of reciprocity are intertwined. This appears still more clearly when 'father' and 'son' farm separately. Thus Saɣabo of Kpata'ar was Nyaaŋzum's late half-brother's son. He occupied the same homestead as Nyaaŋzum, but separate quarters with an independent gateway and farm for himself. When Saɣabo abducted a Gorogo man's wife, the injured husband, supported by his father-in-law, brought a case against Saɣabo at the chief's court. Nyaaŋzum, together with Saɣabo and almost all the other men of their inner lineage, went to answer the suit. Nyaaŋzum's defence was simple and straightforward. He knew of no bar to the marriage. They had no kinship ties with the girl's paternal kin, nor clanship ties with Gorogo. In former times Kpata'ar men and Gorogo men had not hesitated to abduct one another's wives. He was ready to pay the bride-price at once if the 'owner of the child (*büraan*)'—that is the girl's jural guardian in this case, the father—agreed. The latter, however, refused to accept Saɣabo as a son-in-law, so she was returned to her first husband and Nyaaŋzum forfeited his hearing fee of three shillings. Incidentally, this fee was made up of a shilling contributed by Saɣabo, a shilling from Nyaaŋzum, and a shilling from another member of the inner lineage.

Why was Nyaaŋzum so ready to accept the responsibility for Saɣabo's marriage and to answer for him at court, seeing that Saɣabo was not farming with him? In the first place it was his duty as Saɣabo's proxy father; and being a man of principle he would not evade such a duty. Even if he disapproved of the young man's behaviour he must answer for it in public, and he was under a jural obligation to pay the bride-price for the youth's wife, from his own resources if need be. In fact, however, he would not have offered to pay the bride-price with such alacrity if it were a question of using his own resources, for he had his own sons to think of. Another factor came into the situation, as Nyaaŋzum himself explained to me.

When Saɣabo's father, Nyaaŋzum's half-brother Galɔmɔyar, died, Nyaaŋzum inherited a number of cattle from him. Some were cattle Galɔmɔyar had received as bride-price for a younger sister of his and Nyaaŋzum's. These cattle accrued to the *faar*, the patrimonial property, in the strict sense; Nyaaŋzum was entitled to dispose of them as he pleased since he was the last of his father's sons. In addition, Galɔmɔyar's herd included cattle he had himself bought or had received in payment of his daughters', Saɣabo's sisters', bride-price. As Saɣabo was still only a boy, Nyaaŋzum took possession of these cattle too. In theory he could dispose of them as he pleased. In practice Saɣabo had a prior right to them, since they were his father's own earnings and his sisters' bride-price animals, and Nyaaŋzum had merely a nominal over-right. Nyaaŋzum had utilized most of these cattle for his own purposes; but he considered himself morally bound to make an equivalent return for them to Saɣabo. This was the main reason why he was ready to meet Saɣabo's bride-price debt immediately. There was also a religious sanction in the background. Had he refused to support the youth, Galəmɔyar's spirit would have become angry. He would have gone to their father's spirit and protested against the ill-treatment his son was receiving at his brother's hands, and the father would have punished Nyaaŋzum.

In the same way the father is the person who bears the essential jural responsibility for his son if the latter commits adultery. Though the negotiations for the reconciliation with the offended lineage or clan are carried out through the head of the inner lineage or medial lineage or even wider lineage segment to which the wrongdoer belongs, the animals sacrificed in the reconciliation rites are provided by his father.

Similarly a father is responsible for his son in all ritual matters in which the son is concerned as a member of the lineage or as the person through whom his father's line is perpetuated. A man is responsible to the ancestor spirits for performing the rites by which his child, boy or girl, is placed under the mystical care of a spirit guardian (*sɛyɘr*). It is the father's duty to provide the flour, beer, fowls, guinea-fowls, or other animals needed for these rites. If a child gets ill, its father has the duty of consulting a diviner and is obliged to provide any money, animals, or other goods that may be needed for the sacrifices to the ancestors, the treatment, and the payment of the medicine owner. Of course, if it is his own child a man does not think of such obligations as a duty but rather feels them to be a natural action of love and solicitude. But I have known cases where a proxy child was concerned in which the proxy father was less moved by affection than by his sense of duty and fear of mystical retribution. Among the Hill Talis it is a father's duty to provide the animals, flour, and beer required for his son's initiation into the External *Bɔyar* cult. And, to complete this catalogue of examples, a father must take the initiative and provide the 'things' needed for the rites of exorcism, if his son is persecuted by an evil Predestiny (*Yinbe'er*). If his daughter-in-law is the sufferer, he must request her father to come and perform the exorcism and must provide the contributions due from the girl's husband's family.

The mutual rights and duties of parents and children among the Tallensi have a feature of particular interest which has already been indicated in the course of our analysis, but deserves further notice. They can be used as weapons of coercion by one side against the other, the principle of reciprocity being turned into an *ad hoc* sanction. The case of Tampɔyar illustrates how a son can make use of the fact that his working power is essential for the household economy to force his father to get him a wife. This sanction is openly admitted by fathers. One day at Yinduuri I came upon a group of men engaged in a vehement argument. In the middle of the group was a man whose leg was badly swollen with guinea-worm. It appeared that he had recently inherited his late brother's widow and her two children, a boy of about 16 or 17 and a girl of about 15. He had given this girl in marriage to a Sii man, but she had taken a dislike to him and had the previous day run back home again. Now the Sii man was anxious to make sure that the girl would be regarded as his legitimate wife. He feared that she would either be kept at home now, or else take the first chance of eloping with someone else. So he at once sent an intermediary with the prescribed placation gifts, and this emissary had just arrived. But this procedure was quite contrary to custom. The placation gifts must not be sent or accepted if the bride is at her father's house. The group of men was discussing the situation. It was in the course of this discussion that the girl's proxy father said that he could not take any decision without consulting her brother. 'He is a youngster (*bii*)', he said, 'and I own him. But he is the girl's brother. And you see that I am laid up with a bad leg. If I don't consult him, will he help me on the farm and do my errands for me?'

In using these mutual rights and duties as a sanction parents have the advantage over children. Within the limits of the inner lineage a father's payment of his son's bride-price is thought of as an obligation to the son. But as against the society at large it has an extra nuance. A son has no jural *locus standi*. He cannot get a wife unless his father is prepared to accept responsibility for the bride-price, even if he himself provides the means of payment. Thus Naaho, who was earning good wages, paid all the expenses of his courtship. He bought all the 'things' needed for marrying his wife by arrangement, as well as the two cows asked for her, out of his own pocket. But he was powerless to arrange the marriage by himself. He had to appeal to his father's brother, under whose paternal authority he was, to undertake this. It is true that it would be a most unusual thing for any man to refuse to take formal responsibility for his son in such a situation. But the mere fact that the latter cannot do without his assistance reinforces his authority over his son. Again, this consideration is of more importance for a proxy-father's authority than for the natural father's. It is the same, as has been observed earlier, with the ritual sanctions a proxy father commands.

We have spoken of the principle of reciprocity in the preceding paragraphs without attempting to define it. To do so it is necessary to take into account a wider context than the relations of parents and children.

The principle of reciprocity or, more accurately, of equivalent returns[1] is implicit in the relations of parents and children. The natives see it as following on the mutual rights and duties of parents and children, and not as an explicit rule of conduct. There is a large voluntary element in

---

[1] I am indebted to Professor Radcliffe-Brown for this concept and for stimulus in appreciating its significance. I owe much, also, to Malinowski's *Crime and Custom in Savage Society*, both here and elsewhere in this book.

its working, as we have seen. Moreover, it applies equally to all members of a household and is implicit in all kinship and affinal relations. It arises out of common interests, mutual rights, and mutual obligations and is a way of giving expression to them. As these interests, rights, and obligations are of different kinds and degrees, corresponding to the differences in quality and degree of the relations involved, so there are different kinds and degrees of reciprocity. But all forms of equivalent returns have the general purpose of keeping social relations on a stable and mutual footing. The greater the field of common interests between persons, the less does deliberate calculation enter into the working of this principle. Hence the closer and more personal the relationship between people, the less formal is the rendering of equivalent returns for services or loans. Mutual services, between lineage segments, as, for instance, in the performance of one another's funeral ceremonies, are highly stereotyped. A son-in-law's services to his father-in-law must be immediately recompensed with food and drink. But between father and son, brother and brother, or husband and wife there is a continual give-and-take on a basis of all-in reciprocity. Equivalent returns cannot be demanded; it depends upon the good sense of the person concerned as to when and how he makes them, even in situations where custom lays down a definite norm. Meanness or selfishness in this respect gives rise to ill feeling and so to disharmony.

Tallensi sum up the observance of the principle of equivalent returns under the idea of debt (*samər*). Debts are goods or services accepted or requested on the definite understanding that they will be repaid and it is a maxim that debts never die (*sama pu kpira*). A man's heirs are liable for his debts.[1] Where equivalent returns are the customary mode of recompense, accepting goods and services is not a debt. A man 'borrows' (*pɛŋ*) money or a cow from a distant clansman and that is a debt; he 'takes' (*zaŋ*) or 'accepts' (*die*) his son's or wife's belongings if he needs them, and it is not a debt (*la ka samər*).

The most important criterion determining whether or not a particular service or gift or loan creates a debt is kinship. Members of a nuclear lineage and of an expanded family do not incur debts by borrowing from one another. The same rule applies to cognates whose kinship ties are as close as those of members of a nuclear lineage. If a man obtains something from his own mother's brother, for example, it is not a debt. This is definite. In theory there can be no debts either between members of the same inner lineage, or cognates whose kinship ties are as close as those of members of one inner lineage. What happens in practice

---

[1] Unless, as has been mentioned, they were not made a party to the debts at the time they were incurred or were not told of them by the debtor himself. The question of the procedures and sanctions that can be used to secure payment of a debt do not concern us here. One of the chief sanctions is public opinion. A defaulter finds it very difficult to borrow again.

varies from case to case and from lineage to lineage. We have seen how this works out among the members of Ziŋgan biis. Another instance is that of Yinworəb and his 'son' (his grandfather's brother's great-grandson) Kadɛne. Yinworəb gave Kadɛne three shillings to pay the hearing fee when he was summoned to the chief's tribunal. This was not a debt. Three or four months later Yinworəb borrowed a goat from Kadɛne. Again, this was not a debt but it was tacitly understood to be an equivalent return for the loan of the three shillings. By contrast, Ləyani used some sheep belonging to Maantiya, his father's half-brother's grandson and therefore his 'son'. This he regarded as a debt because the sheep were earmarked for the payment of Maantiya's wife's bride-price.

Outside the inner lineage, however, a debt is incurred by accepting goods or services from a clansman. The only exceptions are if the lender is also a matrilateral kinsman of the borrower—e.g. a uterine kinsman—or a close friend.

The principle of reciprocity, as seen in operation in the family and lineage, ties on to a more general theory of social action in Tale society. It is a particular application of the principle of equilibrium in the social system. The idea that in the long run mutual services or favours should balance is inherent in Tale social organization. Canalized by the lineage system, it means that a son or grandson or later descendant can make or expect equivalent returns for an action of his father or grandfather or earlier ancestor. It is a matter of pride as well as of moral or jural obligation to see that one benefit is balanced by another. For example, it is a common thing at an elder's funeral to see a distant clansman of his, who is not obliged to do so, bring a sheep or goat as a valedictory offering to the dead. The donor explains that there is a special reason for this offering. The deceased had been a friend of his father. When his father died the deceased brought a goat as a valedictory offering to his father. His goat is a return gift. The maxim that 'debts do not die' springs from this principle; and it applies not only to the relations of the living among themselves but to their relations with their departed ancestors. A grandson may have to atone for his grandfather's sins, as happened with Kuwaas. Years of constant ill luck were attributed by a succession of diviners to the sins of his paternal grandfather, whose name he bore. Kuwaas I, as Chief of Tongo, had betrayed his office by abandoning his clan and seeking only his personal safety once when the Hill Talis attacked Tongo. This was a grave sin against the ancestors, who demanded a large expiatory sacrifice, and until this was paid the sin would continue to lie heavily on the descendants of Kuwaas I. The right of self-help by raiding, and the notion that retaliatory warfare and retaliatory abduction of women are simply 'cancelling a debt (*lɛrəg samər*)',[1] belong to the same category of ideas. The principle of reciprocity underlies all these categories of social behaviour.

[1] Cf. *Dynamics of Clanship*, pp. 236, 245.

The Duty of Supporting the Parents in Old Age

Parents retain their rights and authority over their children throughout their lives. A man may be so senile that he can take no active part in household or public affairs. He is still the father of his children and the head of the household, the owner of the farms and livestock that belong to the household. Any of his sons living with him is automatically bound to farm for him. On this basis alone, and apart from the dictates of filial piety, an old man who has a son need not lack economic support. It is the same with an old woman who has a son. In her case, however, the stress is on the duty—a duty which is felt to be in part a privilege—of a son to care for his old mother, since she does not own any land.

An old man who has no adult sons need not necessarily lack food or shelter. He either has land of his own or can obtain some from a kinsman, and it is a question then of securing labour to work it. This, however, is no easy matter. Sporadic assistance can be obtained from kinsmen and neighbours, but it is impossible to get regular full-time labour. No one would go and work another man's farms for a whole farming season, either for a wage or as a kinship obligation. Thus an old man in this position is not likely to have more than the minimum of food and other necessaries. Tɛndaan Teroog was in this position. His only adult son was not living with him and he was dependent on others for the cultivation of his land. When his neighbours and kinsmen were too busy with their own farms to help him, his wife did the weeding in a rough-and-ready way. If it were not for the gifts of grain sent to him by his adult son from Mampurugu, Teroog and his family would have lived at starvation level right through the year. As it is they were just managing to subsist.

Cases like that of Teroog are not numerous, simply because the number of old men who are incapable of doing some work for themselves is small. In the whole of Tongo I knew only six old men (apart from chronic invalids) who were completely incapable of work. Another ten or fifteen (according to the criterion of efficiency employed[1]) could work, but would probably not have been able to support themselves and their wives without assistance.

A somewhat different and less frequent case is that of Sabaalug. He is an old bachelor living with his half-brother. But he does not help with the farming and so is not entitled to be supported by his brother. He keeps himself by 'scrounging' (*bimh*) a bit of food or a basket of millet, a few pence or an old garment from his matrilateral kinsmen and friends. A childless old woman like Tɔŋ, who lives with a 'son' of her long dead husband ekes out a poor existence in the same way. Tallensi are very

---

[1] Kuwaas, for example, might have done much more work if he had not had two adult sons; Voŋraan-Tee would certainly have worked less if he had had a son to help him; Ta'aŋ spent so much time on ritual and communal affairs that he did less work on his farms than he was capable of.

tolerant of such old folk, but they consider their mode of life a pitiable one, not so much from the purely material aspect as from the social side. 'Who will mourn his death? Who will give him a proper funeral?' they say. But such cases serve as examples for an argument they often put forward. I once heard it very well put in a comment on life in the coast towns. There, said the speaker, you starve if you have no money. Here, at home, no one need die of destitution. If he has no children he can always find a roof with a kinsman, either one of his close agnates or his mother's brother's people, and keep himself alive by the gifts of food he gets from kinsfolk and friends. Though a man is not bound to be overgenerous, and he is not compelled to feed a kinsman living with him who does not contribute to the common pool, it is an offence against the ancestors to refuse food to a kinsman in straits.

Still rarer are instances of people who come to live with a daughter in their old age. I knew of only two cases, one that of an old man, the other of a woman. It is considered to be unbecoming for a man or woman to live with a married daughter. It is not compatible with 'in-lawship' (*deen*) and Tallensi say it causes friction. A married daughter contributes to her parents' material welfare indirectly. Her chief contribution is through the bride-price paid for her. A cow received for a daughter's bride-price may be the starting-point of the accumulation of more livestock. In times of severe shortage a bride-price animal may be used to purchase grain and so save the family from starvation. Most important, however, is the use of a daughter's bride-price to pay off bride-price debts of her natal family. It helps, therefore, to add to the womanpower of her father's household upon which a large part of the household's productivity depends. The occasional assistance given to a man by his daughter's husband in farming, house-building, thatching, and so forth is a small item relatively to the total labour required to maintain a household, but it is enough to turn the scales in a difficult year. Many of the homesteads that were being built on the Tong Hills in 1936 would not have been completed that dry season if the owners' sons-in-law from other parts of the country had not come to their aid.

In short, a native's chief economic asset in old age (and this applies to sickness too) lies in the possession of sons, best of all own sons, but also proxy sons, that is, all those who have an interest in the patrimonial land which is for the time being in his keeping. As we already know, more distant 'sons' than those of the nuclear lineage are very unlikely to live with and work for a man whom they recognize as a classificatory father. Tallensi say that one of the reasons why sons are preferred to daughters is because they will farm for one when one is old. Women are even more apt than men to emphasize the insurance value of sons just because they are more dependent on a son's sense of moral obligation to care for them.

Yet Tallensi do not explicitly state it as one of the duties of a son to support an old father economically. They assume support of an old father to follow automatically from the economic and jural relations of parents and children and from the moral obligations of filial piety. It is simply an aspect of co-operative production and joint consumption in the household under the household head's management, and a result of the principle of reciprocity. If a man's only son, for example, were living in his native settlement and refused to have his father or proxy father in his homestead, it would be a monstrous breach of ethics. He would lay himself open to immediate punishment by the ancestors; he would, indeed, be unable to participate in the life of the community since he could not act for himself in ritual or jural affairs.

This is an hypothetical instance, for I know of no such case. But nowadays the question of supporting an aged parent does occasionally arise when men emigrate from their native settlements to seek work abroad or to farm outside Taleland. Cases are occurring of men who stay away abroad and postpone their return home from year to year, leaving an aged parent to struggle on alone. They are far from numerous —I knew of some six or seven only, counting two cases where the sons had genuine grounds for their absence.

Native opinion about these absentees is illuminating. They are not criticized for neglecting to send money home regularly. Tallensi do not expect regular remittances from relatives working abroad and still tend to regard the occasional remittances that are sent home as windfalls. Absentee sons are censured rather for deserting their parents, for leaving them without the companionship and the social support of a son. Tɛndaan Teroog's son used to send baskets of guinea corn and maize to his father from Mampurugu. Nevertheless, the old man kept pressing him to return home; and when the son died suddenly people said it was because he had 'rejected' (*zayah*) his father. He should have come home long ago to be his father's companion (*kɔyal*, vb.), to act for him in jural matters, assist him in ritual activities, and manage the household for him. The same sentiment was uppermost in Maantiya's mind when he explained why he could not leave his proxy father Saantarɔba, though the latter was able to support himself and his wife with occasional assistance from kinsmen. Maantiya went down to the coast every dry season carrying fowls to sell and usually stayed away three or four months. He was always home again before the rains began. He said. 'I cannot abandon my father. He has no one else.' When I was going home in 1937 a number of men asked me to find their absent sons in Kumasi or Accra or elsewhere in the south, and to try to persuade them to return home. 'Tell them', said one old man, 'that we do not care about the money or things, but we want them to come home.'

We have said that there is a more definite emphasis on the duty of a son to provide for his mother. There was an old woman at Kpata'ar whose only son had been abroad for some years. She sent him many messages begging him to return, but to no avail. 'That good-for-nothing', said Tiezien, contemptuously, telling me about this youth. 'He leaves his mother to starve here while he goes wandering abroad. He is no person (*u ka nit*).'[1]

This feeling that it is a son's bounden duty to support an aged mother is strongly marked in the case of one's own mother. It sometimes happens that a woman is widowed while still young and is left with one or two young children. She remarries into her late husband's clan and has children by her second husband. When she gets past child-bearing age, even if her second husband is still alive, she usually goes to live with her oldest son of the first marriage. Tallensi say that the right person to support such a woman is this son, as her second husband has no further interest in her after she ceases to be able to bear children.

Any surviving widow of one's own father or proxy father (i.e. a close co-wife of one's own mother) is felt to be entitled to support, but in this case a ritual sanction enters the picture. Tallensi say a man is bound to support his own mother 'because she bore you (*ɔn n-dɔyi la zugu*)'. It is a direct moral duty to her. But one has to support a mother's widowed co-wife because she was one's father's wife and he would be angry if one did not. This rule applies only to widows of fathers of one's own nuclear lineage. Outside that range no obligation is felt to support an old widow whom one's mother would have called her co-wife. It now becomes a question of more abstract ethical values summed up in the concept *dulɔm*. There is no exact equivalent for this concept in English. According to Tale ethics, any act of deliberate malice or even thoughtlessness that causes trouble or suffering to another person through no fault of his own is immoral. For example, deliberately giving a person wrong information that leads him into trouble; or refusing to give or lend a person something that can well be spared, and so causing him to suffer a serious loss; or if one is in a position to prevent a person getting hurt and makes no effort to do so—all such actions come into this category of moral delinquency. They incur *dulɔm*. The concept covers both the sufferer's resentment and the ethical stigma attaching to the wrong done to him by allowing evil to befall him. The native phrase is 'it brings (or is) *dulɔm* (*de mar dulɔm*)'; and *dulɔm* bears mystical retribution in its track.

Tallensi say that if an old woman whom one calls 'mother' (either because she is the widow of a classificatory father, or out of courtesy, because she belongs to one's mother's generation of wives of the clan) has no one to support her and appeals to one, it is *dulɔm* to refuse her. *Dulɔm* is one of the reasons why one cannot refuse food to a kinsman in need. It was the reason Kuŋaaŋba gave for allowing his old 'mother'

---

[1] This expression of contempt contains a wealth of meaning for the native. It means, broadly, someone who has no sense of decency or is oblivious of his social responsibilities.

Tɔŋ to stay with him. Banɔrəg furnished another instance. One afternoon he looked in on his way home from the market and found two elders with me. He told us he was having some trouble with Ziba, a young man of his inner lineage. Ziba had an old woman, whom he called 'mother', living with him; but he had suddenly decided to get rid of her. Banɔrəg told us how he had expostulated with the heartless young man. 'It is an evil thing to do', he concluded, amid murmurs of assent from the two elders. 'A man who drives out an old woman to starve becomes blameworthy before Heaven (*u kpera Naawun taale*); it is *duləm*.' Banɔrəg's efforts, in this case, were in vain since he had no paternal authority over Ziba. The intervention of an older kinsman does not always check disgraceful treatment of domestic relatives, and public opinion only takes notice of it after the event and then often has no power to make the culprit remedy it.

A Methodological Point

The cases we have quoted in the preceding pages are précis of statements, opinions, and explanations given to me by Tallensi themselves. If space allowed, a score of cases could be quoted for each one I have recorded. I mention this because it might seem incredible, to anyone who has not lived amongst the Tallensi, that a people so primitive in their mode of livelihood should balance up rights and obligations in the most commonplace activities of their lives in so calculating a fashion. But the picture I have sketched is not a distortion. Description and analysis inevitably reduce human action to slow motion and men's motives to a seemingly mechanical pattern. In reality Tale parents commonly act as spontaneously and generously as parents in any other country and their children respond as spontaneously and sincerely. But even the most spontaneous actions and feelings of the natives occur within the framework of their social organization and subject to the values postulated in their culture. Social organization and cultural values allow of alternative forms of action and affect in any particular situation, but not of infinitely numerous alternatives. Where the relations of parents and children are involved these alternatives are not unlimited; and allowing for differences of personality and character, as the natives themselves do, we can say that the alternative that will be selected in a particular situation is determined by the structural relations of the individuals concerned. Men's motives and their social relations are closely integrated with one another among the Tallensi, as we have emphasized before. In their actual social behaviour Tallensi do not have to stop and think out every situation before they act. The individual's ideas and attitudes have been shaped by the social structure and the cultural norms. The framework of his social relations is as much a part of him as he is a part of it. He automatically evaluates every situation in terms of his social relations. To put it crudely, every Talǝŋ carries a set of labels bestowed upon him by the social system and a set of ideas and attitudes implanted in him by his culture. In every situation he responds to the relevant labels borne by the other people who enter into it with action springing from his ideas and attitudes. What we have tried to do is to examine this process of response in slow motion and to show how the ideas and attitudes evoked by certain labels can be traced back to the structural relations of the people concerned.

CHAPTER VIII
TENSIONS IN THE PARENT–CHILD RELATIONSHIP
Rivalry between Parents and Children

PERHAPS the most extraordinary feature of Tale parents' relations with their children is the recognition, in custom and belief, of the latent antagonism behind their mutual identification and comradeship, their devotion and co-operation. We have already had some glimpses of this. A psycho-analyst might say that the Oedipus complex is apparently openly recognized in Tale culture. He would have to add that it is built into their social organization in such a way as to enable them to control it. The mystical ideas and ritual symbols in which the rivalry between successive generations is clothed form the cultural mechanism by which it is neutralized and made to serve socially useful ends.

We have discussed the taboos observed by first-born children among the Namoos in our previous book. We showed there[1] that the distinguishing mark of all Namoo clans as opposed to non-Namoo clans is the observance of these taboos. Among all Namoos a man's first-born son and daughter may not eat the domestic fowl, may not wear any of their father's garments or his quiver, or look into his granary during his lifetime. The latter taboos are connected with the fact that a man's clothes and quiver and granary are intimately identified with his social personality. As the natives put it, a man's clothes and quiver are imbued with his bodily exuviae from constant contact with his body, while his granary is associated with his unique status in the patricentral family. It is easy to see that these possessions are peculiarly apt symbols of a man's social self. It is not surprising, therefore, that though these taboos are not formally observed by non-Namoos analogous usages with the same symbolic significance occur among them.

In our previous book we studied the significance of these taboos as quasi-totemic symbols in the system of inter-clan relations; but they have other dimensions of meaning as well, like all Tale customs and ideas that give expression to fundamental elements in their social organization. For they go back to deep and universal tendencies in human psychology. These taboos have a particular meaning in the contemporary structure of Tale society as symbols of corporate units; but underlying this is the deeper meaning they have in the relations of successive generations and for the individual himself in the conduct of his life.

We are concerned here with these latter aspects of their meaning. We cannot attempt to unravel all that lies behind them, but their super-

[1] Cf. *Dynamics of Clanship*, chs. v and viii.

TENSIONS IN THE PARENT–CHILD RELATIONSHIP 223

ficial symbolism is transparent. What they mean is that a child may not be equated with his or her father while he is alive. As we have observed, though these taboos do not occur among non-Namoos, the ideas and sentiments they express are as frankly admitted by them as by Namoos. It was a Tɛnzugu (Talis) man who gave me the clearest statement I obtained on the struggle between the Destinies (*Yina*) of father and son. I remember also being struck by this during the ceremony of exorcising the evil Predestiny of Sinkawol of Kpata'ar's wife. Just as the most important rite of all was begun somebody noticed that Tiezien, Sinkawol's proxy father, was absent. Nyaaŋzum, Sinkawol's proxy grandfather and Tiezien's proxy father, shouted for Tiezien to come out of the homestead. Tiezien shouted back, in some anger, 'No, I won't come. They are exorcising my daughter-in-law's *Yin* and I should be there? Oh no. Is she your (plural) wife or mine? No, it is not for me to be there.' There was a moment's pause and then Nyaaŋzum called back, 'Well, leave it then, you are right.' The point was that a man must not equate himself with his son, particularly where the latter's procreative status is concerned. But grandfather and grandson are equated with each other, as we shall see more fully later. And by the same principle a woman must not be equated with her daughter in her reproductive capacity. Thus when a man's daughter becomes a mother for the second or third time he gives up sleeping with her mother even if she is still of child-bearing age. Tallensi call this an important taboo. It is significant also that among both Namoos and non-Namoos an analogous taboo to that of the father's granary holds between a mother and her first-born daughter. While her mother is alive a girl may not uncover her mother's chief storage-pot (*u pu sugal u ma doko*). This taboo is not stressed so much as those that discriminate a child from its father, as might be expected in a society so thoroughly organized around the patrilineal line. But it does show that the tension between the generations among the Tallensi is not the product of *patria potestas* only, but arises out of the whole network of the relations between parents and children.

The avoidances of first-born children are not the only customary expression of the tension between the generations. A man and his oldest child do not eat together. 'You and your oldest child do not dip your fingers into the same dish of food together,' the natives say, 'for if you did perhaps his finger-nail might scratch you and that would bring misfortune on both of you.' This prohibition is not subject to ritual sanctions, though the misfortune that would follow the symbolic act of aggression would be of a mystical character. Tallensi share a dish with the youngest child for preference; and it is not an uncommon sight to see a man eating with his youngest child while his oldest son is sitting near by eating separately.

Then there are the restrictions we have already mentioned that must be observed at funeral ceremonies by anyone who has a parent of the same sex as the deceased still living. Similarly an oldest son may not deputize for his father in making sacrifices to an ancestor shrine which is in the latter's custody; 'he is too near to inheriting the shrine', the Tallensi say. The implication is that if an oldest son deputizes for his father in relation to the ancestors he is anticipating his inheritance and this is tantamount to wishing his father dead. Even during the interval between the mortuary rites and the final funeral ceremony of a dead father it is his younger sons who make sacrifices in his name to the ancestor shrines that were in his possession and will be inherited by the oldest son.

All these customs indicate how strongly the Tallensi feel that there is an underlying rivalry between parents and children that must not be allowed to drive a wedge between them. While his parent (particularly his father) is alive, a child (particularly a son) must not act in any way that suggests a desire to usurp the parent's place; and this holds vice versa for the parent too, as the incident between Tiezien and Nyaaŋzum shows. It is implicit in the Tale concept of incest. It can be summed up in the formula that father and son may not take each other's place in the procreative relationship, which is the fundamental relationship defining their positions in society relatively to each other; but this principle is extended to all social relations of father and son, particularly the first-born son. Tallensi state this quite openly, and it is worth quoting what Yarəg of Gbizug, who is not a Namoo, said to me once in this connexion. There had been a ceremony the previous night at which the Gbizug tɛndaana had been represented by one of his younger sons. I asked Yarəg why he did not sometimes deputize for the tɛndaana in these ceremonies, for surely he knew more about the rites than his younger classificatory brothers? 'No', he replied, 'that is impossible. I am like the tɛndaana's oldest son, for my father was his full (*soog*) brother; I cannot put on his cap and skin and perform these rites for him. We are Talis and it is not a taboo for us, but it would not be right, it would not be seemly.'

We have seen that the undercurrent of rivalry is most apparent in the relations of father and son. Marriage removes a daughter from the arena of possible conflict with her parents and her social role does not create interests and motives that bring her into competition with either of her parents. She cannot take the place of either her father or her mother. Removal from their control has the effect, if anything, of strengthening her uterine tie with her mother and her lineage tie with her father. The first-born daughter is associated with the first-born son in these taboos by the principle of sibling equivalence.[1] She is the first-born child of her sex, and stands for the filial generation as much as her brother does. It is their first child, whether it be son or daughter, that makes a married couple into parents. Moreover, we must not forget the Tale maxim that

[1] This principle is discussed in Ch. X below.

TENSIONS IN THE PARENT–CHILD RELATIONSHIP 225

she might have been a son but for the accident of birth. A son's situation is entirely different, as we have shown in the preceding chapters. He remains a member of his parental family all his life. He does eventually take the place of his father in the life of the community and could be suspected of wanting to hurry on the day when this will happen. His desire for independence is liable, as we have seen, to run counter to his father's plans and demands. Every advance in his social and economic development might be interpreted as an added threat to his father's dominance. He will not be his own master until he has no father. The very principle of reciprocity which plays such an important part in their economic co-operation conceals mutual jealousy about property. And the social cleavage between his generation and his father's is emphasized by the wider context of fatherhood. A man's father's brothers, who are identified with his father both by generation and by birth, stand between him and his full independence as his father's heir. Even after his own father's death they retain authority over him. As we have seen, the cleavage between successive generations usually comes to a head more decisively with a proxy father than with one's own father.

Tallensi themselves make no bones about the matter. 'Your oldest son is your rival (*I bikpeem a i dataa*)', the men say bluntly. I have heard this phrase used by both Namoos and non-Namoos from every part of the country. 'Look at my oldest son', an elder once said to me. 'He would not care if I should die to-morrow. Then he would inherit all my possessions, he would own the *zɔŋ* and he could take his ease. The things connected with an oldest son are hard (*bikpeem yɛla ntɔ*).'

This candour in fathers is not matched by their sons, who never admit the rivalry. They laugh it off as 'an affair of custom (*de yɛl nla*)', or simply say that it is a ritual matter, a taboo (*kihər*) like any other taboo that one accepts without questioning. And they generally launch out, with obvious sincerity, into the kind of panegyric on the advantages of having a father that has been previously quoted (p. 172). This is as one might expect, for it is the fathers who feel the threat to their dominance; and they feel it the more strongly as they grow older and their powers decline.

The taboos of first-born children begin to be enforced in early childhood. By the age of 7 or 8 a child takes them as seriously as his parents.[1] But it is only after the son is married and has a growing family, when the father is getting on in years, that the opposition symbolized in ritual observances emerges as an opposition in practical life. It coincides with the son's increased striving to free himself from his father's economic control. This is expressly symbolized, among all the Tallensi, in a taboo which the first-born son begins to observe about the time he gets married. He and his father must not meet face to face in the gateway of their common homestead. This taboo is as scrupulously observed as

[1] Cf. *Dynamics of Clanship*, p. 125.

the other taboos of first-born children. Its meaning is plain if we bear in mind what the gateway and the *zɔŋ* symbolize in the structure of the family and the lineage.[1] Significantly enough, a first-born daughter does not observe it.

Eventually, when the son's older children are reaching adolescence, the opposition between his father and himself culminates in his formal separation from his parental family. We have noticed before that fission in the joint family is basically due to structural and economic factors. In the case of an eldest son's hiving off, Tallensi say that it is often brought about by the jealousies of the womenfolk. The son's wife or wives complain that they are not getting a fair deal in the distribution of food-supplies in the joint family. They are always nagging at their husband on that account. So when a son 'goes out on his own (*yi u kɔkɔ*)' natives say it is in order the better to support his wives and children. But the separation is actually due as much to the relations between the man and his father as to the purely economic causes. It is an instance of the convergence and congruence of structural principles and economic necessities.

Most commonly an eldest son separates off formally by cutting a new gateway for himself in the family homestead. The native phrase is *bit u zanɔr* ('slit his gateway'), and it describes precisely what happens. The wall of the homestead is cut through so as to make an extra gateway leading into the son's quarters. Though he and his wife and children will very often use the main gateway, he is by status the owner of his own subsidiary gateway and cannot formally clash with his father. At the same time he achieves a considerable measure of economic independence. He will have his own bush farm and small home farm and be responsible for providing the bulk of the food required by his wife and children. But he still helps his father and younger brothers with their farm work, and receives some food-supplies from his father in return if his own supplies are insufficient for his needs. Sometimes, however, an eldest son moves out altogether. His father may let him build a homestead on a bush farm belonging to the family, or he may migrate to one of the peripheral settlements. As we have seen, it usually takes a few years for a son to achieve this step. I have heard young men who were pressing their claims for a separate gateway express impatience with an obstinate old father and even resentment against his apparent tyranny. But when the parting comes it is usually amicable, and father and son continue to be on excellent and intimate terms thereafter. The son is still under his father's final authority in jural and ritual matters.

The Native Theory of the Tension between the Generations

Tallensi explain the rivalry between father and son by means of the

[1] Cf. Ch. III above.

mystical concept of the *Yin* or personal Destiny.[1] There is, they say, an inborn antagonism between the *Yin* of a father and the *Yin* of his eldest son. While the son is still young his *Yin* is weak, but as he grows older his *Yin* grows more powerful and wants to make him master of his own affairs. The son's *Yin* wants to destroy the father's *Yin*; but the father's *Yin* desires the father to live and be well and remain master of the house. It wishes to continue to receive sacrifices from the father. Therefore it will try to destroy the son's *Yin*, and if it is the stronger *Yin* it will cause misfortune and perhaps death to the son. That is the reason why father and son must avoid meeting in the gateway of the homestead and why it is better for them to separate, after the son has reached a stage of maturity when his *Yin* begins to be as powerful as his father's. In the same way an oldest daughter's evil Predestiny (*Yinbe'er*) is a threat to her mother's life and health. When Sinkawol's wife was waiting for her evil Predestiny to be exorcised she was not allowed to go and visit her sick mother for fear that her *Yinbe'er* might cause her mother to get worse.

To appreciate the profundity of this interpretation we need to understand the Tale notion of *Yin*. It is one of the most difficult of their religio-psychological ideas to translate into our categories of thought. Indeed, it is not a precise notion but, like all Tale ritual ideas, a configuration of mutually overlapping ideas, beliefs, and values.

Yin is the shortened form of *Naawun* or *Naayin*, the Tale term which can best be translated as Heaven. But whereas *Naawun* is concerned with all mankind, each person's *Yin* belongs uniquely to that person. It is the symbol of his individuality, of what makes his life history different in his own eyes from that of every other person. If he falls ill he is enduring something that is the common human lot, and he tries to cope with his illness by the same measures that anybody else would take. But, he asks himself, why should he have fallen ill just at this time and not his brother or somebody else, for instance. When he kills an animal in the hunt, or buys a cow, or marries, or has a child he goes through experiences that every man has, and his social personality takes on attributes that are part of the social personality of every man of about the same stage of social maturity. Yet they are his own private experiences. They form part of the unique continuity of his personal development. None of them was inevitable. They are due to the intervention of chance in his life; or, as the Tallensi believe, to the action of the mystical agencies that dictate the course of human life.

These, very briefly, are the ideas, as nearly as one can translate them into our modes of thought, behind the Tale notion of *Yin*. It is a mystical notion because their ideas of causality are couched in a ritual idiom and are rooted in ritual beliefs; and it serves several ends. Tallensi do not

[1] Cf. *Dynamics of Clanship*, p. 144, for a discussion of this concept from a different angle.

conceive of the inner life of the individual as a distinct phenomenon apart from the external, material, and social facts of his life. But they understand clearly that each person is unique as an individual. The notion of *Yin* is the means by which they visualize the connexion between the material and social facts of the person's life and his individuality. It enables them, also, to see a tendency and a determinism in the life of the individual by reference to which they make the intervention of chance intelligible and emotionally tolerable.

A person's Destiny has various aspects, some or all of which may emerge in the course of his life. There is, first of all, his Predestiny (*nuor Yin*, the *Yin* of the mouth). This is the fate the individual has preordained for himself before birth. In his pre-natal state he 'spoke when he was with Heaven above (*u daa vɔlɔm Naayin zugni*)'. Both men and women have this *Yin*; and it is this *Yin* that sometimes manifests itself as an evil *Yin* (*Yinbe'er*), when the individual is pursued by chronic bad luck in the important things of life—things like health, marriage, parenthood. He (or she) had declared before birth that he does not want to have parents or children or a spouse or any of the good things of life. A child suffering from an evil Predestiny is constantly ailing; a man so afflicted cannot find a wife or is deserted by every wife he marries; or he loses his children one after the other in infancy; or he is for ever having bad crops or losing his livestock; and a woman with a *Yinbe'er* loses her children one after another in infancy, or her husband, or perhaps she herself gets ill of some wasting disease. Moreover, this ill luck that haunts the unwitting sufferer is also a constant danger to his family. A child's evil *Yin* may cause the death of a parent or a sibling; a man's or woman's evil *Yin* spoils the life of his or her spouse, children, and parents as well as his or her own life. The evil *Yin* symbolizes all the subterranean animosities and aggression latent in the relations of members of the joint family with one another. The cure is a ritual exorcism, carried out by the maximal or medial lineage of the sufferer, but this is not always successful.

If a woman's Predestiny is harmless or beneficent it remains latent, as it were. It is not objectified in any way as she has no ritual status.[1] Her *Yin* is subordinate to and submerged in her father's or her husband's *Yin*. But a man's Predestiny, if it is beneficent, may declare itself to him, usually after adolescence, but occasionally before. Thus a young man may kill an animal in the hunt and this will declare itself, through a diviner, to be the vehicle of his *nuor Yin*, and demand that he dedicate a shrine to it.

---

[1] Women have no *Yin* or other ancestor shrines as they have no independent relationship with the ancestors. This is a reflex of their status in Tale society as jural and ritual minors who do not play a part in maintaining the continuity of the society or the equilibrium of the body politic independently of their relationship to their fathers or husbands.

TENSIONS IN THE PARENT–CHILD RELATIONSHIP 229

But a man's most important *Yin* is that with which certain of his ancestors are associated. This too may come to him in childhood, though it does so more commonly in early manhood. Usually it manifests itself to him through an accident or a coincidence. Thus a young man falls ill shortly after he has bought a new hoe or killed an animal in the hunt. The diviners then declare that his illness was caused by his *Yin*; his ancestors so and so, and so and so, are thus revealing themselves as his *Yin*; the hoe or the animal is their vehicle; they brought illness on him because they demand that he should accept them as his *Yin* and sacrifice to them. The young man will then build a shrine dedicated to these ancestors placing the skull of the animal or the blade of the hoe on it, and will henceforth sacrifice to them on this shrine. This is his first and most intimately personal shrine, and it plays an enormous part in his life thereafter. As far as his own personal affairs are concerned, it will always be his most important link with his ancestors. It is through his *Yin* that they exercise the most direct influence upon his life and that he seeks to maintain their goodwill specifically for himself. When he becomes head of his joint family he will entrust most of the children born into the family to his *Yin* as spirit guardian. Every important step in his social development will be registered in his relations with his *Yin*; it may be by a special sacrifice, or it may be by a change in the location of the shrine, or the addition of an ancestor to the group of ancestors who have revealed themselves (*naam*) as his *Yin*. A man's *Yin* is both the chart of his life and the helm with which he steers his way through life.

All the ancestors and ancestresses of a man have a potential mystical relevance for his life, but they have the same potential relevance for any of their descendants. His *Yin* ancestors, on the other hand, are concerned exclusively with him, for his own sake, so to speak. They form a particular combination, usually of very recent forebears, who do not belong together in just that grouping for any other of their descendants. They may be patrilateral or matrilateral ancestors or a combination of both lines. Thus a man might have as his *Yin* ancestors his father, father's father, father's father's mother, and her father, while his brother has their father, father's mother, and father's mother's father as his *Yin* ancestors. Of another pair of brothers, one's *Yin* ancestors may be their mother's father, maternal grandfather, and maternal great-grandfather; and the other's might be their mother's mother, her father, and his father (see Fig. 5, page 230).

Thus when a Talǝŋ says that his *Yin* and his eldest son's *Yin* are mutually dangerous, he is saying that his son's successful growth and development into and through manhood is a threat to his authority and primacy in the family, a symbol of the inevitable decline in his physical and mental power that comes with age, and a warning that he must in due course make way for the next generation; and yet it is also the

230 TENSIONS IN THE PARENT–CHILD RELATIONSHIP

crowning achievement of his life, the most significant sign that his *Yin* has prospered him (*maal*) well. The relations of father and son are a balance between their ties of solidarity and mutual identification, which form the central link of the lineage system, and the cleavage due to their belonging to successive generations. Once more we encounter the fundamental

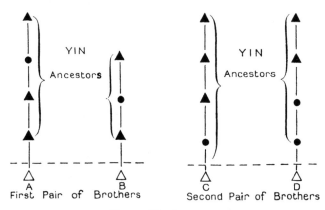

FIG. 5. *Yin* Ancestors.

principle of Tale social organization, that every constellation of social relationships is made up of a polar balance of ties and cleavages.

The Discrimination between Oldest Children and Youngest Children

The cleavage between father and first son obviously plays an important part in the cycle of development of the joint family and lineage. The oldest son's breakaway from the parental home is the first phase of fission of the joint family, and it is not until after his father's death that he and his brothers are likely to become reunited into a single domestic unit.

We have spoken sometimes as if the cleavage between successive generations lay solely between parents and their first-born children, at other times as if it were a gulf between parents and all their children. In practice, tension crops up between a parent and any of his or her adolescent or adult children, but one reason why it is always likely to be sharpest with oldest children is simply because they have gone farthest along the road of social and economic maturity and so symbolize the filial generation most effectively of all the children. Among non-Namoos it does not seem to matter whether the oldest children are first-born or merely the oldest surviving children. Among the Namoos, however, there is the striking peculiarity of their fixing the ritual and affective bar between the generations on the first-born children. If a man's first-born son is dead, and even if he died in infancy, the oldest living son does not assume the taboos of the first-born. The tension that develops between a father and his oldest surviving son is never as great as that which occurs between a man and his first-born son. An oldest surviving son may in time begin to farm on his own, but he will very often stay in his father's homestead, for his *Yin* is not a danger to his father's.

Tallensi have no explanation for this. Their only comment is to point to the fact, which can often be observed, that parents discriminate between their older children and their younger children, especially between the oldest and the youngest. Youngest children are the favourites, upon whom they lavish all their tenderness when they have long ceased to make a show of affection for the older children. A man's or a woman's last child (*bikpa'ar*) is the apple of its parent's eye. Tallensi say that a last child is always spoiled and pampered, and therefore grows up to be vain, lazy, and extravagant. Guna'ab was a man of this stamp, and his older brothers explained contemptuously that he had been their mother's *bikpa'ar* and they had been unable to discipline him after their father's death.

Tallensi say that a person's younger children, and in particular the youngest child, feel their dependence on their parents till the last. There is, as in so many aspects of the relations of parents and children, an element of reciprocity in this. For a man's youngest son, for instance, is still farming with him when his oldest son is farming either wholly or partly for himself—'thinking of how to feed his wife and children rather than of his parents', they often say. 'If I die to-day', men have said to me, 'do you think my oldest son will weep? Oh no; but my youngest son, he will shed bitter tears.' There is much truth in this. I have more than once seen a man's youngest son being harshly rated by an older brother for abandoning himself to grief over his father's death. Because older children no longer need their parents' care they do not inspire the same affection as young children. In the eyes of the natives, therefore, the discrimination between youngest and oldest children is a natural result of the process of upbringing. But I have heard women say, also, that a woman's love for her *bikpa'ar* is due to her seeing in him the sign of the end of her reproductive powers.

It is, however, not merely a matter of the vagaries of parental psychology. This discrimination runs deeply into the social structure of the Tallensi. A curious but enlightening indication of this occurs with divining (*bakologo*) shrines. When a diviner dies, the clairvoyant power associated with his shrine sometimes passes on to one of his sons by a process which the Tallensi think of as a kind of mystical contagion (*lɔŋ*). The son who is selected for this privilege is always a younger son. There is more sympathy between father and younger son than between father and oldest son. But the best indication of this is found at funeral ceremonies, where the oldest and the youngest children of the deceased have distinctive mourning duties. The oldest son and oldest daughter, as the chief mourners, have the most arduous mourning duties. They have to take part in almost every rite, both by day and by night, and these rites are mystically dangerous to those who participate in them. Hence they have to be carried out very carefully. All the participants must, for instance, observe absolute silence throughout these rites. The youngest son and youngest daughter, on the other hand, wear the *dooluŋ* string as a special emblem of mourning. The *dooluŋ* string is decorated with four cowrie shells for a dead mother and three cowrie shells if the deceased is the mourner's father. The youngest son wears it on his hand, looped about his middle finger in a prescribed fashion; the youngest daughter wears it round the neck and waist and down the back.

The most important of these rites are those which conclude the funeral. The rites differ in content from clan to clan, as we have mentioned in our earlier book,[1] but their symbolism is the same for all clans. Everywhere they symbolize the removal of the social personality of the deceased from the world of the living and his or her incorporation among the ancestors. They symbolize also the emancipation of the children from the control of their living parent and the assumption by the oldest son or daughter of the father's or mother's position in society. This is evident from the rites by which the customs, taboos, and articles which stood for the cleavage between the generations are ritually annulled or transferred to the son or daughter. In the case of a woman, among all the Tallensi, the principal rites are 'the sealing of the store-pot (*bɛa dok*)' and the sending of the *kumpiog*.

The rite of 'sealing the store-pot' is the only ritual act performed solely by women for a woman. On the last day but one of an old woman's funeral a group of old women, her co-wives, sisters-in-law, and friends, together with her daughters, gather in her sleeping-room. They take one of her large store-pots, put inside it a ladle, a dish, and other articles characteristic of women's activities that belonged to her, and solemnly seal it with a potsherd plastered over with mud and cow-dung. Beer and porridge are offered on the pot to her spirit. Her oldest daughter takes part in these rites, and then the pot is hidden in a place where she is not likely to see it. She may not come near it until it is finally disposed of. Next day the pot is ritually opened by the old women and the oldest daughter, who thus symbolically discards the taboo which she had to observe all her life if she is a first-born, or since her mother's death if she is not. Later the pot is removed from the house and taken by one of the old women. The daughter must never see it again.

At the end of the funeral ceremonies a dead woman's *kumpiog*, the special pot and calabash which stand for her social personality as a woman and mother, is solemnly and extremely carefully carried to her oldest daughter's house and given to her, as we have noted before.

[1] Cf. *Dynamics of Clanship*, ch. viii.

TENSIONS IN THE PARENT–CHILD RELATIONSHIP 233

For a man these final rites are more elaborate and variable. Among the Namoos the high-water mark of the rites is the induction of the first-born son and first-born daughter, if they survive, into those secret and forbidden things which they have avoided since infancy. The first-born son is dressed in his father's cap and smock, turned inside out.[1] A stick with a loop of string, and a piece of hollow bamboo, specially prepared for the occasion and symbolizing the father's bow and quiver, are hung round his neck. Then a procession is formed of all the children of the dead man, his first-born daughter following immediately behind the first-born son and holding on to the smock. An old man leads them round the homestead three times. Then the first-borns are taken inside through their dead father's zɔŋ, and are taken up to look into his granary for the first time in their lives. The whole rite is felt by the onlookers to be overwhelmingly solemn and the 'showing of the granary (*paal buur*)' is for them an intensely dramatic moment. A hush comes over the crowd of spectators as the son ascends to the granary and his mentor puts a hand behind his head and pushes it forward so that he peers into this hitherto-forbidden place. The son himself appears quite unperturbed, though this is one of the decisive moments of his life. I have been told by men who have been through this rite that they felt quite calm and collected at the time. But Tallensi are that way, and this is perhaps a sign of the efficacy of their ritual practices.

Among the Talis and other non-Namoos, the parallel rite is that of sending the quiver (*ta'ah loko*) of the dead man to the External *Bɔyar*. When an old man dies, his quiver is hidden in his principal granary by one of the elders and his oldest son and daughter are thereafter forbidden to look into the granary until the end of the funeral ceremonies. 'If they did', a Yinduuri elder once explained to me, 'they would see the spirit of the dead man and die.' Younger sons and daughters are free to look into the granary. This is of particular interest as a parallel to the Namoo taboos; but with the Talis the ritual and affective expression of the tension between father and eldest son is concentrated in the period when its meaning is most significant to the son, the transition period between the extinction of his father's social personality and his assumption of his father's place. For the rite of 'sending the quiver', the 'quiver' (consisting of a real bow and a symbolical quiver exactly like that used by the Namoos) is taken from the granary by the oldest son. Followed by his father's senior surviving wife he is escorted by the clan elders to the External *Bɔyar*. Sacrifices are made to the ancestors and especially to the dead man, who now belongs to the realm of the ancestors, and his 'quiver' is left in the *Bɔyar* in token of his final departure from the world of the living.

We must conclude that the distinction Tallensi make, both in custom

[1] To distinguish the context of death from that of life and to symbolize the reversal of the taboo.

and in sentiment, between oldest children and youngest children is of more than casual significance. It is as if the two major aspects of parent-child relations are split apart and distributed so as to make them more easily reconcilable. The mutual identification, mutual love and devotion of parents and children are focused in the relations of parents with their youngest children; the cleavage between successive generations is focused in the relations between parents and oldest children; and we can easily see why this is so. For it is the latter who will take the place of the parents on their death, who seem to be standing on the threshold waiting for them to die. The emphasis of the Namoos on first-born children is, as we have noted, due to the fact that it is the first-born child which makes a man and woman parents. Hence, if a first-born dies, its parents have to undergo a special purification rite; and a wife who has not borne a child to her husband does not undergo the purification rites for a widow when he dies. Later children do not change the role and status of a person in the same way; they do not make him or her more of a parent. Nor does the sex of the first-born matter, though the agnatic principle makes a first-born son of greater importance to a man than a first-born daughter. This and the principle of the equivalence of siblings explain why both sons and daughters are subject to the taboos of the first-born among the Namoos.

The Ancestors as Parent Images

The ambivalence in the relations of parents and children is more dramatically expressed in the ancestor cult than in any other aspect of Tale culture. We cannot discuss this at length here. We can only note that there is a direct continuity between the relations of parents and children in life and their relations after the parents' death. The worship of the ancestors is a culturally standardized projection on to the mystical plane of the tangle of attachments, reciprocities, tensions, and submerged antagonisms that bind parents and children to one another in life. Anyone unfamiliar with the speech and customs of the Tallensi would often find it impossible to tell, in some situations, whether a man is speaking of his living father or his dead father. The dead parents are the prototypes of all the ancestors. Distinctions of name and generation conceal the same primary images. This is clear from the fact that no man can sacrifice to an ancestor or ancestress except through the medium of the spirit of the parent who links him to that ancestor or ancestress.

It will not surprise the psychologist, however, to learn that the attributes with which the spirits of the parents are invested differ in some respects markedly from those that are conventionally assumed for living parents. The disciplinary limitations imposed by the demands of economic and social adjustment and by the rationale of reality are no longer operative. The figures of the dead parents are clothed in qualities that are in part highly magnified versions of their most praiseworthy qualities in real life and in part distorted reflections of the tensions that exist between parents and children in reality. It is no misrepresentation to describe them as a standardized and highly elaborated picture of the parents as they might appear to a young child in real life—mystically omnipotent, capricious, vindictive, and yet beneficent and long-suffering; but the emphasis is far more on the persecuting than on the protecting attributes. The distortion is most striking in the case of a mother's spirit. All ancestor spirits are apt to reveal themselves more often by the misfortune they inflict than by the benefits they bring. They emerge as sanctions of conduct more by reason of the punishments they bring down on wrongdoers than because of the benefits they confer for right doing. But the spirits of female ancestors are believed to be specially hard, cruel, and capricious. This is remarkable when we consider the love and devotion a mother shows for her child throughout his life. As we have observed elsewhere,[1] there is a never-ending struggle between a man and his ancestors. It is psychologically rooted in the relations of parents and children during the lifetime of the parents. Sacrifices and prayers are reminiscent of the principle of reciprocity in the real relations of parents and children. They contain the same elements of acquiescence, justice, and hidden coercion. They show another aspect, though, in the propitiation, reverence, and gratitude they often express.[2]

We can see why filial piety towards the dead parents is more strongly stressed than towards the living. While he is alive a person's father has direct jural and ritual authority over him; when he dies, the father becomes the paramount sanction of moral conduct for him; and this applies, *mutatis mutandis*, in only a lesser degree to the mother. The oath 'by my father and his goatskin (or sheepskin) and his three cowries' discussed in our previous book[3] is one proof of this. The centre of gravity of the whole social system of the Tallensi is the relationship of father and son, and it is the idea of filial piety that keeps this relationship in balance in the face of all the forces that tend to divide father and son. In this as in other respects the Tallensi are typical of patrilineal and patriarchal societies of simple culture from many parts of the globe, both ancient and modern.

[1] Cf. *Dynamics of Clanship*, p. 145.
[2] As death, among the Tallensi, is always believed to be mystically caused by a particular ancestor spirit or a group of ancestor spirits (material causes such as sickness being recognized as necessary but not sufficient without the mystical adjunct), it follows that a dead father or mother can kill (*ku*) his or her own child. The converse is impossible, since children, in life, have no jurisdiction over parents. I have asked Tallensi if patricide ever occurs or is known to have occurred. My most trusted informants said they had never heard of a case and thought the very idea abhorrent beyond measure. The idea of matricide they considered even more vile and unnatural.
[3] Cf. *Dynamics of Clanship*, p. 66.

CHAPTER IX

GRANDPARENTS AND GRANDCHILDREN

WE have mentioned earlier that the relations of grandparents and grandchildren can be regarded as a foil to those of parents and children. Tallensi themselves often draw the contrast. It is particularly striking with the paternal grandparents. For in a three-generation joint family the head is a grandfather and the senior *dugdaana* a grandmother. As head of the family the grandfather holds jural, economic, and ritual authority over all its members, including those whom he calls grandchildren, and there is a contrast between his authority and his familiarity in personal relations with his grandchildren. It reflects the contrast between the cleavage due to difference of status and role in terms of the lineage principle and the ties of cognatic kinship between grandchildren and paternal grandparents. This contrast does not occur with the maternal grandparents, in whose relations with a daughter's child the question of authority does not arise. When Tallensi say that a person can die happily if he or she has 'reached grandchildren (*paa yaas*)' they refer primarily to paternal grandparent and grandchild.

A grandchild of either sex refers to a grandfather of either line as *ba-kpeem*, literally 'older father', or more formally as *yaab*, and to a grandmother of either line as *ma-kpeem*, literally 'older mother', or more formally as *yaab-pɔk*. Grandparents are addressed by personal name or, in the case of grandmothers, by the clan name used for them by their affines. A grandchild is described as *yaaŋ* by any of its grandparents and addressed by his or her own name.

The essential feature of the relationship between grandchild and grandparent is that they can tease and joke with each other and each other's spouses. As we have seen, between parent and child this would be almost equal to sacrilege. A grandchild can tweak his grandparent's ear—hence the diviner's sign for grandparent, pointing to the ear—or pretend to mock him or her as 'an old baggage (*bonkɔrəga*)' or play practical jokes on them such as snatching at their food. Grandparents, reciprocally, tease their grandchildren, calling them 'you ugly thing (*bonlɔrəga*)', or by similar epithets that would be insults in another genealogical context. This joking relationship holds for both sets of grandparents, and serves the purpose of reconciling the potentially conflicting elements in their relationship.[1]

With it goes an intimacy and mutual trust, more particularly between

---

[1] Cf. the similar usage between siblings-in-law, p. 120. Joking in the present case reconciles the familiarity permissible on the grounds of personal interest and the social equivalence of alternate generations, with the respect due to grandparents because of their age and their lineage status.

patrilineal grandparent and grandchild of the same sex, such as is not found between any other kinsfolk, close or distant. Its nearest parallel is the relationship of full siblings. And as a grandchild grows older this aspect of its relations with its grandparent becomes stronger. Nothing delights grandparents so much as to take care of their grandchildren in babyhood or early childhood. Children often sleep with a grandparent, as we have noted. A woman whose father- or mother-in-law is alive always has someone with whom to leave her baby. Joking is one of the ways in which the grandparent shows his or her joy in the child. But as the grandchild grows older and begins to associate on more adult terms with its grandparents, these demonstrations of affection become unnecessary. Occasionally, as mood and situation dictate, a grandfather or grandmother will throw out a jest at a grandchild. Thus I once heard an old man call out to his grandson's wife with a laugh, as she sauntered past, that she ought to get a wider back *voog* (the decorated flap worn by women over the intergluteal fold) as the one she was wearing was immodest. But it is more likely to be the grandchild who occasionally throws a jest at the grandparent.

There is, then, a kind of freedom and equality between grandparents and grandchildren which could not exist between parents and children. A grandparent does not normally discipline a grandchild. A paternal grandmother has no command over her son's children. I have heard a crotchety old grandmother complain of her grandchildren's noisy habits and lack of obedience but have never heard of a grandmother punishing her grandchildren. The gifts given to her by a granddaughter's suitors are brought as a gesture of respect for the senior woman of the house, but she cannot, as a rule, influence her granddaughter's choice. A paternal grandfather often gives an order to a grandchild or administers a scolding. Tallensi, however, think of a grandfather's scolding as something quite different from a father's discipline. They regard it as a friendly correction. If serious disciplinary action against a grandson is necessary, a grandfather leaves it to his son. A grandfather's jural and ritual authority over a grandson or granddaughter follows from his being the head of the joint family, 'owning' all its members. Thus he can override his son in such matters as the marriage of the latter's son or daughter. But if there is a conflict of wills between him and his grandchild in such a matter he will rely on his son to enforce his decision.

I remember the occasion when Maanlɛrəg eloped with his sister's husband's younger sister in defiance of the veto of the elders of the inner lineage. Nyaaŋzum, Maanlɛrəg's own late paternal grandfather's half-brother, as head of the nuclear lineage, stormed and raged but he could do nothing directly. 'Why don't you control your sons?' he shouted at his 'sons' (his late brothers' sons) Tiezien and Bɔyaraam, the culprit's 'fathers'. In fact, it is notorious that grandparents spoil their grandchildren, especially their oldest grandchildren, those whose birth makes them into grandparents. Again, this is especially marked with the paternal grandparents. The first-born son among Namoos, in whom the cleavage between parents and children is focused, is his grandparents' particular favourite. His grandmother will always have some titbit for him to eat, his grandfather tries to shield him from his father's authority. 'Look at Nɔbya', said Samane of his first-born son, 'he spends his time in play [that is, having a good time]. He never lacks for anything. He does not want to work. That is because he is the oldest grandchild. When he was a child he used to be with his grandparents always and they spoilt him. Now he goes to his grandfather if he wants anything.' The story of Kpana-Tee and his grandson, which we have previously related, is typical of many cases in which father and son disagree and even quarrel over the latter's treatment of his son. The alternate generations seem to be in league against the generation between them.

Maternal grandparents spoil their daughter's children in the same way, but there is not the feeling that they are acting in opposition to the parents. Maternal grandparents do not see so much of their daughter's children as paternal grandparents of their son's children. But from infancy a child is often taken to visit its maternal grandparents, and children over 4 or 5 are sometimes left in the care of their mother's mother for days or weeks on end. This is a kind of holiday for the child and is generally greatly enjoyed. Also, as we have mentioned before, a motherless child, especially a little girl, is often sent to her maternal grandmother and may grow up with her.

The death of a grandchild is felt as a heavy blow by grandparents of both lines. But they do not have to undergo special mourning rites as parents have to. Curiously enough, it is the maternal grandparents, and in particular the grandmother, who is singled out by custom as the greatest sufferer by the loss of a grandchild. The maternal grandparents may not attend the funeral of their grandchild, though their children may. They must grieve alone at home. And if it is a daughter's first-born dying in babyhood a special rite of consolation has to be performed at the maternal grandparents' home. After the infant's mother has been ritually purified she goes to her mother's house accompanied by one or two co-wives and carrying gifts from her husband. When she arrives a simple and very moving rite is carried out symbolizing the consolation offered by the child's father's people to its grandmother, almost as if the father's people were apologizing for the child's death. Then mother and daughter weep together and the daughter remains for a few days to keep her mother company. Tallensi say that this is done because the grandmother has lost her *soog*.[1] They have no explanation for the taboo against maternal grandparents attending a grandchild's funeral. It can be con-

---

[1] Cf. Ch. II above. The rite is a reflection of the recognition of the uterine tie as a personal tie. It symbolizes, also, the recognition of a woman's parents, in particular of her mother, as the source of her reproductive powers.

jectured that the taboo is connected with the fact that the rights over a woman's reproductive powers belong to her husband and must not be confounded with her parents' authority over her. If they came to the funeral of their daughter's child they would have to be received with respect, and it might seem as if they were on a par with the child's paternal grandparents. For the same reason, perhaps, a married woman's parents do not attend her funeral in person, but are represented by other members of her natal family and lineage.

For a man his son's children stand for the certainty that his line of descent will go on. The wheel of the generations has come full circle. When he and his wife die it will be announced to all the world. On the day of his or her funeral the youngest grandson will be placed before a drum with the drumsticks in his hands and the youngest granddaughter before a calabash with two pieces of cane in her hands. When the signal is given for the funeral to begin they will strike the drum and calabash and cry out, 'Oh my grandfather, oh my grandfather, oh my grandfather (*N-yaab yee*)'. And when the funeral is concluded the son's children and the brothers' sons' children will have their heads shaved in mourning in the manner prescribed for grandchildren. Half the head will be shaved and half left unshaved.

The equivalence of alternate generations is shown by the fact that a grandson may marry the widow of his paternal or maternal grandfather, or of any man whom he calls grandfather, other than his own grandmother. This rule is of practical significance when an old man dies leaving a young widow, and all the men of his inner lineage are either 'sons' or 'grandsons' to him. Then the grandsons who are old enough are encouraged to woo the widow, and the elders of the lineage put pressure on her to choose one of them so that she can remain a wife of that lineage. It was thus that Tiezien married his own paternal grandfather's youngest widow. At that time she had a young infant at the breast who was Tiezien's own father's half-brother. Tiezien was then about 18 or 19. He thus had the unusual experience of bringing up a child who was his proxy father. To-day Tiezien, a vigorous man of about 70, is ritual head of Kpata'ar; but his proxy father Nyaaŋzum, whom he reared, is the head of their inner lineage. Tiezien was made politico-religious head of the clan (*Kpata'ar na'ab*) over Nyaaŋzum's head according to the rule that 'begetting does not cross the *dug*';[1] but within their *dug* he is nominally subject to Nyaaŋzum's authority. This might lead to considerable friction between them if they were not as devoted to each other as they are. The marriage of a grandson with his grandfather's widow is, however, an uncommon occurrence, chiefly

---

[1] Headship of the clan, in this case, goes by selection from amongst the eligible elders, but usually comes to the oldest man in the clan. Tiezien could, however, not have accepted the offer without the consent of his proxy father, Nyaaŋzum.

because it is not very usual for a man to have a grandson old enough to take a wife, when he dies, and also to leave a young widow.

The converse marriage of a grandfather with the widow of his 'grandson' of the same inner lineage is said to be permissible but not good. Tallensi think it is incongruous and therefore likely to be unlucky. I learnt of only one such case that has occurred in recent years, and my informants pointed out that all the children born of the marriage had died.

Old women make use of this rule when they are left widows. A widow must either remarry one of her husband's clansmen or else go home to her father's house and marry from there as if she were a spinster. For an old widow remarriage is a formality since she is past child-bearing, and will in any case live with her sons. So when she is asked to choose her new husband from amongst those of her late husband's clansmen who offer her marriage *pro forma*, she often announces, 'I choose a grandson (*man luogəra yaaŋ*)'. She thus satisfies the formal requirements and can go on living with her sons.

Within the lineage inter-personal relations of grandparent and grandchild are not extended beyond the inner lineage—that is, the range within which generation differences between individuals are recognized; but the term *yaab* is applied to any patrilineal ancestor except the father. On the mother's side only the mother's own parents and proxy parents are recognized as grandparents; but any lineage with which a person has matrilateral connexions is described as his *yaab yiri*. Thus any patrilineal ancestor's mother's lineage is a *yaab yiri*; and the letter of custom entitles a man to marry the widow of any member of his *yaab yiri*. In practice such marriages are exceedingly rare, for the widow's husband's lineage-brothers and clansmen resent them strongly. But there have been one or two instances in the past generation in which a young widow eloped with her deceased husband's classificatory *yaaŋ*. What the outraged members of the deceased husband's lineage most resent is that they cannot claim the return of the bride-price. The only sanction they can use is to refuse to sacrifice to their ancestors on behalf of the 'grandson' who has so flouted them; but this is a double-edged weapon. They may not use it, since the 'grandson' was within his formal rights in marrying one of their widows. Hence they would arouse the wrath of their ancestors if they sought to penalize their 'grandson' ritually. This extension of leviratic rights to matrilateral kin is associated with the notion that a woman might have been born a man but for the intervention of chance, and her descendants might therefore have been of the true agnatic line. It will be better understood when we have considered the relations of mother's brother and sister's son (Ch. XI below).

CHAPTER X
SIBLINGS IN THE SOCIAL STRUCTURE
The Concept of 'mabiirət'

TALLENSI make a distinction between kinship that implies a difference of generation, summed up in the concept *dɔyam*, and kinship that implies identity or equality of generation, summed up in the concept *mabiirət*.[1] *Mabii* (lit. mother's child) is the general term for a sibling of either sex and of any degree of consanguinity, and it is extended, as we have shown in our previous volume, to corporate groups, linked by patrilineal descent, that are of equal status. Its primary reference is to a sibling by the same parents as the speaker's when only the fact of siblingship is relevant—that is, when difference of age or sex is not relevant to the situation. Tallensi sometimes use the term in contrast with *babii* (lit. father's child), a usage that indicates very neatly the underlying implications of the term *mabii*. Thus Tallensi say that a man's *mabiis* have first claim on the inheritance of his widows, but that his *babiis* are also entitled to marry the widows. To the native this means that a man's brothers of the same *dug* have a stronger claim than his clansmen of other *dugət*—*dug* here being a lineage segment defined relatively to the agnatic distance between a particular suitor for a widow's hand and the deceased. A man of the same inner lineage as the deceased will call himself a *mabii* of the latter by contrast with another suitor of a different inner lineage but the same medial lineage; and the latter will call himself a *mabii* of the deceased by contrast with a more distant clansman, whom he will describe as a *babii*. Thus the use of the term *mabii* implies a relationship between the parties as if they were agnates who have a common progenitrix over and above their patrilineal ties. When a native describes another as his *mabii*, however distant their genealogical ties, he is tacitly implying a close personal element in their relationship for that moment and in that situation, as if they were children of the same parents, by contrast with a pair of distant agnates. A man will speak of a matrilateral relative of a different clan in this way in some situations. Thus a Tongo man, telling me the story of his first visit to Kumasi, related how he had stayed with a *mabii*, a Ba'ari man, who had loaned him the money for his lorry fare. Abroad, in Kumasi or Accra, a Taloŋ speaks of any other Tallensi he meets there as his *mabiis* by contrast with all the foreigners amongst whom they live. And this is not merely a form of words. Abroad, Tallensi who have no ties of kinship or of locality, who would probably never have met or heard of each other at home, assist one another as if they were kinsmen.

[1] Cf. *Dynamics of Clanship*, ch. vii, p. 117.

In the broadest sense, then, *mabiis* are cognates who are on terms of equality with one another and have a mutual interest in one another's welfare. In the narrowest and prototypical sense *mabiis* are siblings by the same parents. The emphasis is on their equality of status due to a common relationship with their parents.

The Equivalence of Siblings

The key to the social relations of siblings in Tale society and to the effects on the whole social structure of the sibling bond is the principle to which Radcliffe-Brown has given the name of 'the social equivalence of siblings'.[1] It is as true of the Tallensi as of the Australian aborigines that 'there is a very strong, intimate and permanent social bond between two brothers born and brought up in the same family', and that they 'occupy similar positions in the total social structure'. As we shall see, the latter proposition has to be translated into terms of the lineage organization to give it the appropriate connotation for the Tallensi. Siblings derive their social equivalence—that is, equivalence in jural, ritual, and economic relations, as opposed, for example, to private marital relations —from their common relationship with their parents. Outside the lineage range of strictly reckoned classificatory kinship, the recognition of siblingship implies not so much similar positions in the social structure as similar roles in certain situations due to membership of the same corporate groups, or, with matrilateral kin, to having common ascendants. We have, in fact, already had a good deal of evidence in preceding chapters of the social equivalence of siblings. We have seen also how the recognition of siblingship varies in significance according to the lineage context. What we wish to do now is to study the sibling relationship in its own right. By bringing the evidence together in a unitary picture we shall be able to see what constitutes the social equivalence of siblings. We shall find it useful for purposes of our analysis to distinguish between the solidarity of siblings and their equivalence.

But before we examine the social equivalence of siblings more fully it is worth noting that there is, among the Tallensi, a correlated principle of social action of very wide application. Individuals who have the same social role or have had similar socially critical experiences are identified with one another whenever their role or these experiences come into a situation. The best instance is the case of co-wives who always speak of each other as sisters. All chiefs are regarded as 'brothers' (*mabiis*) because of their chiefship; so also are tendaanas. We have seen how men who have no father or mother alive are identified with one another at funeral ceremonies by the fact that only those who have undergone this social experience may take part in certain rites. Similarly only those who have themselves lost a wife or a husband may look after

[1] A. R. Radcliffe-Brown, 'The Social Organization of Australian Tribes', Part 3, *Oceania*, I, 1930–1, pp. 428–9.

the widow (or widower) during a funeral, or assist in the rites of purifying the widow or share her meals. Tallensi assert that a breach of this rule is impossible as no man or woman who had not had the experience would take charge of a widow. It is a taboo (*kihar*), and anyone who infringed it would die. Again, owners of diviners' shrines (*bakologo* shrines—the diviner is called *baya*) are identified in certain situations, though they do not form a corporate body of any sort. Thus when a new diviner's shrine is being set up for a man certain portions of the beer used in the rites can be drunk only by men who already have such shrines, and it is they who carry out the final rites by which the actual power of divination is conferred on him. Similarly it is only men who have themselves undergone the experience and the treatment who may assist in the ritual of purifying a homicide or a man who has slain a big game animal such as a bush cow. The list of illustrations could be extended, but this will suffice to show how deeply rooted the idea is. It is, however, only a determinant of individual conduct and sentiment, giving rise to *ad hoc* co-operation in certain situations, and not a principle of association in corporate units.

Factors modifying the Sibling Bond

The solidarity and social equivalence of siblings are conditioned by a number of factors. Differences of sex and, between like-sex siblings, of age are important. But distinctions of equal or even greater significance are imposed on siblings by the fundamental principles of the social structure. Siblingship does not cancel out the uniqueness of the individual, as symbolized in the notion of the *Yin*, and socially crystallized in the precise differentiation of the lineage segment which he or she founds. This factor, with its counterpart in the family structure and the economic organization of the household, is not important in childhood, but increases steadily in influence with the years. It is the basis of the fission between fraternal descent lines and, consequently, of the ramification of a lineage sprung from one progenitrix. How it works out, however, in a particular case depends upon the position of each person in terms of patrilineal descent and maternal origin. Thus the sibling relationship, while itself an important constitutive factor of the lineage structure, is reciprocally moulded by that structure. The relationship of brothers among the Tallensi might very well have been different from what it is if their social organization provided for the continuous merging of collateral lines of descent in lineal lines,[1] so that lineage branches springing from brothers were not specifically recognized, but only the inclusive trunk-line deriving from a distant ancestor.

[1] This appears to be the case with the Nuer at higher levels of lineage structure (cf. E. E. Evans-Pritchard, *The Nuer*, Oxford, 1940, ch. v) and among some Southern Bantu tribes, such as the Zulu (cf. E. J. Krige, *The Social System of the Zulu*, 1936).

The influence of these modifying factors is recognized in the kinship terms used for the sibling relationship. Most of these have already been recorded, but it is convenient to bring them together again in this place. Within the limits of recognized generation differences, siblings never address one another by kinship terms, but always by name. Outside that range it is also not customary to address people by the kinship terms for siblings, in the ordinary way. When the terms are used it is either as a gesture of courtesy or half in jest, to single out a person from a group; or they are used in addressing distant clansmen or members of linked clans with whom one is not well acquainted. The usage conforms to the rule that kinship terms—other than those for mother (*ma*) and parent-in-law (*deema*)—are not as a rule used in addressing close relatives and are chiefly used towards distant relatives as a sign of special respect or courtesy. On the other hand, the terms for siblings are regularly used in referring to or making statements about brothers and sisters.

Tau (pl. *tap*) is the term for a sibling of opposite sex to the speaker or the subject of a statement. A man will say '*N-tau n-ɛl Ba'arɔ*—My sister is married to this place Ba'ari'; and a woman, '*N-yɛa n-tau yiri*—I am going to my brother's homestead.' The term *tau* has no age significance, as age differences do not affect the social relations of opposite sex siblings, but the suffixes *-kpeem* (senior) and *-bil* (junior) can be added for descriptive clarity.

An elder sibling of the same sex is *bier* (pl. *biernam*), a younger is *pit* (pl. *pirəba*).

A sibling by the same mother (whether or not the father is the same) is called *soog* (pl. *saarət*) without reference to sex or age; but sex and relative age can be indicated by combining *soog* with the preceding terms. Thus *tasoog* is a *soog* of the opposite sex; *bier-soog* is an older *soog* sibling of the same sex; *pit-soog* is a younger *soog* sibling of the same sex. These terms, as we have seen,[1] are extended to all uterine kin.

A sibling of different maternal origin is described by the term *sunzɔ* (pl. *sunzɔp*). Anyone who can be regarded as a sibling by the rules of classificatory kinship may be referred to thus, and the term is also used in corporate relations to denote co-ordinate lineage segments.[2] By itself *sunzɔ* may indicate a patrilineal sibling of either sex, but the suffixes *-pɔk* (female) and *-doog* (male) are often added to indicate the sex of the person referred to.

The Solidarity of '*soog*' Siblings

The interplay of the various factors that mould the relations of siblings can best be understood by studying their genetic development. True siblings always grow up together in their natal family through the formative years of childhood, whether they remain together after adolescence or separate. Thus the mutual attachment and identity of

[1] Cf. Ch. II above.   [2] Cf. *Dynamics of Clanship*, ch. xii, p. 201.

interests of siblings, particularly of brothers, is built up on common upbringing and a common body of affective experience. In the older settlements the children of an expanded family, or even of a group of families based on a medial lineage, grow up together. Hence one finds, as has already been recorded,[1] that any member of an inner lineage knows the life-history of every other member.

This common background of siblings is illustrated in children's play-groups.[2] In the older settlements the play-groups of children under 8 or thereabouts rarely include children who belong to different medial lineages. It is the children of a group of adjacent homesteads, who are *ipso facto* members of the same inner or at most medial lineage, that form regular play-groups. Children of one sex of the same joint family or expanded family between whom there is not a wide age-gap always play together in the same group. Siblings of like sex learn together, and to an important extent from one another, the economic skills and practical knowledge they will need in order to get their livelihood. As nearly common a body of experience as is possible for separate individuals shapes their social personalities and directs their interests, ideals, and purposes towards culturally defined goals and values. In Tale society men or women of equal social maturity tend to think and feel alike in the same situation. Thus the similarity of character marking them out amongst their age-fellows which one very often observes in a pair of brothers or sisters is noteworthy,[3] the more so as differences of temperament and intelligence are not obliterated thereby. It is, indeed, just this uniformity of character that makes it difficult for some brothers and sisters to get on well with each other.

The ties of mutual attachment, loyalty, and solidarity in social matters that unite siblings are graded according to their genealogical closeness. They are closest for full (*soog*) siblings and progressively less close for those who have only a father in common, a paternal grandfather in common, a paternal great-grandfather in common, or more remote connexion.

These differences are laid down in earliest infancy. The intimacy and close mutual identification of full siblings is rooted in their common dependence on their mother in childhood. It is to her that they look for food and emotional security, and a mother's care is given to all her small children equally and in a group. In the hunger months if a woman gets hold of a little grain to cook some food for her children, she calls them all to eat of it and they all sit down together around the dish. The first lessons in sharing equally are learnt in this setting. The 6-year-

---

[1] *Dynamics of Clanship*, p. 210.
[2] I have given a short description of these play-groups in my '*Social and Psychological Aspects of Education in Taleland*', previously cited.
[3] The processes of education that lie behind the formation of social personality among the Tallensi are more fully discussed in the paper just cited.

old, admonished sometimes by his mother, tries not to eat too greedily lest his 2-year-old brother or sister eating with him should not have his fill. The 11- or 12-year-old, copying his parents, will take a mouthful or two and then say he has had enough, leaving the dish to be finished by his younger siblings. Thus are the seeds of the concern for each other's welfare commonly found between full siblings planted through the precept and example of the mother.

As we have seen, children sleep with their mother in infancy and early childhood. The feeling of emotional security this gives to a child thus becomes associated with his maternal siblings. Tarəmba, aged about 9, was playing with his usual companions of about the same age— four other boys and a little girl. All but one of these children came from the same expanded family. I stopped to chat to them. After a while we got on to the subject of parents. Yindubil said he preferred his father to his mother. Tarəmba interrupted, exclaiming, 'Hee! he's telling fibs. It's only because his mother has run away. My mother is dead and so I can't help it, I've got to like my father best. But if you have a mother it's different. She is the one who gives you food; and when night comes you sleep beside her, and you don't have bad dreams. If you sleep alone you have bad dreams.' For a Taləŋ sleeping badly or having bad dreams is the arch symptom of a state of anxiety. Tarəmba's wistful remarks sum up vividly what a mother means to a Taləŋ as the focus of his sense of security, and this affect adheres to a full sibling. It forms a strong motive in the reluctance of full brothers to part and set up separate households or separate homesteads. Tɔbəg and Dɔbil were full brothers (saarət), both middle-aged men with adult children. They lived together and farmed together in great amity. I knew them well and had occasion more than once to discuss with them one of my stock subjects, why *soog* brothers do not, like half-brothers, separate when their families start growing up. 'No', they said, 'thus it is pleasant (*ŋwala m-mah*). Being together thus we help each other. We two sitting here, are we not the children of one mother? He and I, we come from one vulva (*ti yi la pɛn yɛnni na*).' This is the standard explanation given for the lifelong partnership of *soog* brothers.

Soog siblings are generally devoted to each other and always, as far as my observation goes, unquestioningly loyal to each other in relation to other people. One sees this very clearly in the behaviour of young children. Babies and infants are often left by their mothers in the care of older children. A woman may ask one of her co-wives' children to keep an eye on her infant for a little while, but it is not usual for an infant to be left for hours on end, or a whole day, in the care of a half-sibling. So if one sees an infant being carried about by a young girl of 10 or 11 one can be fairly certain that they are either full siblings or that the little nursemaid is the infant's mother's classificatory 'sister' or 'child', whom she has specially brought to live with her

SIBLINGS IN THE SOCIAL STRUCTURE

as nursemaid to the baby. If one sees a boy taking care of an infant one can be certain that the children are *saarət*. A boy will gladly keep an eye on a baby half-brother or half-sister for an hour or so, but he will refuse to take care of the baby for a longer period. Not so with his *soog* sibling. Boys delight in carrying their infant *saarət* about or having them with them in the same play-group. All children are very patient and affectionate with younger *saarət*. A homely sight is that of a little boy or girl of about 6 or 7 kneeling beside a baby sibling on the ground and caressing its face with slightly parted lips.

Tale children often squabble among themselves, with that mixture of earnestness and fantasy that runs through so many of their group activities; but I have never seen a child trying maliciously to hurt another. Between siblings, especially full siblings near to each other in age, squabbling is regarded as a normal habit. It is one of the signs of their equality and familiarity. So one sometimes sees a little boy or girl of 3 or 4 angrily pummelling a sibling of 7 or 8 and the older child playfully warding off the childish blows. Or one sees an infant howling in rage for something and his elder brother or sister patiently soothing him. Yindubil, aged about 8, whose mother had run away, was being brought up by his father's younger wife. Her little son, Mɔyar-pu-la'at, aged about 4, was very fond of Yindubil and followed him about wherever he went. Said Yindubil, of his half-brother, with a grin, 'He's quarrelsome, always wants to scrap with me. But I don't mind; he's my *soog*[1] and besides he's not greedy. If our mother prepares some food for us he always waits for me to come and join him.' Passing Bayankura's homestead one morning I found his children standing about in front of the gateway. As I came up, the youngest, a boy of about 3, ran to his brother, a lad of 11 or 12, and clung to him. Their half-sister, aged about 9, laughed and said to me: 'He (the infant) is afraid of you, so he runs to his *soog*.' I asked, 'Why didn't he run to you?'—for a small child runs to its mother or older sister more readily than to a brother or its father for protection. 'Oh', she replied, 'he likes his *soog* better than me.' I asked Kyekambɛ, aged about 11 or 12, whom he liked best, his small *soog* brother Badiwona, aged about 6, or his half-brothers who were his constant playmates. 'Badiwona', he said emphatically, 'we are one mother's children, and some day, when I move out to farm on my own, he will come with me, the others won't.' Similarly, Maɛŋya, aged about 12, and his *soog*-brother Tɛndaanbon, aged about 8, were inseparable. They helped each other to hoe their respective ground-nut plots and always went about together. They ate together regularly out of the same dish; they went on errands together.

---

[1] Not in the strict sense, of course. But this is a very good example of how being brought up by the same 'mother' creates sentiments of attachment similar to those of true *saarət*. I came across several instances of this.

Once a smaller boy who was with them hit Maɛŋya. Maɛŋya turned furiously on the small boy; but it was somewhat comical to see Tɛndaanbon equally angry with the assailant. Like many full or half-siblings of about the same age and the same sex, these two boys were extraordinarily alike in character, modelling themselves obviously on their father. They had his blunt and honest habits of speech, his diligence and readiness to oblige, and a sense of responsibility beyond their years.

Until one of them reaches the age of about 9 or 10, and sometimes even after that age, *soog* siblings are frequently together irrespective of sex. That is why one often sees a little girl with a group of small boys, or a little boy with a group of small girls. Between the ages of about 9 and 12 the sexual dichotomy prevailing in Tale culture begins to have a strong influence on the children, as we have seen. Different economic activities divide boys and girls. One rarely finds girls accompanying the herd boys or boys going for firewood with their mothers and sisters. Boys are beginning to share the interests and activities of the men, girls those of the women. Boys go about with their 'mates' (*taab*, sing. *taraan*) or 'chums' (*dɔlɔntaas*, sing. *dɔlɔntaa*) of about the same age, and girls with their girl chums. Boys of 11 and 12 are apt to be rather scornful of girls, and girls of this age turn up their noses at their boy contemporaries. Overtly, their attitudes to one another remind one of the latency phase in European children. Children round about 11 to 13 do not play together much in groups except on special occasions. Girls, in particular, are at home a good deal.

This is the time, therefore, when the sex factor begins to exercise a strong influence on the relations of siblings; age differences also become significant; and with this emerges a distinction between the social aspect of siblingship and the affective, personal aspect. A boy of 11 to 13 may make a boon companion of a half-brother or a classificatory brother from a neighbouring homestead of about his own age, leaving his younger *soog* brother or sister to his or her own devices if the difference between them is considerable. When Kɔyatee came to see me it was always with one of his chums who belonged to a different branch of his medial lineage, never with his younger *soog* brother or sister.

It is the same with girls at this stage. Ba'anzee's best friend was her classificatory 'daughter' of about her own age from the next homestead. They used to come up to the camp to call on my wife, as they generally announced to me, their arms affectionately round each other's neck. Maanyeya's daily playmate was her classificatory sister of about the same age from a neighbouring homestead—until her mother had a baby who wholly absorbed Maanyeya's delighted attention.

This tendency to seek outside friendships, though still chiefly among siblings of the same inner lineage, increases with the approach of adolescence. From the age of about 14 to 16 up to about 18 to 20 many boys are keenly learning the art of courtship and are experimenting with sex. They have sweethearts (*gab*, pl. *gabnam*), most commonly slightly younger girls of the same clan whom they call 'sisters' in the widest sense. These girls may have serious suitors from other clans, but not being quite ripe for marriage find much more pleasure and excitement in their freer relations with their clan 'brothers'. With them they can indulge in sexual play, not always stopping short of intercourse, without criticism. Now when boys go to visit their sweethearts they often like to have the company of a friend (*zɔ*, pl. *zɔnam*) of about the same age, who has a similar interest in such adventures. For this a boy prefers a friend from another homestead, a not too near classificatory brother, to a close brother. Later on such a pair of friends will help each other in serious courtship, for one cannot carry on a serious courtship without a friend to act as spokesman and go-between. And a distant brother is preferable to a close brother as a friend in affairs of the heart. It helps to keep them secret from the other members of one's family, and that is desirable because it is a point of honour with every young man to find a wife for himself. The same motives operate with girls between the ages of about 13 and marriage at 16 to 18 years of age. A girl likes going to market with a girl friend of about her own age who is equally interested in the young men around. But if a girl is thinking of eloping with a suitor she prefers to confide in her mother or her clan-brother sweetheart. Having no rights in the bride-price they will—for a bribe from the suitor—help her to get away, whereas her own brothers will insist on a marriage by arrangement so as to make sure of the bride-price.

But the divergence of interests and companionship in the years immediately preceding and following adolescence does not disturb the personal intimacy and attachment of *soog* siblings. Custom prescribes that husband and wife should eat separately. So a man eats with one or two of his younger children, and each of his wives eats with one of her younger daughters or an infant. The other children are divided up, one dish of porridge to this pair of boys or that pair of girls or even to a girl and a boy. They may be full siblings or half-siblings, and the porridge they are eating on a particular occasion may be of their mother's co-wife's cooking. Nevertheless, every child continues to think of his own mother as the food-giver and of his *saarɔt* as those with whom he automatically shares food. A boy of 12 does not sleep in his mother's room, yet he still regards her as the source of his sense of emotional security. In a small and harmonious polygynous family the children are almost equally at home in all the women's quarters, but in a large joint family the children of one woman tend to be in her quarters for most of the time that they are indoors.

Of many other signs of the lasting intimacy of full siblings and their closer identification with each other than with their half-siblings, the best is this. A 12-year-old is conscious of his seniority (*kpɛmət*) in relation to his younger siblings. He orders them about and pulls them up if they are not behaving properly. But whereas he would not hesitate for a moment to smack a younger *soog*, he will not go further than scolding a younger half-sibling for the same offence. Tallensi say that if you strike your younger *soog* it does not matter; your mother or your father may rebuke you afterwards and the affair is forgotten. But if you strike a half-sibling—even if the child has behaved so disgracefully that public opinion will be on your side—you cause friction in the family. The child's mother gets annoyed with you and with your mother and quarrels arise.

There is another interesting indication of this. As has been previously mentioned, Tallensi do not designate incest between brother and sister as sinful. When they say it is forbidden (*kih*), as they sometimes do, they mean it rather in the sense that it is disgraceful, scandalous, and unnatural than in the narrower ritual sense. If they are asked why then it is so uncommon, considering the many opportunities and temptations that surely offer, they explain it by the intimacy of siblings in childhood and adolescence. They deny that the temptation exists. 'Look', said Sinkawol, arguing this point with me, 'my sister, is she not marriageable? And here am I, however attractive she is, I do not even notice it; I am never aware that she has a vagina; she is just my sister and someone will one day come and marry her and I will give her to him and get my cows. You and your sister grow up together, you quarrel and make it up, how can you desire to have intercourse with her?' This is a stock argument with the Tallensi.

At the same time the natives are the first to point out that sexual play in childhood generally begins with a classificatory sibling. Family play is a regular thing in the under-8 play-groups; and the final realistic touch is for the 'husband' and 'wife' to pretend to have coitus. This is common knowledge, and adults laugh at it. A standing joke is to tease a small boy about his so-called sweethearts. As we have seen, Tallensi say that small children 'have no sense (*ka yam*)', and therefore it is not a breach of propriety or morals for them to play at coitus with a sibling. Every man I questioned on the subject told me, with a grin of amusement, that his first sweetheart was a 'sister', sometimes of the same expanded family, more often of the same inner or medial lineage. 'We were very small and didn't know better', they said.

But Tallensi maintain stoutly that even small boys of 6 or 7 do not play at coitus with their *soog* sisters or half-sisters. There are exceptions, of course, they readily admit. There are stupid children, precocious children, and badly brought up children. Among such children instances of brothers copulating with sisters are bound to occur. It has been known to happen even with adolescents, who are presumed to 'have sense'. If it is found out, the culprits are given a severe thrashing and are taunted for months afterwards by their fellows. But these are not the reasons why children so rarely commit this impropriety. It is because of the intimacy, the closeness to each other in daily life, of brother and sister. Children do not need to be told that it is wrong to copulate with a sibling of the same joint family; they know it themselves. And, in fact, children from the age of 6 or 7 and upwards always say, with an expression of disgust, that sexual play with one's own siblings is wrong. Moreover, though they are not taught it as an avoidance, they are well aware of the conventional attitudes on the subject from listening to adult conversation.[1]

Incidentally, there are no taboos on conversation on sex matters among the Tallensi. Men, women, and children are all outspoken about sexual matters, though young women are apt to use euphemisms and to talk more circumspectly than men. Some men also say that it is embarrassing to talk about sexual subjects in front of young wives or female relatives-in-law. But no native hesitates to discuss these subjects in the presence of his sister.

These ties of mutual affection and devotion between *soog* siblings last throughout life and are extended to their children too. One sees this most dramatically in the grief people show, and especially women, over the death of a *soog* sibling. Tallensi say that very often the loss of a full brother is a greater shock to a woman than the death of her husband. A husband is replaceable, a full brother not, they add. When Kpe'emi died his wife fainted and afterwards sat about disconsolately, weeping at intervals for days. His *soog* sister also fainted, but, the men said, it had been much more difficult to revive her than her sister-in-law and she became ill with grief. Seeing the two young women together one could not doubt that it was the sister who felt the blow worst.

Another vivid demonstration of the strength of this tie between full siblings occurred when Tɛndaan Teroog performed the succession ceremony on succeeding to the custody of his maximal lineage *bɔyar*. A large crowd had gathered, chiefly men—clansmen, and neighbours and matrilateral kinsmen of Teroog's maximal lineage. Amongst them my

---

[1] The psychological undercurrents of these conventional attitudes do not concern us here, but it may be remarked that there is probably a strong and partly overt sexual component in the affective relations of brother and sister. I was struck by this when I once had an opportunity of observing the behaviour of Yamzooya (aged about 11) and his *soog* sister (aged about 8) who were playing together in a corner of the room where I was chatting to their father. The children, who were quite naked, stood embracing each other, the boy with his legs round his sister's, and they twisted and wriggled about as if they were engaged in a mixture of an orgiastic dance and a wrestling-match. They were both in a state of high excitement, panting and giggling and muttering to each other, with obvious sexual pleasure. They seemed to be oblivious of their surroundings. This game went on for about twenty minutes after which they separated and lolled back as if exhausted. These two children were most attached to each other.

eye was caught by an old woman who seemed to be particularly privileged, as she walked about giving orders, and greeting the guests. I was not surprised to learn that she was Teroog's only surviving full sister (*tasoog*). He presented her to me with great pride, holding her hand affectionately. She sat beside him throughout the rites, listening intently to his long invocation to their ancestors, prompting him once or twice, and helping him as if she and he were jointly succeeding to the ownership of the *bɔyar*. One could see that the notion that any woman might well have been in her brother's place in the social system if it were not for an accident of birth has a very concrete meaning to the Tallensi.

Full (*soog*) siblings, as we have already related, constantly visit one another, bringing and taking away gifts. When a woman has a baby, her full sister hastens to her with a bundle of firewood or a dish of soup ingredients. If a person falls ill, his full siblings come running to see him. When Kuur fell and broke his ankle there was consternation among his immediate relatives. Two of his half-brothers rushed off at once to consult a diviner about the accident—no laughing matter, as they well realized, for a man in the fifties—while his full sister stayed behind to nurse him. His wife hovered about helplessly, only approaching him when his sister called for some more hot water. The sister came to him every day for the next week or so and was his most devoted nurse.

We have described before, also, how full brothers generally hold together, economically and residentially, longer than half-brothers and often throughout their lives. This is due, basically, to their close identification with and attachment to each other. One constantly comes across examples of this. Samane was the Chief of Tongo's right-hand man and probably the only person who had the chief's absolute trust. Why, I once asked Samane, did the chief not put the same trust in his own son Saa? 'Don't you see', said Samane, 'the chief and I are born of one father and one mother. We are as one. He will have no secrets from me or I from him. A man's brother is more to him than his son. Saa wouldn't care[1] if the chief died and he succeeded. I want my brother to live, for his being chief is just as if I were chief myself.' Again, one of the very few cases I knew of men working abroad sending home regular remittances of money was Sɔyar's policeman brother. When I praised him, Sɔyar said, as if in explanation, 'He is my *soog*'.

This comes out very clearly, too, in the property relations of full brothers. Men of the same joint family borrow one another's clothes freely, though the individual ownership of the clothes is never in doubt and the owner's permission is always necessary. But full brothers behave almost as if their clothes were their common property. Hence when a man dies his full brother often takes some of his clothes, instead of leaving all to his sons. There is also a specific ritual sanction in this relationship, the common subjection of full brothers to their mother's

[1] He was the chief's first-born son. Cf. p. 225 above.

spirit, perpetuating, on the religious plane, their common dependence on her in her lifetime.

It must not be thought, however, that friction between full siblings never occurs. That would be contrary to human nature, the natives often declare. As amongst most peoples, sibling solidarity conceals a strong element of rivalry. Indeed there is one circumstance in which it is taken for granted that *soog* siblings will be prone to quarrel all their lives, even if they do not set up separate homesteads. Two successive children of the same mother and father are regarded as born rivals. The second of the two children, irrespective of sex, is called the *nyeer* of the first. The first *nye* (verb = immediately precedes) the second, who *tayal* (verb = immediately follows) the first in birth order. The definition applies strictly to birth sequence, not to survival order. A child is not its older *soog* sibling's *nyeer* if between them their mother had another child who died in infancy, or a miscarriage—for a miscarriage counts as a birth. The concept *nyeer* is regularly used to indicate an infant's degree of maturity. An infant that has a *nyeer*, or is old enough to have a *nyeer*, is entering the second conventionally recognized stage of social development, childhood proper. So if a native is asked about the stage of development reached by a particular child and says, 'It has a *nyeer* (*u mar nyeer*)' or 'It is fit to have a *nyeer* (*u saya nyeer marəga*)', one can infer that the child is between 3 and 5 years old—or, to keep to native categories of thought, that it is weaned, no longer needs the constant care of its mother or a nursemaid, and is beginning to fend for itself, to join in children's play-groups, and to become acquainted with the world outside the homestead walls.

A child and its *nyeer* are believed to be rivals almost from the day the *nyeer* is born. This predisposes them to be ill tempered with each other and wrangle on the most trivial provocation. Often when I have noticed two children bickering or annoying each other in some petty way, my companion—a man or an older child perhaps—has said with a laugh, 'There's someone and his *nyeer* (*nit ni u nyeer nla*)'. Once at a funeral ceremony there was an argument between the two sons of the dead man. It ended with the older giving the younger a buffet across the mouth that drew blood. Relatives intervened and separated them. Then an old woman, their father's *soog* sister, with mingled pleading, protests, and sighs, dragged the younger brother away to attend to his cut lip. He was weeping with injured pride and humiliation, exclaiming, 'If he were not my older brother (*bier*) I would kill him'. The people sitting around commented scathingly on this shameless spectacle. Then someone remarked, 'Oh well, it's a case of a man and his *nyeer*'. It had all begun, I learnt, from the younger lad's accusing the older of having appropriated something belonging to him and the older losing his temper with him for fussing about ridiculous trifles on such a solemn day.

If a person is ill tempered or unnecessarily sharp with him, or appears to dislike him, a Talǝŋ retorts with 'Why do you dislike me? Am I your *nyeer*, or what? (*I yaagǝm bo? Man a i nyeer bɛ?*)' This formula is always spoken half-mockingly; for the rivalry of successive children, though assumed to be in the very nature of their relationship, is not taken too seriously. It is not, like the underlying rivalry of father and first-born son, subject to ritual sanctions. It is simply an acute expression of the familiarity and equality of siblings and does not destroy their solidarity.[1] Tallensi themselves say that successive siblings often get on together admirably and stand together as staunchly as any other full siblings. I have never heard it said that *soog* brothers are quicker to set up separate households if they are successive siblings than if they are not.

Tale custom recognizes the rivalry of successive siblings in a number of other ways. Thus successive siblings (this applies chiefly to brothers) may not be buried in the same grave. If they are, their spirits will be continually quarrelling and persecuting their descendants until they are exhumed and separated. Again, successive sisters may not be married to the same man or even to the same clan. But this rule is, to my own knowledge, often broken. If they do happen to be married into the same clan the sisters must avoid being pregnant at the same time or, if they are, they must not see each other during their pregnancy. If they do one or both will miscarry. Here it is belief rather than practice that is a sign of the rivalry of successive siblings. Tallensi object to having two sisters married to the same man for prudential reasons. They say that it is obviously more difficult to get eight cows out of one man in payment of bride-price than it is to get four cows. Nevertheless it does sometimes occur. A well-to-do son-in-law who has his father-in-law's esteem can often persuade the old man to give him another daughter to wife. If the girls are successive siblings, a very simple magical rite involving the burying of a hoe at the entrance of the husband's homestead serves to 'cut' their *nyeer* relationship.[2]

---

[1] I do not know whether successive siblings quarrel more often than non-successive siblings. Tallensi say they do. Knowing the Tallensi, I have no doubt that conventional expectation itself acts as a stimulus to petty wrangling between successive siblings. Every time they have a disagreement not only onlookers but they themselves put the conventional interpretation on the situation, and this is bound to make them more touchy in relation to each other than to other siblings. In every aspect of Tale social life cultural definitions and expectations direct behaviour in this way. On the other hand, I knew several pairs of successive siblings who got on extremely well together and to all appearances never said a cross word to each other. Tallensi admit that this is quite common and explain it by the invariable stock phrase 'It's all a matter of character'.

[2] A question that immediately suggests itself is, whence does the rivalry of successive siblings arise? I have put this question to many Tallensi. The usual answer is in terms of the cliché that 'it is in the nature of things (*de yɛl nla*)'.

To return to our main subject, squabbles between children, whether they are successive siblings or not, are laughed away. When adult brothers and sisters quarrel it is taken more seriously. The irresponsibility—as the men view it—of women in marriage often leads to family quarrels. A woman who runs away from a husband to whom she has been given, or obstinately returns to one from whom she has been taken, arouses her father's and her brothers' anger. There may be a temporary estrangement between them. But in the end they usually become reconciled again. If she does not give in, her father or brothers do. 'They have no alternative but to give in (*ba kɔŋ ka diegəra*)', the natives say. Before that happens, however, there may be a father's curse on the girl and hard words spoken to her and her husband by her brothers.

Adult *soog* brothers also fall out at times, but in contrast to disputes between half-brothers this seems very rarely to become either the pretext or the stimulus to their deciding to separate. Tallensi ascribe it to peculiarities of personality. The very fact that full brothers are often alike in character may be the cause of friction between them. To give one or two illustrations, there was the case of Zaŋ and his older *soog* brother Pumaan. They were both inclined to be solitary, egocentric, excessively touchy about their status, and suspicious of others. The strong competitive streak in them inevitably coloured their relations. So Zaŋ often complained that he found Pumaan's authority irksome. But there was never, as far as I could discover, an open quarrel between

But one or two more thoughtful informants appeared to have an inkling of the deeper sources of this peculiarity. They connected it with the fact that the older sibling is 'set aside' or 'left to itself (*bah*)' by the mother when she becomes pregnant with its *nyeer*. That is to say, the child's physical weaning is completed and simultaneously its affective attachment to its mother—a very possessive attachment with unweaned Tale babies—is brought to an end. A *nyeer* dispossesses its immediately preceding sibling of their mother's undivided care and devotion in both the physical and the psychological sense. This is a fact of observation and one which has a direct influence on family life. As we know, Tallensi maintain that it is very difficult for a woman to take care of two unweaned infants, hence the prohibition against a woman's becoming pregnant again before her infant is old enough to do without her undivided attention. When this custom is broken, so that a premature pregnancy follows, the parents are said to *nye* their child. As this term, cognate with *nyeer*, suggests, and conventional opinion confirms, a premature *nyeer* is believed to endanger a child's life. On the analogy of what is known to happen in our society, it can be surmised that the open acknowledgement of rivalry between successive siblings is a culturally standardized safety-valve for the jealousy and resentment the older sibling has against the younger for robbing him of their mother's attention. This explains also why successive birth order is the significant feature and not survival order. The older child's resentment will be directed only against its immediately next-born sibling, the one on whose account it was 'set aside', whether that sibling lives or not. It is possible, moreover, that open acknowledgement of the rivalry of successive siblings prevents it from turning into a disruptive element in the relations of siblings.

them, and Zaŋ stood unswervingly by Pumaan, when the latter took sides against the head of their own medial lineage in the dispute over the succession to the clan *bɔyar*. Nindɔyat and Yintee, who, unlike Zaŋ and Pumaan, still farmed together, were cast in the same mould. Both were notorious for their instability and aggressiveness. They were known to quarrel frequently and on at least one occasion came to blows. But no one could have been more loyal to Nindɔyat than Yintee, in particular where the possessions of the family were concerned.

In short, though *soog* siblings come into conflict at times it does not undermine their solidarity. The reason for this is obvious. The crux of the sibling relationship lies in its social definition. Personal qualities may modify its content in particular cases; they cannot break up its structure; and this holds for every degree of sibling relationship. In the case of *soog* siblings the infrangible core is the relation of uterine siblings to and through their mother, as members of the matricentral *dug* in contraposition to the patricentral *yir*, first in the joint family and later in the lineage. The significance of this factor, the notion of maternal origin, can be judged from the relations of *soog* brothers who have different fathers. They may have no common economic interests and may grow up separately, after the early years of childhood. But they have very firm ties of affection and mutual loyalty, which are often expressed through mutual economic aid. Sie and Da'amo'o were *soog* brothers thus related, their mother having first been married to Sie's father and after his death to Da'amo'o's father, who belonged to a different medial lineage of the clan. Sie was the older of the two by ten or fifteen years. Whenever he was in trouble over something Da'amo'o went to seek Sie's advice rather than his proxy father's. This principle, as we have noted before, is of general validity in Tale social structure. It appears in the stronger cohesion and amity always found between individuals and lineages whose progenitors were *saarət* than between those who are only patrilineally connected. Nɛna'ab and Ɔndieso remained great friends in spite of the long-standing quarrel between their two inner lineages, because their mothers were full sisters. At the level of maximal lineage organization, Seug is a much more closely knit section of Tongo than the other three sections, because the founding ancestors of the two major segments of Seug were sons of one mother.[1]

Solidarity and Equality among sunzɔ Siblings

But the critical importance of the idea of their common parentage, bilaterally or unilaterally, in the relations of siblings is best shown in the differences between the relations of *soog* siblings and those of half-siblings and other paternal siblings (*sunzɔp*). Tallensi tend to draw a line between *soog* siblings and all other sibling relatives within the same nuclear lineage or inner lineage. Thus half-siblings (i.e. children of

[1] Cf. *Dynamics of Clanship*, ch. xii, p. 213.

the same father by different mothers) and ortho-cousins (father's brothers' children) are all lumped together as *sunzɔp* of close degree, referred to by sibling terms. Though the exact degree of patrilineal kinship between a pair of siblings has a direct effect on their mutual and common interests and on their place in the family structure, Tallensi tend to feel the same way towards an ortho-cousin as towards a half-sibling. This is natural since brothers' children often grow up together in the same domestic family.

The social and personal relations of *sunzɔp* siblings of the same nuclear lineage are identical in pattern with those of *soog* siblings. But they differ, markedly at times, in degree; for the affective as well as social relations of siblings are a function of their genealogical distance from one another, and in particular of the cleavages fixed by differences of maternal parentage.

Many indications of this have been given in previous chapters and in the preceding paragraphs, for one cannot isolate the relations of *soog* siblings from the total context of family relations or from the total field of sibling relations. Having different mothers or different fathers creates significant differences in the social relations and personal intercourse of children with their parents and with each other. It stamps the child's experience of the common domestic environment and family history uniquely for himself and his full siblings. The structural correlate of this, as we have shown in an earlier chapter, is the distinctive field of cognatic kinship which goes with different maternal origin. Hence his social position in relation to his siblings is directly reflected in his sentiments and attitudes towards them. Differentiation in the field of genealogical ties carries with it differentiation of status, rights, and duties, and this has an immediate counterpart in affective behaviour. Thus, whereas it is assumed that full brothers will remain together for most of their lives, half-brothers are expected to separate in due course; and whereas discord between *soog* brothers is felt to require explanation by reference to personal idiosyncrasies, what is felt to call for such explanation in the case of half-brothers is their adhering to each other when most people would expect them to separate. 'It is only because we are on such good terms that Barimoda (his younger half-brother) still shares the homestead with me', said Naabdiya, when he was describing the organization of his domestic family.

In childhood and adolescence paternal siblings may be the greatest comrades in play and work. The affective cleavage between them comes out chiefly in the domestic circle—when they go off at night to sleep in their respective mothers' quarters; when they seek the solace of their own mothers in sickness or distress; when an older sibling merely scolds his younger *sunzɔ* for a fault for which he would have smacked his *soog*; and so forth. The relations of *sunzɔ* siblings are strongly coloured by the social and personal relations of their mothers. *Sunzɔ* siblings whose mothers are or were classificatory or clan sisters have stronger bonds than those whose mothers were not kin. Such ties, intersecting those of patrilineal kinship, are very common. The children of a woman and her *pɔyasoog*[1] (a 'sister' or other kinswoman she brings into the family as a child to look after her baby, and who later marries her husband or another man of the family) feel almost as close to each other as if they were full sisters' children. Most common, however, are cases such as that of Naabdiya and Barimoda, who trace their long-lasting amicable association back to the excellent personal relations of their mothers.

After adolescence, with the attainment of greater economic responsibility, the cleavage between *sunzɔ* siblings becomes more apparent, though it is still largely masked by membership of the same domestic and economic unit. Paternal control and the common needs of the unit hold their divergent interests in check. Sex differences become significant in the same way as with *soog* siblings; but brothers are usually partners in work and often comrades in leisure.

At this time the pattern of their future relations emerges clearly. Its keynote is a free-and-easy comradeship on terms of equality. Differences of age, formally recognized in the terminology of kinship and socially significant as they are in the distribution of authority, rights, and duties, hardly influence the personal relations of brothers in young manhood, or even later. No Taləŋ, man, woman, or child, will submit to arbitrary authority without resistance. If any demand made on another person in virtue of superiority of generation, age, or sex is felt to be unreasonable or unjust it will be resisted. Quite small children, obedient as they are, jib at commands from parents or older siblings if they think them unreasonable or unfair.

This attitude is particularly strong among siblings. The basis of their social and personal relationships is the principle of sharing (*tɔt*). This principle underlies the social relations of siblings of any degree as well as of corporate units whose relative standing is assimilated to those of siblings, such as co-ordinate lineage segments. As we have noted earlier, it is one of the chief contrasts between the relations of father and son and those of brother and brother. It is summed up in the maxim: 'A man and his father do not share; a man and his brother share (*Nit ni u ba pu tɔta; nit ni u mabiig ntɔt*).'

As will be recollected, this maxim is most clearly illustrated in the rules of inheritance. Brothers are coheirs, even though the effective management of the lands and chattels they inherit from their father is vested in the oldest of them at any given time. Hence if a man has only 'sons' to consider in dealing with property that has come to him by inheritance from his father or brother, he is in theory free to dispose of it as he pleases. But if he is merely the oldest of a group of brothers

[1] Cf. Ch. IV. above.

inheriting from their father he will be effectively restrained by his brothers. This rule is constantly met with in discussions of the pledging of property or the sale of land or cattle. Naabdiya summed up these rules very well in reference to the various farms held by the members of his inner lineage of Kunduzoor biis. First there was the home farm originally inherited and left intact by Kunduzoor at the time of his death, now owned by the last of his and his brothers' sons, Na'am. Na'am could, if he wished, sell some or all of this land, since on his death it will pass to men whom he calls 'sons'. 'We (the sons) could protest but we could not restrain him', said Naabdiya, 'but Kunduzoor (i.e. his spirit) would be angry and would slay Na'am.' Then there was some land Kunduzoor had himself acquired and left intact, heritable only by his direct descendants. The largest part of this was now owned by Na'ampa'ahya, the oldest of his true grandsons. 'He cannot sell this land', said Naabdiya; 'we, his brothers (who will inherit after him) could restrain him. In the old days we should not hesitate to draw arrows in order to do so, but now we would drag him to the chief, who would forbid the sale.'

The records of land sales in the past which I collected at Tongo amply confirm Naabdiya's statement. When Na'ampa'ahya inherited this land from the last of Kunduzoor's own sons it was as oldest of a group of brothers. So he had to 'cut off (ŋma)' portions of it for his other brothers. These distributed portions are normally re-amalgamated with the main block of patrimonial land as the brothers inherit from one another and add their portions to the main block. But if friction develops between brothers over a serious issue, it may result in one of them refusing to let his portion revert to the patrimonial land. Such a case occurred in Naabdiya's inner lineage in his father's time. One of Kunduzoor's sons, having become his father's heir, took offence at an apparent slight put upon him by a son of his father's brother. So he took an oath that his portion of the patrimonial land should never revert to the brother who would inherit from him and made a bond with his brothers that they should act likewise. Such a compact could never have been made by a man with his 'sons'. Characteristically, the compact left uneasy consciences. A generation later deaths occurred in the lineage. Diviners said they were a punishment for certain actions that resulted from this compact and Kunduzoor's grandsons were commanded to annul it. They could no longer do so in fact, but a token annulment and an expiatory sacrifice to their grandfather were considered sufficient.

In accordance with this principle we find that duties and rewards are distributed among siblings on a basis of equality of status, though in proportion to such distinguishing personal attributes as age, ability, need, and in conformity with the demands of the situation. When brothers work together as a team in the production of the household's food resources, each is expected to contribute the maximum share he is capable of; the care of livestock is the responsibility primarily of the younger men and boys, whereas such tasks as house-building and thatching fall principally on the older brothers who have the necessary skill. All labour for the common needs of the household is informally directed by the household head, but every member of the unit is expected to know his duties and to carry them out in co-operation with the others. In this connexion a father may insist on a son's giving up his own plans in order to carry out a job for the common good; a man cannot demand this of a younger brother. He can only give a lead or make a suggestion and rely on the younger man's sense of responsibility and concern for the interests of the household.

Conversely, siblings of the same household are entitled to equal treatment in drawing on the common resources of the household for the satisfaction of their wants. Brothers are entitled to equal treatment in the allocation of food-supplies from the common stock if they are married. If a man has two adult sons—own sons or proxy sons—and pays the bride-price for the wife of one of them, it is considered right for the second to be assisted to marry before his brother is allowed to draw on patrimonial livestock for a second wife. Great importance is attached to this rule in family relations. Injustice in this matter arouses resentment. It is one of the causes of friction between a man and his proxy father, and between half-brothers, that leads to the secession of the injured party, or, very often nowadays, to his leaving home to seek work abroad. Tallensi claim that cases of this sort are not uncommon; but those I was able to investigate show that discrimination in this respect between *sunzɔ* brothers is usually only one element in a complex picture of motives for seceding. The point stressed by the natives, however, is the principle; and observation shows that it is more commonly honoured than not. An almost ludicrous example of this was Yinworəb's dogged efforts to find a wife for his half-brother Yimbɔm. He failed, alas, for no girl would stay with so unprepossessing a man as Yimbɔm.

The notion of sharing is especially important in the ritual relations of brothers or the descendants of brothers. Many examples of this are quoted in our previous book.[1] Its outstanding characteristic is the precise distribution of roles and division of sacrificial or ceremonial foodstuffs, beer, and meat in accordance with the lineage relationships of the participants.

This emphasis on just sharing among siblings begins in childhood, first when siblings sit down to eat from a common dish, and then in the children's play-groups. I have many times stood by watching with some amusement while a group of small children solemnly divided up a small animal they had killed, a lizard or a mouse, for instance. They are always fair, especially to the younger ones; and they follow the pattern

[1] Cf. *Dynamics of Clanship*, ch. xiii.

of distribution employed in the division of sacrificial meat, as they have seen it among adults, with hardly an error. By the age of 8 or 9, boys are sufficiently familiar with the lineage organization to have grasped this pattern.

The division of sacrificial and ceremonial food expresses precisely the genealogical structure of the lineage concerned. The first division is into equal shares for each of the major segments of the lineage; then a further division takes place on the same lines within each segment; and so on down to the smallest segments. Thus one can see the children of an expanded family of two homesteads divide a mouse first into halves, one for children of one homestead, the other half for the children of the other homestead, and then each group apportioning their share equally amongst the children of different mothers in the same joint family.

As these rules show, the configuration of social relations characteristic of brothers is generalized throughout the social structure, not, of course, in all its intimate nuances and particularities but in its structurally relevant norms. Where two persons or corporate groups are defined by descent as 'siblings' or 'brother-groups' they act towards each other as brothers would in a comparable situation. This, as we have previously found, is a fundamental principle of lineage organization and action.

The equality *inter se* of siblings, except for sex and age differences, postulates equality of rights in relation to their 'fathers' and to one another. The fiction by which the token rights of a woman and her children in her father's house are upheld—the theory that but for the accident of birth she might have been a son vested with a son's rights— is evidence of this. These rights become significant when a young man enters into the full productive activities of the household and when a girl gets married. It is in virtue of the labour he contributes to maintain the household, and in virtue of the bride-price she brings in, that youth and girl claim these rights. Thus these rights exist, by definition, only within the lineage framework, in relation to the corporate unity of the lineage. They are epitomized in the rule that brothers are equally entitled to inherit patrimonial property, especially land.

We have previously seen, however, that the entry of a youth into full economic responsibility coincides with the increasing progress of his self-differentiation as a social personality in his own right. There is no inconsistency in this. The unity and cohesion of family and lineage depend upon a balance of rights and duties among all the individuals involved. And the recognition of their rights and duties presupposes their self-differentiation as individuals, partly in terms of their respective maternal origins, but equally in terms of their developing social maturity and productive capacity.

The climax of this process comes with marriage, or more accurately with the establishment of a family on becoming a parent. This brings the cleavages between *sunzɔ* siblings, both on the level of jural and economic relations and in sentiment, more prominently to the fore. It is the starting-point of those intra-familial tensions that, according to native views, stir up jealousies between co-wives who are wives of brothers. As we know, these tensions are said to culminate, very often, in quarrels over alleged unfairness in the apportionment of food-supplies, or over the treatment of children, or other ostensible acts of discrimination between co-wives. This is one of the reasons most often adduced for a man's leaving the paternal homestead to farm on his own. From these tensions arise also those disagreements between brothers over petty trespasses on one another's property or independence, summed up in the conventional formula of 'quarrels about chickens and eggs'. The stage is thus set for the typical process of residential and economic fission in the joint family along the genealogical lines of cleavage inherent in it. The equality in status and rights of brothers in relation to one another within the lineage thus attains its maximum emphasis in the social structure. The natives are well aware of the economic pressures behind this process; but they also see that these pressures would not work out in just the way they do if it were not for the inherent dichotomy in the structure of the family and the lineage. These two factors mutually determine and reinforce each other.

This brings up a point of some importance. It is conceivable that tension between brothers, whatever it is a symptom of, might result in young men separating after the death of their father, or after marriage, to take up land wherever they can find any. Thus a group of brothers would be scattered without respect to their lineage ties; and this process would in a few generations lead to the disintegration of the present highly localized lineage structure, and the emergence of a system of dispersed intermingled clans such as is found in many West African societies.[1] In fact, as previous chapters have shown, there is a slow process of dispersion in progress among the Tallensi all the time, but it has not led to a breakdown of the lineage system. The lineage ramifies, it does not break up into independent units that sever their genealogical ties with the main branch.

The basis of this is the fact that brothers separate but do not thereby relinquish membership of their maximal lineage. They do not sever their social and personal bonds with one another; which means that they do not forfeit any of their rights or relinquish any of their duties as sons and brothers. They are independent only within the bounds set by the corporate unity and the common interests of the lineage system. For it is only through his position in the lineage system that a Talɔŋ is able satisfactorily to secure his rights and perform his duties as a

[1] This would appear to be the case among the Ashanti (cf. R. S. Rattray, *Ashanti Law and Constitution*, ch. viii) and the Jukun (cf. C. K. Meek, *A Sudanese Kingdom*, ch. ii), to cite only two widely separated examples.

responsible member of his society. Of this we have had ample evidence.[1] Again, there are strong economic elements in the individual's adhesion to the lineage. There is the pressure due to the form and organization of Tale economy as a whole, which tends to restrict excessive mobility. As Tallensi themselves often put it, shrewdly picking on the key item in their productive cycle, it is all a question of manure, including human excrement. A home farm in one of the old settlements kept at a high level of fertility by continuous manuring is not light-heartedly abandoned.[2] This fact, and the scarcity of unutilized and unowned farmland in the old settlements, puts a premium on the right to inherit land in them. To-day, it is true, the pressure of these forces has been relaxed by the opening up of an easily accessible external labour market and of facilities for trade both in Taleland and with other areas. These extraneous outlets have made life easier for the natives but they have not, as we have observed before, materially altered their traditional mode of livelihood. In fact they serve to emphasize the contention of the natives that economic motives are of secondary consequence in maintaining lineage unity.

It is not joint interest in, and equal rights to the inheritance of, their patrimonial lands which alone hold a group of brothers together. Men who leave their natal settlements on account of land shortage do not return home eventually only because they have at last inherited their patrimonial lands. The decisive sanction, as we have shown in an earlier chapter, lies in the obligation of filial piety and what it stands for in terms of the jural and ritual functions of the lineage. The focus of unity for every lineage is the authority of the father, either the real authority of the living father or the mystical supremacy of the dead father or his surrogate, an ancestor spirit. Men like Yinworəb and Da'amo'o gave up wage labour in Kumasi very reluctantly to return home because the death of their fathers left them at the head of their respective joint families, and other similar cases have been quoted in an earlier chapter (p. 179). Similarly, a group of brothers may be scattered, some at home, some in a peripheral settlement, some in Mampurugu, some working abroad. On certain ritual occasions those who are near enough make a point of returning home. Family funerals, in particular, bring the scattered members of the family together. The three chief mourners at Tɛndaan Gieŋ's funeral were his brothers' sons Gikoo-Duun, who lived near Sameni in Mampurugu, Saanbuohba, who had been farming near Tola on the Red Volta for some years, and Baŋ-Duun who had been living at Biuŋ for nearly twenty years. They all

---

[1] In preceding chapters as well as in *Dynamics of Clanship, passim.*

[2] We have touched on this subject in our earlier book, chapters i and xi. It is more fully considered in C. W. Lynn's report, *Agriculture in North Mamprussi* (Dept. of Agriculture, Gold Coast, Bulletin 34, 1937), and in M. and S. L. Fortes, 'Food in the Domestic Economy of the Tallensi', *Africa*, IX, 1936.

spoke of their ancestral home at Zubiuŋ as their 'real home (*ti yir ni yɛlmɛŋər*)' to which they would all return sooner or later. Two years later, in fact, both Saanbuohba and Baŋ-Duun did return to Zubiuŋ.

As these examples show, though the solidarity of siblings derives its psychological content from the fact of their growing up together, its validity as a norm of social relations among siblings is a function of the total field of lineage relations. In other words, whatever the personal relations of siblings may be, their indestructible social bonds spring from their common jural and ritual relationship to their parents; and 'sibling' in this context stands not only for individuals but for lineages, while 'parent' stands for any ancestor that may be relevant in a particular situation.

We must add that the friction which sibling rivalry between brothers occasionally gives rise to does not come to an end with their economic and residential separation. Self-interest among Tallensi provokes clashes of personality and of rights as much as anywhere else in the world. Tallensi say that the gravest disputes between brothers of the same nuclear lineage arise over land, though such disputes are very rare. Unlike the petty squabbles of day-to-day life, they are apt to end in blows and even bloodshed. I heard of several instances that had occurred during the previous thirty years, but only one came to my notice during my stay among the Tallensi. It was, however, a typical case. When Gunyam died, his sons Taagbin and Zayahkpɛmǝre inherited his lands and chattels, with Taagbin, the oldest son, as the senior heir. Taagbin allocated a portion of their late father's home farm to his younger brother. But the latter objected that he was being unfairly treated. The dispute ended in a fight in which Zayahkpɛmǝre was injured in the hand. Public opinion was severely critical of Zayahkpɛmǝre; for, as a Tale saying goes, an older brother who inherits his father's property and position is like one's father and should be treated with similar respect. But, as an elder of their section shrewdly pointed out when we were discussing this case, stupid as he is reputed to be, Zayahkpɛmǝre would never have raised his hand against Taagbin if the latter had been his proxy father and not his brother. Brothers quarrel just because they have equal rights in relation to one another.

There are two offences, however, which irrevocably disrupt the bonds of brotherhood if one brother commits either of them against another. As we have previously stated, it is a grave sin for a man to seduce the wife of a brother of the same inner or medial lineage. If this happens, the Tallensi say, the injured man and the culprit 'will never eat together again, will never sacrifice together again'. Because of this taboo a man may not sit on the same sleeping-mat as his brother's wife. 'It is as if he wanted to sleep with her', the natives say. Hence, also, it is considered to be improper for a man to address his brother's wife while he is alive as wife (*pɔya*), though he may speak of her to non-members of the same inner lineage as 'our wife (*ti pɔya*)' or even as 'my wife (*m-pɔya*)'; and, reciprocally, a woman speaks of her husband's brother of the same inner lineage as 'my husband (*n-sɛt*)' or, preferably, as 'my husband's older (younger) brother (*n-sɛt-bier* or *n-sɛt-pit*)', but does not address him thus. The proper reciprocal term of address is *n-kpee* ('my neighbour'), or *n-dakii* ('my sibling-in-law'). The terms for husband and wife are used in address only between a man and a distant clan-brother's wife.

The penalty for breaking this taboo has both a literal and a figurative meaning, in the sense that the brothers will never share anything again or take part in corporate activities as co-members of the same lineage. It amounts to social and religious ostracism for the sinner, and Tallensi say he would not long survive or his line of descent would perish. A similar penalty is said to follow the killing of a brother, whether it happens by accident or design. As we know, incest with a brother's wife is said to occur, though extremely rarely; fratricide by a brother of the same inner lineage as the victim is felt to be so abhorrent as to be likely to happen only by accident in exceptional circumstances. It has happened once or twice in the past, informants say, when brothers fought over the division of farm-land, but I have not heard of any cases having occurred in the last thirty years or so.[1]

The strength of the sanction we are considering can be judged from its incidence, in an attenuated degree, in cases of intra-clan homicide where the parties are not brothers of the same inner lineage. If this happens, whether intentionally or by accident, the maxim 'A cow has trampled her calf to death (*naaf n-nɔ bu bii ku*)' applies—that is to say, it is as if a cow had trampled its calf to death; so it is forbidden, on pain of bringing down the wrath of the ancestors, for the victim's close agnates to 'cancel the debt' by killing one of the slayer's close agnates. This rule holds also for lineages or clans interlinked by clanship or ritual ties. The guilty party offers expiatory sacrifices to the Earth and then a ritual reconciliation is effected between the two units concerned. But thenceforth the close agnates of the slayer—members of his nuclear lineage, usually—will not participate in a sacrifice in which the close agnates of the victim take part. If the homicide was deliberate, this taboo will even extend to all the patrilineal descendants of the two men. Thus Wakii-Sagbarug yidɛm and Kuruugdɛm are adjacent maximal lineages linked by clanship and ritual ties. On certain occasions they meet to sacrifice together at an Earth shrine common to them. The Kuruug people refrain from attending these sacrifices if the chief officiant is a member of a particular segment of Sagbarug yiri. A Kuruug man told me the reason for this in confidence. Some four or five

---

[1] There is a legend that one of the early chiefs of Tongo slew his brother in order to get the chiefship. Tallensi say this was following the customs of the Mamprusi. Cf. *Dynamics of Clanship*, ch. iv.

generations ago the ancestor of this segment of Sagbarug yidɛm slew the ancestor of a segment of Kuruug, hence the two units may not sacrifice together. To do so would be to court the wrath of their collective ancestors.

Our analysis shows that what makes a rupture of the ties of brotherhood, at any level of lineage organization, so grave a matter, is the fact that it involves a rupture of the common filial relationship of the parties to a parent or ancestor. For it is from this relationship that the persons or units concerned derive their status of brotherhood relatively to one another.

In the preceding discussion we have spoken of brothers or siblings sometimes in the primary sense of these terms, sometimes in the classificatory sense. That is exactly how the natives use the kinship terms for siblings; and the speech context by itself does not always indicate the exact genealogical degree of the relationship between the speaker and the person referred to. Like the terms used for parents and children, these kinship terms only have a strict connotation, implying specific sentiments, rights, and duties within the standard classificatory range. Within the inner lineage, or at the utmost, in lineages of narrow span, the medial lineage, a person described by the speaker as his sister (*tau*) or older brother (*bier*) or younger brother (*pit*) can be shown by genealogical reckoning to be of his or her generation by birth, even if he or she belongs to a totally different age stratum. Thus Badiwona, aged 6, describes Tiezien, aged about 70, as his older brother because they have a common patrilineal grandfather; and Zoobon-Tɔŋ-Tɔbəg's children call their contemporaries, Kurug's children, brothers and sisters because they have a common patrilineal great-great-grandfather and belong to the same inner lineage. The pattern of conduct and sentiment we have been describing holds within this range, with the qualification that the solidarity of siblings tends to be shallower and their equality of less personal consequence the more distant their genealogical connexion within the inner lineage. But so close-knit is the inner lineage as a corporate unit in relation to wider corporate groupings that these differences of degree very often vanish altogether, except for the difference between *soog* and *sunzɔ* siblings.

As usual, it depends on the situation and on the kind of interests involved. The situation steers conduct and sentiment; it is an infallible guide to the connotation of the kinship terms used in it. To take a few examples: A man may be nearly starving; he will be much more likely to receive a gift of grain from one of his matrilateral kinsmen than from a distant *sunzɔ* brother of the same inner lineage. Similarly, if a man is hard pressed in his farming programme, he will ask a uterine kinsman or an affinal kinsman to assist him and not a *sunzɔ* brother of the same inner lineage. These are personal problems and they are dealt with by invoking cognatic kinship ties. But in ritual and jural affairs it is the other way round. These involve not individual economic or social interests but the common interests of the lineage. If a man has to answer a charge of having abducted another man's wife, or meet a demand for the payment of bride-price or the surrender of the custody of a child, his 'brothers' and 'fathers' of the same inner lineage will rally round him unanimously. For marriage affairs (*pɔyadir yɛla*) involve the common interests of the whole lineage. The observer cannot deduce from the opinions or actions of any member of the inner lineage, in such a situation, whether he is the full (*soog*) brother or the paternal (*sunzɔ*) brother, or a more distant classificatory brother or father of the main actor.

The differences of degree in the solidarity of siblings is most apparent in residential, economic, and domestic arrangements. So if one asks a man whom he lives with and he replies 'I share a homestead with my older brother (*man ni m-bier la kab kpeerəme*'—lit. 'I and my older brother enter together'), one can be certain that the older brother referred to is not more distantly related to him than a father's half-brother's son. But the term *bier* has a different connotation in marriage affairs. For instance, Yin's son's father-in-law came one day to see Yin about the payment of his daughter's bride-price. There was a long and at moments acrimonious argument, with the intermediary (*pɔyasama*) acting as conciliator. At length Yin said: 'I agree to your terms; but of course I must first consult my older brothers (*biernam*).' Everybody understood that what Yin meant was that he should first have to obtain the formal consent of the elders of his inner lineage.

As we have learnt before, generation differences are not reckoned beyond the limits of the inner or at most medial lineage. Beyond this range, therefore, all clanswomen are called sisters (*tap*) and all clansmen who are one's contemporaries or one's own siblings' contemporaries are described as siblings. In relation to them the pattern of sentiment and conduct that holds between true siblings only comes into action *vis-à-vis* non-clansmen, and then in a very attenuated form. It is a question chiefly of united action and mutual loyalty in the service of the corporate interests of the maximal lineage or clan. So any man will come to the assistance of a clansman in an argument or fight with a man of another clan, irrespective of the rights or wrongs of the case. This is vividly seen in hunting or fishing battues. It is a very common thing for two or three men to lay claim to having killed an animal, especially if no arrow is found embedded in the animal's flesh. Then the clansmen of the claimants rally round them and their dispute turns into a violent altercation between two or three solid phalanxes of hunters. As we have previously narrated,[1] a famous war of the old days began in this way. Similarly, market brawls occasionally arise from a man's clansmen coming to his support in an argument. The commonest

[1] Cf. *Dynamics of Clanship*, ch. xiii.

cause of such brawls is women. A man sees a man of another clan talking to the wife of a member of his inner or medial lineage—or even to the wife of a distant clansman of his. He suspects the couple of plotting the woman's abduction and accuses them of this. In a few minutes clansmen of the two disputants who happen to be near come to their support; and so a brawl may ensue.

But where the ideal of the equality and solidarity of siblings is most apparent in social relations outside the inner lineage, is in the institutionalized co-operation of lineages and lineage segments. It is most conspicuous in important ceremonial and ritual matters such as funerals or changes in the custody of lineage shrines. But it emerges also in jural affairs such as marriage transactions and reconciliation ceremonies. The maxim 'Brothers look after one's affairs (*Sunzɔp mmaan yɛla*)' sums this up for the native. Thus, as we have described in our previous book,[1] at funeral ceremonies all the *sunzɔ* lineages of the group celebrating the funeral are bound to be present, and it is the representatives of these lineages that supervise and mostly take the lead in the various rites. When Kpe'emi died, the messengers bearing the sad tidings did not go straight home to his father. They went first to an elder of a different section (*yizug*) of the clan; he took them to the head of a segment of Kpe'emi's section different from that to which Kpe'emi belonged; and this man took them to the head of Kpe'emi's segment, who conducted them to Kpe'emi's father. Thus the blow was softened by the presence, the condolences, and the immediate ritual action of *sunzɔp* of different degrees. Similarly, if a man seduces a clansman's wife, he appeals not to his own immediate lineage head but to the head of an inner or medial lineage closely related to his to intercede on his behalf. The reciprocal of these and similar acts of assistance given to *sunzɔp* is the strictly defined rights of *sunzɔp* lineages to certain shares of sacrificial or ceremonial meat, beer, flour, and so forth. But the Tallensi do not regard these rights as rewards for 'looking after' the affairs of a *sunzɔ*. The rights and the duties coexist as equally essential features of the relationship of 'brother' lineages.

As these examples show, there are, in fact, no person-to-person social relations between individuals who are only clan-siblings of the same quality as sibling relations in the narrow sense. Their solidarity is a consequence of the general solidarity of the clan in situations affecting the common interest. Thus clan-brothers have no property relations *qua* clansmen. But the chief distinction between clan and inner lineage siblings lies in the sphere of sex. As we are aware, sexual relations with clan sisters outside the medial lineage are not regarded as disgraceful, and to have sexual relations with a distant clansman's wife is considered to be adultery, not incest. Tallensi, thinking of these matters in their inveterate socio-spatial terminology, say that clan siblings are 'too far'

[1] *Dynamics of Clanship*, pp. 215 ff.

to be treated as real siblings and 'too close' to be treated as if they were non-clansfolk in these matters. So one cannot marry a clan-sister but may have sexual relations with her, and one cannot abduct a clansman's wife, but to seduce her is not a sin. That adultery with a clansman's wife is very rare and is vehemently reprobated is a sign of the strength of clan solidarity, not of the strength of the sibling tie between clansmen.

A further point of significance is that whereas competition between brothers of the same inner lineage for wives or for politico-ritual office is held to be improper, distant clan-brothers may and do compete. No self-respecting youth would court a girl whom his brother of the same inner lineage is seeking in marriage unless it be on his brother's behalf; but it is a very common thing for several young men of the same maximal lineage or clan to court the same girl in friendly rivalry. Again, Tallensi say that until very recently, when the white man's criteria of suitability for a chiefship superseded the traditional standards, two men of the same inner lineage would never or very rarely compete for a vacant chiefship.[1] In the past, if a chiefship fell vacant, it was generally the oldest men of the clan, heads of at least medial lineages, who competed for it. Speaking of these matters Tallensi say: 'A man and his brother[2] do not like each other (*nit ni u mabiiga pu boot taaba*).' To win a chiefship, they assert, a man will not hesitate to resort secretly to medicine shrines, or to make extravagant promises to his ancestor shrines and the Earth, in order to compass the defeat of his rivals.

The Social Equivalence of Siblings Reconsidered

The solidarity and equality of siblings is a reflex of their social equivalence, but these do not mean the same thing. Equality exists between siblings; their social equivalence lies in their relations with the community at large, as has already been indicated. Many features of the configuration of sentiment and conduct we have analysed in the preceding pages acquire a new shade of meaning if we recognize them as indices of the social equivalence of siblings as well as being expressions of their equality.

Siblings are socially equivalent by reason of their genealogical identity, in whole, as between full (uterine, i.e. *soog*) siblings, or in part, as between patrilineal siblings. There are degrees of social equivalence corresponding to degrees of genealogical identity; so that *soog* siblings are more nearly equivalent than half-siblings and half-siblings than ortho-cousins, and so on.

In regard to their social roles, their rights, and their duties, wherever these are determined by descent, siblings are therefore the more closely identified the nearer they are to one another genealogically, and that

---

[1] A chiefship is always vested in a particular clan or maximal lineage. Cf. *Dynamics of Clanship*, ch. iv.

[2] A 'brother' of a different medial lineage is meant here.

covers almost every standard social relationship of siblings in Tale society. Siblings are laterally identified with one another, so to speak; brothers can replace one another in the social structure in a way that gives rise to a minimum of readjustment in the social relations of any other people affected. This contrasts with the vertical identification of parent and child, which rests on the continuity of the descent line not on actual or potential identity of social roles. This is a generalized formula. It leaves out of account a very important item, the effect of the sexual dichotomy of Tale culture. The distinctive social roles imposed on men and women by this factor restrict the identification of brother and sister to a narrow sphere, and the functions of women limit the social equivalence of sisters to their relationship with each other's children.

In infancy and childhood the equivalence of siblings is of little consequence. It comes out chiefly in the rule that parents should not discriminate between their children (proxy children as well as own children). Tallensi say that, in practice, one cannot help preferring one son to another or one daughter to another. One child may be more obedient or industrious or better tempered than his brothers and sisters, so one will be inclined to favour him; and there is the admitted bias in favour of younger children, especially the youngest, as we have seen. Moreover, proxy children are rarely as dear to the heart of a parent as own children are. Even a mother, whose love for all her children (except the youngest) is proverbially without bias, sometimes has favourites among them. There is plenty of evidence for these admissions. The Chief of Tongo had well over two-score children; among them his favourites were a son and a daughter of about 18, born soon after he was appointed chief. Nor do such preferences stop with childhood. Tiezien reposed his trust in his late brother's two sons, who had grown up in his care. The only son he had of his own who was old enough to assist him in public affairs was, he said good humouredly, too stupid.

But, say the Tallensi, this is a matter of *feelings*—what 'your heart desires (*i suh mboot*)'. When it is a matter of *rights*, to discriminate between children is bad, almost sinful; it is like rejecting one child for the sake of another. It would be regarded as iniquitous for a man to let some of his children go hungry while others were well fed. With two adult sons, as we have seen, it is considered right for both of them to be assisted to marry before either is allowed to have two wives. It is the same with other things in which there is an element of right or duty; and the majority of natives are very conscientious in this matter, at least as far as their own children are concerned. Nowadays, in particular, as has often been emphasized to me, if a man has two sons and does not deal with them equally, the one who feels himself unjustly treated soon finds an opportunity for running away to seek work abroad. Sensible parents follow this rule conscientiously even in trivial matters. Ɔmara had two little daughters, aged about 3, by different wives. One day the two children appeared very proudly each wearing a strip of cotton print about the waist. Ɔmara explained that he had bought them these 'skirts', which had to be exactly the same in size and pattern. Had they been different in colour or size, or had he bought the children different presents, they would have been very upset and their mothers angry. He would have been accused of discriminating between them.

As this instance suggests, the closer children are in age or parentage or both the more should they be treated alike. The limiting case is that of twins and this deserves a special note. Twins (*leeba*)[1] are not greeted with joy among the Tallensi; but they are not destroyed; nor are they regarded as sacred in any circumstances; nor is the mother subject to moral censure or ritual penalties. But no woman desires to bear twins. One of the most efficacious medicines that can be placed in a ground-nut plot or among *ma'ana* (*Hibiscus esculentus*), *bɛt* (*H. sabdariffa*), or *bɛris* (*H. cannabinus*) plants—all of which supply favourite ingredients for sauces[2]—to prevent women from pilfering these crops is the medicine of twins (*leeba teem*) used in purifying the parents of twins. Anyone who defies this charm will have twins, it is said. I have seen women run on catching sight unexpectedly of a twin medicine charm dangling in a farm.

Tallensi believe that twins may not be 'human (*ninvoo*)'—i.e. complete social beings—at birth. As soon as they are born, a man who owns twin medicine is asked for medicine to mark their sleeping-place. If one or both die shortly after birth that is proof positive that he or they are *kɔlkpaaris*, malicious bush sprites, not human beings. They are then buried ignominiously in a special uninhabited place. A twin that survives the first month or so of life is tacitly assumed to be human and treated as an ordinary child. But if it dies in early infancy it may still prove to have been a *kɔlkpaarɔg*, when the cause of its death is sought by divination. Its death will cause great distress to its parents, for it will have been treated with as much affection and devotion as a normal child, but it will not receive normal burial. Only when it reaches the age of about 4 [i.e. is old enough to have a following sibling (*nyeer*)] and is placed under the spiritual guardianship of an ancestor spirit, is a twin definitely regarded as a complete social being.

Tallensi seem to expect, as a matter of course, that at least one of a pair of twins will die in very early infancy.[3] The survivor then has to be

[1] They are always named *Yin* (Heaven) for the older and *Zuur* (tail) for the younger—*Yin*, 'because he sees the light of day first'; *Zuur* 'because he comes last'.

[2] *Vide* previously cited paper 'Food in the Domestic Economy of the Tallensi', by M. and S. L. Fortes.

[3] I can state with absolute certainty that every effort is made to keep twins alive. But the natives assert that the sheer physical strain of nursing and caring for twins is too much for most women. This is highly probable considering that

ritually 'pegged (*ba'*)'—fastened to life, as it were—and is henceforth regarded as human. But whether either or both of the twins survive, the parents have to undergo a course of ritual purification after their birth. This is believed to act as a magical safeguard against the recurrence of such a misfortune besides cleansing them of the ill luck that has occurred.

In spite of this mystical background, twins that survive are regarded and treated as ordinary human beings. But there is one point on which very great stress is laid. Twins must be treated exactly alike by their parents. 'If you give one a portion of porridge you must give the other an equal portion; if you give one a penny you must give the other a penny', said one informant. If they are brothers, they will live together all their lives. If they are sisters they must be married to the same settlement[1] or to adjacent and interlinked settlements. For it is as if they are one person and yet are two. They are completely equal, completely equivalent siblings; and if they are not so treated, *ba ku nye sɔmma*, things will not turn out well for them.

Rights and duties become important in adulthood, when they are actively claimed and discharged; and it is in the social relations of adults that the equivalence of siblings becomes conspicuous. It is best exemplified in three institutions, the levirate, the rules of inheritance and succession, and the extension of patrilineal, matrilateral, and sororal kinship ties. We have dealt with various aspects of these subjects in preceding chapters. Brief recapitulation with reference to the present context is all that is needed here. The kinship aspect comes up again in the following chapter. But before we look again at the levirate and at the rules of inheritance, it is worth noting some of the minor indications of the equivalence of siblings.

There is, firstly, the idea that the bride-price received for a girl should be earmarked for the payment of the bride-price for the wife of her closest brother. This convention is not strictly upheld, for the deciding

---

artificial feeding is unknown to the Tallensi. During our stay among them two pairs of twins and a set of triplets (who are treated in exactly the same way as twins) were born to people known personally to my wife and me. Even to a layman's eye it was obvious that the triplets were doomed from the first, both because they were so puny and because the mother was so utterly exhausted. Of the two pairs of twins, only one child survived the first few weeks of life, and this child, when last heard of, did not seem to have a very good chance of reaching childhood. I do not know what the incidence of twin births is among the Tallensi. The best-known owner of twin medicine at Tongo told me he had had five cases during the past two years or so and of these only one child was still alive. I knew only one pair of living twins, aged about 7 or 8, among all the children—easily running into three figures—whom my wife and I got to know throughout Taleland. Single survivors of twins are more common and I knew four. Thus the native view of the high mortality of twins appears to be justified by the facts.

[1] They are, of course, not a pair of successive sisters, so the concept of *nyeer* (*v. supra*, p. 253) does not apply.

PLATE 13

a. Children of a single domestic family. From left to right: Da'ano'o's child, his late father's child, his agnatic cousin's (i.e. classificatory brother's) child

b. Four generations. From left to right: Nyaaŋzum, his own mother with his infant son, his older (deceased) half-brother's son, who married his mother after his father's death and brought him up

PLATE 14

a. Siblings by the same parents have breakfast together. The bigger children are a boy and a girl. Note that they are eating out of the same dish

b. Successive (*nyeer*) *soog* brothers

voice in the disposal of bride-price payments always lies with the head of the joint family. He has to strike a balance between the different claims that have to be met; but other things being equal he will earmark at least a portion of a daughter's bride-price for her *soog* brother's use in espousing a wife, or if he has a wife, her nearest *sunzɔ* brother. Tallensi say that a self-respecting man should be specially scrupulous in this matter with his proxy children, but that sometimes proxy fathers are not. I have known elders of the inner lineage put pressure on a man to abide by the rule. Thus one of the grouses Sinkawol had against his proxy father Tiezien was that the latter had refused to part with cattle received for Sinkawol's *soog* sister in order to secure a second wife for Sinkawol or his *soog* brother. By contrast, one of the few things in favour of Na'abzɔ was that he allowed his proxy son Siŋ (who was farming on his own) to keep the money received in payment of Siŋ's half-sister's bride-price, against the day when Siŋ would need it himself to pay bride-price. Siŋ, incidentally, prudently handed over the money for safe-keeping to a friend, lest he himself should be tempted to fritter it away in meeting petty needs, or, worse still, lest Na'abzɔ should suddenly demand it for the payment of some debt that had meanwhile become urgent. This convention, in short, represents not a right to a sister's bride-price but an acknowledgement of the social equivalence of siblings.

Conventionalized joking between a man and his wife's siblings (in the widest classificatory sense of all her clan-siblings), and of a woman with her husband's sisters and his more distant clansmen, is another indication of the social equivalence of siblings. We have discussed this before and need only draw attention here to the associated custom by which a man is allowed to sleep with a wife's unmarried sister who comes on a visit. It is very difficult to ascertain how far this custom is actually practised. Men say it was commoner in the old days when girls were not married off, as they often are now, before puberty, but at a somewhat later age. None of the men I knew best claimed to have slept with a sister-in-law; but several said they had 'played' (*deem*)—a euphemism for flirtation ending in stealthy sex relations—with visiting sisters-in-law of one of their near clansmen. At the same time, in joking with a sister-in-law or talking about a sister-in-law men always emphasize this custom, as if it were an unchallengeable right.

Another illustration associated with the joking relationship between siblings-in-law is the terminology used between them. A man's sisters speak of his wife—and sometimes address her, half jokingly—as 'our wife (*ti pɔya*)' and the wife uses the reciprocal term 'husband' (*sɛt*) in the same way of them. I once heard a girl of about 9 address her sister-in-law thus. Pretending ignorance, I asked her why she did so. 'Our wife (she is)', came the answer, with a gesture of disdain that amused the wife, 'Have we not given cows for her?'

In ritual activities the social equivalence of siblings is constantly apparent, and in its most flexible form. For example, in almost every one of the elaborate series of rites that make up funeral ceremonies certain duties fall on particular kin of the dead person. A typical instance is the cooking of 'sisters-in-law porridge (pɔyakiis sayabo)', one of the inaugural rites of every funeral. Two 'wives' and a 'daughter' of the clan together cook porridge in a prescribed ritual fashion. Usually the rite is performed by daughters and wives of the inner lineage that is celebrating the funeral, but any daughter of the clan and any wife of the clan can serve. The rite ends with a 'sister's son (ahəŋ)' pretending to whip the women who cook the porridge with a twig. As there is not always a true sister's son present, a member of the clan has to act instead. There is never any difficulty in finding somebody who is qualified to do so. By going back far enough almost anybody can trace a matrilateral link with his own clan and can therefore act as a 'sister's son' for the purpose of the rite. Thus at Sayawuob's mother's funeral Latarəg acted as 'sister's son'. His father's mother's mother had been a daughter of the clan section to which Sayawuob belongs and that made him a classificatory 'sister's son' for purposes of this rite. A double identification lies behind such assimilations of remote to near kin. There is the lateral identification of any daughter of the clan with any other daughter of the clan, living or dead; and there is the vertical identification of a person with any of his ancestors in certain situations.

A somewhat different illustration is the following. We have seen, in our earlier book,[1] how the genealogical equality ('but for the accident of birth') of women members of the lineage and clan with their brothers is recognized both in secular and in ritual custom. Among all the daughters of a lineage—from the minimal to the maximal span, as it emerges in a particular context—the oldest of them, the pɔyayabəlǝgkpɛŋ, has special prestige. She stands for the genealogical equality of women and men in the lineage. She has a kind of honorary equality with the male head of the lineage. She has no authority in lineage affairs; but if she happens to be present when they are being discussed she may speak her mind freely and will be listened to with respect. In the case of the senior daughter of a medial or lesser lineage, she has the right to be informed in advance of every important ceremonial event in the lineage. If she attends, she is entitled to a special portion of the sacrificial meat usually allocated to the daughters—the backbone, upper ribs, and intestines. But there is a curious custom which shows her symbolic equivalence with her brother, the lineage head, best. She may never sleep under the same roof with him, even if he is her own full brother. If she did, one of them would die. There is a feeling that in the eyes of the ancestors the oldest male and oldest woman of a lineage are so nearly equivalent that the latter could easily replace the

[1] Cf. *Dynamics of Clanship*, p. 52 and ch. ix.

former. The taboo emphasizes the superiority of the male members in spite of genealogical equivalence. There is an obverse to this taboo. The token funeral performed for a woman by her father's people, after her real funeral at her husband's home, is made for a *pɔyayabəlag-kpcŋ* not by her own father's heirs but by the head of the inner or medial or even maximal lineage, her status-brother, so to speak. Tallensi say she belongs to the whole lineage not to her paternal family.

To revert to the levirate, the fundamental rule is that a man's widow may be inherited only by a 'brother' or a 'grandson' in his own clan or a linked clan, or by a 'sister's son' in an unrelated clan. The two principles involved are those of the equivalence of siblings and of the equivalence of alternate generations. A 'sister's son's' leviratic rights go back to the notion that his 'mother' might have been a man and a 'brother' of the dead man. He is exercising the rights that might have been his 'mother's'; hence this, too, is a recognition of the equivalence of siblings. What is absolutely prohibited is to inherit the widow of a 'son' or a 'father'.

In theory, as we know, these rights extend to 'brothers', 'grandsons', and 'sisters' sons' in the widest connotation of these terms. Joint leviratic rights is one of the critical norms of clanship,[1] implying that all men of the clan are 'brothers'. In practice these rights are neither absolute, nor are they equal for all men who are ostensibly entitled to them. Various factors enter into the picture, but the most important are the widow's preferences and the genealogical distance between her dead husband and whoever is seeking her hand. The strongest efforts are made to prevent a widow of child-bearing age from remarrying out of the nuclear, or at most inner, lineage of her late husband. His full and half-brothers have the strongest claim to the widow. This is based not only on the argument of genealogical proximity but on what this implies. They have contributed by their labour to the bride-price that was paid for her, and if she marries a distant clansman of theirs they lose the returns on this that children represent; for a man marrying a distant clan-brother's widow need not, in theory, refund the bride-price the latter's nuclear lineage gave for her. Actually a refund of the bride-price is often demanded in such cases and usually paid to avoid ill-feeling between the two inner lineages concerned. In addition, full and half-brothers are the dead man's coheirs. They take possession of the patrimonial property he administered during his lifetime. They accept responsibility for his debts and assume the custody of his children. For all these acts the Tallensi use the concept *vaa* (to inherit or succeed to). So they say a man *vaa* (inherits) his late brother's land, livestock, and children; and it is just, therefore, that he should also inherit his privileges and rights, especially in the matter of his widow. As brothers of the same nuclear lineage are coheirs of their patrimonial

[1] Cf. *Dynamics of Clanship*, p. 41.

property it is good enough if she marries any one of them. In practice, a widow of child-bearing age who has children by her late husband usually consents to remarry one of his close brothers.

Next to a brother of the nuclear lineage, a brother of the late husband's inner lineage is considered to have a strong claim to his widow's hand. If a man dies leaving two widows of child-bearing age it is considered proper for one of them to be given to a member of her late husband's nuclear lineage and for the other to go to another nuclear segment of the same inner lineage. If a widow appears to be unwilling to marry her late husband's half-brother, for example, and is prepared to marry one of his 'brothers' of the same inner lineage, she is usually allowed to do so by the head of her husband's nuclear lineage. The new husband is still spoken of as having inherited the widow. In every case that came under my notice widows of child-bearing age married into their late husband's inner lineage if they had young children. But in a few cases, amounting to about three out of ten, these second marriages broke down after a time. Childless young widows often prefer to go back to their parental home and try their luck again on the marriage market.

Beyond the range of the inner lineage a 'brother' of the dead man has only the rights of a clansman. If the widow is of child-bearing age he will have to be very circumspect in courting her; for he can only marry her if she chooses him in preference to other claimants, and this means she must be courted. Hence it is more usual to speak of 'marrying' (*di*) a widow than of 'inheriting' (*vaa*) her in such cases. But it would be a very bold woman who, left a widow while still capable of bearing children, rejected a husband's brother of the same inner lineage in favour of a clansman of his. Only in exceptional cases would such an action not create ill feeling between the two clan segments concerned. Such an exceptional case occurred when Baroog died leaving nine widows. His father tried hard to persuade several distant clansmen of his to seek the widows in marriage. The reason was that Baroog had no adult brothers in his nuclear lineage and so few in his inner lineage that they would not be able to inherit all the widows. For few men wish to inherit more than one widow at a time. Rather than let them return to their fathers and be sought in marriage by men of other clans, Baroog's father preferred to see them marry distant clansmen of his.

Widows beyond the age of child-bearing have complete freedom of choice in selecting a new husband from among their late husband's clansmen. Often such marriages are merely nominal. The woman continues to live with a grown-up son and her new husband comes to visit her occasionally and sends her a little grain now and then. If the widow has no adult son she will live with her new husband, adding to the labour power of his household and to its indirect sources of income through the gifts she obtains from her patrilineal kin, for example, or any private property of her own, such as a couple of sheep or goats.

SIBLINGS IN THE SOCIAL STRUCTURE

Inheritance of a grandfather's widow by a grandson, in the patrilineal line, is confined to the inner or at most the medial lineage for the simple reason that generation differences are not reckoned beyond those limits. Such marriages are not common because few men live long enough to have adult grandsons. The case of Tiezien, previously recorded, who married his grandfather Kuŋkɔŋki's young widow is the only one of its kind I encountered. For at least another generation or two the custom of inheriting a grandfather's widow will probably survive in that lineage. For Nyaaŋzum, Tiezien's proxy father whom he brought up, is the last of his generation in that medial lineage, hence his widows will have to go to his own or classificatory grandsons.

A sister's son (*ahɔŋ*) cannot marry his true mother's brother's (*ahɔb*) widow. That would be incest, since he identifies his *ahɔb* with his mother and therefore thinks of him as a quasi-father. He can marry his *ahɔb*'s son's widow or his *ahɔb*'s father's widow; for he regards the son as a 'brother', and the father is his grandfather. If the sister's son and mother's brother are uterine kin (*saarɔt*), marriage of the latter's son's widow to the former is generally approved of by the dead man's inner lineage—provided, of course, there are no better claimants among the dead man's brothers—for a uterine *ahɔŋ*, as we shall see more fully presently, is considered to be almost as closely related to his mother's brother's nuclear lineage as a born member of it. Nevertheless, such marriages are rare, and the few instances I heard of all seemed to be due to special circumstances. In one case, in which I knew the parties personally, the woman was suspected of being sterile, and the sister's son was known to be a special favourite of his mother's brother; in others the women were apparently too old for child-bearing.

In theory any member of another clan who can trace kinship with the clan of a widow's late husband through an ancestress can be called a 'sister's son' or a 'grandson (*yaaŋ*)' in the widest classificatory sense. I heard of two or three cases of such distant *ahɔs* marrying the widows of members of their classificatory 'mother's brother's lineage', but the women were all elderly and the marriages were purely nominal. There was one case, however, in which a man eloped with the widow of a member of the inner lineage from which his paternal great-grandmother had come. This was widely spoken of as a scandal, and the pair were never forgiven by the first husband's nuclear lineage; but nothing could be done about it as the *ahɔŋ* had the support of the letter of custom. The truth is that a 'sister's son' has no chance against the corporate solidarity of his 'mother's brother's' lineage. He can succeed only if they tacitly withdraw their claims or openly give him permission to court the widow.[1]

The levirate thus brings out clearly the social equivalence of siblings and shows how it is graded in accordance with genealogical distance.

[1] Cf. p. 240 above, and Ch. XI below.

We might mention here that the institution of the sororate, which is considered by some authorities[1] to be the natural complement of the levirate, only exists in a rudimentary—some might say vestigial—form among the Tallensi. It comes up if a man loses his only wife and is left a lone widower. Then his father-in-law sends a party of mourners to the funeral who take with them a young girl of his clan—perhaps one of his own daughters, perhaps the daughter of a 'brother' of his inner or medial lineage. This girl, a real or classificatory sister of the dead wife, is presented to the grief-stricken widower. She has been brought, the father-in-law's messengers say, 'to sit on your knees, to console you, to dry your tears, to be your wife' and so take the place of her dead sister. It is, however, more a gesture of condolence than a real offer of a substitute for the dead wife. Tallensi say that very occasionally the girl might stay on as the wife of the widower; most commonly she goes home immediately after the funeral or within a few weeks. Her deputy wifehood is purely ceremonial, for she is usually too young to do all the housekeeping or to be slept with.

The rules of inheritance among brothers also illustrate the gradation of their social equivalence in accordance with their genealogical distance. These rules have been considered from various angles in earlier contexts and little remains to be added. Their operation, as we have seen, depends on the conditions of economic co-operation to a very considerable extent. If two brothers farm together they automatically have joint rights in all lands, livestock, and other resources they possess. If one dies the other does not so much inherit his property and position in society as amalgamate it with his own. What was formerly managed by two men conjointly now becomes the concern of one man. There is practically no change, to begin with, in the social relations of their dependants as the result of the death of one brother. When Nindɔyat died his *soog* brother Yintee inherited the homestead they had both occupied. Nindɔyat's wives at first stayed on as Yintee's wives, his children naturally remained in the homestead. They had lost their own father, but there was no change in their social position or their economic condition as a result of his death. If brothers farm independently they inherit from each other in order of seniority and of degree of consanguinity. Patrimonial property, rights, and ritual objects that have been transmitted intact from their fathers are inherited strictly by seniority amongst the group of brothers who trace their descent to the original holder of these possessions. But property acquired by the deceased's own father goes only to his brothers by the same father, in order of seniority. And the custody of his children will pass to his genealogically nearest brother whether or not he is the heir to the patrimonial property.

Here a revealing jural fiction deserves mention. Brothers are thought

[1] Cf. Lowie, R., *Primitive Society*, p. 33.

to be closer to one another than father and son—this is one aspect of their social equivalence, as we have previously observed. In theory this holds for any brother of the same inner lineage, in practice it is only full or half-brothers who feel such close bonds. Now any land a man acquires by his own efforts goes to his sons, not to his brothers. There is no question about this. The sons have contributed by their labour to the acquisition of the land and this is their title to it. Cattle acquired by purchase also belong to the man's sons; but the heir to the patrimonial property, if he is a proxy father to or a father's brother's son older than the man's own sons, has titular control over the use to which they may wish to put any of their father's livestock. It is different with clothes and weapons; and here the fiction we have mentioned comes into the picture. Clothes are very intimately associated with a person; they are a sort of extension of his individuality, as was suggested in an earlier chapter. A man's bow, his quiver of arrows, his knife, and his spear are also thought of as symbols of himself as an individual in a way that land is not. The fiction is that such personal effects should be inherited by a man's brothers, not by his sons. Thus when a man's funeral is finished his brothers of the inner lineage assemble in his *zɔŋ*. His oldest son fetches all his personal effects in. But the brothers do not divide them amongst themselves. At most they might take an arrow apiece from the dead man's quiver. The other personal effects they will restore to the sons. 'We have seen it and now you keep it', they say. A full or half-brother, especially one who has farmed with the deceased, may, if he desires, take some garments. He may take all if the dead man's children are all too young to farm for themselves, as he then becomes their proxy father in fact as well as in name. Even then he might return some of the clothes to the sons when they are old enough to use them.

In the same way a woman's personal effects go to her daughters on her death, but her close sisters may claim some of them if they wish. For example, every woman accumulates a number of calabashes (*ŋman*, pl. *ŋmana*) during her lifetime. There is a good material reason for this, for there is hardly a more useful domestic utensil than the ubiquitous calabash dish. A woman will, however, store away her best calabashes for use on special occasions only. As she grows older she collects more and more of these select calabashes, and an old woman may have as many as forty or fifty. She keeps them in her large string bag (*zaalɔŋ*), hung up in the darkest corner of her sleeping-room. At the bottom of the *zaalɔŋ* bag is the largest and finest calabash. This will be part of her *kumpiog* (basket of death) when she dies. In it she keeps her particular treasures. Because of this an old woman's *zaalɔŋ* is as sacrosanct as a man's granary—to which, in fact, Tallensi compare it. No one but the old woman herself ever looks into the bottom calabash of the *zaalɔŋ*. When she dies an old woman's *kumpiog* is taken to her oldest daughter, who also gets the *zaalɔŋ* bag. But she does not get all the calabashes. The old woman's close sisters have first pick of the calabashes and the remainder are divided among her daughters and daughters-in-law.

Outside the inner lineage, as has been previously indicated, succession goes by age seniority. Succession to the custody of a maximal lineage *bɔyar* or to a politico-ritual office such as a chiefship or tɛndaanaship follows this rule. This, as we can now see, is in conformity with the principle that members of the same maximal lineage or clan who are not of the same inner lineage are titular 'brothers'.

It is in the usages of extended kinship, however, that the social equivalence of siblings is most apparent. We have already dealt at length with the extensions of parental roles within the lineage and it is necessary only to observe that they are based on the principle of the social equivalence of brothers. We shall find, in the next chapter, that it is an equally important factor in the web of matrilateral and sororal kinship ties, outside the agnatic lineage.[1] We shall see that, as in the ramification of lineage structure, so in extra-clan kinship bonds the tie of siblingship is the principal mechanism of their wide-spreading reticulation.

[1] This is Radcliffe-Brown's theory of the chief mechanism responsible for classificatory kinship in primitive societies. Tale material amply supports him. See Radcliffe-Brown, 'Social Organisation of Australian Tribes', previously cited, and his articles on 'The Mother's Brother in South Africa', *South African Journal of Science*, xxi, 1924, and on 'The Study of Kinship Systems', *J.R.A.I.*, lxxi, 1941.

CHAPTER XI
THE WEB OF EXTRA-CLAN KINSHIP
Some General Points Restated

WE propose now to bring together and amplify a number of lines of argument that have been introduced in previous chapters concerning the place of matrilateral and sororal kinship ties in Tale social structure.

According to our argument in Chapter II, there is a distinction of primary significance between agnatic bonds and those kinship relations that unite members of different maximal lineages and clans. The former constitute the foundation of corporate social units; they cannot be understood except within the framework of such units. The latter are personal, linking individual to individual or an individual to a corporate unit with which his or her agnates have not necessarily any genealogical relationships. Thus they do not form the basis of corporate associations. They may and often do, in fact, entail loyalties that run counter to those evoked by membership of the agnatic lineage. They imply different kinds of interests from those that unite members of a lineage. They are, as we have previously learnt, widely diffused, both for the individual and for the members of a particular lineage; and they are, in theory, without limit, both in respect of geographical range and of generation distance. In practice only a limited number and a limited range of a person's matrilateral and sororal kin ever become socially relevant for him. Geographical proximity, genealogical proximity, and the nature of the situations in which extra-clan kin normally play a part determine this.

We can describe these kinship ties as matrilateral and sororal ties because the crucial link in the genealogical chain is always a woman, whom Ego calls either his mother or his sister or father's sister, using these terms sometimes in the primary sense, sometimes in a derived, classificatory sense. Tallensi, speaking of this subject, have a saying: 'It is women who cause kinship to spread widely (*Bumpɔyas nkye ka dɔyam ɛŋ yalaŋa*)'.

There are two types of extra-clan kinship ties, as we know from previous chapters. There are the ties of uterine kinship (*soog*) which we have described in Chapter II. These are symmetrical relationships derived from the genealogical and social equivalence of sisters. Uterine kinship unites individuals on a basis of equality, as if they were siblings. Their friendship, mutual affection, and mutual interests are modelled on the relations of uterine sisters. There is no compulsion about these ties; they are not visualized in terms of binding rights and duties, but as being at bottom voluntary.

The characteristic example of the other type of extra-clan kinship ties

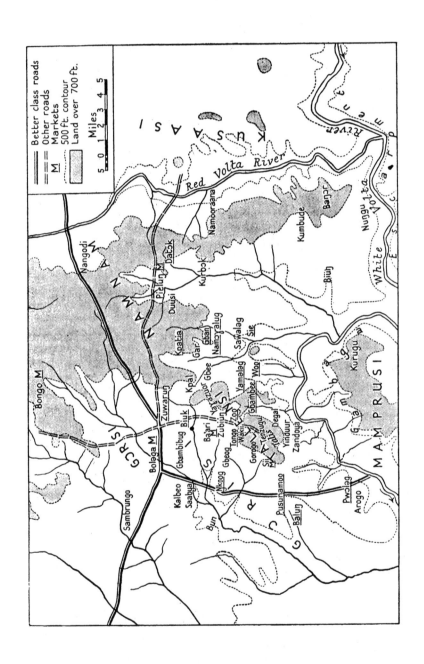

is the relationship of mother's brother (*ahəb*) and sister's son (*ahəŋ*). In a broad sense it is true to say that all matrilateral-sororal kinship ties except those of *saarət* have the same form as the relations of mother's brother and sister's son. This is a reciprocal relationship of the same class as that of parent and child. Thus Tallensi always say of any sororal kinsman 'I (or we) begot him (*man* [or *tam*] *dɔyuwa*)', and of any matrilateral kinsman 'he (or they) begot me (*u* (*ba*) *dɔyəma*)'. This phraseology is reminiscent of the way in which the relationship of successive generations within the agnatic lineage is defined. It points to an aspect of the mother's brother–sister's son relationship which is absent in that of *saarət* linked through their mothers only. A mother's brother, being a man, has jural and ritual rights, duties, and powers in virtue of his membership of his patrilineal lineage, and they condition his social relations with all his kinsmen. Moreover, they are not extinguished by his death. They pass to his heirs and descendants as part of the network of rights and duties embodied in the structure of the lineage. A man's relationship to his sister's son, as we shall see presently, necessarily has a jural and ritual coefficient. It is not a voluntary relationship and it is necessarily extended to include, in different degrees, the whole of the mother's brother's inner lineage. Being thus tied to the lineage structure it is perpetuated in accordance with the lineage principle.

The statement that extra-clan kinship ties are relationships between individuals, or between individuals and corporate groups, has therefore to be qualified in one particular. As the preceding paragraph implies, and as evidence cited in our earlier book shows,[1] lineages can be related as 'mother's brother' to 'sister's son'. We have seen that this is the relationship assumed to exist between accessory and authentic lineages in some clans, and between some linked lineages of different clans.[1] But conceptually in all cases, and, no doubt, historically in some, these linkages between corporate units go back to a mother's brother–sister's son bond between individuals, perpetuated in accordance with the lineage principle.

This description represents native thought and behaviour more accurately than generalizations about the classificatory extensions of the primary relationship. The chief criterion by which a native identifies his mother's brother or a lineage standing in the relationship of a 'mother's brother' to his lineage is that 'he sacrifices on my behalf (*ɔn nkaabət tirəma*)' or 'they sacrifice on our behalf (*bam nkaabət tiit tam*)'. This implies a specific ritual duty and privilege vested in a particular person or lineage, not a vague general relationship with a certain class of relatives.

We shall find that the structure of all extra-clan kinship relationships of the form we are discussing is the product of three factors: the principle of the social equivalence of siblings; the principle of generation

[1] Cf. *Dynamics of Clanship*, ch. iv.

differences; the principle of lineage continuity. It is because all three principles enter into it that the relationship of mother's brother and sister's son has a jural and ritual coefficient.

Kinship Terms

Before we go any farther it will be convenient to list all the kinship terms used in this context by the Tallensi (see diagram, p. 285). As usual, they are primarily terms of reference, rarely used as terms of address between direct relatives of the particular classes. A man never addresses his own mother's brother as *ahɔb*, but always by his name, and vice versa. These terms are used as terms of address only in speaking to distant relatives of that class who are not personally well known to the speaker and therefore have to be addressed somewhat formally, or as a special gesture of courtesy. Thus Kpanaraana, during a case at the chief's court, said to the girl whose marriage was in dispute: 'My grandmother (*m-ma-kpeema*), tell us your story.' This was a gesture of courtesy because the girl was a clanswoman of his paternal grandmother. Similarly Ga'ab always addressed my clerk Naaho, who was probably his junior by twenty-five years, as *n-ahɔba*, because his mother was a clanswoman of Naaho, and his relationship with the latter was purely formal.

A person describes his or her mother's brother as his or her *ahɔb* (pl. *ahɔbnam*), and is described as *ahɔŋ* (pl. *ahɔs*) irrespective of sex. There is, significantly, no term for mother's brother's wife. She may be described as 'the wife of my *ahɔb* (*n-ahɔb pɔya*)', and be addressed by her clan name; or she may be described metaphorically, and addressed respectfully, as 'mother (*ma*)'. Similarly, there is no term for the spouse of an *ahɔŋ*. I have heard men speak of a sister's son's wife as *ahɔŋ*—by identifying her with her husband—and as *deema* (in-law), or *bii* (child)—by the speaker identifying himself with his sister. By a similar identification a man may address his sister's son's wife as *ma* (mother), just as if he were her husband's father, or he may use her clan name. Corresponding usages apply in speaking of and addressing a sister's daughter's husband.

A mother's father is referred to as 'grandfather' (*yaab* or *ba-kpeem*) and a mother's mother as 'grandmother' (*ma-kpeem*). The reciprocal term is *yaaŋ*, grandchild of either sex. But grandparents and grandchildren address each other by name.

The mother's brother's children are described and referred to as 'mother's brother's children (*ahɔb biis*)' or as 'siblings of the same (or opposite) sex (*bier, pit, tau*)'. But, as we shall observe presently, there are many significant situations in which a mother's brother's son is identified with his father and called *ahɔb*. Mother's brother's child and father's sister's child address each other by name. They describe one

THE WEB OF EXTRA-CLAN KINSHIP 285

another's spouses as siblings-in-law (*dakii*) and address them by name, or by the kinship term if they wish to be specially courteous. But as Tallensi often point out, all such terms transferred by metaphor from the lineage context to a matrilateral context are used in a figurative sense. 'It is a figure of speech only (*la a nuoni maa*—lit. it is only of the mouth)', they say.

The father's sister, it should be added, is described as *ba-pɔk* (pl.

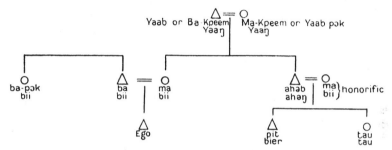

Fig. 6. Kinship terms used by Ego (top) and their reciprocals (bottom).

ba-pɔknam) (female father)—an apt description of her social position in relation to Ego—and is addressed by her name. Another term of reference for the father's sister is *pugəraba*.[1] It is not commonly used for the father's own sister, however, but for a classificatory father's sister or father's father's sister. The father's sister's husband is referred to descriptively or metaphorically as *ba* (father) and is addressed by his name, or as 'father', as a mark of special courtesy. A woman refers to her brother's children as her 'children (*biis*)', identifying herself, as this suggests, in sentiment and behaviour with their father. She and their spouses call one another *deema* (in-law). She may use this term in addressing them and they in speaking to her, if they are not well acquainted; or the father's sister may address her brother's son's wife by her clan name or as 'mother', as if she were the girl's parent-in-law; and she will usually address a brother's daughter's husband by his name.

An incidental point of interest emerges from a consideration of the kinship terminology used in this context. It appears, and observation shows this to be a fact, that the spouses of matrilateral and sororal kin do not come into the picture directly. A man is only interested in his mother's brother's wife, for instance, in so far as her welfare and behaviour affect his mother's brother's and his children's welfare. He has no direct social relationship with her.

The classificatory extensions of these terms will be considered later.

---

[1] This is the Mampɛle variant of *ba-pɔk*, commonly used instead of the latter term among the Mamprusi. Etymologically *ba-pɔk* is 'father-female' and *pugəraba* is probably compounded of 'woman (*puɣ*)' and 'father (*ba*)'.

The Socio-spatial Aspect of Extra-clan Kinship

From the point of view of the total social structure the most important function of extra-clan kinship is to make a number of breaches for the individual in the rigid genealogical boundary of the maximal lineage and clan. It creates bonds of amity and loyalty for him with members of other clans, irrespective of the corporate, political relations that may prevail between his clan and those other clans. The individual is not confined within the boundaries of his clan for social purposes. He has not only channels of communication with other clans, but sources of material aid and moral support outside his own clan. In the past this was of great practical importance. As we saw in the case of uterine kin, it meant that people could move about the country with some security, in spite of the absence of centralized government and in spite of the tendency for each local clan to be politically self-contained and on terms of latent hostility with other geographically near clans. Under the safe-conduct of a mother's brother or sister's son or other relative of these classes a Tongo Namoo, for instance, could go among the Hill Talis. He could rely on receiving hospitality from his Talis kinsfolk and on assistance from them in carrying through the business that took him amongst his clan's potential enemies.

In theory, it will be remembered, kinship ties are never extinguished. This has a bearing on our present topic. If the extra-clan kinship ties of any native are investigated one finds that they spread, like the spokes of a wheel, to most of the clans in the neighbourhood of his own clan. Naabdiya of Tong-Seug, for example, had his mother's brother at Wakii, his father's mother's brother at Ba'ari, more distant matrilateral kinsmen at Ķpata'ar, Gorogo, and Yinduuri, and uterine kin in the Sie district (see map on p. 282). He had his own sister's sons at Wakii and father's sister's children in the Sie district. Every native has such a constellation of cognatic kin among neighbouring clans. This is one reason, perhaps, why all Tale rules of hospitality can be summed up in the single rule of obligatory hospitality to kinsfolk. Everybody has close cognates in five or six neighbouring settlements, and more distant kin, most perhaps unknown to him, in half a dozen more settlements. As the natives themselves say, if a person knew all his extra-clan kinsfolk, he would find a kinsman in every settlement in Taleland. The trite observation so often made by European travellers in Africa, that natives seem to have 'brothers' in every village, is only too true of the Tallensi.

The consequence is that a continuous and vigorous flow of interpersonal social relations between clans and beneath the surface, as it were, of the constituted lineage structure, goes on all the time. Disputes between members of different clans can be adjusted through the mediation of common kinsmen without setting in motion the organs of corporate political life. This is one of the chief functions of the *pɔyasama* (see p. 318) in marriage affairs, for example. However the lineage system separates individuals and corporate groups from one another, or sets them against one another, this underlying network of extra-clan bonds knits them together; and this is a very powerful factor in maintaining the equilibrium of Tale society. In the social structure as a whole it has a complementary function to that of clanship. In the old days it acted as an unseen brake on the tendency of clans to resort to fighting as a means of settling their differences; and if fighting did break out it gave an extra stimulus to any efforts directed towards making peace. For, as likely as not, every man on either side had relatives among the enemy and was swayed by divided loyalties. These bonds probably helped to keep down the number of casualties in inter-clan fighting. For it is a sin to slay a kinsman in war. 'If you saw a kinsman on the other side', said Tiezien, 'you shouted to him to get away lest your arrows hit him by mistake; or else, you yourself moved away to another place.' One could not shoot off one's arrows at random but had to pick out an enemy, making certain that he was not a kinsman.

These extra-clan kinship ties are not indiscriminately distributed. They fall into an order in accordance with the field principle which our investigation of clanship brought to light.[1] That is why they reinforce the forces of social integration in the society at large rather than the forces that encourage clan isolation. Though every member of a clan has his own particular bonds of extra-clan kinship, the tendency is for most members to have extra-clan kinship ties with the same clans. Thus members of one clan tend to have a common field of extra-clan kinship ties; and as the lineage principle encourages the attachment to a whole lineage or clan of sentiments and interests directed towards one of its members, the result is that members of one clan all tend to have personal sentiments of amity and loyalty for the same neighbouring clans. In accordance with the field principle this means that members of any particular clan will have more and closer extra-clan kinship ties with adjacent clans than with more distant clans, and with clans linked to theirs by special ties rather than with clans with which theirs has no political or ritual ties.

This appears quite plainly if a distribution map is made for a sample of the wives of men of a clan, showing the natal clans of these women. Since it is through marriages that extra-clan kinship ties are woven into the lineage fabric, such a map shows the distribution of the most important ties of matrilateral kinship for a particular clan, the ties they have with their mothers' brothers.

We reproduce here a diagram (Fig. 7) constructed for a sample of wives of Tongo men. Similar diagrams for a sample of Kpata'ar wives

[1] Cf. *Dynamics of Clanship*, ch. vi.

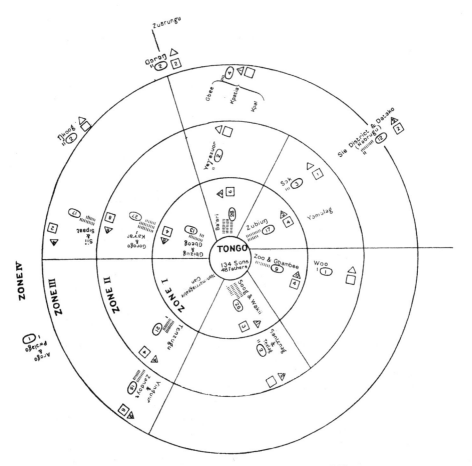

Fig. 7. Distribution of matrilateral kinship ties of Tongo men.

The diagram shows the geographical distribution of wives and mothers of a sample of Tongo men and hence their field of matrilateral kinship.

Wives of men shown thus ㉖.
Mothers of men shown thus △₁₁.
Mothers of men's fathers shown thus ③.

The diagram divides the socio-spatial field of matrilateral kinship into four zones: Zone I, immediately adjacent clans; Zone II, clans immediately adjacent to clans of Zone I; Zone III, clans beyond Zone II clans; Zone IV, non-Tale clans.

The location of clans or groups of clans on the diagram corresponds to their territorial relations to one another; but the zones are socio-spatial not territorial regions. Most clans of Zone I are within 2 miles of Tongo; most clans in Zone II are between 2 and 5 miles of Tongo; most clans of Zone III between 4 and 7 miles of Tongo. But some clans in Zone III are spatially nearer to Tongo than some clans in Zone II, and vice versa, and one or two non-Tale clans are spatially nearer than some clans in Zone III. Though there is a high positive correlation between social distance and territorial distance, the correspondence is not perfect. The emphasis of the diagram is on the social distance from Tongo of the clans included.

PLATE 15

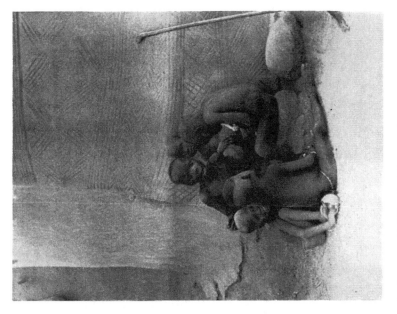

a. Classificatory sisters' sons (*ahas*) partake of the porridge ritually cooked by the *ppyakais* during one phase of the maternal uncle's (*ahab*) funeral ceremonies

b. A group of 'siblings' of the same inner lineage dividing a lizard which they have killed

PLATE 16

a. The members of a segment of a maximal lineage gather at the homestead of the head of the segment to sacrifice to their immediate founding ancestor. 'Sisters' sons' of the segment have the right to be present. The sacrifice has been performed and the goat offered is now being divided up. The two 'sisters' sons' (nearest the camera, wearing caps) sit waiting for their portion of the meat. Note the active interest in the process of cutting up the goat taken by the members of the lineage, most of whom are standing up, by contrast with the passive interest of the 'sisters' sons' on the fringe

b. Matrilateral kin come to set up a new shrine (the mud cone against the wall, right background) for the grandmother of Pirbazaa (extreme right)

and a sample of Sie wives have exactly the same form and show that the same principles operate throughout Taleland.[1]

A sample of 134 men from all four sections of Tongo, who were living at Tongo at the beginning of 1934, was chosen for this test. The distribution according to their natal clans of all their wives—living, dead, or separated—who had borne children to them was marked on a map. The distribution by clan of origin of the mothers of these men was plotted on the same map. As a number of the men were brothers and some were polygynous the total number of mothers recorded is smaller than the number of wives. Lastly, the distribution by clan of origin of these men's fathers' mothers was plotted on the same map; and as their fathers were fewer than they are and some were polygynous, the total number of their paternal grandmothers recorded is less than the number of their mothers and much less than the number of their wives. The diagram therefore shows the socio-geographic distribution of (a) these men's fathers' mothers' brothers' (ba ahəbnam) clans; (b) of their own mothers' brothers' (ahəbnam) clans; (c) of their children's mothers' brothers clans.

Table showing the Field of Extra-clan Kinship Ties

Total number of men, all sections of Tongo . . . 134
Total number of their wives 205
Total number of their mothers 64
Total number of their father's mothers 46

Zonal Distribution of Kinship Ties

Zone	Incidence Mothers' brothers of		
	Men's children	Men themselves	Men's fathers
Zone I . .	93	33	21
Zone II . .	56	12	13
Zone III . .	47 ⎫ 56	18 ⎫ 19	9 ⎫ 12
Zone IV . .	9 ⎭	1 ⎭	3 ⎭
	205	64	46

It will be seen that the total field of extra-clan kinship ties for Tongo is directly complementary to the total field of clanship ties, and largely congruent with the field of politico-ritual ties we have previously established for this clan.[2] Within this field there are four zones of density graded in accordance with spatial and social distance from Tongo. Thus

[1] They also operate among the Gərisi, as a sample of marriages collected in one of the sections of Boləga showed.
[2] Cf. *Dynamics of Clanship*, ch. iv and v.

Tongo people, individually, have closer and more numerous kinship ties with the immediately adjacent clans of Zubiuŋ, Ba'ari, Wakii, and Zoo than with clans in the next zone, such as the Tɛnzugu clans. On the other hand the incidence of such relationships with Yinduuri is markedly greater than with any other clans of Zone III, because Tongo and Yinduuri have a bond of friendship through the chiefship of Sii, as has been explained in our previous book.[1]

It will be seen, moreover, that the field of extra-clan kinship is relatively constant for a particular clan through several generations. For its form is approximately the same for children, fathers, and grandfathers. This suggests a regular tendency in the social structure rather than a chance result of the random choices of individuals. As we have previously stated, men seek for wives preferably amongst the nearest eligible women—that is amongst the women of clans that are spatially or socially nearest to their clan. The whole weight of the social structure lies behind this tendency. The restrictions on mobility in the past encouraged it. But the most important factor was, and is, the circular relationship that exists between marriage and extra-clan kinship ties. Marriages create extra-clan kinship ties; social contacts between members of different clans are largely canalized by extra-clan kinship ties; and these ties lead to contacts that in turn bring about new marriages. The modifications that are coming into this sequence nowadays are proof of this argument. The freedom of movement now possible has led to a great expansion of the social space of the younger men. They are beginning to take wives from distant parts, very often outside Taleland, in increasing numbers.

As every Tale clan has a similar field of extra-clan kinship ties, the fields of adjacent clans overlap. The bonds of extra-clan kinship between any two adjacent clans are not only reciprocal but bilateral. Just as many Tongo people, for example, have mothers' brothers at Ba'ari, Zubiuŋ, and Wakii, so many Wakii, Ba'ari, and Zubiuŋ people have mothers' brothers at Tongo. Lɔyani of Zubiuŋ Yakɔra provides a good instance of multiple bilateral ties between men of adjacent clans. His mother was a woman of one segment of Tɔŋ-Puhug; one of his sisters married into another segment of Puhug; one of his daughters married a member of yet a third segment of Puhug. If we multiply such cases by the total population of Taleland we can get some impression of the intricacy of the web of extra-clan kinship ties. I have never yet been in a situation where a group of natives have gathered for some activity, whether secular or ceremonial, in which it was impossible for any person present to establish some genealogical (or, if it came to the worst, affinal) link with the lineage principally concerned. Merely being sisters' sons—actual or classificatory—of the same clan can become an effective bond of amity in certain circumstances. The following is a trivial illustration of this.

[1] *Dynamics of Clanship*, pp. 89 and 121.

Early one morning I met Baripɛta. His hoe on one shoulder, and a chicken coop suspended from the other, showed that he was bound for his bush farm. But he was not taking the path that led there. I asked him where he was going. 'Oh', he said, 'I am going to congratulate Tinta'alǝm on his succession to their lineage bɔyar. He and I are both Yinduuri ahǝs and so his good fortune naturally makes me happy.'

The result of this overlapping of the fields of extra-clan kinship of adjacent clans is that these ties are interwoven to form an elaborate mesh, parallel, on the level of individual relationships, to the mesh of clanship on the level of corporate group relationships.[1] Hence the native thinks of his matrilateral kinship bonds as linking him to such-and-such a person of a different clan, who is himself linked similarly to someone in yet another clan, and so on to the limits of his social horizon. Nor are these connexions confined to Taleland. Tallensi often emphasize their cultural and social distinction from Gɔrisi, Builsa, Namnam, and other neighbouring peoples. But they are quite likely to end a discourse on this theme by saying, 'However, our kinsfolk are among them (ka ti dɔyam le bɛ nɛŋha)'.

It must be remembered, though, that most of these ties are only potential for a person for most of his life. He does not, as a rule, know of his more remote extra-clan kinsfolk until they become relevant for him on some special ritual occasion. This may happen once or twice in a lifetime. But when the need arises he can always trace them by following out (tumh) his kinship ties step by step, as we shall see presently. On account of this, and of the complex interweaving of these kinship ties, it is a common thing for individuals to be connected by more than one route, or to be distant kin without knowing it. Thus when I asked Puɛŋyii why he had formerly attached himself to the Gɔlibdaana, whom he now professed to regard as the arch-enemy, his answer was 'because we are kin (ti a dɔyam la zugu)'. He went on to explain that, firstly, the Gɔlibdaana was a distant 'sister's son' of his (Puɛŋyii's) inner lineage, and, secondly, he and the Gɔlibdaana 'both come from Gorogo' on the maternal side. Puɛŋyii's mother's mother and the Gɔlibdaana's mother were both daughters of the same inner lineage of Gorogo. 'If my mother's mother's brother's (ma ahǝb) people make a sacrifice to their lineage bɔyar, the Gɔlibdaana and I both go to it', he said. This is a simple instance. More complicated multiple relationships are very common, cases in which, as the natives put it, 'they have begotten each other (ba dɔya taaba)'. That is to say, two persons may be related in such a way that by one route A calls himself a 'sister's son' of B and by another reckoning the relationship is reversed. The relationship of Puɛŋyii and the Gɔlibdaana can, in fact, be interpreted in this way. Identifying himself with his inner lineage, Puɛŋyii can say, 'I have begotten the Gɔlibdaana'—since the Gɔlibdaana looks upon

[1] Cf. *Dynamics of Clanship*, chs. iv, v, vi.

Puɛŋyii's inner lineage as his distant 'mother's brother's lineage'. On the other hand, the Gɔlibdaana can make the same claim in regard to Puɛŋyii by identifying himself with his 'sister', Puɛŋyii's mother. In the ordinary intercourse of daily life it is immaterial which relationship is stressed. The blanket concept of kinship (dɔyam) covers all. But in special ritual situations a specific relationship emerges as the decisive one. For example, if the head of Puɛŋyii's inner lineage were to die, the Gɔlibdaana might, if he were on good terms with the deceased, as a gesture of respect, send a gift of millet flour and a fowl as a contribution to the funeral, on the grounds that he is a 'sister's son' of the lineage.

Many instances could be quoted of people discovering hitherto unknown extra-clan kin by chance, as it is a common occurrence. It was on a chance visit to Tɛnzugu that Kuŋaanba learnt that Nyaaŋzum was the head of his father's mother's brother's inner lineage. Since then Kuŋaanba has become a regular visitor to and a great personal friend of Nyaaŋzum's family. In the same way it happens that people get married and discover later that they are kin. Tallensi say this probably happens very often but seldom becomes known. It is only if the couple lose several children one after another that it comes out. A diviner then reveals it as the cause of their misfortunes. Thus apprised of it, they consult the elders of their lineages and try to 'trace out (tumh)' their kinship. Whether they are successful or not—and they usually are—they then perform the rite of splitting kinship (bɔk dɔyam), and this makes it permissible for their marriage to continue. It happened thus with Pukiehɔt, and this was one of the reasons why his in-laws were so angry with him for not paying his wife's bride-price. It was bad enough, they complained, that their daughter's marriage should be a breach of kinship; but, on top of that, here was her husband for ever hedging over the payment of the bride-price.

The natives know very well that they have closer and more numerous matrilateral and sororal kinsfolk among adjacent clans than among more distant clans. We have seen (Ch. II) how they visualize this situation for uterine kin (saarət). They tend to think of their close matrilateral kin as being spatially near and their more remote extra-clan kin as being far away geographically as well. But they do not, of course, realize that all the extra-clan kinship ties of a lineage or clan, taken together, fall into a regular and definite socio-spatial order. They think of these relationships from the individual angle always. At the same time they are very conscious of the mutual reaction on one another of the clanship and lineage structure and these extra-clan kinship ties. Thus Tongo people say that it is much more satisfactory to have one's mother's brother at Zubiuŋ or Zoo than at Ba'ari or Wakii. The local and political cohesion of Zubiuŋ and Zoo with Tongo make it easier to keep in touch with one's mother's brother, make one readier to accept and be accepted by his clansmen as a classificatory kinsman, and predispose *ahǝb* and *ahǝŋ* to greater mutual confidence, than if one's *ahǝb* belongs to the traditionally hostile Talis. On the other hand, a man whose mother's brother is at Wakii does not wish evil to befall that clan, and he may find himself in an embarrassing position if there is conflict between his own clan and that clan.

Kinship Amity

Outside situations in which specific extra-clan kinship ties correlated to defined modes of conduct emerge, the social relations of kin are governed by a general rule of amity. A kinsman of any degree is a person in whose welfare one is interested and whom one is under a moral obligation to help in difficulties, if possible. A good illustration of this occurred one day when I was on a visit to Kpata'ar. Nyaaŋzum asked, in the customary way, what was the news from Tongo. I ran through the conventional items—the chief, the crops, current gossip, births, marriages, and deaths. When I told him that Gbɛn-Tɔŋ's mother had died he exclaimed, 'Eee! And why haven't I been told? I'll have it out with Gbɛn-Tɔŋ next time I see him. This is his maternal ancestors' home (*u yaab yir nla*). I sacrifice on his behalf so that he may sleep peacefully; and now that he is not sleeping well (i.e. has trouble), if he does not send to tell me, is that as it should be?' Thus also Banɔrǝg complained that he had given away about twenty baskets of grain in a period of one month after his harvest to kinsfolk who had come to 'beg (*soh*)' gifts to tide them over a time of food shortage. But, he concluded, 'you can't refuse a kinsman (*i ku tuo nzayah i dɔyam la*). One day I myself may have to go and ask my kinsmen for some grain.' A kinsman in need of hospitality cannot be refused, though there is no obligation to go out of one's way to persuade him to accept it. In the old days if a person saw anyone wantonly molesting a kinsman of his from another clan, it was his duty to intervene. It is wrong to seek a kinsman's harm and a sin that will bring down the wrath of the ancestors to cause his death. In 1936 the Tɔŋraana and the Gɔlibdaana were compelled to meet in order to try to settle one of the latter's grievances against the former. At the end of the long and fruitless discussion the Tɔŋraana burst out, with scarcely veiled vexation, 'You and I, Gɔlibdaana, are kin. We have begotten each other. Why do you seek my enmity always?'

As we have previously learnt, one of the most important duties of kinship in the old days was to protect a kinsman in one's own clan territory. A typical example is the story of Baŋam-Teroog's journey to Sandema in the Builsa country, some fifty or sixty years ago. Had he gone openly by himself he would certainly have been caught and sold into slavery by the Builsa. He had been commanded by an ancestress, through a diviner, to go to her home in Builsa country and perform the rites of setting up a shrine dedicated to her. For safety's sake all the travelling on such journeys was always done at night. During the day the traveller lay low in a kinsman's house. So Teroog set off one night. He went first to his father's mother's brother's home at Gorogo. Thence he was escorted to his father's mother's mother's natal home at Sii. The Sii people took him to a more remote kinsman at Balung and from there he was conducted, by similar stages, to Sandema. His return journey was made in the same way. The whole trip took nearly a month. The same journey can be done on foot, nowadays, in three or four days each way.

Similarly Zubiuŋ men relate how in the old days their Tongo neighbours, being of a different and unconnected clan,[1] used sometimes to raid their livestock to recover bride-price debts. As the people of Tongo were much more numerous than those of Zubiuŋ resistance was generally impossible. But if a Zubiuŋ man had a close matrilateral or affinal kinsman at Tongo, this afforded him some protection. His kinsman would intercede to get any livestock of his that had been seized restored to him, or, if the debtor were a very close agnate of his, to arrange a settlement between creditor and debtor. Often the head of an intercalary lineage, such as Nɔŋsuur yidem,[2] undertook this on behalf of his classificatory mother's brother's lineage.

Nowadays the most important obligations extra-lineage kin have towards one another are in ritual matters, and these are unavoidable obligations. This applies especially to kin of a senior generation in relation to those of a junior generation. A person owes ritual allegiance to his matrilateral ancestors as well as to his paternal ancestors. In fact, in the strictly personal affairs of the individual, his matrilateral ancestors have as decisive a role in his life as his patrilineal ancestors. This accords with the recognition given to maternal origin in the social structure and with the rule that kinship never dies out. Hence there are many occasions in the life of a man when he has to go to his mother's brother or to someone standing in that order of relationship to him to ask him to sacrifice on his behalf. For it must be remembered that the canon of agnatic descent prohibits anyone other than a true patrilineal descendant from sacrificing to an ancestor or ancestress. Thus if a man wants to sacrifice to his mother's spirit guardian he has to go to her natal home and ask her father (or his heir) to perform the sacrifice. Herein lies the force of the statement commonly used to define extra-clan kinship ties, 'I sacrifice on his behalf', or 'he sacrifices on my behalf'. The whole weight of the ancestor cult stands behind these and other ritual obligations of extra-clan kin to one another and no Talɔŋ would violate them.

If we add to this the rule that marriage between extra-clan kin of any degree is forbidden, we can see that there is much in common between

---

[1] Cf. *Dynamics of Clanship*, ch. vi.
[2] Cf. ibid., pp. 59 and 78.

the basic rules of inter-personal sentiment and conduct for extra-clan kin and for members of one clan or lineage. As in the lineage, so among extra-clan kin, the pattern of sentiment and conduct we have sketched has greater force with close than with distant kin. The differences between kinship within the lineage and kinship outside the lineage lie less in the sphere of individual sentiment and conduct than in the different structural implications of the two kinds of social ties.

The Classificatory Extension of Extra-clan Kinship

At the outset of this chapter we referred to the classificatory extension of extra-clan kinship ties. This requires further elucidation. In the early stages of my field-work this aspect of Tale kinship seemed to me extraordinarily confused. The natives seemed to label any extra-clan kinsman a 'mother's brother (*ahəb*)' or 'sister's child (*ahəŋ*)' quite indiscriminately. The only distinction they appeared to make was in terms of generation differences. A person was apparently labelled a 'sister's son' if he was related to the speaker through any ancestress who was a member of the latter's clan, and he was described as a 'mother's brother' if the woman forming the link was the speaker's mother or ancestress and a member of the other person's clan.

This apparent confusion soon resolves itself into an orderly picture if the three principles in accordance with which kinsfolk are identified with one another are applied. In addition we must take into account the socio-spatial distribution of these kinship ties, and, especially, the time dimension without which no aspect of Tale social structure can be understood. Naturally the natives themselves do not consciously use such general conceptions in sorting out their kinship bonds; to them it is simply a question of spontaneous adjustment within the everlasting stream of social relations.

The most important of these factors is the lineage principle. An indication of this is found in the constant reference made by natives to their mother's brother's lineage (*ahəb yiri*) or maternal grandfather's lineage (*yaab yiri*). If a native is asked about his matrilateral kin the first thing he mentions is his *ahəb yiri*—the clan and perhaps clan segment of his mother's brother. The interpretation given to the concept *yiri* varies according to the situation, and follows the rules that govern its usage within the clan or lineage. For instance, I went to Tɛnzugu one day accompanied by two Tongo men. When we reached Kpata'ar one of them said 'This is my *ahəb yiri*', and explained that his mother was a Kpata'ar woman (*pɔɣayabəlaɡ*). A little later he stopped and broke off a couple of heads of ripe millet in a farm through which the path wound. I twitted him with stealing other people's crops. 'No', he replied, 'this is my *ahəb yiri*. This is La'ab's farm and I am an *ahəŋ* of his *duɡ*. They won't object to my taking a few heads of millet.' Thus at first he was using *ahəb yiri* to refer to the clan and later he used it for the inner lineage of his mother's brother.

In keeping with the principles of lineage structure, a man visualizes his relationship with his mother's patrilineal kin as having three degrees. There is, firstly, his bond with his 'true *ahəb (ahəb ni yɛlmɛŋər)*'—his mother's full (*soog*) brother, if she has one, or her oldest paternal half (*sunzɔ*) brother. This is the man who will sacrifice on his sister's son's behalf (if *his* father is dead). Apart from this there is no distinction between the 'true *ahəb*' and his brothers of the same nuclear lineage. The next level is that of the mother's brother's *dug*, his inner or at most medial lineage. A sister's son describes this *dug* collectively as his *ahəb yiri*, or, by contraposition with the clan, as his *ahəb dug*. Like any member of this inner lineage he distinguishes between its members in accordance with the rules of classificatory kinship. That is, the men whom his *ahəb* calls 'father' he calls 'grandfather', and he jokes with them; the men and women whom his *ahəb* calls siblings he calls *ahəb* or mother; and he describes those whom his *ahəb* calls his children as brothers and sisters. He may not marry a daughter of this inner lineage, and if he has sexual relations with one it is as disgraceful as if she were his close agnatic sister. He may not court a widow of any man of this inner lineage whom he calls *ahəb*, and if he seduces the wife of such a man it is incest. He may in theory court the widow of a member of this *dug* whom his mother's brother calls 'son' and whom he, therefore, regards as a sort of brother.

Finally, there is the level of his mother's brother's clan beyond the range of his inner lineage. Again the rules of classificatory kinship in the clan context apply. Beyond the range of his mother's brother's inner lineage a man does not distinguish between members of his mother's brother's lineage (his *ahəb yidɛm*) by generation. He can marry a daughter of the clan, or court a widow of any man of the clan, at this range.

Reciprocally, a man calls a child of a daughter of his inner lineage 'an *ahəŋ* of our *dug* (*ti dug ahəŋ*)', and a child of a daughter of a different inner lineage of the clan 'an *ahəŋ* of our lineage (or clan) (*ti yir ahəŋ*)'. There are a number of ritual ceremonies at which all the segments of a clan or maximal lineage must be present. Funerals of politico-ritual functionaries such as tɛndaanas, and the ceremony by which a man takes over the custody of a lineage *bɔyar* shrine, are ceremonies of this kind. *Ahəs* of every branch of the clan usually attend such ceremonies. Then they are divided into two groups: *dugni ahəs*, those who are linked through their mother or an ancestress to the inner lineage responsible for the ceremony; and *yɛŋha ahəs*, outside *ahəs*, whose mothers or ancestresses came from other segments of the clan.

The lineage principle operating in relation to the flux of time introduces a new feature. A man dies and in due course his social roles pass to one of his sons. The son now assumes the duties his father had as a mother's brother. He now sacrifices on behalf of his father's sister's sons and becomes their *ahəb* in function. So a mother's brother's son is, in certain situations, called *ahəb* by identification with his father in accordance with the lineage principle, even while his father is still alive— in anticipation, as it were, of the role he will one day have. On the same principle a sister's son's son may be identified with his father in relation to the latter's mother's brother's sons and lineage. Thus Ɔmara once introduced a young man from Gorogo to me as his *ahəb*. I expressed surprise, as I knew his mother came from Woo. He then explained that the young man was really his father's *ahəb* (*ba ahəb*)—not, of course, his father's true mother's brother, but the grandson and successor of the latter.

Through the operation of the lineage principle such a relationship can, in theory, go on for ever. The mother's brother's role—progressively attenuated, as we shall see presently—passes from one generation of the original mother's brother's agnatic descendants to the next. And this brings out a point of importance. The crucial element in the mother's brother's role is his duty to sacrifice to his ancestors on his sister's son's behalf whenever the latter requests it. By the lineage principle the latter cannot sacrifice to his maternal ancestors directly at their original home. The mother's brother is bound to perform this duty or else suffer the wrath of his ancestors. He can refuse only if his *ahəŋ* has very gravely offended him. Then this duty becomes a right which he uses as a sanction. He receives no recompense for this other than his prescribed share of the animal sacrificed, which must always be provided by the sister's son. The mother's brother's role goes with this right of sacrificing to his lineage ancestors' spirits. Hence, after the death of all of the grandfather's sons—all the true mother's brothers—it is in fact vested in the head of the lineage descended from the grandfather.

Now let us glance for a moment at the other side of the relationship, the sister's son's position. A man has no interest in or bonds with any of his sister's children's agnates except her children. They are not his kin through his sister. In theory he or his son can marry any of his sister's children's female agnates if they are not related to one another by another link. In practice such marriages with a woman member of the sister's husband's inner lineage are not countenanced. One objection is that the girl might be a proxy or classificatory daughter of the sister, which would make the marriage seem incestuous. A stronger objection is that such a marriage would amount to exchanging one woman for another. This the Tallensi disapprove of on the grounds that it must inevitably breed discord between the two lineages concerned. It is incongruous for the same inner lineages to be both sons-in-law and fathers-in-law to one another. You cannot, as the natives put it, both owe bride-price to and claim bride-price from the same man, or owe filial respect to and be entitled to filial respect from the same person. The objection does not hold outside the range of the sister's husband's inner lineage. An *ahəb* is concerned only with his sister's own children; and *his* agnatic descendants are genealogically related and socially concerned only with *their* descendants—that is to say, with the matri-segment (sprung from the sister of the original *ahəb*) of the lineage sprung from her husband. Such is the history—or, more frequently, the putative history—lying behind the *ahəb–ahəŋ* relationships of lineages of different clans with one another. Every lineage and every segment of a lineage has its *ahəb yiri* in this sense. When the relationship (whether real or putative) is assumed to be remote it may have only a ceremonial function or may serve as an explanation of clanship linkage; when it is not too remote it emerges from time to time in ritual or jural activities. And it follows from the structure of the lineage that the farther back by number of generations the relationship is located, the wider will be the span of the lineages concerned.

There is a further complication. A woman's children have a tie, through her, with her *ahəb yiri*—their mother's mother's brother's lineage (*ma ahəb yiri*). This is a bond of a rather limited and formal significance; nevertheless it is kinship (*dɔyam*); it prohibits marriage between a man and a woman who are directly related by such a route, and it often emerges in ritual relations. Indeed a man and his sister's, or father's sister's, daughter's son may be on terms of friendship and special intimacy, if, as is quite possible, they are clansmen or neighbours. The friendship of Pumaan and Sayəbazaa, both of Tongo, went back to a relationship of this kind; and Sayəbazaa, who was in the mother's father's position, spoke of Pumaan as his 'grandson (*yaaŋ*)'. By the lineage principle a relationship of this kind can be sustained for several generations, but it tends to fade out with the passage of the generations. Still more roundabout extra-clan genealogical connexions are recognized in special circumstances, the parties being linked by various combinations of male and female antecedents.

A relationship such as that of Sayəbazaa and Pumaan is assimilated to the pattern of mother's father–daughter's son relationship. As this shows, there are two categories of extra-clan extended kinship ties. One type is assimilated to the *ahəb–ahəŋ* (mother's brother–sister's child) tie, and the other to the *yaab–yaaŋ* (mother's father–daughter's child) tie. The criterion is simple. If two individuals or lineages are linked through one woman (i.e. at a remove of one generation) only, they are *ahəb* and *ahəŋ* to each other: if the chain of genealogical connexions includes more than one woman (i.e. more than one female generation—a woman and her mother), making it a secondary matrilateral tie, the parties are *yaab* and *yaaŋ* to each other. Thus Lɔyani called himself, in various contexts, an *ahəŋ* of Tɔŋ-Puhug, because his own mother came from there; an *ahəŋ* of Gorogo because his father's mother came from that place; and also an *ahəŋ* of Sie and of Tɔŋ Kuorəg because other patrilineal ancestors of his were *ahəs* of those clans. But when he was explaining his various ancestor shrines to me he accounted for his possession of one on the grounds of his being a *yaaŋ* of Sɔk—his patrilineal great-great-grandfather's mother's mother having been a daughter of Sɔk; and for another on the ground of his being an Arogo *yaaŋ*, since his mother's mother's mother came from Arogo. The distinction between *ahəŋ* and *yaaŋ* in this sense implies corresponding differences in social relations. It follows, as can easily be seen, from combining the principle of lineage continuity with that of sibling equivalence.

Our analysis shows that the extension and transference of extra-clan kinship ties through the social system is not an indiscriminate lumping together of classes or groups of relatives. It is strictly regulated by the basic principles on which that system is built up. We must not forget, however, that the majority of these derivative social ties are only potential. The more distant or indirect they are the less frequently and the less effectively do they emerge in the form of actual social relations. We shall come back to this presently.

The diagram overleaf summarizes the results of the preceding analysis.

The Nuclear Relationship of Mother's Brother and Sister's Son

All extra-clan kinship ties, except those of uterine kin, are rooted in the relationship of mother's brother and sister's child. We proceed now to study this relationship in greater detail.[1]

Tallensi say that a mother's brother is a 'sort of father (*u ŋman ni i ba*—lit. he is like your father)', and a sister's child is 'like your own child (*u ŋman ni i bii*)'. These expressions conjure up, to the native, a picture of a personal and lifelong mutual interest and attachment similar to that of parent and child. How deeply it goes depends on the character and disposition of the individuals concerned, but it is always there. In part it is no more than a continuation of the interest a woman's close lineage kin have in her children, but it has distinctive features of its own and is counted of more value and importance than a maternal grandparent's interest in a daughter's children.

When a girl becomes pregnant for the first time her husband sends a message to her parents. Later, about the fourth or fifth month of her pregnancy, her mother sends one of her close co-wives to bind the girl with a perineal band (*suol voog*). This is a proud moment for her, as the perineal band shows her to have left maidenhood behind and to have entered the ranks of the matrons (*pɔyaŋaaŋ*, pl. *pɔyaŋaas*). Then, before

---

[1] The starting-point of this analysis is Radcliffe-Brown's theory of the social equivalence of the mother's brother to his sister in relation to her children, first expounded in his article 'The Mother's Brother in South Africa', loc. cit. 'Sister's son' in this chapter stands for 'sister's child of either sex', except when the context shows that a male is meant.

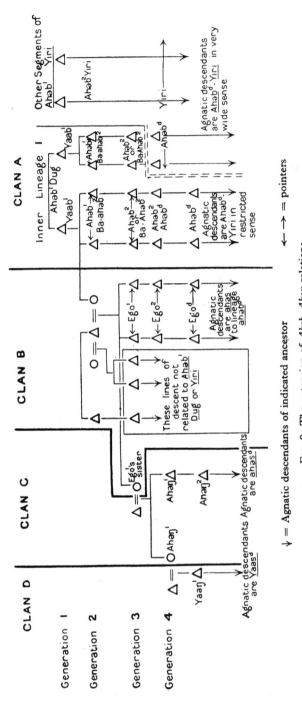

FIG. 8. The extension of *Ahab–Ahaŋ* relations.

The diagram reads as follows: Ego¹'s true mother's brothers are designated *Ahab*¹, Ego¹ calls them *Ahab*, Ego² (Ego's son) calls these men *Ba-ahab*, hence they are also designated *Ba-ahab*². Ego^d (Ego¹'s agnatic descendant) calls *Ahab*¹'s agnatic descendants *ahab*, hence they are designated *Ahab*^d. Similarly with all the other relationships placed on the diagram. The index figure or letter shows what the Ego bearing the same index calls that person or group.

the child is due, her husband sends a sacrifice for her spirit guardian to her father, to secure the blessing of her patrilineal ancestors on the ordeal she is soon to undergo. When the child is born, a messenger is again dispatched to announce its birth to the girl's parents. He is received with the hospitality due to a bearer of particularly glad tidings. Now the girl's mother sends her four new calabashes. These are the infant's toilet-vessels—one for giving the infant its daily medicated water to drink, one as a dipper for use when bathing it, one as a slop basin, one for scooping up its excrement. These private toilet utensils are in part a magical protection for the baby. The occasion is also marked, as we have learnt, by a special gift of foodstuffs to the new mother from her father. All these formalities are not necessary for children after the first; it is enough to send a message on the birth of the child. But the woman's paternal relatives are no less interested in these later children than in her first child.

A child makes the acquaintance of its mother's paternal family very early in life. Its mother's sisters and mother's mother, if she is not too old, are frequent visitors to its mother. Its mother's brothers may be frequent visitors too, especially if they are on friendly terms with its father. But it is not till the child reaches the age of about 5 or 6, when it begins to be taken on visits to its *ahəb yiri*, that it clearly distinguishes these relatives. The person who matters most to a small child at its mother's brother's house is its maternal grandmother (*ma-kpeem*), in whose quarters and under whose care the child lives.[1] Old people, both men and women, love to have their daughters' young children to stay with them, and pet and spoil them quite as much as their sons' children. As will be remembered, grandchildren joke with their maternal grandparents. At harvest time, in particular, old women often have daughters' children to stay for a week or two, so that they can enjoy the good food available at that time. Playing and eating and sleeping with the children of the house, a child learns to regard them as siblings, and partly through imitating them, partly through coming directly under the discipline of his mother's brother, a child thus visiting its *ahəb yiri* learns to think of its *ahəb* as a 'sort of father'. He hears all the gossip of the family. When a domestic sacrifice is performed he is present and receives the portion of the animal—the neck (*naŋgoor*)—prescribed for an *ahəŋ*. I have more than once seen a small boy of perhaps 8 receive the neck of a sacrifice, amid an amused chuckle from his mother's brothers. If a woman dies leaving a young child of less than 5 or 6 years old it is a common thing for the child to be sent to live with its maternal grandmother for a year or two until it is old enough to need only a minimum of maternal care.

Thus, a child learns to think of its *ahəb yiri*, in the strict sense of its mother's brother's homestead, at first, in the more extended sense, later, as a place where it is given food, shelter, affectionate attention, and

[1] This follows directly from the constitution of the joint family.

status in almost the same way as in its own home. It is not surprising to find that most Tallensi know almost as much about the affairs of their mother's brother's family as they do about their own family, and that they often have a very good knowledge of the distinctive ritual practices and ideas of their mother's brother's clan. For though a sister's child is not admitted to the esoteric ritual ceremonies of his maternal kinsmen's clan, he often hears them discuss the less sacred aspects of these ceremonies and takes part in the domestic rites that are interspersed with them.

A great attachment may thus grow up between mother's brother and sister's child, in particular, the sister's son. This is especially the case when *ahɔb* and *ahɔŋ* are uterine kin (*saarɔt*), that is when the mother's brother is the full brother of the mother of the *ahɔŋ*. The sentiments and attitudes a person has towards his mother are extended in a modified form towards her brother, and the latter extends to the sister's child the attachment he has to his sister. When I first met Barimoda at Baŋgam-Teroog's house the latter said, pointing to Barimoda, 'This is my child (*m-biig nla*).' Knowing that Barimoda and Teroog belonged to different clans, I demurred. Whereupon Teroog said: 'He is my full (*soog*) sister's son; and if you and your *soog* sister together have a child, is he not your child too? (*N ta-soog biig n-a-u; ka nyɛn ni i ta-soog n-kab dɔya bii, daya i biiga?*).' Barimoda was as much at home in Teroog's house as in his own. Seldom a day passed without his visiting the old man. Since Teroog's only adult son lived far away, Barimoda did for him many of the things a son would have done. He enlisted the help of his brother's sons to get Teroog's small home farm hoed and was his counsellor in all his problems, as sons usually are to a father enfeebled with years. Being an old man and head of his lineage, Teroog very often had to make sacrifices to his ancestors. On these occasions he always sent for Barimoda. Once, through a trifling disagreement with Teroog's younger wife, Barimoda refused to attend a sacrifice at Teroog's house. Naabdiya, Barimoda's half-brother and a friend of Teroog's, and I happened to be present. After the sacrifice Teroog offered the neck of the goat sacrificed to Naabdiya. Another man, able, like Naabdiya, to claim a distant matrilateral connexion with Teroog's clan, would have considered himself a 'sister's son' in this situation and have accepted the prescribed portion. But Naabdiya refused. No, he said, everybody knew that Barimoda was Teroog's favourite *ahɔŋ* and always came to such sacrifices. If he, Naabdiya, now accepted the sister's son's portion Barimoda would resent it. In a few days his sulky mood would pass and he would resume his usual relations with Teroog. Teroog agreed and added that he would send the goat's neck to Barimoda with a conciliatory message. Everybody in Zubiuŋ knew of Barimoda's devotion to his *ahɔb-soog* and spoke highly of him for this. So when Teroog's son died and he insisted that Barimoda should be allowed to inherit one of the widows, it met with general approval among the men of Zubiuŋ.

The relationship of Kpɛlimɛrəme and his mother's full brother Kuur was similar. One incident may be quoted as a particularly forcible illustration of the intimacy and attachment that often exist between *ahəb* and *ahəŋ*. Kuur was suffering from a very painful and repulsive skin disease which had finally attacked his genitals, turning them into a disgusting, ulcerated area. When Ləyani, Kuur's younger paternal brother, came to ask me for some medicine to treat this sickness, he said that the mere sight of it made him vomit—and, as he remarked, he was known to be a man of stout heart (*suhkpeemərdaan*) in dealing with sickness or death. I gave Ləyani some disinfectant, and advised cleansing and bathing the affected parts with it. Ləyani looked dubious and then explained that Kuur was in too great pain to carry out the treatment himself, Kuur's children were all too young to do it, and his disease was so revolting that none of his more distant relatives would undertake the task. Then an idea struck him. There was someone who would do it—Kpɛlimɛrəme. And in fact Kpɛlimɛrəme did undertake the unpleasant task and performed it faithfully for several weeks. 'Do you think,' said Kpɛlimɛrəme to me, 'I would let my *ahəb* die if I knew of any way of saving him?'

Such a relationship is common between sister's son and mother's full brother. As a rule there is not such great intimacy and devotion between a man and his half-sister's son. It is, however, only a matter of degree. Ɔmara was very attached to his half-sister's children, especially to her eldest daughter. He was as proud of her marriage to the Chief of Bongo as her own father was. Yɛanbərigya, like most Tallensi, was a constant visitor to his *ahəb* at Samiit. Once at a public sacrifice at which he was the only non-member of Samiit present, his mother's brother's clansmen teased him saying that he might as well come and join them for good. Anyhow, they chaffed him, he was really a son of Samiit since his mother's bride-price had not been fully paid.[1] He rejoined, jokingly, that he belonged both to Samiit and to his own clan.

As a rule, too, a sister's daughters do not after marriage have such constant and close contacts with their mother's brother's people as a sister's sons. Any interest a woman has in relatives other than her husband's people is chiefly directed towards her parental family, and she keeps in touch with her mother's brother's people through her mother and brothers. A woman lacks the bond of common interests due to identity of sex that reinforces the ties of mother's brother and sister's son. A woman also has no need to maintain ritual relations with her

---

[1] If a woman dies leaving adult sons before the fourth cow of her bride-price is claimed, her paternal kin are normally obliged to waive it in favour of her sons. This is interpreted as a sign of their quasi-parental interest in the sons' welfare and marriages

ahɔb. Nevertheless she has much the same attitude to him as her brothers have and will, if need arises, go to him for help as if he were her father. A woman will go to her mother's brother for a basket of grain at harvest time if her husband's grain supplies are very low and she knows that her father or brother has none to spare.

These personal bonds are transferred, in accordance with the principles we have previously made clear, to sons and grandsons and collateral relatives, as well as to the lineages, of *ahɔb* and *ahɔŋ*. Yarɔg of Gbizug was a close friend of his paternal grandfather's mother's brother's family at Puhug. Sayəbazaa, who was both a neighbour and a distant classificatory *ahɔŋ* of Zubiuŋ (since both the founding ancestor of his maximal lineage and one of his inner lineage forbears were sister's sons of a Zubiuŋ lineage), took great pride in being the *ahɔŋ-kpeem*, most senior of the 'sisters' sons' of that clan. He took a keen interest in its affairs and never missed attending important ceremonies anywhere in Zubiuŋ. The elders of the clan spoke of him with respect as 'our elder brother (*ti bier*)'. But naturally, the more distant the relationship is, the less intimate and the more formal do the mutual interests of *ahɔb* and *ahɔŋ* tend to become.

Death is the key test of kinship sentiments. The day after Kpe'emi's death I happened to call at the house of his mother's full brother, Lɔyani. I found Lɔyani and his brother sitting listlessly at their gateway and the house was as quiet as if there were a person on his death-bed inside. The women, who should have been out collecting firewood, were at home, and the children, usually playing boisterously at that time of the day, sat in corners, talking in subdued voices. When I asked what was the matter, Lɔyani said mournfully, 'Have you not heard of our child Kpe'emi's death? That is our grief (*ti suhkpɛlɔg nla*). We sitting here, our bodies are prostrate (*ti nɛŋgbina nkpi*—lit. our bodies are dead). We have no thought for food or drink or work.' Barimoda was deeply affected when his *ahɔb* Teroog died, though he was then a very old man. Barimoda could not publicly manage the funeral but he did in fact manage it behind the scenes. As we shall see later, an *ahɔŋ* has certain customary obligations to fulfil at the funeral of his *ahɔb*. The feud between the Gɔlibdaana's faction and the Kpata'arna'ab's supporters at Tɛnzugu placed many men in the camp opposed to that of their *ahɔb* or *ahɔs*. Kpata'ar men and Bunkyiuk men stopped having any contacts with each other. But just then the mother's brother of Nayabil of Kpata'ar died. I was with the Kpata'arna'ab, the head of the maximal lineage, when Nayabil came to tell him of this. 'I want to tell you', he said, 'because he (the dead man) is my true *ahɔb* (i.e. mother's full brother) and if I do not go to the funeral to mourn his death it would be unseemly (*de ku maali*). Besides', he went on, turning to me, 'if I don't go my mother (also dead) would be angry because I was scorning her brother's funeral.' The Kpata'arna'ab at once gave Nayabil permission to go, saying that the quarrel between the two clans had nothing to do with the question of personal kinship ties. As this example shows, there is a strong element of moral (but not jural) compulsion in the respect owed by a sister's son to his mother's brother, and the sanction behind it is the allegiance every man owes to his maternal ancestors.

On the level of sentiment and affective attitudes there is clearly a close resemblance between the relationship of mother's brother and sister's child and that of father and child. The difference, and it is a fundamental difference, lies in the fact that *ahɔb* and *ahɔŋ* have no common economic or jural interests. Thus a man can be familiar with all the affairs of his *ahɔb* or *ahɔŋ* and be keenly concerned that they should go well, but he is under no responsibility for their satisfactory outcome. The tension underlying the relationship of father and son is absent, and in this important respect the relationship of *ahɔb* and *ahɔŋ* resembles that of mother and child more closely. An *ahɔb* must be respected by and he has considerable moral authority over his *ahɔŋ*; but he cannot demand obedience from him as of right. This will be clearer from what follows.

Here it is pertinent to ask why the mother's brother and not her father—though he is the head of her natal family—holds the key position in the network of social relations that bind a person to his mother's patrilineal kin. As our analysis makes clear, it follows from the interaction of the principle of the equivalence of siblings and the principle of the cleavage between successive generations. A person cannot identify himself with his mother in relation to her father. He cannot have the status of a son and the status of a grandson in relation to the same person. On the other hand, as the preceding discussion makes clear, it is in conformity both with the logic of the social structure and with the pattern of sentiments uniting parent and child, for a person to extend to his mother's brother the filial attitude he has towards his mother. He can consistently be his mother's son and at the same time have a quasi-filial status in relation to her brother.

The Place of Gifts in the Relations of Ahɔb and Ahɔŋ

An *ahɔb* demonstrates his interest in his sister's son's well-being by the gifts (*piini*) he occasionally gives him. The theory is that they are given freely out of kinship amity. By the rule of reciprocity there should be a similar freely-given flow of gifts and services from *ahɔŋ* to *ahɔb*, but the emphasis lies on the generosity of the *ahɔb*. A man is under no jural or ritual obligation to give things to his sister's child; he does so voluntarily as a quasi-paternal gesture. And though an *ahɔŋ* has no property rights in the lineage or clan of his *ahɔb*, he is, in theory, allowed certain liberties with things belonging to them, as if he were a kind of son of the clan. This is explained by the formula that but for the accident of birth his mother might have been an owner of these things. In the past, when people moved about less freely than now, a man passing through the clan settlement of his *ahəb* could seize any guinea-fowl he saw and collect any guinea-fowl eggs he came across[1] irrespective of which member of his mother's brother's clan they belonged to. Nowadays this custom is objected to. Tallensi say that with people moving about so freely and frequently as they do now, it would soon lead to the destruction of all their flocks of guinea-fowl. But an *ahəŋ* is still at liberty to cut himself a few heads of guinea corn or millet from any farm when walking through the settlement of his *ahəb*, if he is feeling hungry.

Women *ahəs* have an analogous privilege of much more practical value. As we have learnt, if a woman has a small baby she often gets a young sister of her own inner lineage or clan to come and live with her and be the infant's nursemaid. If there is no suitable girl in her father's lineage, she is entitled to ask her *ahəb* or her father's *ahəb* to give her a little girl. This is a very common practice.

Sister's son and mother's brother cannot contract debts towards each other. If a man borrows money or livestock from an *ahəb* or *ahəŋ* repayment cannot be demanded. It rests with the borrower to make an equivalent return in due course. Ɔndieso provided an amusing illustration of this rule. He borrowed three shillings from Naambuləg, a member of the lineage of his paternal grandfather's *ahəb*, and a friend of his. For about a year nothing was said about this loan and the friendship of the two men continued as before. Then a disagreement developed between Kutɔbis, head of Ɔndieso's inner lineage, and the head of Naambuləg's clan, for which the latter was in part responsible. As it was a question of a right vested in the inner lineage, Ɔndieso supported and indeed instigated Kutɔbis. He was particularly angry with Naambuləg. Thereupon the latter immediately demanded repayment of the loan, thus symbolically relegating Ɔndieso to the class of non-relatives, and Ɔndieso ostentatiously repaid two shillings. Repaying Naambuləg in kind, he had deducted one shilling for two fowls Naambuləg had borrowed from his brother two or three years previously.

When Bontuya died his son Ba'andoog had to sacrifice a white bull to the dead man's *Yin* shrine before starting the funeral ceremonies. Ba'andoog went to his father's sister's son, who, he knew, had a white bull, and asked for the animal. Very reluctantly the *ahəŋ* parted with his bull. As he explained to me afterwards, it was a very fine young bull. 'But', he said, 'Bontuya begot me and I have no power to refuse him anything.' Several months later the father-in-law of the *ahəŋ* came to him demanding a cow of his daughter's bride-price. The young man promptly went

---

[1] Guinea-fowl are only semi-domestic birds. They live out of doors and are very difficult to catch alive. They also lay their eggs out of doors. The privilege of an *ahəŋ* therefore had more of a token value than any practical worth. But I know several men who claim to have used their privilege at least once.

to his mother's brother's house and Ba'andoog gave him a cow of somewhat greater value than the white bull to give to his father-in-law. But such exchanges are exceptional. A fowl, a sixpence, a slab of tobacco, a few kola nuts, these are the more usual kinds of gifts that pass between extra-clan kin.

There are two gifts from a mother's brother to which great significance is attached. One of these is the gift of a hen to a lad from his *ahəb* when he becomes capable of productive labour. This is almost a universal custom among the Tallensi. As we have shown in an earlier chapter, its importance lies in that it marks the beginning of the economic (and, therefore, in due course, social) self-differentiation of a boy within the joint family. It symbolizes, and in many cases actually serves as, the starting-point of the accumulation of wealth by individual effort. It was the proud boast of Barimoda that starting as a small boy with a fowl given to him by his father's *ahəb* he had eventually 'achieved' (*paa*) a cow from which he had had several calves. In every settlement one can find two or three men who have matched this achievement, but it is more common to find men who have 'achieved' a goat or a sheep in this way. And though Tallensi always speak as if they began with one hen this is not strictly true. A boy may receive fowls from two or three matrilateral kinsmen, and he may be given more than one fowl by an *ahəb* who is specially attached to him. Kɔyatee was unlucky with the first hen his true mother's brother gave him. When it died he told his *ahəb*, who gave him another. He successfully bred a brood of chickens from this hen and was given yet another hen by the same mother's brother.

An *ahəb* has no claims on livestock bred in this way by his sister's son. Very often, if a man needs a fowl for a sacrifice and has none that is suitable, he will send to ask his sister's son for one; but this is not connected with the gift of a hen he may have made to the latter many years before. The equivalent return for the mother's brother's hen is made in another way. As has been previously mentioned, when a man 'achieves' a cow, after starting with his mother's brother's hen, he owes this cow to his mother's brother's lineage ancestor shrine (*bɔyar*). He keeps the cow until it is too old to calve and then takes it to his mother's brother's lineage as a thank-offering to his maternal ancestors. For, say the natives, it must surely have been their beneficence that gave him prosperity, since the hen came from their son.

Far more important is the gift of land by an *ahəb* to an *ahəŋ*. There are degrees of finality about such a gift. It is a very common practice for both men and women to beg a plot of land from an *ahəb*—or any other extra-clan matrilateral kinsman—living in an adjacent settlement to plant with ground-nuts or sweet potatoes. The land given for these purposes generally lies on the outskirts of the donor's settlement, near that of the recipient. As often as not, it is land too exhausted for grain crops; or else it is land not required by the *ahəb* that season. Use of the land is granted for one season only, but the *ahaŋ* is often allowed to retain it for several years with the tacit understanding that it must be surrendered whenever the donor asks for it, as he will do a season in advance when he wishes to resume cultivation of it. The gift is made without any special ceremony and the recipient pays no rent. If he gets a good crop he usually gives his *ahɔb* a basket of ground-nuts or sweet potatoes as a token of gratitude. But this is entirely optional. A person may borrow a ground-nut plot in the same way from a uterine or other matrilateral or sororal kinsman in his or her own clan and the same rules apply. Women also borrow plots for ground-nuts from their own kinsmen belonging to their husbands' clans. This practice is so common that it can be described as the normal thing for young men, especially if they are unmarried and farming with their fathers. Nor is it shortage of land that makes young men ask an *ahɔb* for a ground-nut plot rather than their fathers. Nayabaal, Nalɛbseug, and Mosuor, all youths aged between 15 and 20, had borrowed ground-nut and sweet potato plots from their mothers' brothers' people, but the fathers of all three had ample land. Indeed, Nayabaal's father allowed two of his *ahas* to grow ground-nuts on a distant piece of fallow land belonging to him. A strong motive is the knowledge that a youth's father will, as a rule, not interfere with the manner in which the youth may wish to dispose of a crop grown on his mother's brother's land as he might if it were grown on land belonging to the nuclear lineage. There is always the feeling that anything obtained through the use of lineage resources must be at the disposal of the whole domestic group if it is required. Thus borrowing a ground-nut plot from one's mother's brother reflects the association we have previously stressed of individual self-differentiation in economic and social terms with maternal origin. But there is also a more important jural reason. A man cannot refuse his son or brother's son if the latter asks for some land to use for himself and the father has spare land. But then he cannot take possession of the land again without very good reason. The result is that if a man obtains a plot of land from his father or the head of his nuclear lineage for growing ground-nuts he tends, in due course, to establish *de facto* possessory rights over it and it never reverts to the patrimonial land. Unless, therefore, a man wishes deliberately to endow a son or brother's son with land, to be held in perpetuity by the latter's agnatic descendants, he prefers not to grant such a dependant a plot for his private use. He cannot make such a grant to one son or brother's son only; he would have to give similar plots to his other sons and proxy sons. Resort to matrilateral kin avoids this dilemma.

This arises also in the more serious business of borrowing land to cultivate as a regular bush-farm for a period of years. A man who wants a new bush-farm commonly tries to get one from a matrilateral or sororal kinsman or lineage. It is very rare for land to be borrowed from a clansman who is not also a matrilateral or sororal kinsman, for permanent cultivation. It is felt to be incompatible with clanship ties. Clansmen form a corporate unit, in theory made up of a vastly expanded group of brothers. In theory, every member of a clan or maximal lineage has an interest in and a potential right to inherit the property of any other member of the clan. Hence if a lineage segment dies out all the land formerly owned by its members passes into the ownership of the next higher lineage of which it forms a segment, and is vested in the head of that lineage. Thus if a man were to lend land for permanent farming to a clansman he would never be able to demand its return. The lender, moreover, would not give the land with that feeling of personal interest in the recipient's welfare and desire for his prosperity that an *ahəb* has towards his sister's son or an *ahəŋ* towards his mother's brother. A matrilateral kinsman gives freely, solely out of consideration for the needs of his kinsman, not because the latter has a right to what he asks for; and the spirit in which the gift is made carries with it the blessings of the giver's ancestors. There is an advantage to the giver in that what is voluntarily given can be taken back without affecting the relationship of the parties, and an advantage to the recipient in that restoring the borrowed land to its owner does not mean a surrender of a right.

I have recorded the ownership of a large number of bush-farms. They fall into three approximately equal groups: those which are said to have belonged to the lineage from time immemorial; those which it is claimed were bought by an ancestor; and those which, it is said, were obtained by an ancestor by gift from a mother's brother or other matrilateral kinsman. The latter explanation is so common and so stereotyped that it may well be mythical in many cases. But cross-checking and the fact that such gifts are still commonly made show that the claim is true for most cases. I witnessed the whole procedure twice, when two men well known to me obtained gifts of bush-farms from matrilateral kinsmen. Ɔmara, a Zoo man, obtained his from the head of the inner lineage at Zubiuŋ to which his paternal great-grandfather's *ahəb* had belonged; and Sɔmbura from Ba'ari obtained his from his paternal grandfather's mother's brother's lineage at Tongo. These cases are the more significant in that it has been the practice, for several generations, for Tongo people to get land from their matrilateral kinsmen at Zoo, and for Ba'ari people to resort to their kinsmen at Yayazoor for grants of bush-farms.

The procedure is as follows. A man looking for a new bush-farm sees a suitable piece of land which he knows belongs to his true or to a classificatory mother's brother's lineage (*ahəb yidɛm*). He ascertains that it has not been cultivated for the last ten or fifteen years, which suggests that the owners are not hard pressed for land. He then goes to 'beg' (*soh*) the land from his *ahəb yidɛm*. The land Ɔmara desired belonged to his lineage *ahəb*[1] Dawoog's inner lineage; and partly for this reason,

[1] i.e. the progenitrix of Ɔmara's medial lineage had been a daughter of Dawoog's inner lineage.

partly because Ɔmara's relationship was with the whole inner lineage, not with Dawoog personally, the request had to be placed before the assembled elders of the inner lineage. The land could not have been granted without their unanimous consent. This having been obtained, a day was fixed for handing over the land. Early in the morning of the appointed day Ɔmara, followed by his oldest son, arrived bringing a fowl and a guinea-fowl and a large basket of guinea corn. Dawoog then summoned all the men of his inner lineage, and proceeded to sacrifice the birds to his lineage ancestors at the lineage *bɔyar*. Addressing the ancestors he explained all the circumstances of their 'grandson' Ɔmara's request and exhorted them to bless his labour and to grant that the new farm might bring him prosperity. It was a long prayer detailing exactly how Ɔmara was related to Dawoog's lineage and promising that he would bring further offerings in gratitude to the *bɔyar* whenever the new farm produced good crops. The flesh of the birds was divided amongst all present, including Ɔmara, in accordance with the customary rules.

Ɔmara and his son, accompanied by two young men and an elder of the *ahɔb yiri* deputed by Dawoog, then repaired to the bush-farm. The elder showed Ɔmara the boundaries of the farm and the young men hoed a strip along one boundary to symbolize marking them out (*kyie*). They then set to, with the aid of Ɔmara and his sons, to hoe a small patch, and so symbolically to hand over the right of working the farm. This was symbolized, also, in a simple rite in which the elder handed Ɔmara a large pellet of soil from the farm, mixed with a handful of the flour used in the sacrifice to the *bɔyar*, to eat.

The procedure was identical in the case of Sɔmbura, with one exception. The land belonged to his *ahɔb* Sayamane's nuclear lineage, so there was no need to obtain the consent of the elders of his inner lineage. Sayamane did, however, inform them because, as he put it, 'you cannot undertake so important a transaction without the knowledge of your "brothers" and "fathers", and besides, telling them makes them witnesses to the act'. It means that there will always be some member of the inner lineage who knows the circumstances and conditions of the gift.

Tallensi attach very great importance to the ritual steps in this transaction. They secure the blessing of his matrilateral ancestors for the recipient of the land. Without this, they believe, failure and even disaster would overtake him when he starts farming the new bush-farm; for, they say, the land really belongs to the ancestors who first cultivated it. Moreover, the ritual formalities also have an explicitly stressed jural function. It is a solemn covenant between the parties, made in the presence of the ancestors, in which all those who have rights in the land avow their consent to the gift and the recipient pledges himself to abide by the implicit conditions of the tenure of the land. The arrangement has the sanctions of the ancestor cult behind it, and the guarantee of having been made with the public consent of all who have an interest in the land.

The recipient pays no rent or dues for the land. During the first three or four years he must give a basket of guinea corn or millet to the grantors after every harvest. If he has had good crops it will be a large basketful; if he has had a poor season it will be a small basket. In subsequent years he need only bring a gift of grain if his crops are good and if he wishes to do so. Some of this grain will be ground into flour and a libation poured to his matrilateral ancestors at their *bɔyar*, expressing thanks for their beneficence. This serves also to reaffirm the ownership of the land by the grantors. Occasionally, too, he may bring a fowl to offer at the ancestral *bɔyar* of his *ahɔb* lineage in gratitude for the beneficence of the ancestors whose land he is working.

In principle, the lineage that grants the land can recover use of it at any time by giving the recipient a year's notice. But this right would only be exercised, in practice, if the latter offends them in any way—for instance, by withholding the gifts of grain in spite of having excellent crops. As a rule, therefore, the *ahaŋ* retains the use of the land until he no longer requires it. It then reverts automatically to its proper owners. If the original recipient dies, his son may continue to use the land without specially renewing the arrangement with his *ahɔb yidɛm*.

Now supposing the farm is so large that the recipient need not cultivate all of it at one time. By cultivating and fallowing different portions of the farm in rotation he and his sons after him may keep it in use continually. If this goes on for two generations, by which time all the individuals who were present in person at the original transaction are probably dead, the land passes into the effective ownership of the original recipient's lineage, in the third generation. The successors of the original grantor no longer have the right of recovering the land but they are still the nominal owners of the land. If it is wholly abandoned they may resume occupation; the users may not sell the land; and if they grossly offend the nominal owners, the latter can, in theory, turn them off it.

This right is most emphatically claimed, though it is, by all accounts, very rarely exercised. An incident concerning Ɔndieso is suggestive of what might happen. Ɔndieso quarrelled with his neighbour and the head of his paternal grandfather's mother's brother's lineage, the Gbizug Tɛndaana. The latter, in his anger, ordered Ɔndieso to leave the land he was farming. This land had been given to Ɔndieso's grandfather by his mother's brother, the then Gbizug Tɛndaana. Ɔndieso, previously defiant, was filled with dismay. Not to comply with the tɛndaana's demand meant risking both the wrath of his matrilateral ancestors and the vengeance of the Earth whose cult is so closely bound up with Gbizug. So he went across to Deemzeet, the head of Puhug section of

Tongo and therefore the senior lineage head of all Tongo, and begged him to intercede. As Deemzeet was also the head of the Gbizug Tɛndaana's grandfather's mother's brother's lineage, the choice was doubly fortunate. Deemzeet thereupon sent two of his sons to plead with the tɛndaana, who consented to withdraw his demand if Ɔndieso would bring a fowl and a guinea-fowl to sacrifice to the ancestor who had originally made the gift of the land, in sign of contrition.

Though Ɔndieso climbed down for fear of mystical retribution, both he and others maintained that the tɛndaana had exceeded his rights. The land Ɔndieso's grandfather had been given was no longer a bush-farm. Ɔndieso's father's brother had been given leave to build on it and the homestead had stood there for two generations. This, they considered, gave Ɔndieso a title amounting to complete ownership of the land. Had his *ahɔb* been an ordinary person and not a tɛndaana, whose ritual position gives his fulminations the force of a curse, Ɔndieso could have ignored his demand.

It has always been and still is a frequent practice for men to solicit a site for a homestead and a piece of land to make a home farm, from a matrilateral kinsman, if they wish to set up an independent homestead. As we have recorded in our earlier book, this is how many Tongo people have come to live at Zoo and this is how many immigrants into the peripheral settlements find sites for their homes.[1] We mentioned there that it is considered to be morally wrong to refuse such a request if one has land to spare.[2] The rules of tenure are the same as for a bush-farm borrowed from a matrilateral kinsman. But if the house site and home farm have been continuously occupied by the same nuclear lineage for two or three generations, their ownership is considered to be entire. Their title rests not only on the passage of the generations but on the fact that they have begun to bury their dead there and to transmit the land in accordance with the rules of inheritance. Indeed, Tallensi say that only the person who originally granted the land can really recover it. Even his immediate heir could not compel the recipient to surrender the land. The latter could, if he wished, refuse to go. He would invoke the common ancestors of his hosts and himself and this would be sufficient—unless he had committed some particularly heinous breach of kinship amity against his hosts. Pa'anbobis furnishes a case in point. Many years ago, owing to a quarrel with his older half-brother he went to build his homestead on a bush-farm he had borrowed from his matrilateral kinsman and clansman Mambaŋya. There he lived for perhaps twenty years. Then Mambaŋya asked him to relinquish the land. He said his sons were growing up and wanted more land to cultivate. So Pa'anbobis went back to his original home. Both men understood and admitted in private that Mambaŋya's story was a polite

[1] *Dynamics of Clanship*, pp. 161, 221.
[2] Ibid., p. 163.

pretext. The point was that he did not wish this land to be lost to his sons altogether; and he therefore took the precaution of getting it back in his own lifetime.

If a man gives land over which he has full rights of disposal to his own sister's son, this amounts to an outright gift. The land belongs to the sister's son and his heirs in perpetuity. This is always explained by the jural fiction that the *ahɔb* (identifying himself with his sister) has, like a father, bestowed a portion of his own land on 'his child'. When the *ahɔb* dies the *ahɔŋ* has the same rights in respect of the share of the patrimonial land allocated to him as the *ahɔb*'s own sons have in respect of any shares he might have given them. It is an application of the rule that siblings are equals. Barimoda and Kpɛlimɛrɔme both had farms given to them on these terms by their mothers' brothers and both said they would never part with their farms. Wherever a branch of one clan is found settled on land coming under the ritual jurisdiction of a neighbouring clan, the origin of the relationship is traced back to such a gift of land. Thus Nɔŋsuur yidem of Tongo occupy and own land under the ritual jurisdiction of the Zubiuŋ-Yakɔra Tɛndaana.[1] They ascribe their rights in their land and the fact that they are living on Zubiuŋ land to their founding ancestor's having been a true sister's son of the Zubiuŋ-Yakɔra Tɛndaana of his time. He was given a very large piece of land by the tɛndaana and came to live there. It is this land that his descendants now occupy.

The Status of an Ahɔŋ as a Foster-child in his Ahɔb's Family

We have mentioned before that a boy who loses his own parents and cannot settle down with a proxy father sometimes goes to live with his mother's brother. A few cases of this sort are found in every settlement. As a rule the boy eventually goes back to his natal home to settle down there; occasionally he settles permanently in his mother's brother's settlement. In any case, he never loses touch with his natal home and never forfeits his rights and status in his own lineage and clan. He does not, as we know, become a member of the lineage or clan of his *ahɔb*. This brings us back to the question of the jural relations of *ahɔb* and *ahɔŋ*.

A boy who grows up in his mother's brother's household is treated exactly like a son and is indistinguishable from a son of the family, to the outsider. Thus it was many months before I discovered that Puvɔlimra was not the Gbizug Tɛndaana's son but his sister's son. He was probably in his late twenties and had lived with the tɛndaana since boyhood. He continued to farm with the tɛndaana after the latter's oldest son had established his own household. He was, indeed, the tɛndaana's right-hand man, more trusted by him, in some ways, than

[1] Cf. *Dynamics of Clanship*, p. 59.

his own sons. More surprising, Puvɔlimra was admitted to all the esoteric rites of the Earth cult and often represented the tɛndaana in ritual activities. He was permitted to do this because he belonged to a lineage holding a tɛndaana-ship allied to that of Gbizug. Had he been a Namoo, he would have been excluded from all but the domestic religious rites of the tɛndaana.

He was a great favourite, too, with the tɛndaana's children. But one of the sons once made a revealing comment on Puvɔlimra's position. He spoke in a slightly patronizing tone, though not offensively so. 'Puvɔlimra', he said, 'is our child (*u a ti bii*). We like him to stay with us and we may not deny him anything. But one day he may decide to go home and we can't restrain him; or if he offends us we can tell him to go. He is not our person (as a member of the lineage is). However much the tɛndaana may like him he cannot inherit our ancestor shrines or our farms or our homestead. It is because he gets on so well with the tɛndaana that he stays.'

This comment is typical of conventional opinion on the position of an *ahəŋ* in the family of his *ahəb*. Puvɔlimra himself, Gikoo-Duun, and Bayana, three young men who either lived or had lived with their mothers' brothers, defined their position in exactly the same terms. It would be an offence against the ancestors to deny an *ahəŋ* a home, but he has none of the fundamental rights of a son; his position depends on the personal attachment to him, and concern for him, of his mother's brother. An *ahəŋ* in Puvɔlimra's position, it is sometimes suggested, is apt to be more compliant than a son, so as to ingratiate himself with his *ahəb*. He cannot make demands as of right, as a son may do. Said Gikoo-Duun: 'I was a small boy when I went to live with my *ahəb-soog* at Saamər (in Mampurugu). Later I went out on my own to build my homestead and farm for myself near him. It was not because of a quarrel. But my mother's brother will not take care of (i.e. take responsibility for) my affairs (*u ku maal n-yɛla*). He will not marry a wife for me. If he does give me one cow to help pay my wife's bride-price and we should some day quarrel, he will say I must pay it back. He is not of my people. My people are here at Zubiuŋ. Even though I am far away, they (the Zubiuŋ people) will look after my affairs. If I were to die to-day they would make my funeral and inherit my things. Do you not see that I come here (to Zubiuŋ) regularly to sacrifice to my ancestors?'

As we know, one of the major jural responsibilities of a father for his son is in marriage affairs. Hence the fact that a sister's son has no claim, as of right, on his mother's brother's assistance in this important matter is a good test of their jural relations. Puvɔlimra's marriage created the first rift between him and his mother's brother. The marriage was beset with difficulties. The girl's father feared that he would never get the bride-price as Puvɔlimra's proxy father was a blind old man who lived on the charity of his kinsmen and friends. The Gbizug Tɛndaana refused to promise anything in advance. When at length Puvɔlimra succeeded in persuading his prospective father-in-law to give him the girl, all the formalities were carried out by his paternal relatives at Kpatia. Then came the question of bride-price. The demand was made to the head of Puvɔlimra's inner lineage at Kpatia, who transmitted it to Puvɔlimra himself, since his 'father' was obviously unable to meet it. It was then that the Gbizug Tɛndaana made Puvɔlimra a present of a bull, without, however, assuming any responsibility for handing it over to Puvɔlimra's father-in-law. The situation was saved for the time being; but that dry season Puvɔlimra went, for the first time in his life, to seek work abroad, hoping thus to earn enough to buy another bull to give to his in-laws.

Sometimes, however, a mother's brother accepts responsibility for the bride-price of the wife of his sister's son who has grown up as his foster-son. A curious situation arises then. For this amounts to adopting the *ahɔŋ* into the inner lineage of the *ahɔb*. It is as if his mother's bride-price is paid back to his paternal lineage so that he becomes a son of his mother's brother's lineage—much like an illegitimate son. And this is symbolically shown by his children being entrusted to the care of spirit guardians from among his mother's brother's ancestors instead of his paternal ancestors. Though he does not acquire rights of inheritance in his adoptive lineage, the *ahɔŋ* settles permanently in the clan settlement of his *ahɔb*. He retains only ritual ties with his paternal clan. This is one of the ways in which accessory lineages are founded in clans to which they are related as *ahɔŋ* to *ahɔb*. At Gbeog, for instance, there are two homesteads occupied by the sons and grandsons of a Gorogo man who came to live with his mother's brother and settled there when the latter paid the bride-price for his first wife. In ritual matters these men still belong to Gorogo. They keep the totemic taboos and funeral customs of Gorogo. When there is a death in their families their Gorogo clansmen come to bury the dead and celebrate the funeral. When the Great Festivals arrive they join with their Gorogo clansmen in celebrating them. But in another two or three generations it is quite possible that their lineage will become an established accessory lineage of Gbeog.

The corollary to the foregoing is that a person's patrilineal kin do not forfeit their rights over him merely because he has grown up in the care of his mother's brother. These rights are often jealously guarded. For example, Nabil, a lad who lived with his mother's brother, one day killed a hare. Instead of delivering the carcass to the head of his own nuclear lineage, as he was bound to do by custom, he brought it home to his *ahɔb*. The latter divided the bulk of it amongst the constituent segments of his own inner lineage and sent only one hind-leg to Nabil's 'father'. His reaction was an indignant protest, backed by the other members of his inner lineage, at what he called the deliberate flouting of his rights as *biiraan*, owner of the child. A long squabble between the two lineages followed which eventually petered out in a compromise. This may seem a storm in a teacup; it was taken very seriously by a dozen Tale elders.

The outstanding example of the retention of patrilineal rights is found in the case of a girl who grows up at her *ahɔb yiri*. Whatever her personal relations with her father's lineage may be, it is they who receive the placation gifts and the bride-price when she marries. The *ahɔb*'s share is only the 'cow of rearing'.

Cases of girls living as foster children at their *ahɔb yiri* up to marriageable age are uncommon. I knew of only one girl who was living with her *ahɔb* and would probably not be taken back by her father's people before she reached marriageable age. A girl living with her mother's brother is usually there because she was sent to her maternal grandmother in early childhood owing to the death of her mother. She may be left there until she is 11 or 12, but she is then generally fetched by her father's people. A boy has more freedom. He cannot be forced to return to his paternal home if he does not wish to do so.

An interesting reflection of the conventional ideas on the relations of an *ahɔb* and his foster *ahɔŋ* is found in the story commonly told of how certain politico-ritual offices came to be transferred from one clan to another. The tale is so stereotyped that it can be regarded as a standard myth. It is alleged of several of the lesser chiefships that they were originally vested in different clans from those that now hold them—usually clans that are closely related to the present holders by local or ritual ties. The last chief of the original line, the myth relates, had his sister's son, a member of the clan now holding the chiefship, living with him. The chief put great trust in his *ahɔŋ*; and, either because he had no sons or because his sons were indifferent to politico-ritual affairs, the chief always delegated his *ahɔŋ* to represent him. Thus, he used to send the *ahɔŋ* as his messenger whenever he had to communicate with the senior chief who was the elector to that chiefship. In this way the *ahɔŋ* became known to the elector. When his *ahɔb* died he hastened stealthily to the elector with the news, taking lavish gifts along with him. Knowing him so well from their previous contacts and persuaded by the rich gifts he brought, the elector thereupon immediately conferred the chiefship on him. Thus the chiefship came into the possession of its present holders. A similar story is told to explain the dominant position of the lineage of Lakum yiri in the politico-ritual structure of Ba'ari, in spite of their being an attached lineage.[1]

When it is pointed out that such actions are contrary to custom and would not be allowed at present, the natives have two answers. Firstly, they say, unscrupulous people never hesitate to break a customary rule

[1] *Dynamics of Clanship*, p. 88.

if it suits their purpose. Men have always been prepared to go to great lengths to win an office so coveted as that of a chief or tɛndaana. In addition, they argue, the breach of custom is not so outrageous as it seems. For the *ahɔŋ* can claim that if his mother had been born a man he would have had an unquestionable right to the office.

This argument gains strength from the fact that in certain cases an *ahɔŋ* or a sororal lineage is delegated to exercise rights vested in a particular office or lineage. Thus the people of Tongo maintain that in former times the Chief of Tongo always had the right to 'strip (*yɛa*)' all locust-bean trees in Tongo and the adjacent settlements, including Tɛnzugu. Now it would have been neither tactful nor dignified for the chief to send his wives or clansmen to strip locust-bean trees growing in another settlement. Therefore every chief delegated one of his 'sister's sons' in each settlement to harvest the pods for him. The *ahɔŋ* was entitled to keep some of the locust-bean pods he harvested, but had to send the bulk to the Chief of Tongo. Tongo people say that the 'sisters' sons' gradually ceased sending the chief's share to him and took full possession of the trees, in much the same way as a man obtains *de facto* possession of land loaned to one of his ancestors by a matrilateral kinsman.

Certain powers normally held by tɛndaanas only are sometimes vested in lineages that do not have tɛndaanas. Thus at Tongo the people of Seug live on land that comes under the ritual jurisdiction of the Zoo Yiraaŋ.[1] But when they dig a new grave they do not send for the Yiraaŋ to come and 'mark out the grave (*kyɛbɔg voor*)' ritually, as they should do, according to the letter of custom. The head of one segment of Seug performs the rite instead. He keeps the carcass of the goat sacrificed, but sends the head and skin to the Zoo Yiraaŋ. This arrangement is found wherever people of one clan live on land that falls under the ritual jurisdiction of another clan. The regular explanation is that an ancestor of the lineage head who actually marks out the grave was an *ahɔŋ* of the tɛndaana who had ritual jurisdiction over the land when the lineage first settled there, and that the tɛndaana delegated this ritual duty to him and his successors.

The Ahɔŋ as Intermediary

By his genealogical position an *ahɔŋ* forms a link between his father's lineage and his mother's lineage; and by extension this applies to every degree of matrilateral kinship. Hence an *ahɔŋ* is always chosen as intermediary in all private jural and ritual transactions between a segment of one clan and a segment of another. Marriage is the most important of these transactions. A key role in all the jural and ritual formalities necessary for the conclusion of a marriage is that of the

[1] Cf. *Dynamics of Clanship*, p. 169.

pɔyasama. As has been previously stated, he is a clansman of the bridegroom who is also an *ahəŋ* of the bride's clan—*ahəŋ* being understood to include any sororal kinsman of whatever degree. The reason for this choice was well put by a group of elders with whom I discussed this subject. 'He (the *pɔyasama*) is our (the bridegroom's clan's) person and is also their (the bride's clan's) person. He may not deceive us nor may he deceive them. If he deceives either of us the ancestors will not permit it.'[1]

The *pɔyasama* appears in every transaction between the two parties to a marriage. He takes the placation gifts (*lu sɛndaan*) to the bride's father. When, later, the bride's father sends messengers (*duondɛm*) to demand the bride-price, the *pɔyasama* conducts them to the person responsible for paying the bride-price and assists in the negotiations. Many a marriage is saved by the skill and patience of a *pɔyasama* in persuading the bride's people and the bridegroom's people to a compromise on the question of bride-price payments. He must be present whenever bride-price payments are made; for if, at any subsequent time, a dispute should arise as to what was paid, his word is final. The *pɔyasama* also acts as intermediary in all the formal claims, services, and duties that arise between the parties as a result of the marriage. He is the messenger who goes to announce the birth of her first child to the bride's parents. If a woman's father or mother dies, the *pɔyasama* conducts the party sent by her husband with his obligatory food contributions to the funeral, and he hands these contributions over to his 'mother's brother's lineage (*ahəb yidɛm*)'. In this and similar jural or ritual relations between the husband's people and the wife's people, the *pɔyasama* has to be present both as a witness of the transaction and as a mediator, in case the recipients object to the quantity or quality of the food contributions or the payments offered. For though the obligations of the parties in such situations are clearly defined by custom, there is room for much quibbling over details. Custom declares that a man must kill and cook a goat or a sheep to send to his father-in-law's funeral at a certain stage. But one man will, out of generosity or as a special sign of respect, kill a large goat, whereas another will be mean and choose a puny animal. I have seen violent arguments arise between a son-in-law's messengers and his late father-in-law's lineage over a point of this sort. The mere presence of the *pɔyasama*, even if he is but a young lad, has a conciliatory influence. As will be remembered, the *pɔyasama*'s role does not come to an end on his death. It passes to his brothers and sons, like any other attribute of his social personality.

There are other situations in which an *ahəŋ* acts as intermediary between the members of his paternal clan and his matrilateral clan. For example, the setting up of a divining (*bakologo*) shrine for a man is done

[1] '*U a tam nit ka le a bam nit; u ku too m-paah tam, u ku too m-paah bam-mi; ɔn paah ti sɔ kpiinam la ku sayi.*'

for him by the lineage of the ancestress who has demanded the erection of the shrine. The diviner-to-be is himself a 'sister's son (*ahəŋ*)' or 'grandson (*yaaŋ*)' of the men who come to perform the ceremony of establishing the shrine. But in addition, a member of his clan who is also an *ahəŋ* of the visitors' clan is deputed to act as intermediary. He goes out to meet the visitors when they approach and escorts them to the homestead of the diviner-to-be; and he acts as spokesman for the latter throughout the ceremony. Thus he formally 'shows' (*paal*) the visitors the beer and the fowls and the goat that have been provided for the ceremony and acts as mediator if there is a disagreement about the amount or quality of these provisions. In the ritual situations that make up the ceremony the visitors sit together in a group and the diviner-to-be and his clansmen sit together in a group. Between the two groups sits the selected *ahəŋ*. As is customary in all such situations, the two parties do not address one another directly. They address the intermediary, who 'passes on (*zaŋ ti*)' what was said to the other party.

Similarly, if a dispute occurs between segments of different clans, for instance over the abduction of a wife, the injured group might send one of their members who is a 'sister's son' of the abductor's clan, with a message of protest and a demand for the return of the wife. An *ahəŋ* is the appropriate person to act as go-between in negotiations between different clans. In the system of clanship ties, it will be remembered, intercalary lineages are sometimes credited with being the agnates of one clan and the 'sister's sons' of the other.[1]

As has been suggested, Tallensi maintain that an *ahəŋ* acting as an intermediary in inter-clan transactions is bound to be equally faithful to both parties. This does not mean that an *ahəŋ* is always equally loyal in sentiment to both his patrilineal and his matrilateral—especially his immediate maternal—kin. Tallensi say that when there is a clash of interests a man will always side with his patrilineal kin while endeavouring, if possible, to refrain from bringing harm on his maternal kin. The behaviour of an *ahəŋ* in war between his and his mother's brother's clan is a case in point.

But there is a belief which suggests that the loyalty of an *ahəŋ* to his mother's brother's lineage may, in some circumstances, outweigh his loyalty to his own clan. In the old days of warfare, it is said, if a man was killed in fighting, there was a way of taking vengeance on the slayer by means of sorcery. The arrow that slew the victim was extracted, and the clan and lineage of the slayer were ascertained. This was easy. Every inner or medial lineage of a clan usually has a distinctive mark (*daan*). One lineage, for example, may tie a tiny guinea-fowl feather at the base of the arrow-head, another may use a particular species of grass. By inquiring from their sororal kinsmen in the enemy clan the victim's lineage brothers soon discovered which lineage the slayer

[1] Cf. *Dynamics of Clanship*, pp. 44 ff.

belonged to and who he was. The method of sorcery was to dip this 'evil arrow (*peembier*)' secretly into some food or drink the slayer was about to take. If this was done he would die. The problem then was to find someone who would carry out this task. It could not be done by any of the victim's clansmen since it required intimate contact with the slayer's family.

If there was a daughter of the victim's clan, or better still, inner lineage married to a member of the slayer's inner lineage, she might be persuaded to do it. Such an action would be a grave sin, for which the woman's husband's ancestors would punish her with death. But sometimes women hate their husbands so much in their hearts, Tallensi say, that they will risk anything to injure them and their clan. And if the dead man was a close agnate of the woman, she might put vengeance for his death above her duty to her husband's clan. Alternatively, an *ahəŋ* of the victim's inner lineage or clan, who is a member of the slayer's inner lineage or clan, might be persuaded to undertake the commission. Only a man who had a deep grudge against the slayer would undertake so wicked an action for which the clan ancestors would certainly punish him with death. But enmity between clansmen, even between brothers of the same inner lineage, is not unknown; and as Tallensi often assert, the belief that the ancestors may punish an action with death does not always restrain an unscrupulous man. Whether or not this act of sorcery was ever carried out I cannot tell. It is impossible to obtain verifiable information on a point of this sort. But what is of interest is the belief itself. Assuming that it is founded on fantasy, it still suggests that the loyalties of an *ahəŋ* are felt to be more evenly divided than is conventionally admitted.

There is other evidence for this view. The Gɔlibdaana of Tɛnzugu earned the hostility of most of the maximal lineage and clan heads of the Tongo district by his high-handed drive to aggrandize himself.[1] In public his opponents had the support of practically all their clan or lineage elders. But amongst them there were, in every clan, one or two private sympathizers of the Gɔlibdaana. The usual explanation was that these men were 'sisters' sons' or 'grandsons' of his inner lineage or clan. One of the Chief of Tongo's most trusted and devoted elders used to visit the Gɔlibdaana regularly. Another elder of the chief pointed out to me, in explanation, that the first was an *ahəŋ* of the Gɔlibdaana's inner lineage. He quoted several other men who were *ahəs* of the Gɔlibdaana's inner lineage and maintained close contact with him. It was through them, he added, that the Gɔlibdaana kept himself so well informed of everything that happened at Tongo, even of matters that should not be known outside the chief's family. He admitted that the Chief of Tongo probably had similar contacts with the Gɔlibdaana's faction and kept himself informed of the Gɔlibdaana's activities in the same way.

[1] Cf. *Dynamics of Clanship*, pp. 251 ff.

The Ritual Relations of Matrilateral and Sororal Kin

We have previously observed that the distinguishing attribute of an *ahəb* in Tale thought is that he sacrifices on behalf of his *ahəŋ*; and *ahəŋ* in this context includes all sororal kin, both those who are strictly *ahəs* and those who are strictly *yaas*. This is an indication of the importance attached to the ritual relations of extra-clan kin.

As with all the social relations of mother's brother and sister's son, their ritual relations vary in frequency and degree according to their genealogical distance. Thus a male *ahəŋ* is obliged to send a ready cooked fowl to be 'set out (*zien*)' in commemoration of his *ahəb* when the latter's funeral is being celebrated. A child of 3 or 4 will have the fowl sent in his name by his parents; a man of substance might, as a special gesture of affection and respect, send a sheep instead of a fowl. No *ahəŋ* would fail in this duty where his true mother's brother is concerned. I have known men who were small children when a mother's brother died, and whose parents omitted to send fowls to the funeral in their name, make up for it years later on the occasion of a funeral in the family of their *ahəb*. Not infrequently, men will voluntarily send a fowl or a sheep as a tribute to the funeral of a father's mother's brother. But it is exceptional for such a tribute to be offered at the funeral of a more remote 'mother's brother'.

When a man sacrifices to an ancestor spirit, any descendant of that ancestor has the right to be present and to share in the sacrament. The only exceptions are the cult of the clan or maximal lineage *bɔyar* and, among the real Talis, the cult of the Earth and of the External *Bɔyar*. It would be incompatible with the functions of these cults as foci of social integration on the highest level of corporate structure to allow non-members of the lineage concerned to take part in them. But an *ahəŋ* may attend domestic sacrifices to any of his matrilateral ancestors and sacrifices to the founding ancestor's shrine (*bɔyar*) of the lineage of his true or classificatory mother's brother.

If a man proposes to make a sacrifice to one of his immediate antecedents (say, his father or grandfather), and if he is going to sacrifice anything larger than a fowl or guinea-fowl (say, a goat or a sheep or a cow), he is in duty bound to inform his sisters. He is not bound to tell his deceased sister's sons, but he generally does so, particularly if it is so important a sacrifice as a cow. A cow is seldom sacrificed to a shrine of lesser standing than a lineage *bɔyar*. Hence when such a sacrifice is planned, the man who is making it should, in theory, inform all the sororal descendants of the lineage. He does not actually do so; he informs his own sisters' sons and his father's sisters' sons and leaves it to the other members of the lineage (who will, of course, automatically be present) to inform their close *ahəs* if they wish to. But news of such a sacrifice travels fast owing to the complex interweaving of kinship ties, and few people who have an interest in it escape hearing of it in advance. It is the same with funerals. Close extra-clan kin of the dead are informed, distant extra-clan kin, unless there is some special reason for sending them a message, find out indirectly.

An *ahəŋ* is not obliged to attend a sacrifice at his mother's brother's house (*ahəb yiri*); but if it is an important sacrifice, or if it is being made by his own mother's brother, he generally makes an effort to be present. Again, an *ahəŋ* whose home is near to that of his *ahəb* will be more likely to come than one who lives farther away. Thus, as has been recorded, Barimoda seldom missed a sacrifice at his true mother's brother's homestead which was very close to his own. Yinworəb, on the other hand, did not attend a single sacrifice at his mother's brother's house at Yinduuri during the year he was with me. It must not be thought, though, that a sacrifice at one's *ahəb yiri* is considered to be of no consequence. Tallensi say they would always go if they could, for their matrilateral ancestors have powers of blessing only little less than their agnatic ancestors; but it is not compulsory when the sister's son is not himself bringing the sacrifice. As every man has shrines consecrated to those of his matrilateral ancestors who have revealed themselves as directly concerned with his life, in his own home, he generally attends sacrifices at their lineage home only on special occasions or when they command him to offer sacrifice there.[1]

Thus when a man performs a private sacrifice in his own home a close sister's son or two may be present; it would be most unusual to find an *ahəŋ* more distant than a father's sister's son present. But in the majority of such private sacrifices, judging from the several score I have witnessed, sisters' sons are not in attendance. When, however, a cow is sacrificed to a lineage *bəyar*, there are always *ahəs* present; perhaps only one, perhaps half a dozen, including both near and distant sisters' sons.

As we have mentioned before, the right of a sister's son to be present at ritual ceremonies at his mother's brother's house is recognized by the allocation to him of a prescribed share of the sacrificial meat. He receives the neck of every animal sacrificed. One of the lighter moments at the end of a major sacrifice is the good-humoured wrangling of a group of

[1] We are here touching on one of the most complex features of Tale religious custom. The shrines consecrated to a man's matrilateral ancestors in his own homestead provide him with an indirect route to them. When he sacrifices to them on these shrines, he is, as it were, approaching them through an intermediary spirit or group of spirits. He is never able to approach them directly. Only their agnatic descendants can do that. Generally a matrilateral ancestor spirit (male or female) who has a shrine consecrated to him or her by a daughter's son or descendant demands sacrifices on that shrine. But there are many occasions on which the spirit demands that the sacrifice be offered to him or her directly on the shrine consecrated to him or her at a son's or agnatic descendant's house. It is on such occasions that the 'sister's son' or 'grandson' has to take the animal he has been commanded to offer to the homestead of his 'mother's brother' or 'grandfather'. See below, p. 324.

ahǝs, representing perhaps five or six clans, over the division of the cow's neck amongst themselves. It is on such occasions that the *ahǝs* divide into two groups, the *dugni ahǝs*, who are sisters' sons of the inner lineage responsible for the ceremony, and the *yɛŋha* (outside) *ahǝs*, whose matrilateral links are with other segments of the clan. Etiquette dictates that the choicest and largest part of the meat apportioned to the *ahǝs* should be given to the 'outside *ahǝs*'. The *dugni ahǝs*, it is argued, have many more opportunities of attending ceremonies of this inner lineage and receiving their shares of the sacrificial meat.

There are certain ceremonial occasions on which sisters' children of all degrees usually turn up in large numbers.[1] They include not only *ahǝs* of the lineage immediately responsible for the ceremony but also remote *ahǝs* and 'grandsons (*yaas*)' of the clan. The death of a senior elder or of the holder of a politico-ritual office brings 'sisters' sons' and 'grandsons' from a wide range to the funeral. They are present at all stages of the funeral, but the largest number usually come on the day of the burial, on the day the funeral proper (as opposed to the burial rites) commences, and on the two occasions when a diviner is consulted to ascertain the mystical author of the death. These are all occasions when animals are slaughtered as offerings and tributes to the dead, or else food or beer is used in the rites and shared amongst all present. The meat and the drink form a big attraction to all who have kinship ties with the lineage celebrating the funeral. It is no mean attraction either, considering that at a big funeral, such as that of the head of a section (*yizug*) of a clan or of a maximal lineage, two or three big beasts (cows and donkeys) and from twenty to forty small stock (sheep and goats) will be slaughtered, not to speak of innumerable fowls. In addition there will be great quantities of porridge and other cooked food. And *ahǝs* have prescribed shares of all these items. Similar prodigality is shown in the brewing of beer for a big funeral.

But greed is far from being the chief motive that brings matrilateral and sororal kin to an important funeral. The profusion of food and beer—both of which are distributed only on specific ritual occasions—serves chiefly to create and maintain the right atmosphere of pride and kinship amity. For it must be remembered that most of the 'sisters' sons' will bring a gift, if it is only a meagre chicken and a small basket of grain; and if there are twenty or thirty 'sisters' sons' present the share of meat and beer each will receive is of less value than the things he brings.

A 'sister's son' or a 'grandson', like everybody else who attends such

---

[1] As these ceremonies are almost always conducted by men and belong to the ritual and jural spheres of activity dominated by the men, the *ahǝs* who come are principally males; but often one or two female *ahǝs* come as well. The neck of the animal sacrificed belongs in theory to the *ahǝs* of both sexes, but I have never seen it given to a woman.

funerals, comes because of the social importance of the occasion. The funeral of a section or maximal lineage head is of exceptional public interest. It marks the end of a phase of lineage history and the beginning of a new phase, involving realinements in the social relations of many people and probably of all segments of the clan. That is why every branch of the dead man's clan, representatives of related clans, and many matrilateral and sororal kinsmen come to take part in the funeral.

For similar reasons the ceremony by which the *bɔyar* of a lineage of a high order, such as a medial lineage or a maximal lineage, is formally taken over—'inherited (*vaa*)', as the natives put it—by a new lineage head is also attended by many 'sisters' sons' and 'grandsons' of the lineage and the clan. This ceremony marks the re-establishment of the structural equilibrium of the lineage around a new lineage head after its temporary disturbance by the death of the previous lineage head. It is an event of special importance for reaffirming the bonds of lineage solidarity and of kinship amity—for renewing, in the presence of their founding ancestors, the covenants of clanship and of kinship. All the males of the lineage, including the small boys, and representatives of all the other segments of the clan attend; and extra-clan kinsfolk from far and wide are present. I have counted as many as thirty, ranging from the full sister's son of the new lineage head to a distant 'sister's son', whose matrilateral ties with the clan went back to the founding ancestor of his maximal lineage, at such a gathering. Though it is a festive occasion, the attraction of food and drink is unquestionably of minor significance. Only two or three sheep, at most, are sacrificed, in addition to a large number of fowls; but every adult who attends is expected to bring a fowl to be offered to the *bɔyar* on his behalf. 'Sisters' sons' and 'grandsons' take special pride in offering their fowls, for this is the essence of the sacrament. An atmosphere of great goodwill and fellowship prevails, suffusing the most solemn moments of the sacrifice itself.

It is very much the same with the installation ceremonies of a newly appointed tɛndaana or other holder of a politico-ritual office. Extra-clan kin, clansmen, representatives of linked clans and of ritually associated clans, all come in great numbers to the ceremonies, bringing fowls, dishes of cooked food, baskets of grain and of ground-nuts, and other voluntary gifts to congratulate the new chief or tɛndaana and to testify to their kinship bonds with him and his clan. These ceremonies are, in effect, simply an elaboration of the ceremony of 'inheriting' a lineage *bɔyar*. Their significance is the same, but in a heightened degree, corresponding with the wider social sphere to which they refer. 'Sisters' sons' and 'grandsons' closely related to the new chief or tɛndaana are as proud of his elevation in status as are his close agnates.

This is one aspect of a man's ritual relations with his 'sisters' sons' and 'grandsons'. There is another, and in some ways more important, aspect. Every man sacrifices to both his agnatic ancestors and his maternal ancestors, as we have seen. He has shrines consecrated to ancestors of both lines in his homestead. The ancestors who constitute his *Yin* are very often matrilateral or include matrilateral ancestors. Indeed this is so common that a *Yin* that has no matrilateral ancestors is somewhat unusual. Knowing the significance of the *Yin* shrine as a symbol of a man's individuality, we can see why his connexion with his mother's side is apt to be stressed in it. Again, every man erects a shrine to his mother when she dies, which in the course of time may develop into a very important shrine for him. There are other shrines, too, which are consecrated to matrilateral ancestors. The most important of these are divining shrines (*bakologo*) and *bɔyar* shrines.

A *bakologo* shrine is, by definition, a 'female (*bumpɔk*)' shrine. That is to say, the ancestors associated with it come, by definition, from a matrilateral lineage of the diviner; and the dominant figure among them is usually a woman, a 'mother'. It is a point of striking significance in the social psychology of the Tallensi that the spirits through whom a diviner makes contact with the ancestors of his clients should constitute a 'feminine' group,[1] the more so when the character of the *bakologo* complex is understood. The *bakologo*[2] is the very incarnation of the vindictive and jealous aspect of the ancestors. It persecutes the man in whose life it has intervened relentlessly, until he finally submits and 'accepts (*die*)' it—that is, until he undertakes to set up a shrine to the *bakologo* spirits in his own home so that he can sacrifice to them regularly. He then promises, also, to use the shrine for divining. But not every man has a talent for divining, so most men simply have the shrine and do not use it for divination. It is interesting to note that nine out of ten men over 40 have *bakologo* shrines. Every man, and not only those who have suffered exceptional misfortunes, is directed by the religious system of the Tallensi to project his deeper feelings of guilt and insecurity largely on to the mother image embodied in the *bakologo* complex. Usually, also, a man does not immediately yield to the demands of the *bakologo* ancestors. He temporizes, evades, and resists, perhaps for years, until he is at last forced to submit and accept the *bakologo*. This 'cools (*maa*)' or subdues the *bakologo*. By giving the spirits a home in his own house, where they can be cared for, their victim transforms their hate into love. They may still inflict misfortunes on him, but he has a means of placating them since he can sacrifice to the shrine. In return for the sacrifices they

[1] Cf. what was said on p. 235 above about the cruelty attributed to female ancestor spirits.

[2] As with all religious terms of this class among the Tallensi, *bakologo* is used both for the shrine (*bɔyar*)—the tall, conical object built of mud and smeared with the dried blood and feathers of sacrifices—and for the group of ancestors to whom the shrine is dedicated. It signifies also the whole configuration of ideas and beliefs associated with the shrine.

will henceforth bring blessings upon him, too, from time to time. And if he becomes a diviner the erstwhile persecutrix becomes his benefactress. The *bakologo* becomes a source of income instead of a standing menace.

As has been mentioned before, a divining shrine is set up for the man it has 'reached (*paa*)' by his matrilateral lineage from which the dominant ancestress of the complex came. For example, Pal-Zɔŋ's *bakologo* ancestors consisted of his father, paternal grandfather and great-grandfather, and the latter's mother, who was the dominant figure of the group. She had been a daughter of the Gbambee Tɛndaana's maximal lineage. Zɔŋ, therefore, had to go to the present head of this maximal lineage to arrange for the setting up of his *bakologo* shrine. Taking a fowl, a guinea-fowl, a basket of grain, and a pot of beer, Zɔŋ went to the Gbambee Tɛndaana to lay his request before him. The tɛndaana sacrificed the two birds to his lineage shrine (*bɔyar*) on Zɔŋ's behalf, explaining in his invocation to his ancestors the occasion that had brought their *ahɔŋ* to plead with them. He ended with the customary exhortation to the ancestors that they should bless the setting up of the new *bakologo* shrine, assist Zɔŋ to become a successful diviner, and grant him prosperity, children, and health. He finally 'scooped' (*fiŋ*) the lineage *bɔyar* for Zɔŋ. That is to say, he put a little of the sediment accumulated at the bottom of the pot, which is the most important part of the paraphernalia of a *bɔyar*, into a tiny pot for Zɔŋ to take home to add to his new *bakologo* shrine. In this way the direct continuity of the new *bakologo* shrine with the matrilateral lineage *bɔyar* is tangibly symbolized.

Next evening a party from Gbambee arrived at Zɔŋ's homestead to perform the ceremony of actually setting up the new shrine. The party consisted of the Gbambee Tɛndaana's own son, representing his father, and several other members of his maximal lineage; for though the immediate responsibility for the ceremony falls on the head of the lineage, the whole lineage is concerned in this ritual service to their *ahɔŋ*. At Zɔŋ's house they found a number of members of his inner lineage and clan as well as three *ahɔs* of Zɔŋ's inner lineage. The ceremony lasted all night. The details are not relevant here, and it need only be said that it consists of a series of ritual episodes with interludes of conviviality and hilarity. It is one of the paradoxes of the *bakologo* complex that the setting up of a divining shrine is one of the least solemn of Tale ceremonies.

The ancestors associated with Zɔŋ's *bakologo* comprised a fairly simple combination. Naabdiya's *bakologo* ancestors consisted of his mother's father, *his* mother, and *her* mother. It was the clansmen of the last who came to set up the shrine for their 'grandson' (*yaaŋ*) Naabdiya. To reach them Naabdiya had first to go to his mother's brother's people; they escorted him to his maternal grandfather's mother's brother's lineage, and thence he was escorted to his maternal grandfather's mother's mother's brother's lineage. At each place he had to sacrifice a fowl and a guinea-fowl to the lineage bɔyar. Nayabil's bakologo ancestors were his mother's father, *his* father, *his* mother, *her* mother, and *her* mother. Zɔŋ knew of the ancestress who was the dominant figure in his *bakologo*. He had been to Gbambee to attend sacrifices to the lineage bɔyar as an *ahəŋ*, both as a child, accompanying his father, and as an adult by himself. Naabdiya and Nayabil had never heard of the ancestresses who dominated their *bakologo* shrines before they revealed themselves as *bakologo* ancestresses. They had never before been to the natal clan settlements of these women; and once their divining shrines were established would probably never go there again.

One reason for this difference is spatial proximity. Zɔŋ lives about three miles from the Gbambee Tɛndaana; the matrilateral kinsmen who set up Naabdiya's shrine live about twelve miles from him, and those who set up Nayabil's shrine nearly fifteen miles from his clan settlement. But more important is the genealogical distance involved. Zɔŋ is considered to be a fairly close *ahəŋ* of the Gbambee Tɛndaana, Naabdiya and Nayabil count themselves distant 'grandsons' (*yaas*) of the matrilateral kinsmen who thus almost accidentally became socially relevant for them.[1]

Though matrilateral ancestors are particularly conspicuous in connexion with the *bakologo* complex, they can be associated with many types of ancestor shrines. Hence few men pass through life without having at least one such experience as that of Naabdiya and Nayabil. Tiezien, for instance, had a magnificent baobab tree outside the entrance to his homestead. It was a stalwart sapling when Tiezien was born and

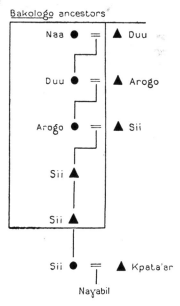

[1] Nayabil is a Kpata'ar man, and the matrilateral kinsmen who came to set up his *bakologo* were not Tallensi but Mamprusi from beyond the White Volta. This is an interesting illustration of how extra-clan kinship in this part of the Northern Territories of the Gold Coast cuts across 'tribal' and political boundaries. As the attached genealogy, showing Nayabil's genealogical connexion with his *bakologo* ancestors and ancestresses, indicates, it is also a beautiful illustration of how matrilateral kinship 'travels' (*kyɛŋ*) through intermarriage between adjacent clans. The result is that genealogical distance by matrilateral ties is closely correlated with socio-geographical distance, as in this instance.

could not have been less than 80 years old. This tree was the centre of the communal life of the neighbourhood. It was, as every native would automatically expect, also an important ancestor shrine. A few years after it sprouted Tiezien's paternal grandfather discovered through a diviner that his mother's father and *his* mother, a Pusunamoo woman, had chosen the baobab as their shrine. The Pusunamoo woman's maximal lineage consecrated it for Tiezien's grandfather. Thereafter sacrifices were regularly offered on the tree. In due course Tiezien succeeded to the custody of this shrine. Then came the influenza epidemic of 1918. Many people died at Kpata'ar, including members of Tiezien's inner lineage and wives and children of the lineage. A diviner revealed that these deaths were being inflicted by the Pusunamoo ancestress in retaliation for long neglect. She demanded that Tiezien should collect a large number of fowls from all the members of his inner lineage and take them to Pusunamoo to be sacrificed to the lineage *bɔyar* of her medial lineage as an atonement. This was Tiezien's first and last contact with his matrilateral kin at Pusunamoo up to 1936.

It is evident, from these examples, as has been previously suggested, that the majority of a man's remote matrilateral kin are not socially relevant for him. All, however, are potentially so and may become so at some time or another; and when they do enter his field of social relations it is chiefly in their ritual capacity.

We said that the most important ancestor shrines linking a man to a matrilateral lineage are *bakologo* and *bɔyar* shrines. Of the two the *bɔyar* shrine is, in fact, the more important. As we have shown in our earlier book,[1] the ancestor cult of the Tallensi culminates in the conception and cult of the *bɔyar*. This notion and the cult that expresses it form the centre of gravity of the lineage system. Hence it seems strange, at first sight, to find that every *bɔyar* must necessarily be derived from a matrilateral lineage. We can understand this, however, if we consider the significance of the *bɔyar* in the lineage system.

A *bɔyar* is the shrine consecrated to the founding ancestor of a lineage and his mother. It symbolizes the identity of that lineage and its differentiation from other lineages of the same order within a more inclusive lineage or within a clan. A lineage expands by a process of internal segmentation and differentiation that follows the lines of cleavage inherent in the structure of the joint family.[2] The component segments of a lineage are differentiated from one another primarily by reference to their descent from different 'mothers'—that is different wives of their common founding ancestor. But a woman does not sever her ties with her lineage when she marries and becomes a mother; and in kinship questions Tale thought is dominated by the lineage concept. Hence Tallensi think of a lineage progenitrix not only as such-and-such a

---
[1] Cf. *Dynamics of Clanship*, p. 137.
[2] Ibid. ch. xii.

named person but also, and chiefly, as a member of such-and-such a clan and lineage. When Tallensi discuss the internal structure of a maximal lineage what they emphasize is the clan and lineage origin of the several 'mothers' of its segments.

When a new segment begins to crystallize out in any lineage, it requires a *bɔyar* of its own to symbolize its identity. And since its genealogical distinctness comes from its progenitrix, its *bɔyar* must come from her lineage. This is simply a consequence of the fact that the notion of the *bɔyar* is a ritual conceptualization and sanction of the singularity, as well as of the unity and the continuity of the lineage. A new lineage segment can only arise, among the Tallensi, by derivation from an existing lineage. It is, one might say, a rearrangement within the existing social system, and does not represent a breach of continuity. The *bɔyar* symbolizing it is, similarly, an offshoot and replica of an existing *bɔyar*. To put this in another way, a person's status (i.e. the sum total of his rights and duties in relation to Tale society at large and to all the other members of the society) is at bottom determined by his or her descent, as we have previously shown. When he becomes an ancestor spirit his mystical attributes and powers are not absolutely autonomous arising solely from the fact that he begot sons and then died. Whatever their real psychological roots may be, in Tale religious thought these attributes and powers belong to an ancestor spirit because when he died he 'went to join his forefathers (*kyɛŋ paag u banam*)' and because he represents his whole line of ancestors in a particular situation or context. Hence every ancestor shrine either is or in course of time becomes the altar for a group of lineally related ancestors and ancestresses, never for one ancestor alone. A shrine consecrated to a particular ancestor is *ipso facto* consecrated to his agnatic descendants that come between him and the owner of the shrine. Sacrifice is offered and prayer addressed to the whole sequence of ancestors, in order of ascent; for the more remote ancestor can only be approached through the less remote. This principle is well illustrated in the examples of *bakologo* complexes quoted earlier. It applies to both patrilineal and matrilateral ancestors. Even when a man sacrifices to his own father's or mother's spirit he invokes them to 'attend with all their forefathers (*ba dɔl ni ba banam waabi*)'. Conversely, when an ancestor intervenes in his descendant's life he can only do so through the medium of those who came between him and his descendant.

It would take us too far afield to discuss all the evidence of the significance of this principle in Tale religion. One more item must suffice. According to Tale thought, an unnatural death is one that is shown by divination *not* to have been mystically caused by the ancestors. The physical cause of the death makes no difference to the issue. A person may die of old age; if none of his ancestors claim to have caused his death, this is a sign that he was not 'human (*ninvoo*)'—that is a full social being. He was a disguised bush-sprite. He is not given human burial, he does not join his forefathers, he does not become an ancestor spirit. This shows that it is not the fact of death that turns a person into an ancestor spirit but the fact that, as Tallensi believe, he is summoned (*buol*) by his ancestors and goes to join them.

Thus when a lineage progenitrix becomes an ancestor spirit, she does so as the bearer of mystical powers and attributes that reside in the collective body of her lineage ancestors, symbolized and made accessible to man in their lineage *bɔyar*. Looked at in this way, too, the *bɔyar* consecrated to her and her son must be an offshoot of her lineage *bɔyar*.[1]

In addition, there is the obvious point that a segment of a lineage cannot symbolize its distinctness by means of a *bɔyar* derived from their own lineage *bɔyar*, which is the symbol of the genealogical and social unity of the lineage, not of its internal differentiation. The lineage *bɔyar*, as is evident, is the most esoteric symbol of the principle that runs right through Tale social structure, that social differentiation within the lineage framework springs from maternal origin. This principle operates in lineage structure;[2] and we have seen how, at the other end of the scale, it constitutes the springboard of individual differentiation in the structure of the joint family.[3] This is a further instance of the consistency of Tale social structure at all levels conferred upon it by the kinship system.

A new segment of a lineage begins to crystallize out as a recognized corporate unit in the time of its founding ancestor's grandsons. For it is not until then that the process of fission in the lineage has gone far enough to separate his grandchildren and his brothers' grandchildren into distinct nuclear lineages. Thus it is a man's grandson or great-grandson who sets up a *bɔyar* consecrated to him and his mother. According to the idiom of Tale religious thought, the ancestor demands that a *bɔyar* be set up for him and his mother. A day is appointed for the ceremony, and all the descendants of the progenitrix, through both males and females, are informed. In the morning or early afternoon the head of the new segment takes a fowl, a goat or sheep, and a pot of beer to the head of his grandmother's inner lineage, or in some clans, medial lineage. The men of that lineage assemble so that all of its branches are represented and the animals are sacrificed to the lineage *bɔyar* on behalf of the *ahɔŋ*. Then the *bɔyar* is 'scooped' for him, in the same way as was described in the case of the diviner's shrine. The *ahɔŋ* goes straight

---

[1] In theory, obviously, the only lineage *bɔyar* that need not be derived from another *bɔyar* is the *bɔyar* of a maximal lineage. Actually most maximal lineage *bɔya* conform to the pattern we have described. The only truly sovereign *bɔya*—i.e. *bɔya* not derived from other *bɔya*—are the External *Bɔya* of the Talis and their congeners. And it is significant that the component maximal lineages of these clans generally have two *bɔya*, one the domestic representative of the External *Bɔyar*, the other a distinctive *bɔyar* derived from their founder's mother's lineage. Cf. *Dynamics of Clanship*, ch. vii.

[2] Ibid., ch. xii.

[3] *Supra*, Ch. III.

home, where in the meantime the other members, both men and women, of the new segment and the 'sisters' sons' and 'grandsons' of the segment who have been able to come have gathered. The head of the new segment arrives, followed, as the Tallensi think, by the spirits of his grandmother's ancestors. He now performs the sacrifices by which the new *bɔyar* is consecrated. He himself offers a sheep. All the other male members of the new segment bring a fowl each to be sacrificed on their behalf and *ahəs* and *yaas* all do so too. A large pot or earthenware dish, inside which the small pot containing the sediment 'scooped' from the grandmother's lineage *bɔyar* pot is placed, forms the altar. Henceforth this will be the *bɔyar* of the new lineage segment; and there will be a similar communion rite embracing all the descendants of the founding ancestor and his mother whenever the *bɔyar* is inherited by a new lineage head.[1]

We have now considered the most important ritual services matrilateral kin render to their sororal kin. The ritual services rendered by sororal kin to matrilateral kin are, as might be expected, of far less consequence. In funeral ceremonies, for example, there are a number of rites in which it is necessary to have the participation of an *ahəŋ* of the deceased. The rite of cooking 'the porridge of sisters-in-law (*pɔyakiis sayabo*)', which has been previously mentioned, is typical of these rites; and it is typical of them, also, that anybody who can, by any stretch of the term, be described as *ahəŋ* can serve in them. All these rites express the fact that a person's death is of concern to his or her sororal kin as well as to his or her patrilineal kin, and affects the field of social relations of the former as well as that of the latter. Hence in all funeral rites a special portion of the meat, cooked food, and beer used is allocated to the 'sisters' children', whether few or many are present. Matrilateral and sororal kin do not, however, undergo mourning rites.

Apart from funerals, there are one or two other special ceremonies in which the services of an *ahəŋ* are needed. Thus in the ceremony of exorcising an evil Predestiny (*Yinbe'er*) an *ahəŋ* is required to perform the final act of sympathetic magic. This consists in collecting the magical paraphernalia used in the ceremony—all of which symbolize the wish that the evil Predestiny may depart and conceal itself for ever—and throwing them away in some barren spot. A 'sister's son' is called upon

---

[1] There is a point of religious doctrine that cannot be fully discussed here but must be mentioned to avoid confusion. Every important ancestor shrine is a means of making a whole line of ancestors accessible to its possessor. Now the collective mystical power of a patrilineal line of ancestors reposes in the lineage *bɔyar*. Hence every important shrine has to be linked up with the lineage *bɔyar* of the dominant spirit to which it is consecrated. That is why when a *bakologo* is set up, the *bɔyar* of the matrilateral lineage from which it is derived is 'scooped' for inclusion in the new shrine. Broadly speaking, the ritual validity of every ancestor shrine goes back to a *bɔyar*. But the setting up of a new lineage *bɔyar* is a very special ritual landmark.

to do this service because, as a kinsman of the sufferer, he naturally wishes to see him free of his evil fate. He is held to desire this the more strongly because his *ahəb* sacrifices on his behalf. Hence his welfare depends on the continued life and the perpetuation of the lineage of the *ahəb*, both of which are threatened by the evil Predestiny. Lastly, he is specially suitable because a complete stranger might use the opportunity to do the sufferer magical harm, while a patrilineal kinsman of his might be contaminated by the evil Predestiny. Again, anybody who can be identified as an *ahəŋ*, in however remote a classificatory sense, may be asked to perform this service.

The Father's Sister

We have left the discussion of the relationship of father's sister (*ba-pɔk*) and brother's child (*bii*) for this chapter, although it is not a relationship of extra-clan kinship. Father's sister and brother's child are members of the same clan and lineage. But Tallensi associate the father's sister with relatives outside the clan. This is due to her marrying out of the clan, to her having no significant public voice in the affairs of the lineage, and to her being unable to inherit lineage property or ancestor shrines.[1] Thus a native usually compares his relationship with his father's sister to his relationship with his mother's brother, not to his relationship with his parents. It is thought of more as the opposite of the relationship between sister's son and mother's brother than as an item in the scheme of intra-familial or intra-lineage relationships.

As in the case of mother's brother and sister's child, the bond between father's sister and brother's child tends to be more effective for brother's sons than for brother's daughters. In the case of the brother's sons it is reinforced by the ties a woman has with her paternal lineage and by the ties her children have with their mother's brother and his sons. In the case of brother's daughters, it is attenuated because the daughters tend to be dispersed by marriage and their relationship with their father's sister is much more a purely personal affair.

Compared with the mother's brother, the father's sister (*ba-pɔk*) counts for little in the web of extra-clan kinship. Tallensi say this is because she is a woman. 'It is not she who sacrifices for you but you (her brother's son) may one day sacrifice on her behalf.' At the same time they declare that 'she is your father'. I have several times had an old woman introduced to me by a man or a woman as 'my father'. Eŋwala, explaining her affection for her full brother's son, Anaaho, said in the stock phraseology, 'Is he not my child? If you and your brother together have a child, is he not also your child [as much as your brother's]?

[1] Except, as has been mentioned before if she is the last surviving member of the lineage. Even then she does not inherit the ancestor shrines but merely sacrifices to them, as if she were acting on behalf of her deceased father. She can never inherit lineage land.

(*Pa m-biiga? Nyɛn ni i tau n-kab dɔya bii, pa nyɛnmi biig n-a u?*)'. As will be remembered, men quote the same maxim when they are asked why mother's brother and sister's son are generally so attached to each other. In support of this Tallensi usually quote two customs. Firstly, when an old woman dies, the oldest of her brothers' sons has his head shaved in mourning, as if for his father. He represents all his siblings, Tallensi say, in this act of filial respect. Secondly, a *ba-pɔk* has the power of pronouncing a curse against a child of her brother. She can, conversely, withdraw a curse pronounced by her brother if he dies without having done so, and if he has no surviving brother of the same nuclear lineage. But the social equivalence of a woman with her brother in relation to his children is limited by her sex. She is barred from exercising the jural and ritual authority and the rights of a father. In fact, the tendency is for her to look up to her brother's son as the future heir of her brother and the potential repository of authority in the affairs of her lineage.

Two examples will suffice to show how limited in fact are the jural rights a woman has in relation to her brother's children. They have principally a token value. When a funeral is being celebrated by a woman's husband's nuclear lineage her close lineage kin send a party of mourners to bear their condolences to the lineage of their lineage-in-laws. The party includes a number of young girls whom the woman calls her sisters and daughters. Before they leave again for home these young girls are gathered together and surrounded by a crowd of young men of the host clan. Amid laughter and good-humoured teasing the girls are invited to choose a 'future husband' each from among the young men. It is all a game, part of the hospitality accorded to the visitors. The selected 'husband' has to give a parting gift to the girl who has chosen him, so that she shall go home pleased with her visit. Among these girls might be a daughter of one of the woman's brothers of the same nuclear lineage. If the woman is particularly interested in the young man this girl selects, she may declare publicly that she is giving him the girl as his wife. Everybody pretends to accept this declaration as if it came from the girl's father, but in fact everybody knows that it has only a token significance and no jural force whatever.

Again, if a woman deserts a husband to whom she has been given by her father without having previously arranged to go to another man, she very often takes refuge with a *ba-pɔk*. There she is, so to speak, under a parent's protection but not subject to her father's authority. She knows that her *ba-pɔk* will sympathize with her and cannot in any case force her to return to the man she has left. Her father, satisfied that she is in parental care, will not seek to put pressure on her, at least for some time. However, a girl in this position soon attracts suitors, though courtship has to be clandestine, for she is still formally the wife of another man. But sometimes a suitor succeeds in ingratiating himself with the *ba-pɔk* and persuades her to connive at an elopement, a thing which a father would never do. In theory, this means that the *ba-pɔk* consents to the new marriage. In practice, her action has no binding force on her brother. This rule applies also to an unmarried girl who is given in marriage by her *ba-pɔk*. A woman might have one of her brother's daughters living with her as a nursemaid for her baby. She might promise the girl as a wife to one of her husband's brothers. But her brother need not consider himself bound by this promise if he has objections to the marriage.

A father's sister is, in short, a kind of female 'father', but without the jural and ritual attributes of fatherhood. A father's sister must be treated with respect. It would be grossly improper, for example, to joke with her as one jokes with a wife's sister; and to strike or abuse her, even if she were much younger than oneself, would be a sin. But the respect accorded to her is only a pale reflection of the attitude implicit in filial piety. It is much more a matter of etiquette than of emotion, as if it were merely conventional and not evoked by a feeling of moral obligation.

A marked characteristic of a person's relations with his or her father's sister is the absence of specific mutual obligations. Just as a *ba-pɔk* has in reality no rights over her brother's children, so she has no specific duties of either a ritual or a secular kind towards them, or they to her. This is the chief contrast between this relationship and that of parent and child or that of mother's brother and sister's child. Only a shadow of a ritual sanction comes into the relationship, in the form of the belief that the curse of a *ba-pɔk* can harm her brother's child, and in the notion that she stands under the protection of the same ancestors as the latter. Hence, though she cannot demand services from her brother's child, it is felt that a request for help from her should be met, even at the cost of some inconvenience. If a person offends his father's sister and she reproaches him saying, 'I bore you (identifying herself with her brother) and this is how you treat me. My ancestors have seen it, my fathers have seen it (*Man dɔyi la k-i ɛŋɔm la ŋwala; n-yaanam nyeya, m-banam nyeya*)', this has the force of a curse because she is invoking her ancestors who are also his ancestors. Such a curse would disturb a native. but not nearly so deeply as a father's curse or if a mother's brother refused to sacrifice on his behalf.

Because their relationship is devoid of a definite jural coefficient and is not subject to organized ritual sanctions; because, also, a father's sister stands outside the scheme of economic and domestic associations in which the relationship of parent and child is set, the relations of father's sister and brother's child are free of the undercurrent of tension found in those of father and child. A woman's bonds with her brother's children are fundamentally bonds of sentiment. That is why they seldom endure beyond one generation, or extend beyond the nuclear lineage.

The personal relations of father's sister and brother's child have much in common with those of mother's brother and sister's child. They are similarly influenced by the closeness of the sibling tie between the brother and the sister, as is to be expected. There is this difference, however, that the contacts between *ba-pɔk* and brother's child are chiefly maintained by the *ba-pɔk*'s visits to her parental home, and not by the brother's child's being taken, or going on visits to her. They are largely a by-product of the woman's contacts with her parental home, and they diminish as she grows older. A man has no occasion to visit his *ba-pɔk* regularly, and a woman is apt to do so only if she lives near her. Opportunity and disposition count for more than in the personal relations of true mother's brother and sister's child. Thus a *ba-pɔk* sometimes has a brother's child to live with her, but this is rarer than for children to stay with an *ahəb*, and there is usually a utilitarian motive on the side of the *ba-pɔk*. Ɔmara's sister had their late brother's two sons staying with her for two or three years each, in succession. She had them to stay with her so that they could look after her son's horse, and they went home again as soon as they were big enough to farm. If a girl stays with a *ba-pɔk* it is almost always as a nursemaid to her baby. A boy does not go to live with a *ba-pɔk* and grow up in her household, as he might with an *ahəb*. There is an obvious reason for all this. A *ba-pɔk* does not 'own' her household as an *ahəb* does. She cannot have her brother's child living with her except with her husband's consent; and though he would, out of consideration for her, not withhold his consent, he might demur against the burden of supporting another man's child, who is no kin of his, for a long time. A woman cannot give her brother's son a place in the household economy as an *ahəb* can to his sister's son.

With these limitations, the personal relations of father's sister and brother's child are often extremely cordial. Anaaho was a constant visitor to his father's sister's house when he was working near where she lived. He often went there for meals and sought her advice about his affairs. Da'amo'o was welcomed with open arms by his *ba-pɔk* when he travelled with me to her husband's clan settlement. She gave him some presents for his wife who had just had a baby and got permission from her husband for him to take away a large log of a tree that had fallen down near their homestead. A *ba-pɔk* shows her interest in her brother's children by giving or sending them gifts. A person visiting his or her *ba-pɔk* seldom leaves without some such token of her interest and affection. It may be a chicken or a few pence for a nephew, or a basket of shea nuts, a dish of dried vegetables, or a new back-flap to wear at the next festival dance for a niece. The death of her brother's child, especially of a young adult son or daughter, is often a great shock to a *ba-pɔk*. A *ba-pɔk*'s death, on the other hand, seldom grieves her brother's children as much as the death of a favourite *ahəb*, and they have no formal obligations to attend the funeral with prescribed gifts, or to undergo mourning rites other than the head-shaving of the eldest son.

Our discussion has been concerned with the relationship of a person to his or her own father's sister, and we have noted that the bonds of sentiment between father's sister and brother's child seldom extend beyond the nuclear lineage of the latter. A person recognizes the sister of any man in the inner lineage or medial lineage whom he calls 'father' as his *ba-pɔk*. But whereas a woman has a strong personal interest in and often affection for her full or half-brother's children, and generally also takes a personal interest in her father's brothers' sons' children, the tendency is for the relationship to become more formal beyond that range. This is largely due to the fact that contacts between a woman and the children of her distant brothers of the same inner or medial lineage are usually rare, as compared with her contacts with children of her own nuclear lineage. But the appropriate norms of behaviour hold to the limits of the range of recognized generation differences and may be evoked in suitable circumstances. Beyond the range of the inner, or at most medial lineage, a woman of a person's father's generation is not recognized as a *ba-pɔk*, but is described as a 'sister' (*tau*) and thus classed with all the non-specifically related clanswomen.

A woman calls her brothers' children's children her grandchildren (*yaas*), and she may be very fond of them, if she has opportunities of seeing them often. Gɛlima, a childless old widow who had come to live out the last few years of her life at her oldest brother's house, was often teased good-humouredly by her brothers and brothers' sons because of her attachment to the latter's small children. In theory the joking relationship holds for grandchild and grandfather's sister. In practice it is modified by the tendency to class together father's sisters and agnatic grandfather's sisters, who are usually described by the term *ba-pɔk* or its equivalent *pugərəba*. A person identifies himself (or herself) with his father in relation to the latter's father's sister, not only on account of the dominance of the lineage principle, but also, and mainly, because he does so in relation to the woman's husband and children. He thinks of the woman's husband as an 'in-law (*deema*)' and of her children as *ahəs*. And this is facilitated by residential separation and the identification of an old woman with the affairs and interests of her husband's lineage and clan. Thus cases like that of Gɛlima are the exception. The majority of old women see so little of their brothers' grandchildren that their relationship with them is purely formal and perfunctory.

CHAPTER XII
THE FUNCTIONS OF KINSHIP

OUR study has made it clear that the recognition of genealogical relationships in the ordering of social life has an extremely wide range of application among the Tallensi. To be sure, some classes of social relations in which individuals or organized groups normally participate do not necessarily imply cognizance of genealogical connexions. There are the activities of buyers and sellers in the market-place, for example. These are transactions in which kinship may, but for the most part does not, play a critical part. If it comes into the picture it does so as an adventitious factor, not as an intrinsic constitutive element. Even between kinsfolk transactions in the market are ruled by considerations of price, costs, profits, supply, and demand. A man who goes to market to buy a cap will not patronize a kinsman who has caps for sale if he can get one cheaper from a stranger. But it may happen that a seller of caps will be satisfied with a slightly smaller margin of profit if the buyer is his kinsman than if he is a stranger.

Apart from such ephemeral inter-personal relations, there are lasting social ties, such as those of friendship (*zoot*), which do not necessarily presuppose genealogical connexions. It is a common thing for Tallensi, especially for men, to have friends (*zɔ*, pl. *zɔnam*) in other clans than their own, and nowadays in neighbouring tribes. Friends visit one another occasionally, help one another sometimes, and give one another gifts. A man may also have a woman friend (*sɔm*), usually the wife of one of his clansmen. The man takes small gifts to his *sɔm* from time to time and she reciprocates by cooking a meal for him. She may assist him to find a wife from among her clan sisters. But if friends are not necessarily kinsmen, they very often have common kin. In fact friendships between unrelated Tallensi are most often formed through one of the parties visiting a kinsman of the other party and so making his acquaintance. Many friendships arise from contacts at funeral ceremonies or when hoeing or building parties come to help a father- or brother-in-law. In any case, the commonest and most prized form of friendship is friendship with a clansman or a neighbour of a related clan. Many such friendships go back to childhood and are the more highly prized because they are voluntary, personal, and not subject to hard-and-fast rules.

In the same way, though the Tallensi do not have institutionalized age-grades, men or women of about the same degree of social maturity are often grouped together in situations in which many people of all ages play a part. One sees this very clearly on ceremonial occasions. At funeral ceremonies, for example, there is first of all the usual separation of the spheres of the two sexes. The sphere of the women is within the homestead. There they stay most of the time and there they carry out the duties that fall to them. The sphere of the men is outside, in front of the gateway, in the cattle yard and the zɔŋ (cf. p. 53). All the public rites take place outside. But in addition there is a distribution of tasks, duties, and privileges in accordance with a broad stratification by seniority. The oldest people in both spheres are spoken of as the elders (*kpɛm*). They have the seats of honour. For the most part they merely advise, and if hitches arise exercise a somewhat distant supervision over the activities. If they take an active part it is only in the most important of the rites. But they have the highest privileges. When food or meat or beer is distributed it is the elders who receive the portions due to the lineage units they represent and take the largest share of these portions. It is the old women, too, who take the lion's share of the gifts and obligatory contributions of foodstuffs handed over to the womenfolk. The burden of managing the ceremonies, performing the complicated series of rites, and attending to the many practical tasks involved, such as digging the grave, slaughtering sacrificial animals, and preparing food and beer, falls on the men who 'come after the elders (*kpɛm tayalis*)' and their female counterparts. The *kpɛm tayalis* are the men of mature experience but still able-bodied, men in the late forties and early fifties, the corresponding stratum among the women being those who have adolescent children. The young men and women, assisted by the adolescent boys and girls, do the fetching and carrying and give any casual help that may be required. The boys have the privilege of plucking and roasting any fowls that are slaughtered and keep some of the titbits for themselves. The girls surfeit themselves with frequent tasting of porridge and oily bean stew while they are cooking. This pattern can be observed in any collective activity.

Such arrangements, informal products though they are of the pragmatic requirements of the situation, are so stereotyped that they can be called customary. They arise without reference to genealogical connexions. But it is characteristic of Tale social life that they do so in situations whose structure is determined by kinship and clanship institutions. In fact the ideology of kinship is so dominant in Tale society, and the web of genealogical connexions so extensive, that no social relationships or events fall completely outside the orbit of kinship. In this respect the Tallensi resemble very many other primitive societies among whom, as Firth puts it,[1] kinship is the articulating principle of social organization. Just because kinship acts as a major determinant of social behaviour in every aspect and department of social life, it is the basis of the machinery of social integration in societies of this type, as many studies in Africa, Oceania, and America have shown. The result, as we have seen, both in this book and in the first part of our study, is that

[1] Raymond Firth, *We, the Tikopia*, 1936, p. 577.

the concept of kinship is the primary category of Tale thought about the social relations of individuals and the structure of the society.

Firth has stated (op. cit., p. 575) that kinship institutions can be studied from many different angles. But clearly, all kinship institutions have only two major facets or, if we like, functions. They serve as a mechanism of organizing social activities and co-ordinating social relations, either in a limited sector of the social life or in relation to all social interests; and they at the same time constitute the primary mould of the individual's psycho-social development. To assert, as Malinowski virtually does,[1] that the latter aspect gives the master-key to the understanding of primitive kinship institutions is as one-sided as to deny its relevance for their sociological study altogether. Much futile controversy has turned on a confusion of these two aspects of social relations. It is true that the affective relations of parents and children during the latters' infancy, the sentiments, habits, and emotional attachments acquired in the setting of the domestic family in childhood, and the deeper-lying factors of personality, all colour the behaviour of kinsfolk of every degree to one another. But it is equally true that the socially effective ties of kinship and the values correlated with them, which exist as a part of the social system at a given time irrespective of the individual, have a powerful selective influence in the shaping of his psychological environment and, consequently, on his eventual personality. We are concerned with two distinct levels of organization and expression in the structure of human social behaviour, and neither can be reduced to the other.

A complete understanding of the significance of its institutions for a particular society calls for an investigation on both levels. That is not what we have attempted in this book. Our study has been focused on the function of kinship as the articulating principle of Tale social structure. We have taken into account the genetic development in the individual of the modal patterns of thought, action, sentiment, and emotion which emerge in kinship relations, only in so far as this development is a dynamic factor in the social structure or can be directly correlated with the operation of kinship in standard and recurrent social relations. We have, for example, given little space to the genetic development of speech habits in the child, though this is relevant for the understanding of how kinship terminology is learnt, because this would shed little light on our main inquiry.

Among the Tallensi kinship relations are a major determinant of the pattern of organization of all activities through which the ruling interests of the people are satisfied. This holds for all departments of Tale social life—for the activities concerned with the production and consumption of food and all other material goods, for those involved in the reproduction and rearing of offspring, for those concerned with maintaining the rights and duties of individuals and corporate units towards one another,

[1] See his article s.v. 'Kinship', *Encyclopaedia Britannica*, 14th ed.

and for religious and ceremonial activities. By abstracting the constant features in the patterns of organization of all the activities in which a particular kinship relation is significant, we arrive at a formulation of that relation as an element of the social structure. Tale kinship relations are embedded in social activities, but they are not coterminous with any one category of social activities. They are not reducible to economic relations either in their technological or in their social aspects; nor can they be derived exclusively from Tale jural concepts, or ritual beliefs, or political institutions. They are expressed and maintained by all these elements of the social system, but they exist in their own right. And the evidence of comparative studies, which show that similar kinship systems are found in different economic, jural, and ritual contexts bears this out. It is as plausible to argue that kinship ideas lie behind the economic or jural or religious customs of the natives as the other way round. Nor can the Tale kinship system be accounted for on the grounds of utility. Kinship relations are useful to the individual and serve the ends of social well-being for the society as a whole. But they are also very often extremely onerous for the individual; and their social utility springs simply from the fact that they play a vital part in the organization of all the activities that make up and maintain the social system.

Kinship, in short, among the Tallensi as among many other primitive peoples, is one of the irreducible principles on which their organized social life depends. Another irreducible factor in their social life is their traditional economy; and a third is their system of ritual beliefs and values. In the Tale social system these three categories of social facts are so closely interdependent that they cannot be satisfactorily understood in isolation from one another. They appear as functions of one another in the structure of society. But kinship taken as a system of values, a body of rules of conduct, and a scheme of social relations, is unique in that it is the master principle of organization both for particular activities and for the social structure as a whole. Thus we find that there cannot, for example, be gross divergence between the rules governing the ownership and use of land or other productive property, and those governing the application of labour to production or the consumption of the products of labour, since both sets of rules are aspects of the jural relations of a specific group of kinsfolk by birth and marriage. Similarly, the religious beliefs of the natives cannot be grossly inconsistent with their actual social behaviour since they have a common context of social organization in relationships determined by kinship. The wrongdoings or aberrations of individuals do not alter this fact; sooner or later the norms are vindicated and their consistency *inter se* is reaffirmed.

We have been speaking of kinship in the broadest sense of all socially recognized genealogical ties. In this sense Tale social structure is, fundamentally, kinship writ large. But we have found that it is essential to distinguish two aspects of kinship relations, that of lineage organization and that of inter-personal kinship ties. We have particularly stressed the major distinction between these two aspects. The lineage system is built up exclusively on the recognition of the agnatic line of descent and provides the framework of corporate groupings upon which Tale political and jural institutions are founded, whereas inter-personal kinship ties are recognized between cognates of all degrees through either or both parents. These two aspects fuse in what we have called the focal field of kinship, the domestic family. All kinship ties, for the individual, are created in the domestic family; and the family is the mechanism by which the genealogical basis of the social system is continually renewed.

Tale society is an organic society. That is to say, social organization is governed by the same principles at all levels and in every sector of the social structure. The different configurations of social relationships characteristic of different sectors of the social structure are the result of different ways of combining and elaborating the basic principles. The focal field of kinship shows us the basic principles of social structure at work in their simplest and prototypical form.

The structure of this field is determined by the interaction of two categories of social ties, those of parentage and those of marriage. Their interaction gives rise to two concepts of descent that operate as polar principles in the structure of this field.[1] The concept of paternal origin is counterpoised by the concept of maternal origin in every aspect of family life. The structural equilibrium of the domestic organization depends on their complementary functions. At the level of corporate social relations we find a similar structural equilibrium in the lineage system and also in the politico-ritual system that embraces the whole society.[2] At every level the structural equilibrium depends on the mechanism of polarity. It is the play of polar social forces organized round institutions like the chiefship and the tendaanaship, conceptualized in the ancestor cult and the Earth cult, and crystallized in the segmentary structure of the lineage, that gives the equilibrium of Tale society its dynamic character.

The polarity of patrilateral and matrilateral kinship regulates the development of kinship relations in time, as well as their configuration at a given time. If we consider the polarity of patrilateral and matrilateral descent as it works over a stretch of time—e.g. in relation to the cycle of development of the domestic family—a significant generalization emerges. We see, then, that the patrilineal principle is the primary factor of stability and continuity in the organization of the family and

---

[1] Malinowski brought this out in his writings on kinship theory (e.g. in his essay on *The Father in Primitive Psychology*, Psyche Miniatures, 1926) though he stated it in different terms.
[2] This is described in the *Dynamics of Clanship*.

hence of the entire social structure. Conversely, the recognition of kinship ties through the mother is the primary factor of dispersion and segmentation in the family and the social structure. The values symbolized in the concept of patrilineal descent constitute the chief centripetal force, those summed up in the concept of matrilateral kinship the chief centrifugal force in the structure both of the family and of the society at large.

If we visualize the social structure as a sum of processes in time, then the lineage system, which embodies the patrilineal principle, emerges as the source of the enduring pattern, the relatively fixed form of Tale social organization, and matrilateral kinship is seen to be the source of the variability and flexibility in the groups or in the standard interpersonal relations that make up the social structure. The lineage system unites the ancestors, the living, and the yet unborn in a uniform integrated sequence actualized at a given time in determinate corporate groups.[1] The emphasis of matrilateral kinship is on the peculiar social ties of individuals with individuals, living or dead; and every generation brings a shift in the web of matrilateral kinship bonds for the members of a particular lineage. Thus it is the polarity of these two basic concepts of kinship that brings about the striking balance between stability and continuity on the one hand, and segmentary differentiation with its tendencies towards the splitting up and dispersion of social units on the other.

We have spoken of the lineage *system* and the kinship *system* of the Tallensi. The hypothesis that the various features of any particular people's kinship institutions have a 'complex relation of interdependence' and constitute 'an organized whole' has been specially stressed by Radcliffe-Brown.[2] Our study has brought forward ample evidence in support of this hypothesis, as far as the Tallensi are concerned. What it means for the practical life of the individual is that there are no irreconcilable contradictions between the different institutions in which any one category of kinship bonds is effective, and no insoluble conflicts of loyalties arising out of incompatible rights, obligations, or sentiments, based on kinship ties.

This is partly a question of the kind of kinship ties recognized for particular social purposes and partly of the accepted order of differentiation (both as to quality and as to degree) among these ties. We have seen, for example, how the Tale notion of incest is related to the segmentation of the lineage, and how a sister's son never acquires true filial rights in his mother's brother's lineage.

[1] This has frequently been stressed by Radcliffe-Brown in (unpublished) lectures. See also his papers, 'The Study of Kinship Systems', *J.R.A.I.*, vol. lxxi, 1941, and 'Religion and Society' (Henry Myers Lecture, 1945), ibid., vol. lxxiii, 1943.

[2] Cf., for example, his previously cited paper, *J.R.A.I.*, vol. lxxi, 1941, from which the above quotations are taken.

The pivot of the system is the dominance of the patrilineal line in Tale thought and custom. We thus get a systematic interdependence of all recognized kinship ties, with the bond between father and son as the focal point.

The interrelation of all Tale kinship institutions in a coherent system is shown in another way. Our study has shown that the lineage is the basis of a widespread and close-knit network of clanship and politico-ritual ties that embraces the whole socio-geographic region we have called Taleland[1] and even spreads over the frontiers of the region. There is nothing fortuitous about this system of social and political relationships. It is precisely organized in accordance with what we have called the field principle. In the same way we have found that the extra-clan kinship ties of a given Tale community form a close-knit web the pattern of which follows the field principle. In any defined sector of the society the network of clanship and politico-ritual ties is congruent with the web of extra-clan kinship ties. The two systems reinforce each other as unifying media in the social structure, on the level of corporate group organization, and on the level of inter-personal ties of amity, respectively. Simultaneously, they also counterbalance each other in the total flow of social life and so strengthen the general social equilibrium.

Taking Tale social structure as a whole, it can be visualized as a complex structure of different categories of social relations, correlated to different kinds of social and individual interests, rights, duties, sentiments, and values. The lineage system primarily serves jural, ritual, and political interests. The rights and duties of individuals appear as elements of corporate rights and duties. The solidarity of the unit is stressed at the expense of the individual's private interests and loyalties. The submergence of the individual's interests in those of the corporate unit is even more noticeable in the clan organization. Corporate rights, duties, and interests, however, serve not only to unite maximal lineages but also to differentiate them sharply. The cleavages between corporate units loom as large as their ties. At a higher level of the system the network of ritual collaboration and interdependence between corporate units serves as the most powerful control on the autarchic tendencies of the lineage and the resulting danger of the cleavages between lineages becoming too strong for the common good. The politico-ritual system takes care of the common good of the whole society. The interests of the individual are entirely subordinate to those of the community.

Ties of cognatic kinship, both within and across lineage boundaries, form the lowest level of social relations in the hierarchy. They differ from the social relations that exist between corporate groups in one important respect. They are ties of amity and mutual interest between individuals. Private rights and duties and personal loyalties prevail as against corporate rights, duties, and interests. Ties of cognatic kinship

[1] Cf. *Dynamics of Clanship*, ch. xiii.

breach the barriers between individuals erected by the lineage system. They represent the recognition by the society that the direct social bonds of individual with individual are as vital for the well-being of the society as the fixed framework of corporate groupings. The intricate, ever-changing web of inter-personal kinship creates a diffused sense of mutual interest and dependence among the people of neighbouring communities. This sense of the interdependence of men as individuals in the hard struggle of ordinary living, thus canalized by kinship, not only transcends the more rigid solidarities of family, lineage, and local clan, but also counteracts the frictions and disturbances that constantly spring up in the relations of individuals with one another. Inter-personal kinship ties thus act both as a diffuse force of social cohesion in opposition to the sectional bias of the lineage structure, and as a moral sanction of conformity to custom. The concept of kinship amity as a basic premiss of the relations of kinsfolk of every degree reflects this aspect of kinship.

Consideration of the significance of kinship for the individual brings up the most difficult problem in the study of primitive kinship systems. In psychological terms kinship for the individual means a system of habits, sentiments, and affective ties gradually acquired in childhood. In sociological terms it means a system of rights and obligations, privileges, and duties of various degrees of definiteness, in relation to other people, a code of conduct also varying in precision from item to item and geared to a body of moral values and religious beliefs, and embracing all this, in a sense, a concept of the person himself as occupying a definite status and position in society.

What lies behind all this? What makes kinship an irreducible principle of Tale social organization? The economic and cultural homogeneity of the Tallensi to which we have frequently referred does not account for this quality of their kinship institutions. It is true that their society exists on one plane, so to speak—that is to say it exists solely in the living contemporaneity of their social life; for as we have shown in the first part of this study the Tallensi have no conscious historical perspective stretching beyond living memory. In such a society only those principles of social organization can remain valid which require no historical foundations or sanctions but are carried in the day-to-day life of the people. Again, the exiguous range of material goods, productive skills, means of communication, and empirical knowledge, all serve to keep the social division of labour down to a minimum and the range of social relations within correspondingly narrow limits. This, too, puts a premium on principles of social organization that can be maintained in action by direct inter-personal relationships. These factors undoubtedly form essential prerequisites for the existence of an all-embracing scheme of genealogical relationships as the articulating principle of social organization. But comparative research shows that they do not wholly account for the irreducible character of the norms of social organization based on the recognition of kinship, in any human society. We know from comparative studies that kinship bears a similar stress (though its scope is often more limited) in the social organization of peoples with far more highly differentiated social systems than that of the Tallensi.[1]

The usual solution to this question, explicitly stated by Malinowski, Firth, and others,[2] and implicit in the descriptive work of most social scientists who write on kinship, puts the emphasis on the facts of sex, procreation, and the rearing of offspring. There is obvious truth in this view. But like all attempts to explain one order of organic events by invoking a simpler order of events necessarily involved in the first, it borders on over-simplification. It is like trying to explain human thinking by the anatomy of the brain, or modern capitalist economy by the need for food and shelter. Such explanations, which indicate the necessary pre-conditions of phenomena, are apt to short-circuit the real work of science, which is the elucidation of the sufficient causal or functional determinants involved in the observed data of behaviour. They are particularly specious in social science. It is easy and tempting to jump from one level of organization to another in the continuum of body, mind, and society when analysis at one level seems to lead no farther. As regards primitive kinship institutions, the facts of sex, procreation, and the rearing of offspring constitute only the universal raw material of kinship systems. Our study has shown that economic techniques and religious values have as close a connexion with the Tale lineage system, for example, as the reproductive needs of the society. Indeed, comparative and historical research leaves no doubt that radical changes in the economic organization or the religious values of a society like that of the Tallensi might rapidly undermine the lineage structure; but some form of family organization will persist and take care of the

[1] Including, of course, our own social system. As is well known to students of Roman Law, the Romans had a kinship system comparable in many respects with those found amongst primitive peoples to-day (cf. Sir Henry Maine, *Ancient Law*). Similar kinship systems were found among the tribes of central and northern Europe in antiquity. The patrilineal joint family system, in fact, survived in parts of eastern Europe until the latter half of the nineteenth century (cf. Vinogradoff, op. cit., vol. i). A lineage system having many analogies to that of the Tallensi is found amongst Arab villages of to-day (cf. Hilma Granqvist, *Marriage Conditions in a Palestinian Village*, Societas Scientiarum Fennica, Helsingfors, 1931), among the Chinese (cf. Hsiao-Tung Fei, *Peasant Life in China*), and amongst the Hindu (cf. H. S. Gour, *The Hindu Code*, ch. viii).

[2] Cf. Malinowski's article in the *Encyclopaedia Britannica, cit. supra*, and Firth, op. cit., p. 577. Historically this view owes much to Westermarck's *History of Human Marriage*, and has been strongly reinforced in recent years by psychological theory as expressed, for example, in J. C. Flugel's book, *The Psychoanalytic Study of the Family*. It is the current view amongst most sociologists. (Cf. for a clear and succinct recent statement of it, R. MacIver, *Society*, ch. xi.

reproductive needs of the society. The postulate we have cited overlooks the fact that kinship covers a greater field of social relations than the family.

The problem we have raised cannot be solved in the context of an analytical study of one society; it requires a great deal of comparative research. We can, however, justifiably suggest an hypothesis on the basis of our limited inquiry. One of the striking things about Tale kinship institutions is the socially acknowledged sanctions behind them. When we ask why the natives so seldom, on the whole, transgress the norms of conduct attached to kinship ties, we inevitably come back either to the ancestor cult or to moral axioms regarded as self-evident by the Tallensi. To study Tale kinship institutions apart from the religious and moral ideas and values of the natives would be as one-sided as to leave out the facts of sex and procreation. On the other hand, our analysis has shown that it is equally impossible to understand Tale religious beliefs and moral norms apart from the context of kinship. A very close functional interdependence exists between these two categories of social facts. The relevant connecting link, for our present problem, is the axiom, implicit in all Tale kinship institutions, that kinship relations are essentially moral relations, binding in their own right. Every social system presupposes such basic moral axioms. They are implicit in the categories of values and of behaviour which we sum up in concepts such as rights, duties, justice, amity, respect, wrong, sin. Such concepts occur in every known human society, though the kind of behaviour and the content of the values covered by them vary enormously. Modern research in psychology and sociology makes it clear that these axioms are rooted in the direct experience of the inevitability of interdependence between men in society. Utter moral isolation for the individual is not only the negation of society but the negation of humanity itself.[1] Our suggestion is that the essence of a highly elaborated kinship system like that of the Tallensi lies in its function as the primary mechanism through which the basic moral axioms of a society of the type represented by the Tallensi are translated into the concrete give and take of social life. This is perhaps more obvious if we remember that the experience of the inevitability of human interdependence is implanted in the individual in the initial situation of kinship (as Malinowski called it), the dependence of the child on its parents. The focal field of kinship is also the focal field of moral experience; and the psychological and social factors that generate it are symbolically projected in religious beliefs. The hypothesis that all kinship institutions derive from the facts of sex, procreation, and child-rearing is acceptable if the emphasis is laid not on their biological or

---

[1] Vide Fromm, E., *The Fear of Freedom*, London, 1941, for a recent exposition, on the basis of modern psychological and sociological findings, of this ancient thesis of moral philosophers.

utilitarian value but on the moral values attached by society to these facts, and perpetuated through the social relationships brought into being by their conjunction.

This inference is strengthened when we consider the evidence of comparative studies. Patrilineal societies, for example, are found in many parts of the world, including our own culture area. Lineage systems similar to that of the Tallensi occur in a large number of patrilineal societies in Africa, Asia Minor, and the Far East. There is wide variation in the conventions and customs governing sex relations, procreation, and child-rearing in these societies. But there appear to be certain basic features common to all patrilineal societies in the form of the moral values attached to social relationships within the focal field of kinship. Incest taboos; the stress on sexual fidelity in marriage; the supremacy of the husband-father; filial piety counteracting the suppressed antagonism between father and son and mother and daughter—these are some of the main features common to the schemes of moral values found in all patrilineal societies.

These values embody the fundamental moral axioms of the society; and it is this that makes kinship, regarded as a mechanism for the ordering of social relationships within a given society, one of the irreducible principles of social structure in such a society.

INDEX

Abortion, 167.
Adolescence, in parent-child relationship, 198, 203 ff., 230; social development during, 20, 199 ff., 228, 248 ff.
Adoption, into mother's brother's clan, 315.
Adultery, 23, 56, 109 ff.; and lineage ties, 56, 109 ff., 115 ff., 268; with son-in-law's wife, 124; reconciliation for, 117, 124, 212; and possession of children, 170; father responsible for son's, 212; and clanship, 269.
Affines, definition of, 17, 118; as *soog*, 37; relationship with, 93 ff., 105, 118 ff., 122, 123, 125; terminology of address between, 94, 96 & n., 118, 265, 273, 284 ff.; sexual relations between, 93, 96 & n., 112, 120, 122 ff., 273; funerals of, 120 ff.
Affinity (*deen*), and marriage, 15, 16; and *dɔyam*, 16 ff., 119; nature of, 17, 118 ff.; classificatory extension of, 37, 91.
Age, estimates of, 66 n., 187 n., 198 & n.; significance of age differences, 71, 142, 248, 258, 261, 271; and personal history, 78, 245; and social maturity, 147; in succession and inheritance, 156, 158, 279 ff.; respect paid to, 181.
Age-grades, lack of, 337.
Age-sets, lack of, 46.
Agnatic descent, in lineage structure, 4, 7, 11, 13 ff., 22, 135, 281, 341 ff.; in family structure, 11, 14 ff., 45, 204; and social status, 14, 22, 32, 161, 329; dominance of, 22, 30, 55, 324; and maternal origin, 15, 28, 30 ff., 135, 341 ff.; ritual coefficient of, 28 ff.; and liability for sins, 37, 113; and sacrifices, 40, 294, 321; in sibling bond, 243; in parent-child identification, 270; and ancestor cult, 329.
— ties, and cognatic ties, 13 ff., 341; and marriage, 126 ff., 224; in father-son relationship, 181; and *mabiirɔt*, 241; extension of, 272.
Agriculture, *see* Food production.
Ancestor cult, in social structure, 2 ff., 6, 34 ff., 263, 321; as sanction for kinship norms, 18, 24, 28, 158, 217, 294, 305, 346; and incest, 96, 171; place of men and women in, 98 ff., 174; and parent-child relationship, 171, 181, 218, 234 ff.; as filial piety, 173 ff.; in leechcraft, 174; reciprocity in, 215, 235; in moral and political conduct, 235, 265, 318, 320; and land transactions, 311 ff.; and *Bɔyar* cult, 328; and Earth cult, 341.
Ancestor founding, in lineage structure, 4, 7, 10 ff., 181, 328, 330. *See also* Progenitrix.
— shrine, 44, 49 ff., 59, 329; not possessed by women, 61, 228 n.; inheritance of, 157, 159, 280, 313; matrilateral, 321 ff., 324. *See also Bɔyar*.
Ancestors, significance of bond with, 18, 28, 154, 168, 172, 179, 229; as cause of death, 36, 329, 335 n.; women and, 90, 98, 106; as spirit guardians, 165, 212; as parent-image, 168, 176, 234 ff.; father's spirit as intermediary with, 138, 144, 147, 172, 174, 181, 186, 329; attributes of, 173, 234 ff., 329, 325; matrilateral, 294, 322, 325 ff.; land owned by, 310. *See also* Sacrifice.
Ancestral home (*daboog*), significance of, 44 ff., 174, 179, 185 ff.
Avoidance, between husband and wife, 93, 124; avoidances of firstborn children, 57, 67 n., 222, 225, 230, 233 ff.

Ba'ari, 119, 290, 292; land of, 309; structure of, 316.
Babii (father's child), significance of, 241.
Bakologo, 325 & n., 329. *See* Divination.
— shrine, significance of, 51, 318 ff., 325 ff.; transmission of, 231; identification of owners of, 253; and matrilateral lineage, 326, 331 n.
Betrothal, 201.
Biis, 10.
Bɔyar, in lineage system, 6, 111, 186, 328 ff.; succession to, 24 ff., 90, 113, 156 ff., 174, 280, 324, 331 ff.; origin of, 326, 329 ff.; succession ceremony to, 268, 296; in homestead, 55; sacrifice at, 321 ff.; and *bakologo* shrine, 326.
Bɔyar, External, cult of, among Talis, 3, 6, 150, 233, 321, 330 n.; confession at, 117; initiation into cult of, 6, 198, 212; attendance at, 321.
Bow, as symbol of man's personality, 57, 108, 279.
Brideprice, responsibility for, 85 ff., 91 ff., 138, 172, 208 ff., 213; in affinal contract, 17, 86; taboos, 30, 164; non-payment of, 72, 85 n., 86; in father-

350   INDEX

son relationship, 207; significance of, 92, 114; forfeiture of, 108, 123 ff.; rights over, 27, 138, 146, 206, 217, 272 ff.; remission and refunding of, 240, 275, 303 n.; equality of siblings and, 260 ff., 270; payment of brideprice by mother's brother, 25, 315; of foster-daughter, 27, 136, 316; and lineage segments, 9, 113, 146, 209, 213, 261, 273.
British administration, 1, 2 n., 42, 72, 138, 153 ff., 269.
Brother-in-law, 119.
Brothers, relationship between, 145, 158, 243, 245 ff., 252 ff., 256 ff., 264; full (*soog*), 67 ff., 71, 160 n., 245 ff., 252 ff., 257; inheritance by, 158 ff., 258 ff., 261, 275, 278; marriage of, 260, 270; 'sharing' between, 258 ff.; relationship generalized throughout social structure, 261, 264, 266; killing of, 265; basis and sanction of relationship between, 252, 263 ff., 266; terminology for, 266; rivalry between, 159, 264 ff., 269; identification of, 270; beyond inner lineage, 267, 280; separation of, 67 ff., 252, 255, 257, 260, 262; sharing homestead by, 67 ff.; age differences between, 71; equivalence of, 67 ff., 160 n.; children of, 332 ff. *See also* Siblings.
Burial, 179, 254, 271, 323, 329.

Calabash, as symbol of women, 61 n.; at funeral, 239; distribution of, 279 ff.; at childbirth, 301; in divorce, 38.
Cardinall, A. W., 45.
Cattleyard, significance of, 54 ff., 67, 338.
Chance, 227; as Heaven (*Naawun*), 21.
Chiefs (*na'ab*), privileges of, 25, 55, 119; families of, 72; wealth of, 82 n., 83 ff.; have 'no father alive', 154; regarded as 'brothers', 242; installation of, 324.
Chiefship, and Namoos, 3; sanctions for, 3 ff.; and tendaanaship, 3, 6, 341; succession to, 269, 280, 317; myths of origin of, 316.
Childbirth, place of, 28 ff., 46, 60, 125; ancestors at, 28 ff., 301; spirit-guardian and first, 90, 301; care of women in, 28, 130, 133, 164 ff., 252; hygiene of, 166; gifts and formalities at, 133, 165 n., 203, 252, 301; announced to parents, 203, 301, 318.
Child-rearing, in father's home, 29, 46; significance of, 136 ff.; by proxy and classificatory parents, 136, 140 ff.; duties of mother in, 139 ff., 167, 170, 245; methods of, 187 ff., 245 ff.; and kinship systems, 339, 345 ff.
Children, in lineage structure, 4, 130; importance of, 16, 82, 97, 113, 130 ff., 136, 168, 181, 186, 197; relationship with fathers, 16, 168 ff., 186, 223, 232; adulterine, 22; illegitimate, 24 ff., 28, 72, 110; first-born, 57, 67 n., 222, 225, 230, 233 ff., 238; in domestic organization, 62 ff., 130, 192 ff., 249, 301; inheritance of, 71, 275; in marriage, 86 ff., 90, 97, 170; sexual play of, 112, 250 ff.; rights and authority over, 114, 146, 192, 204; care and upbringing of, 130, 137, 141, 144, 162, 164 ff., 167, 187 ff., 190 ff., 245 ff., 254 n., 258 ff., 270, 271, 301; 'separation' of, from mother, 137, 170; pawning of, 138; relation to proxy parents, 140 ff., 144, 270; death of, 165, 167, 253; at funerals, 179, 231 ff.; stages of development of, 187 n., 194 ff., 198 n., 201, 253; play of, 190, 245, 260; and totemic taboos, 192; betrothal of, 201; discrimination between, 230 ff., 270; last-born, 231.
Clan, definition and structure of, 2 ff., 4, 262; clans and interpersonal kinship ties, 3, 31, 38, 142, 286; membership and status, 22, 24, 147; and uterine kinship, 31, 38; solidarity, 83, 109 ff., 116, 119, 267, 269; name, 126; and local cohesion, 181 ff.; headship, 239 n.; property and land in clan structure, 309; politico-ritual relations between clans, 286 ff., 317, 319; friendship ties between clans, 337.
— composite, definition of, 4; *bɔyar* of Talis', 6.
— extra-clan kinship, *see* Kinship.
— inter-clan linkages, 5, 283, 319; and sorcery, 319 ff.
— segment, *see* Segment.
Clanship ties, and extra-clan kinship ties, 286 ff., 290 ff.; reaffirmation of, 324; range of, 343.
Clanswoman, see *Pɔyayabəlag*.
Cognatic ties, significance of, 13 ff., 18, 242, 266, 341, 343 ff.; range of, 14, 43, 80, 286; of women, 47 n.; and adultery, 116; in kinswoman-wife marriage, 126; and debts, 214; between grandparents and grandchildren, 236; and maternal origin, 257.
Conception, theory of, 19 ff.; place of, 28.

INDEX

Continence, sexual, 108.
Courtship, behaviour in, 80, 91, 139, 249; sexual relations in, 115, 249; and puberty, 201.
Courtyard, (*dendɔŋo*) description and significance of, 58 ff.
Cousin, 68 ff., 146, 257, 269.
'Cow of rearing', 27, 136, 316.
Co-wives, tension between, 33, 87, 107, 128, 131 ff., 262; classificatory, 88, 126; mutual adjustment of, 78, 126 ff., 133 ff.; terminology between, 126; equivalence of, 127, 242; co-operation between, 128 ff., 133; authority among, 127, 133; as proxy parents, 141.
Cowrie shells, 121 n., 232.
Culture contact, effect of, 49, 72 ff.
Curse, 44, 46; of parent, 46, 175, 190, 203; of chief, 46; of father, 86, 255; of father's sister, 333 ff.

Dayət ('dirt'), 58, 117, 179.
Daughter, relationship of, to parents, 138 ff., 195, 201 ff., 224; relationship of married daughter to parents, 86 ff., 202, 217, 224; incest with, 111, 114; first-born, 224, 226; and mother, 202, 223, 227.
Daughter-in-law, 93 ff., 112.
Death, social status and personality at, 55, 118; and property relations, 157 ff.; and pregnancy, 163; joining ancestors on, 59, 90, 179, 329; causes of, 228, 235 n., 329; as test of kinship sentiments, 304; divination at, 99, 167, 323, 329; of 'non-humans', 271, 329.
Debt, definition of, 121, 214; liability for, 103, 138, 209, 214; sanction for repayment of, 214 n.; 'cancelling', 117, 215; inheritance of, 275; debts between mother's brother and sister's son, 306.
Deen, see Affinity.
Dichotomy, sexual, in Tale culture, 78, 248, 270.
Divination, practised at home, 46, 55; at ancestor shrine, 90; after death, 99, 167, 271, 323, 329; in illness, 138, 172, 212; responsibility of father for, 172, 212; and *Yin*, 228 ff.; acquisition of power of, 231, 243, 319; occasions for, 33, 45, 90, 138, 163, 165, 172, 176, 179, 186, 292; shrine, see *Bakologo*.
Division of labour, 344; economic, 47 ff., 101 ff.; sexual, 190 ff., 201, 248.
Di⋯ e, 38, 85 ff., 104, 108, 124; between *saarət*, 38; custody of children in, 137.

Dɔyam, definition of, 16 ff., 241; significance of, 17 ff., 78, 135, 137, 162, 209, 292; and procreation, 19 ff.; 'splitting', 38, 292; seniority by, 156, 158.
Dooluŋ string, 232.
Dug (room), definition and significance of, 11, 58 ff., 62 ff., 66, 69, 98, 102, 111, 131, 201; mother's brother's, 30, 296; component rooms of, 60; polarity of *dug* and *yir*, 63, 68 ff., 78, 100, 128, 130, 194, 256; siblings in, 71, 256; and food supply, 128 ff.; and levirate, 241.
Dugdaana, status of, 58 ff., 98, 127, 132, 236.
Duləm, concept of, 219.

Earth cult, 2 ff., 6, 34, 321; women excluded from, 99; and ancestor cult, 341.
— shrine, 6, 49, 55; taboo of, 49; sacrifice to, 265, 321.
Education, received at home, 46; in babyhood, 189; in childhood, 190 ff., 245; in adolescence, 199.
Elders, consent of, 23, 209, 309; 'men who come after the', 70, 338; status of, 153; funerals of, 178, 323 ff.; role of elders at funerals, 338.
Elopement, 91, 139, 201, 208, 249, 333.
Evans-Pritchard, E. E., 2 n., 243 n.
Exogamy, clan and lineage, 4; and kinship, 16, 40.

Family, agnatic descent in, 11, 45, 204; as focus of agnatic and cognatic ties, 14 ff., 341; effect of culture contact on, 72 ff.; structure and development of, 78; line of cleavage in, 63, 79, 128; property relations in, 102 ff.; sexual relations in, 107; cohesion of, 113, 131 ff., 200, 203, 205, 263; as process in time, 63; kinship relations in, 78 ff.; and sibling bond, 243, 257.
— domestic, definition of, 9, 44; cycle of development of, 12, 63, 70; and homestead, 47 ff., 63, 74 n.; size of, 64 n.; and polygyny, 67; privacy in, 79 ff.; economic reciprocity and co-operation in, 101 ff., 105 ff., 123, 128 ff.; tensions in, 128.
— elementary, definition of, 50; in joint family, 63, 65 ff., 98.
— expanded, definition of, 9, 69; cycle of development of, 69, 74, 77; and incest, 111, 123, 126; and classificatory kinship, 141, 161; relations between children of, 245, 250.

INDEX

Family head 12; death of, 66; authority and status of, 78, 102, 204, 260, 273.
— joint, as model for lineage constitution, 11; tensions in, 33, 132, 228, 250, 260; cleavages in, 67, 77, 79, 134, 140, 328; composition and structure of, 63 ff., 81, 330; antithesis between *dug* and *yir* in, 194, 256; cycle of development of, 69 ff., 74, 157, 230; fission in, 12, 57, 66 ff., 74, 140, 157, 175, 185, 206, 226, 230, 262, 328.
Father, authority of, 86, 137 ff., 143, 186, 191 ff., 195, 199, 204, 206, 207, 209, 213, 226, 235, 263; dominance of, 137, 347; rights and duties of, 138 ff., 146, 164, 172; social role of, 143, 146, 174; meaning of in lineage structure, 149, 154; death of, 156 ff.; responsibility of father in marriage affairs, 138, 143, 170, 208 ff., 314; ritual responsibility of, 29, 138, 165, 203, 212; jural responsibilities of, 172, 199, 203 ff., 209, 212; as intermediary with spirit-guardian, 174; and ancestors, 144, 147, 172, 174, 181, 186, 234; attributes of, 198; dependence on, 172; relationship of father and daughter, 201 ff.; proxy, 147 ff., 158, 204, 208 ff., 212, 218, 260; tension between father and eldest son, 225 ff., 230 ff.; father's brother, 140 ff., 225.
Father-son relationship, 78, 135, 189, 192, 196, 198 ff., 200, 203 ff., 230 ff., 235; ambivalence in, 171 ff., 197, 230; identification in, 135, 198 ff., 235, 336; avoidances in, 67 n., 222 ff., 227; rivalry in, 67 n., 223 ff.
Father's brother, position of, 140 ff., 225.
— sister, as link in extra-clan kinship, 281, 332; terminology of address to, 285; status of, 332 ff.; death of, 333, 335.
Father-in-law, relationship of wife with, 93 ff., 96; duties at funeral of, 318.
'Fatherless', significance of being, 147 ff., 154 ff., 161, 179, 224 ff., 242; ambivalent meaning of, 171.
Firth, R., viii, 338, 339, 345.
Fission, in joint family, 12, 57, 66 ff., 74, 140, 157, 175, 183, 206, 226, 230, 262, 328; between brothers, 67 ff., 252, 255, 257, 260; within the lineage, 156, 183, 330.
Flugel, J. C., 345 n.
Food, importance of, 56 ff., 82; distribution of food in household, 57, 98, 260; cooking and storage of, 59 ff.; production, 42, 80, 101 ff., 128 ff., 122, 125, 139, 172, 191 ff., 205, 259; kinship in relation to food production and consumption, 7, 339 ff.; at funerals, 121, 149, 180, 215, 323, 331, 338; taboos in pregnancy, 166; gifts of food to kinsfolk, 217, 219; gifts of food at first childbirth, 203, 252, 301; ritual distribution of, 260, 268, 301, 321 ff., 331, 338.
Forde, C. D., 32 n.
Foster-child, 313 ff.; brideprice of, 315; patrilineal rights over, 315 ff.
Foster-parent, 24, 313 ff.; share of brideprice given to, 27, 136, 316.
Friendship (*zoot*), 337.
Fromm, E., 346 n.
Funeral, expungement of social personality by, 55, 118, 179, 232; and relatives of successive generations, 149, 157, 161, 224, 232, 242; symbolism of, 157, 232 ff.; and pregnancy taboos, 163, 166; function of, 178, 263, 324; food at, 121, 149, 180, 215, 323, 331, 338; gifts at, 121, 203, 318, 321, 323, 338; distribution of property at, 279; division by sex and seniority at, 180, 231 ff., 337 ff.; organization and performance of, 51, 55, 59, 88, 149, 233, 279, 338; mystically dangerous, 232; 'owner of the', 180; sister's sons at, 274, 296, 323 ff., 331.

Gateway, description and significance of, 51 ff., 55, 67, 74, 225 ff., 338.
Generation, cleavage between successive generations, 95, 193, 204, 222 ff., 225, 230, 232, 234, 305; relationship of successive generations, 142; equivalence of alternate generations, 135, 197, 236 n., 239, 275; recognition of generation differences, 9 ff., 141, 150, 156, 200, 240, 267, 271, 277, 296, 336; significance of generation differences, 71, 111, 142, 149 ff., 283 ff., 294 ff.
Gifts, between kinsmen, 42 ff., 202, 252, 305 ff., 335; at funerals, 121, 203, 318, 321, 323, 338; at Harvest Festivals, 132, 139; at childbirth, 165 n., 203, 252, 301; to girl's mother, 139; at harvest, 42, 203, 304; of fowls by mother's brother, 194, 207, 307.
Gold Coast, labour migration to, 49, 72, 73, 89, 140, 173; Northern Territories of, 1, 72.
Gour, H. S., 345 n.

INDEX

Granary, description and significance of, 56 ff., 222, 233.
Grandchildren, 'reaching', 136, 236, 239.
Grandparents, status of, in joint family, 236 ff.; significance of maternal, 30, 194, 203, 236 ff., 301; maternal grandparents' lineage, 295.
Grandparent-grandchild relationship, 15, 146, 203, 236 ff.; joking relationship in, 197, 236, 301; range of, 147, 240; terminology of address in, 236.
Granquist, H., 345 n.
Graves, 178 ff., 182, 254, 317.
Great Festivals, 3, 55, 105, 112, 118, 187 n.
Grinding-room (*neer*), description and significance of, 61 ff., 129.
Grove, sacred, see Earth shrine.

Hailey, Lord, 72 n.
Harvest, 42, 88 ff., 101, 105, 128, 203, 304; festival, 6, 132, 139.
Headmen, 72, 82 n., 83 ff.
Hill Talis, 55, 99, 185; cult of External Bɔyar among, 117, 198, 212.
Homestead, and family, 44 ff., 63 ff., 66, 74 n.; siting and building of, 5, 44 ff., 47 ff., 50, 125, 139, 163, 260, 312; values and significance of, 45 ff., 63, 182; layout of, 50 ff., 58 ff., 62 ff., 66; shared by brothers, 67 ff.; rebuilding of, 173, 185.
Homicide, 243, 265, 286, 293.
House, see *Yir*.
Household, significance of, 50, 74; and homestead, 74 n.; economic organization in, 57, 101 ff., 128 ff., 139, 204 ff., 259 ff., 278; responsibility of father for, 172, 204; setting up independent, 67 ff., 73, 139 ff., 146, 175 ff., 226, 230, 260, 262.
Hsiao-Tung Fei, 345 n.
Hunting, 108, 163, 267, 315.
Husband, authority of, 104 ff.; relationship with affines, 91 ff., 118 ff., 124; ritually responsible for wife, 90, 106, 301; duties at wife's confinement, 164; rights of first husband to take precedence, 170; eats apart from wife, 249.
— and wife, relations between, 81 ff., 85 ff., 92 ff., 97 ff., 104, 124, 128 ff., 249; economic and property relations of, 57, 101 ff.; sexual relations of, 81, 107 ff., 167, 194; sexual taboos of, 28, 115, 124, 126; terminology of address between, 94, 98; dissension between, 104, 108.

Identification, of parent and child, 136, 181, 198, 234, 270, 274; of father and son, 135, 199 ff., 230, 297, 336; of mother and daughter, 202; of parents and proxy parents, 141; of siblings, 252, 269, 270, 274; with ancestors, 274.
Illegitimate child, 24 ff., 72, 110.
Incest, between *saarət*, 38; between affinés, 93, 96, 112, 265; with mother, 96 n., 112; range of, 9, 109, 111 ff., 115, 123, 141, 161, 224, 265, 268, 296; sanctions and retributions for, 111 ff., 117, 265; reconciliation for, 113 ff.; between siblings, 111, 114, 250; with mother's brother's widow or lineage, 277, 296; and lineage segmentation, 342; in patrilineal societies, 347.
Inheritance, of widows, *see* Widows, Levirate; of land, 9 ff., 141, 146, 157, 159, 182, 205, 278 ff.; by women, 22, 332 & n.; rules of, 22, 156 ff., 275, 278 ff.; of woman's property, 103, 158 n., 279; after funerals, 118, 279; of rights over people, 159; of duties and debts, 177, 275; by brothers, 158, 174, 258 ff., 261, 275, 278; sharing in, 258; equivalence of siblings in, 272, 275 ff., 278 ff.; of social personality, 318.
Initiation, lack of initiation schools, 46; into External Bɔyar cult, 6, 198, 212.
Intermediary, in marriage formalities, 91, 200, 209, 249, 287, 317 ff.; sister's son as, 317 ff.

Joking relationship, 197, 273, 296, 334, 336; between affines, 94, 120, 273; ambivalence in, 94, 120; between grandparents and grandchildren, 197, 236, 301; prohibition of, 197, 334.

Kinship, extent of web of, 2 ff., 343; concepts in social structure, 12 ff., 330, 338 ff.; breach of, 13; ties rooted in family, 15, 78 ff., 81, 341; generic concept of, 16 ff., 241; norms, 18, 346; nature of kinship relations, 18 ff.; 'splitting of', 38, 292; ties in new settlements, 71; inertia of, 126; parent-child relationship and kinship ties, 135, 181; in inner lineage, 143; range of classificatory, 141, 155 ff., 161, 217, 240, 266 ff., 296; sentiments, 195; extension of kinship ties, 272, 280; permanence of kinship ties, 286, 294; duties of, 292 ff.; reaffirmation of ties, 324; functions of, 337 ff., 343 ff.; patrilineal and matrilateral,

INDEX

341 ff.; sanctions for kinship institutions, 346.

Kinship, extra-clan, nature and types of, 281 ff., 283 ff., 299; social relevance of, 281, 291, 298, 328; terminology in, 284 ff., 296; function of, 286 ff., 343; and lineage system, 287, 291; and marriage, 287, 290 ff.; and warfare, 287; multiple kinship ties, 291 ff.; socio-spatial pattern of, 286 ff., 295, 327 n.; obligations and sanctions of, 294, 305 ff.; inheritance of kinship ties, 297, 304; classificatory extension of, 143, 281, 295 ff.; ritual relations in, 321 ff., 328 ff.

— fictional, and accessory lineages, 4.

— matrilateral, and patrilateral kinship, 15, 28, 31, 135, 341; and social mobility, 42; extension of, 240, 272, 280; as basis of extra-clan kin ties, 281 ff., 290 ff.; function of, 342. *See also* Levirate.

— patrilineal, *see* Agnatic.

— sororal, extension of, 272, 280; in extra-clan kin ties, 281 ff., 292, 321 ff.

Kinsmen, help and hospitality to, 217, 219, 286, 293.

Kinswoman-wife (*pɔyasoog*), 126 ff., 258.

Kɔlkpaarəg (non-human sprite), 271, 329.

Krige, E. J., 243 n.

Kumpiog (basket of death), 61, 232, 279.

Labour migration, to Ashanti, 49, 72, 73, 89, 140, 173; and family structure, 72; incidence of, 72; and family tensions, 73, 206; motives for, 140, 206, 260, 270; and neglect of parents, 162, 218; return from, 179 ff., 207; and land scarcity, 263.

Land, inheritance of, 9 ff., 141, 146, 157, 159, 182, 205, 278 ff., 332; utilization of, 50, 68, 102, 128 ff., 163; acquisition of, 73, 205 ff., 307 ff., 311 ff., 317; rent, 311; reversion of, 311; rights over, 74, 159; purchase of, 82 ff., 259; disputes over, 83, 159, 264 ff.; and social structure, 157, 181 ff., 309 ff.; begging of, 194, 307, 312 ff.; ownership of, 102, 146, 157, 204, 217, 309 ff., 313; shortage of, 263, 308; ancestor cult and, 310 ff.; tenure and kinship relations, 340; holding and clanship ties, 157, 309.

Legitimacy, 22, 24, 28, 82, 110 ff.

Levirate, and clan and maximal lineage, 4, 83, 110, 156, 275; and constitution of joint family, 71; rules of, 240, 275 ff.; functions of, 83, 85, 272, 275 ff. *See also* Widow.

Lineage, constitution and characteristics of, 6 ff., 45 ff., 78, 155, 341; terminology for, 10 ff.; ramifications and segmentation of, 10, 71, 135, 157, 243, 262, 280; fission in, 12, 155 ff., 330; operation of lineage principle, 18, 26, 44, 79, 96 n., 209, 236; succession in, 24, 28; range of permitted sexual relations in, 28, 115 ff., 123 n.; continuity of, 55 ff., 135, 284, 299; organization and kinship, 71 ff., 283, 287, 295 ff., 341; ties in new settlements, 71; and family reintegration, 74; solidarity of, 79 ff., 109 ff., 113, 116, 179, 181, 200, 263, 267; marriage into, 126 ff.; status in, 147 ff., 262; sanctions for authority in, 186, 263; property, 157, 308 ff.; equilibrium in, 324, 341; expansion of, 328 ff.; segments, *see* Segment; ties, *see* Agnatic.

— accessory, 4, 24, 283, 315.

— attached, 108.

— effective minimal, definition of, 9, 63; and family organization, 12, 64, 67, 69.

— head, role of, 9 ff., 326; and *bɔyar*, 156, 159; death of, 324.

— inner, definition of, 9, 11, 141; incest in, 9, 115, 264; and land, 83, 114; and marriage, 115, 153, 209, 267; and classificatory kinship, 141, 156, 158, 161, 266 ff.; and generation differences, 9, 141, 150, 156, 240, 267, 277, 296, 336; kinship within, 143, 156; and inheritance of widows, 153, 156, 239, 275 ff.; and brideprice, 209, 213, 267, 273; in lineage fission, 156; in other significant situations, 156, 200, 212, 214, 256, 266 ff., 269, 336.

— intercalary, 294, 319.

— maximal, definition of, 4 ff.; internal constitution of, 6 ff.; significance of, 115, 159, 228, 309.

— medial, definition of, 10 ff.; sexual relations within, 10, 111, 113, 115, 264; and generation differences, 10, 267, 271; in other significant situations, 28, 123 ff., 127, 132, 154, 212, 266, 336.

— minimal, 7, 9, 99.

— nuclear, definition of, 9, 114; and brideprice, 113, 146, 209; levirate in, 114, 275; and incest, 114; and filial status, 149 ff., 156, 171; cycle of development of, 182 ff.; in lineage fission, 330; in other significant situations, 141, 149, 161, 214, 217, 219, 256 ff., 334, 336.

INDEX

Lineage, sororal, 317.
— *sunzɔ*, 11, 244, 268.
— structure and affective relationships, 144; and sibling bond, 243; and distribution of food, 261.
— system, function of, 12, 143, 341 ff.; and domestic organization, 12 ff.; and continuity in time, 135; as sanction of filial piety, 181; and principle of sharing, 258.
Livestock, significance of, 54, 82; ownership of, 102 ff., 157, 206, 279; inheritance of, 158 n., 278 ff.; bred from gift fowl, 2q7, 307; sale of, 259; responsibility for, 260.
Lowie, R., 278 n.
Lynn, C. W., 263 n.

Mabii, 142, 241 ff.
MacIver, R., 345 n.
Males, dominance of, 4, 15, 22, 275, 347; symbols for, 61 n., 108, 222, 279; and ancestor cult, 174; at funerals, 338.
Malinowski, B., viii, 213 n., 339, 341 n., 345, 346.
Mamprusi, 3, 265 n., 285.
Mampurugu, 3, 72, 173.
Marriage, patrilocal, 4; prohibited degrees of, 7, 10, 16, 37 ff., 43, 269, 294, 296 ff.; and lineage, 7, 24 ff., 47, 109, 115, 153, 203, 209, 267, 316; significance of, in kinship system, 16, 40, 81, 90 ff., 314, 341; and uterine kin, 37 ff., 43; significance of, for individual, 47, 81 ff., 95, 111, 201 ff., 224, 261 ff.; stability of, 84 ff., 86, 90, 97; age for, 84 n., 201, 273; experimental, 84 ff.; jural formalities of, 27, 85 ff., 91, 122, 208; sexual relationship in, 28, 100 ff., 106 ff.; of widows, 106, 118, 239 ff.; consummation of, 106; sins against marriage, 108 ff.; and legitimacy, 110; preferences, 127, 290; responsibility of father in, 138, 143, 170, 208 ff., 314; mystically dangerous, 163; by arrangement or elopement, 208; and extra-clan kinship ties, 287, 290, 292, 294, 297 ff.
Maternal origin, significance of, 22, 30 ff., 161; and paternal origin, 30, 63, 256 ff., 341; and cognatic ties, 257; in lineage structure, 328 ff.; in family structure, 330.
Maturity, social, 73, 147, 154, 171, 337; physiological, 201.
McLennan, J. F., vii.
Medicine, 165, 174, 189, 212, 271; shrines, 59, 81, 199.
Meek, C. K., 262 n.
Menstruation, 19, 201.

Miscarriage, 166, 253, 254.
Mobility, 42, 286; and parental authority, 206; restriction of, 263; and marriage, 290.
Mole-Dagbane, 1, 142 n.
Morgan, L. H., vii.
Mortuary ceremonies, 51, 88, 120 ff., 163, 178.
Mother, -child relationship, 78, 96 n., 130, 170, 173, 187 ff., 196, 198, 224; -son relationship, 100, 194, 200 ff., 216; -daughter relationship, 135, 173, 201 ff., 223; incest with, 96 n., 112; rights and duties of, 58, 139, 167, 170, 173; mother's spirit, 174 ff., 235, 325; symbol of motherhood, 189; curse by, 190; support of aged, 216, 218; relations with mother's patrilineal kin, 296; as link in matrilateral kinship, 181, 281; proxy, 161.
Mother-in-law, relationship of spouses with, 93 ff., 118, 201.
Mother's brother (*ahɔb*), as fosterfather, 24, 113 ff.; and sister's son, 19, 30 ff., 214, 283 ff., 295 ff., 301 ff., 304 ff.; acquisition of land from, 194, 307 ff., 312; sacrifice by, 282, 294, 296 ff., 321, 332; lineage of, 295 ff., 301 ff., 315, 321; death of, 304 ff.; authority of, 305; funeral of, 321.
— father-daughter's child relationship, 298.
— mother's brother's lineage, 298.
'Motherless' ('having no mother alive'), 160, 179, 242.
Mourning, for relatives, 117, 168, 179, 231 ff., 238 ff., 333 ff.; shaving the head in, 179, 239, 333, 335; emblems of, 232; for matrilateral kin, 331.
Myths, 2, 3, 316.

Na'ab, see Chief.
Naawun (Heaven), 21, 227.
Namoos, 2, 3; *bɔyar* of, 55; taboos of first-born children among, 57, 67 n., 222, 225, 230, 233 ff.; funeral rites among, 233.
Nyeer (successive siblings), *see* Siblings.

Ordeal, for witchcraft, 33, 131; for adultery, 56.
Orphans, status and care of, 71, 130, 142, 313 ff.; purification of, 161.

Parent-child relationship, in joint family, 15; in kinship system, 16, 18, 135 ff., 168, 186; reciprocity in, 136, 204 ff., 207, 209, 212 ff., 225, 231; classificatory extension

of, 140 ff., 143, 161; sanctions for, 142, 162, 170, 181, 186, 218; and ancestor cult, 168, 172 ff., 178; analysis of, 169 ff., 197 ff., 220, 339, 346; ambivalence of, 171 ff., 181, 197, 204, 222 ff., 229, 234 ff.; development of, 187 ff., 195, 198 ff., 203 ff.
Parenthood, 162.
Parents, rights and duties of, 137 ff., 162 ff., 212; proxy, 140 ff., 144 ff., 170, 179, 204 ff., 213, 225, 270; care of aged, 162, 175, 181, 216 ff.; as prototypes of ancestors, 168, 175 ff., 234; death of, 178 ff.; pride in, 180 ff.; terms of address to, 196; killing of, 235 n.
— -in-law, relationship of spouse with, 93 ff., 105, 119; funeral of, 120 ff., 200, 318.
Paternity, 21 ff., 24, 26 ff., 136 ff.; importance of, 82, 110, 164; and marriage ties, 341.
Patricide, 235 n.
Personality, effect of, on conduct, 13, 50, 79, 118, 143, 150, 255, 257, 339. *See also* Social Personality.
Piety, filial, 171 ff., 173 ff., 235; as sanction, 195, 216 ff., 235, 263, 347.
Placation gift, 85 n., 86, 92, 208 ff., 316, 318.
Pɔyakpeem (senior wife), 132 ff.
Pɔyasoog, *see* Kinswoman-wife.
Pɔyayabəlɔg (clanswoman), 88, 98, 115, 165, 274 ff.
'Pollution of the room', 28, 123 ff.; purification of, 123 n., 124, 125.
Polygyny, incidence of, 65 ff., 72, 84 n.; sexual relations in, 107; and kinswoman-wife marriage, 126.
Predestiny, 90, 228; evil, 203, 212, 227 ff., 331; seniority by, 156, 158.
Pregnancy, and dɔyam, 20 ff.; and permitted extra-marital intercourse, 23; premarital, 101, 126; ceremonial at first, 130, 164, 299; taboos at, 30, 125, 163 ff., 166; premature pregnancy in nursing mother, 167, 188, 254 n.; of successive sisters, 254.
Progenitrix, in lineage structure, 11, 126, 181, 328 ff.; as ancestor spirit, 330.
Property, in family, 46, 60, 62, 68, 81, 102 ff., 204; woman's, 89, 102 ff., 158 n., 279; management of dead man's, 118; father's rights over son's, 139, 143, 146, 204 ff.; inheritance of, 22, 157 ff., 278 ff.; and lineage structure, 157, 308 ff.; individual and patrimonial (*faar*), 157; rights and principle of reciprocity, 207, 225; pledging and sale of, 259.
Proxy, 23, 118. *See* Parents.
Puberty, and dɔyam, 20; significance of, 195, 201; estimation of, 198 n.; and marriage, 201, 273.
Purification, 36, 123, 125, 161, 234, 238, 243, 271 ff.

Quiver, in taboo of first-born children, 57, 222; care of, 60; at Talis funeral, 233; as symbol of man's personality, 222, 279; inheritance of, 279.

Radcliffe-Brown, A. R., viii, 22, 103 n., 242, 280 n., 299 n., 342.
Rattray, R. S., 32 n., 96 n., 262 n.
Reciprocity, economic, 18, 42, 102, 204; principle of, 121 ff., 135 ff., 198 ff., 204 ff., 207, 209, 212 ff., 217, 225, 231, 235, 305.
Reconciliation, 113 ff., 117, 123 n., 124, 265, 268.
Religion, and kinship, 18, 340, 345. *See also* Ancestors, Ancestor cult.
Ritual, and family ties, 167, 263, 268, 274; and extra-clan kinship, 294, 321 ff.; in land transactions, 309 ff.; kinship and, 339.
Rivers, W. H. R., 14 n.

Saarət, *see* Soog.
Sacrifice, by senior generation, 19; attendance at, 40, 321 ff.; by father, 147, 172, 181, 186; through father's spirit, 144, 147, 174, 186, 234; and patriliny, 274, 294; place of women at, 90, 98, 174, 199, 332 n.; to ancestors, 138, 163, 172, 212, 233, 311; to personal shrines, 59, 154, 229; to spirit-guardian, 90, 174, 294, 301; division of food at, 260, 268, 301, 321 ff.; for homicide, 265; by mother's brother, 283, 294, 296 ff., 321, 332; at bɔyar, 321 ff., 331.
Sanctions, 3, 4; in kinship ties, 18, 121, 294 ff., 318, 334, 346; in incest, 38, 111, 265; in family relations, 67, 105, 252; in sexual relations, 116 ff., 123, 170; principle of reciprocity as, 121 ff., 212 ff.; in parent-child relationship, 139, 142, 162, 170 ff., 181, 186, 218 ff., 314; in property relations, 158, 214 n., 311 ff.; filial piety as, 11, 81; ancestors as, 235, 265, 318; against sorcery, 320.
Segment, *see* Lineage, Clan; distinguished by bɔyar, 6, 329; of maximal lineage, 7, 329; matri-segments, 126; sunzɔ-segments, 11,

244; differentiation of segments by descent, 11, 328 ff.
Segment, major, definition of, 7.
— minimal, nuclear, inner, medial, see Lineage.
Segmentary differentiation, 2, 7.
Segmentation, order of, 7 ff.; in family, 12, 149 ff.; factors of, in lineage, 110, 116, 328 ff.
Settlements, age of, on Tong Hills, 5; social structure of, 44 ff., 71 ff., 119; peripheral, 226, 312; kinship links between, 286.
Sex, attitude to, 100 ff., 196 n., 251; differences between siblings, 241, 243 ff., 248, 258, 261; in adolescence, 249; and kinship systems, 345 ff.; and dɔyam, 20 ff.
Sexual intercourse, taboos on, 20, 28, 115, 124, 167; posture in, 108 n.; prenuptial, 101, 110, 115, 201, 249; and procreation, 101, 107, 114.
— relations, extra-marital, 23, 110; and family organization, 46, 126; in marriage, 81, 100 ff., 106 ff., 194; range of permitted, 110 ff., 115, 120, 141, 264, 268 ff., 273, 296; in childhood, 250 ff.
Shrine, see Ancestor, Bakologo, Earth, Medicine, Mother, Sacrifice, Yin.
Sibling, and cognatic ties, 14; significance of sibling relationship, 18, 241 ff., 248, 257 ff., 264, 266; incest with, 111 ff., 114, 250 ff.; ties, degrees of, 245, 256 ff., 269 ff.; identification, 270.
Siblings, age differences between, 71, 248, 258, 261, 271; equivalence of, 224, 234, 242 ff., 269 ff., 272 ff., 305, 315, 333; sex differences between, 241, 243 ff., 248, 258, 261; terminology for, 244, 266; full (soog), 244 ff., 251, 256; rivalry between, 253 ff., 264; successive (nyeer), 253 ff., 271; sunzɔ, 257 ff., 262; sharing between, 258 ff.; domestic organization and, 259 ff.; lineage relations and, 264 ff.; in extra-clan kinship, 272, 280, 283 ff.
Siblings-in-law, 120.
Sie, 62 n., 289.
Sii, Chiefship of, 119, 290.
Sister, identification with brother, 270, 333.
Sisters, co-wives as, 127; relationship of, 252; successive, 254; equivalence of, 270, 281.
Sister's daughter, 303, 306, 316, 323.
Sisters-in-law, 94, 120, 273.
Sister's son, status and role of, 24, 71 ff., 274, 277, 302, 313 ff., 317,

321; gift of hen to, 194, 307; death of, 304 ff.; inheritance by, 316. See also Mother's brother.
Slaves, 25 ff., 138.
Social equilibrium, 3, 5, 6, 135, 287, 341.
— organization, basic units of, 4; in home and settlement, 45; polarity in, 197, 341 ff.; and behaviour, 220; lineage structure in, 243; kinship in, 338, 340 ff.
— personality, expunging of, 55, 118, 179, 232; symbols of, 61, 222, 232, 279; development of, 194, 227, 261; inheritance of, 318; kinship as mould of, 339 ff.
— structure, 1, 181, 342 ff.; temporal dimension in, 135, 295, 342; equilibrium in, 341 ff.
Son, see Father.
Son-in-law, 120 ff., 217.
Soog (pl. saarət), concept of, 31 ff., 38, 131, 161, 202, 281; personal bond between, 37 ff., 40, 238 n., 281; sexual relations between, 38, 112; dispersion of, 38, 40 ff.; terminology between, 41, 43; tie between mother and child, 131, 170, 202, 224; tie in kinship relationships, 170, 238, 244, 302. See also Brothers, Siblings.
Sorcery, 319 ff.
Sororate, 278.
Spirit, see Ancestor, Father, Mother.
Spirit-guardian, woman under care of, 90, 174; sacrifice to, 90, 174, 294, 301; for child, 165, 212, 229, 271, 315; father as intermediary with, 174, 203; Yin as, 229.
Status, conferred by descent, 14, 32, 136, 161, 262, 313, 329; conferred by marriage, 82, 111, 201 ff.; and 'having no father alive', 147, 149 ff., 171; and property relations, 156 ff.
Stepchild, 25, 27, 71.
Sterility, 21 ff., 87.
Sub-clan, definition of, 4.
Suicide, 91, 168.
Sunzɔ (pl. sunzɔp), 11, 244, 256 ff. See also Cousin.

Taboos, of Namoos, 25, 57, 67 n., 222 ff., 225, 230, 233 ff.; of Earth, 49; of first-born daughter, 61, 223; between father and son, 67 n., 225 ff., 232; in marriage, 124 ff., 243; in relations of parents and children, 149 ff., 160; of External Bɔyar, 150; absence of, in menstruation, 201; between grandparents and grandchildren, 238; in homicide, 265.

INDEX

Taboos, sexual, 28 ff., 115, 124 ff.; between kin, 38, 111; between affines, 96.
Tale society, characteristics of, 1–5, 13, 78, 341, 343 ff.
Talis, and Namoos, 2 ff.; and tɛndaanaship, 3 ff.; and External Bɔyar cult, 3, 6, 55, 321, 330 n.; and Earth cult, 6, 321; and granary, 58; and first-born child taboos, 222 ff., 230, 233; funerals among, 233.
Tallensi (*sing.* Talǝŋ), 1 ff., 2 n., 241 and *passim*.
Tɛndaana, office of, 3 ff.; tɛndaanaship and chiefship, 6, 341; duties of, 45, 49, 55; installation of, 55, 324; succession to tɛndaanaship, 159, 280, 317; funeral of, 178, 296; equivalence of tɛndaanas, 242; delegation of tɛndaana's rights, 317.
Terminology, classificatory, 140 ff., 196, 244, 266; for relatives beyond inner lineage, 142, 154, 267; courtesy, 154, 196, 244, 284; age differences recognized in, 258; *diagrams showing*, 148, 285. *See also* Kinship.
Tong Hills, 2 n., 5, 66 n., 217.
Tongo, 3, 25 n., 64; relations with other clans, 119, 294, 309, 312; kinship ties in, 287 ff.; rights of tɛndaana in, 317; Chiefship of, 45, 265, 317, 320; Chief of, 72, 83, 270, 317, 320.
Totem, totemic taboos, 2, 22, 90, 98, 192, 222.
Trade, 103, 129, 201, 263, 337.
Twins, 271 ff.
Tyuk, concept of, 35 ff., 40.

Uncleanness, see *Dayǝt*.
Uterine kinship, see *Soog*.

Vinogradoff, L. P., 14 n., 345 n.

Warfare, 3, 5, 91, 108, 215, 287, 319.
Wealth, 54, 82, 207 ff., 307.
Westermarck, E., 345 n.
Whitehead, A. N., vii.
Widows, inheritance of, 4, 71, 113 ff., 153, 156, 161, 275 ff.; remarriage of, 71, 106, 118, 239 ff., 275 ff.; sexual relations of, 106, 117 ff.; support of aged, 219; purification rites for, 234, 243; equivalence of, 242; grandfather's or grandson's, 239 ff., 277; mother's brother's, 277, 296. *See also* Levirate.
Wife, senior (*pɔyakpeem*), 58, 132; room of, 60; abduction of, 83, 267 ff., 319; and paternal kin, 87 ff., 202, 333; divided loyalty of, 90 ff., 99, 194, 202; status of, 92 ff., 96 n., 98 ff., 102, 104 ff., 118, 201 ff.; relationship with affines, 93 ff., 105, 123; kinswoman, 126. *See also* Husband and Wife, Marriage.
Witchcraft, 32 ff.; accusations of, 33 ff., 40, 87, 131 ff.; and agnatic descent, 32, 35, 131; and *soog*, 32 ff., 131.
Wives, plurality of, 65 n., 66, 70 ff., 83 ff.; value of, 82 ff. *See also* Cowives.
Woman, status of, 22, 47, 99, 114, 118, 228; inheritance by, 22, 232; at father's home, 28, 92, 124, 261; care of, in childbirth, 28, 130, 133, 164 ff., 252; and ancestor cult, 61, 90, 174, 179, 228 n., 332 n.; symbols for, 61, 108, 232; significance of marriage and children to, 84, 111, 131; property of, 89, 102 ff., 158 n., 279; death rites of, 90, 203, 232, 275, 279, 333; *Yin* of, 90, 228; and male rights, 203, 225, 240, 252, 261, 274, 306, 317; abduction of, 215; as link in extra-clan kinship ties, 281.
Work-parties, 120, 125, 337.

Yidɛm (clan kin), 142.
Yin (destiny), 227 ff., 229, 231, 243, 325; shrine, 49 ff., 59, 154, 228 ff., 325. *See also* Predestiny.
Yir (house), 9 ff., 44, 69, 124; and family structure, 63, 128 ff.; polarity of *Yir* and *dug*, 63, 68 ff., 78, 100, 128, 194, 256; and witchcraft, 131.
Yirdaana (household head), 54 ff., 57 ff.

Zanɔne (space in front of gateway), 51, 154, 195, 338.
Zɔŋ, definition and significance of, 54 ff., 67; in funeral rites, 55, 149, 233, 279, 338.